BORN _TO_ POWER

HEIRS TO AMERICA'S LEADING BUSINESSES

JAN POTTKER, Ph.D.

BARRON'S

Dedication

This book is dedicated to the next generation:
to my own children and to the children
of the men and women profiled

Copyright © 1992 by Writer's Cramp, Inc.

All inquiries should be addressed to:
Barron's Educational Series, Inc.
250 Wireless Boulevard
Hauppauge, New York 11788

Library of Congress Catalog Card No. 92-6534

International Standard Book No. 0-8120-1456-1

Library of Congress Cataloging-in-Publication Data
Pottker, Janice.
    Born to power : heirs to America's leading businesses /
    Jan Pottker.
        p.   cm.
    Includes index.
    ISBN 0-8120-1456-1
    1. Family-owned business enterprises—United
States—Management—Case Studies.   I. Title
HD62.25.P68   1992
338.6'42—dc20   92-6534
                                                 CIP

PRINTED IN UNITED STATES OF AMERICA
2345   5500   987654321

TABLE OF CONTENTS

iii

Section IV—THE BENCHWARMERS

Section V—THE STEWARDS

ACKNOWLEDGMENTS

My parents, Ralph Eugene Pottker and Olga S. Pottker, were the first to lead me to reflect on family businesses. My late father was a partner with his brother-in-law in a second-generation furniture business in the Midwest and my mother was an editor at *The News-Sun* (Waukegan, Illinois), a third-generation family newspaper owned by novelist Ward Just's family. For their many discussions on the topic of family business, some of them overheard by me as a child, I thank them.

I also want to thank my mother for conducting a substantial portion of library research needed for a book on 50 different heirs and their companies. Despite her long hours in musty stacks, she never failed to be cheerful or to be helpful to me.

My sister, Mary Heléne Rosenbaum of Black Bear Productions, provided substantial editorial assistance to me as I wrote this book. She also took time away from her own book, *Celebrating Our Differences: Living Two Faiths in One Marriage*, to serve as a sounding board throughout my project.

My husband, Andrew S. Fishel, spent many hours discussing these families and their histories with me. Andy also provided substantive feedback on the book's organization and content, chapter by chapter. When my interest flagged over the course of the book's research and writing, he was there to encourage me.

Tracy and Carrie Pottker-Fishel, our children, kept me going through their pride in having a mother who was also a writer. I appreciate their patience and understanding of deadlines.

My father-in-law, Stanley Fishel of Bears, Stearns Companies, Inc., was always there to provide me with a figure or a fast stock quote.

My friends also should be thanked. First, M Kathleen McCulloch, who never once asked the question writers dread to hear, "How much more do you have to go?" Thanks also go to Larry Dickter for performing dual roles: that of a friend and of a professional librarian. I would also like to thank Nancy and Richard Alper, Karen Billingsley, Steven Brady, Doreen Conrad, David

Cutler, Lisa Freeman, Jeffrey Gusfield, Susie Hester, Becky Hoover, Nancy Kaplan, James Blair Lovell, Catherine O'Donnell, Brent Minor, Arlette Perruchas, S. Ned Rosenbaum, Karen Seals, Bob Speziale, Eleanor Steen, Ray Smith, Moira Sullivan, Jim Swan, Gloria Threadgill, Lepa Tomic, Catherine Taubman, Jack Weiser, Cynthia Vartan, Lucy Yee, and Steve Yamamoto for their interest throughout the research and writing of this book.

Thanks also go to Hugo Rizzoli of The Bookstall and to Katherine Meyers of his staff for their help. Also of help were Bea Armstrong, Carol Nussinson, and Mike Pickett. I also want to thank Brian Kelly and the staff of *Regardie's* for running "The Family Circus," which was later adapted for this book as "Flying Without A Net."

Timothy Sommerhauser, my close friend and researcher, died of AIDS after having completed preliminary research for this book. I deeply missed Tim's full participation in the project.

I want to thank my editor at Barron's, Max Reed, for her guidance and good spirit throughout this long project.

Thanks go to my agent, Ron Goldfarb of Goldfarb, Kaufman and Graybill, for his optimism and work on my behalf, and to his staff, agent Nina Graybill and assistant Ann Clark.

I am deeply indebted to literary attorney Ken Burrows and I also want to thank Helen Stephenson and Maria Pallante of The Authors Guild.

I would also like to thank the library staff of Montgomery County (Maryland) Public Libraries, especially the business reference librarians at the Bethesda Regional library and Barbara Harr of the Potomac Community library. Thanks also to the staffs of the Martin Luther King Library of Washington, D.C., Montgomery College Library, and McKeldin Library at the University of Maryland; to the Nite Owl staff at the Baltimore Public Library; to GLIS of George Washington University Library; and to The Foundation Center.

Thanks for the assistance provided by Gail Klotz of The Home Office and by Paul Goldstein of Mail Boxes Etc. And I never would have been able to put in long hours in front of the computer if it weren't for Callanetics of Potomac, especially Nina Schattner, Joan Danick, and Sharon L. Witt.

The managers and staff at the companies profiled who gave unstintingly of their time and provided a high caliber of assistance were: Todd Appleman of Adolph Coors; Ken Schmidt and Steve Schmidt of Harley-Davidson; Amy Paris Wiener of Lazare Kaplan; Arthur Minson and Judy Gordon of Georgette Klinger; Kim Klein and Robert McCulloch of The Funding Exchange; Erica Roseman of Barneys New York; Marc Leland and Jo Anne Burke of P.A.J.W.; Mary Wills of Tootsie Roll; Sue Willis of Wendy's; Arnold Cohen of J. Crew; Liz Reilly of Kiplinger Washington Editors; Virginia Butts of Field Corporation; Kathleen Spencer of AFLAC; Ed Rider and Karee Bologna of Procter & Gamble; Nicholas Hill of Marriott; David Phillips of Congressional Human Rights Foundation; Steve Poole of Gerber; Bill Norman of U-Haul; Cathy Bellemy of Baskin-Robbins; Susan Urbanetti and Cheryl MacKintosh of Cabot; Patricia Carney and Mary Quillens of EarthSave; Gwenn B. Baker of Hammond; Mary Vogel of H&R Block; Bob Ratliffe of McCaw Cellular; Pauline Jacobowsky, Pete Wetz, and Diane Falanger of Helene Curtis; Joan Gold of Phillips-Van Heusen; Bob Burkett of Interscope; Dave Thompson of Marion Merrell Dow; Gayle Compton Huff and Howard Cooley of Jockey; June Forsythe and Allen Bloom of Ringling Bros.; Arthur Speare, former CEO of Mattel; Trish Tardibuono of Lillian Vernon; and Bridget Berk of Ford. Thanks also to Mary Lou Brady of Liz Tagliarino Public Relations Inc.

Of course, the people who deserve the greatest gratitude are those interviewed for this book. By giving me hours of their precious time, they let me know what it is like to be Born to Power.

FOREWORD:
THE FACE OF THINGS TO COME

Everyone knows the familiar faces of Business Present. They belong to such men as Bill Marriott, Leonard Lauder, and Bill and Joe Coors. Now it's time to take a look at Business Future—the young heirs, born to power, who will be leading this country's most prominent businesses well into the next century. The stories of this younger generation of men and women, heirs to America's best-known private and publicly held corporations, have so far been unknown.

It's time to recognize the men and women who succeed a family member in a nationally known business. There are dozens of younger executives whose last names turn heads because they're Hefners or Gerbers. These offshoots of celebrated business families have inherited companies, and then recast them in their own images.

Their dynastic fathers and grandfathers—and sometimes mothers and grandmothers—are celebrated for empire building. But the silver-spoon children have been largely ignored or lumped into a "rich kid" stereotype. Rarely are these young heirs given the recognition they merit for having the spirit to join, shape, and often revamp their family's already-successful businesses.

It's as if their ambition, superb education, hard work, and thirst for challenge are nullified by inherited wealth. That misconception deserves a burial.

Occasionally, heirs with such brand names as Pillsbury, Reynolds, and Gamble choose to make careers in organizations very different from those founded by their forebears. They, too, achieve new heights—although in ways their parents didn't anticipate and sometimes don't appreciate. The stories of these old money heirs who opt out of corporate life are also intriguing.

About one-third of the men and women profiled here were born into today's Forbes 400 families. Some of these heirs even have their own listings, separate from their family group's. A glimpse of the statuspheres they occupy—and how much wealth they have—is captured in their profiles. There's something inherently fascinating about the rich who are, after all, the only aristocracy this country knows.

The 50 profiles in this book highlight the personalities and styles of heirs to famous American companies. These heirs fall naturally into seven different roles or styles. Each of the seven sections is anchored with a larger portrait that provides a longer look at an heir who is typical of that style.

Innovators seek challenges and often change the direction of an already successful company. They are risk-takers who seem visionary to those of us who try to keep up with them. Craig McCaw of McCaw Cellular, the largest provider of cellular telephone service in the United States, is an innovator.

Replicators consciously model their parents' business traits. They stick to the tried and true—if it worked in the past, it will probably work in the future. Tom Bloch of the H&R Block tax service says that he's very much like his father Henry and would be reluctant to jump into uncharted waters.

Conservators see the long-term maintenance of their companies as their most essential task as business leaders. Pete Coors of Adolph Coors Co. says that he is trying to bring the brewery to its next plane so it will continue for many more generations to come.

Benchwarmers are younger executives whose parents still play a dominant and highly visible role in the business. Some benchwarmers experience teething problems as they watch their parents make all the important decisions. Others, like Bill Marriott's benchwarmer sons Steve and John, admit that it will be a while before they are able to step up to bat. As 32-year-old Steve says, "I've got a long way to go."

Stewards are younger family members who do not play a role in the daily management of their companies. Often, they retain board positions to protect their equity status. Rob Walton, Sam's son, uses his board directorship of Wal-Mart in part to represent the enormous financial interests he and his siblings hold.

Family feuders fight over money and company control. These battles are protracted and often lead to litigation. In these feuding families, it's son against father, daughter against brother, and cousin against cousin. U-Haul deserves a special place in this hall of defame—it is the bad dream of family businesses. The kids who ousted their father from the company he founded are divided among themselves; swinging punches at the 1989 annual meeting, these corporate officers had to be restrained by security guards.

Rebels are strong-minded heirs who seek their own way in life, usually in contradiction to what their parents had planned for them. Although some rebels have started businesses that are very different from the ones their families own, others devote themselves to social causes that are similarly out of the mainstream. Adam Hochschild's family helped build the global mineral and mining corporation AMAX; Adam, on the other hand, is cofounder of the left-of-center magazine *Mother Jones*.

These seven different categories are intended to be value-neutral. It's no better to be, say, an Innovator than a Conservator. All of these next-generation men and women have found their own places in life and are successful working within those niches. Even some Family Feuders run enormously profitable companies. We should evaluate these heirs' accomplishments against what they seek to do, rather than compare them to what others are doing.

Of course, prominent families and their businesses undergo change just like everything else. About ten years ago, when Gordon Getty was breaking up the Sarah C. Getty trust, the family's strained relations would certainly have identified them as Family Feuders. Now each Getty branch has its own immense gush of Getty Oil dollars, and Gordon has pacified even those relatives who had litigated against him. Gordon's recent concentration on music composition—as well as his earlier behavior, dropping in and out of the family business when his father J. Paul was alive—place Gordon squarely in the Rebel category.

The richness and diversity within prominent business families is exemplified by the two half-brothers who are separately profiled, Marshall Field V and Ted Field. Their divergent traits are recognized by their separate categorizations: Marshall as a Steward philanthropist, and Ted as a Rebel movie-maker.

I selected a broad range of subjects to portray. Some of these heirs are from families that own private companies; others are public. Some businesses are best known in North America; many others are global. Some are monoliths, such as Procter & Gamble; others have higher recognizability than revenues, such as the Ford Model agency.

I also thought it was important to portray both women and men, and to include companies that represent a broad spectrum of American businesses. And I sought a geographic range.

But the crucial criterion for selection was whether the heirs and their companies had interesting tales to tell.

I extensively researched and analyzed these families and their companies, although no mainframe can measure the heartbeat of a family business. But getting the interview was also very important—and sometimes difficult. The members of America's most prominent and wealthy families are notoriously reluctant to be interviewed. Often they're tightlipped because they want to avoid attention from such feared terrorist groups as the IRS.

But they were usually willing to talk with me. They seemed to be taken with the idea of these snapshot profiles of successors to famous businesses. Sometimes they would turn the interview to ask me specific questions about the families I'd already visited.

These men and women also recognized that this book's point of view would be unique. After all, there have been other books published on family businesses, but those books focus either on unknown small family businesses or on the older family leaders. This is the first look at the younger generation of prominent, sometimes global, family businesses.

Family businesses do well in this country. Two-thirds of public family businesses outperform the Dow Jones index, as one late '80s study showed. The top managers of family businesses provide greater leadership continuity to their companies because of their long-term commitment, despite any initial doubts they may have had about entering the family business: Half of all second generation family business heads reported in a 1990 survey that they seriously questioned the wisdom of entering their parents' companies.

Family businesses are also run differently from other businesses. They have strong cultures that emphasize quality and service—for instance, the Kiplingers and Marriotts. Family businesses take fewer risks in their borrowing practices and in their growth plans. They also rely less on market research and more on intuition, as in the case of Lillian Vernon and Crain Communications. And whether they are private or public, they are all focused on long-term goals, with the end being the preservation of the company for generations to come.

Three of four Americans reported to *Time* magazine that their dream job is to run their own thriving business. People want to be in charge of their own company at an age when they can enjoy it and shape the business to their personal vision.

Here are 50 authentic tales about lives most of us can only imagine. Through their profiles, the heirs in this book communicate what it really means to run a company when you're young. Their stories also let us know how it is being the child, or grandchild, of a business leader who's considered the epitome of the American success story. These heirs also speak out on what it's like to grow up with a last name that's also a famous brand name, recognizable to everybody.

If inheriting and then running a profitable, well-known company is truly the American dream, then here's the chance to get a feeling for whether the reality is as satisfying as the fantasy.

J.P.

SECTION I

THE INNOVATORS

Innovators are assertive people who take the companies they've inherited and venture approaches that are different from the tried and true. They'll typically take charge of a family business that's already sound and dramatically shift its focus to make it more successful. Innovators are not afraid to change direction to ensure growth and avoid stagnation.

Rance and Keith Crain of Crain Communications, for example, have acquired and developed new trade publications, bringing the total to 26 magazines from the seven published while their father was alive. Another publisher, Christie Hefner of Playboy Enterprises, took a shaky business with a tired image and revitalized it. Micky Arison of Carnival Cruise Lines began the most ambitious cruise ship construction program the industry has ever seen.

INNOVATORS USUALLY...

1. say they're competitive and open to risktaking. They might have been entrepreneurs themselves if they hadn't inherited a company.
2. model themselves after their parents when the parents were younger.
3. are unemcumbered by parents still involved in the company's daily operations.
4. have parents who valued self-reliance and encouraged them to be independent, both as children and when they entered the business as adults.
5. have parents and siblings who support change.
6. are first-born or only children.
7. have parents who are well educated.
8. gained experience working outside the family business.

If these Innovators hadn't inherited family businesses, the chances are good that they would have become entrepreneurs. These men and women would not be willing to remain working in someone else's business for very long.

These risktakers have no excuses genes. They realize that their calculated risktaking makes them particularly accountable to shareholders and family members with equity positions. Innovators welcome this challenge. Ron Gidwitz of Helene Curtis says with a shrug that his hair-care company didn't have long-term debt before his leadership "because it didn't do anything." Through his new product development, Ron shows another characteristic of Innovators: They resemble their parents when those parents were younger, more open to change, and taking greater risks to allow the company to grow.

Two of the companies in this section, McCaw Cellular and King World Productions, had family heirs whose fathers died unexpectedly. These older men, risktakers themselves, hadn't planned for succession and left their companies awash. For Craig McCaw and for Roger and Michael King, it was a case of sink or swim. Their audacious business strategies were born from their determination not to go under.

What gives these Innovators the courage to make hard choices? Often, it's the support they've been given by well-educated parents who valued and encouraged their independence. These same parents stepped aside relatively early in their careers to give the up-and-coming heirs mobility and freedom to guide the company. The resulting self-confidence is characteristic of Innovators.

The joint venture of Barneys New York and Japan's retailing giant Isetan Co. Ltd. was promoted and developed by Bob and Gene Pressman within nearly complete latitude given them by their parents. Similarly, when Dean Hammond and his wife Kathy wanted to originate a unique database and software system to modernize mapmaking, Dean's father was supportive—and uninvolved.

Innovators share another characteristic: Their competitive spirit means they don't like to lose. They will use their considerable talents to ensure that this doesn't happen. Instead of becoming entrepreneurs, Innovators have applied their entrepreneurial spirit to an established company.

Innovators are fortunate. They start with a company already profitable and so don't need to fritter away their entrepreneurial talents on such basics as obtaining financing. Instead, they can find personal fulfillment by taking their businesses in new directions. And their companies benefit from innovative leadership within an established business structure.

"What Curtis needed was a new challenge."

Helene Curtis Industries, Inc.
Chicago, Illinois

Business:	Personal care products
Best Known Products:	Finesse; Salon Selectives; Suave; Quantum salon perm; Degree anti-perspirant/deodorant; Vibrance
Founded:	1927 by Gerald S. Gidwitz and Louis Stein
Family Executives:	Ronald J. Gidwitz, President and CEO Gerald S. Gidwitz, Chairman Joseph L. Gidwitz, Vice Chairman
Family History:	Second generation
Family Ownership:	33 percent
Family Board Membership:	3 family members of 9 directors
Employees:	3,000
Traded:	New York Stock Exchange, HC
Net Sales:	$1,020,000,000 1992 867,700,000 1991 736,000,000 1990
Net Earnings:	$19,200,000 1992 6,500,000 1991 16,800,000 1990

HELENE CURTIS INDUSTRIES, INC.

Handsome Is as Handsome Does

Ronald J. Gidwitz, President and CEO

The man is attractive, and he knows it. But he also knows that good looks are good business, because at age 34, Ron Gidwitz was made president of Helene Curtis Industries, Inc. CEO since 1985, Ron has brought what analysts called a stodgy and imitative hair care company into the '90s, giving his company a solid place in that very competitive world.

Not that there weren't a few risks and a couple of glitches along the way. Ron quadrupled advertising in his first year as president and went into long-term debt when he abandoned the drab Chicago westside headquarters for the glossy, newly renovated Exhibitors Building on the north bank of the Chicago River. Then he poured cash into promoting his new upscale Finesse and Salon Selectives lines, along with the less successful Atune shampoo, and stressed growth by emphasizing R & D. In 1990 Curtis brought out its first major non-hair care brand, Degree deodorant, with an expensive $50 million launch.

Now Ron has the satisfaction of having seen Curtis' sales rocket from $123 million in 1980 to $736 million in 1990. More gratifying is that Curtis was recently added to the Fortune 500. These factors and others led *USA Today* to portray Curtis as a "hot stock" of the '80s and *Business Week* to characterize the company as one of the world's top marketers.

Speaking in his tenth-floor glass-walled office, he maintains he never considered himself a risktaker. "My decisions are so obvious on the face of it that if people had the same set of information that I had, with a very moderate amount of intelligence, they'd make the same decision."

Ron speaks coolly and self-confidently, his dark-brown hair slicked back Gordon Gekko style. His gaze is steady, and at 45, his eyes are developing flesh folds around the lids, resulting in a slightly hooded look. He settles into a contemporary beige-cushioned aluminum chair and starts to talk.

"You manage people differently today," he says. Involving people in their work is just one indication of how business leadership has changed since his father's management.

Curtis has come of age since its 1927 start in a small Chicago factory producing facial clay. (An early partner, Louis Stein, had a wife named Helene and a son named Curtis, thus the corporate name.) Gerald S. Gidwitz, Ron's father, nurtured the company until it dominated the professional beauty supply business for four decades, selling its permanent waves, hair driers, and shampoos to beauty salons.

In 1940 Curtis entered the consumer market with Suave shampoo, the best-selling low-cost shampoo in history and one that remains strong today. Its golden age was in the '50s, when Curtis introduced Spray Net—the first successful aerosol hair spray—and Enden, the first non-prescription dandruff shampoo.

By the early '70s, soon after Ron Gidwitz arrived at Curtis a year following his graduation from Brown University, Curtis' future looked unclear. Consumer products accounted for most of their sales, yet an older management didn't seem to be keeping up with the new trends in hair care. Add to this the incredible cost of launching a new shampoo line, especially when added to the major ad dollars needed to protect even modest shares of the market.

Factor in a fickle consumer, one who likes to change her shampoo brand as often as her bath towel, and, as Ron says, "You have a success rate not too dissimilar to the major motion picture industry."

And problems were intensifying. Ron Gidwitz became president in 1979, when net earnings failed to increase. The decade had gone down the drain as other hair care companies poured six new shampoos into the market at the same time. Another problem facing Ron was Curtis' long-standing practice of imitating the competitor's products, finally to the point of copyright violation. Two lawsuits were filed, and Curtis lost both. Indicating, of course, that imitation may be the most expensive as well as the sincerest form of flattery.

After two loss years (1973 and 1979) in one decade, Forbes magazine was calling Curtis the "worst-managed personal care company." Gerald Gidwitz was stymied by circumstances. Curtis was still an entrepreneurial company that had never been able to progress despite its successful products. It would move forward, then fall backward again. Industry analysts were looking forward to Ron Gidwitz taking over.

Unruffled, Ron moved forward and brought Curtis with him. Believing that you have to spend money to make money, he explained to concerned shareholders, "We didn't have any debt before because we didn't do anything."

Curtis is sited in a mature industry suffering from flat shampoo sales, and Ron knew that to develop Curtis as a growth leader while broadening its margins, he'd need to be innovative and aggressive, requirements which didn't bother him at all. By the fifth year of his presidency, sales had doubled and profits quadrupled.

Against this backdrop, Atune was introduced, a specialized shampoo for permed hair. Curtis—and Ron—were being scrutinized to see whether the recent success would hold. It didn't; Atune bombed. With several companies introducing perm shampoos at the same time, Atune was lost in a sea of competition, and even heavy advertising couldn't save it.

It was a total washout, but Ron was philosophical. "You can't hit home runs every day of the week. You're always going to have a certain erratic earnings pattern until you get so big that one 'up' balances out with a 'down' at the same time."

The problem is, Curtis isn't big enough yet for that buoyancy. When it hits a rock, it dips. Ron says, "Curtis has a fundamental question before it, and it's that growth costs money, and so the faster you go, the greater the impact on your margins."

Other companies have deeper pockets that are sorely needed in an industry whose new products have only a one-in-three chance of succeeding. And this two-thirds failure rate comes after a company has spent $50 million on a launch.

This would be costly in any industry, but a company with net sales in 1990 of a "mere" $736 million and with only about 2,500 employees is hit harder because of its relative smallness. On the other hand, Curtis is a leader in the U.S. hair-care market and ranks seventh in the personal care market. (Of the top ten personal care companies, the only other family business is ESTEE LAUDER INC.) Its advertising dollars fall behind only the Goliath, Procter & Gamble. As Ron Gidwitz plaintively said of Curtis' David image, "When do you get to be a large company in their eyes?"

Observers who analyze Ron's lifestyle as closely as his quarterly profits point to an alleged need to play with the big guys and, at the same time, to stamp his personal image on the predictable Curtis. Such commentators conveniently ignore that wanting your job to reflect your personality is a common holdover from the '60s. Instead, they criticize Ron's European double-breasted suits, white Jaguar, fashion-model wife, and his very social nightlife, which includes appearances at glossy Gold Coast store openings and Chicago Symphony benefits in Ravinia Park.

One year, pricey fashion photographer Skrebneski was hired for the company's Annual Report pictures. Ron's compulsion to have his products personify his own chic image, say snipers, pushes him to go after the top of the market.

And when he chose a wife, Ron again went for the top. At a fashion show in 1973, he saw model Christina Kemper and asked a mutual friend to introduce him. In many ways, it is a perfect match. Not only is Christina Kemper Gidwitz smart and good-looking, but she is the daughter of James Kemper, chairman of Kemper Corporation, the giant insurance enterprise headquartered in suburban Chicago. (In fact, the two companies jointly sponsor the top drawer Pro-Am Helene Curtis-Kemper Ladies Golf Tournament.)

The handsome and well-connected couple married in 1975, and now have two young sons, Scott and Alexander. Like all modern dads, Ron has done his share of diaper detail.

Christina Gidwitz continued modeling through the early years of their marriage. Two decades ago, a corporate president's wife rarely worked after marriage. Christina took her career one step further: "She worked for our competitors," Ron points out.

After the typically short career of a model, by the early '80s she had stopped. A wall-size, matte black-and-white photograph of Christina—facial profile, chin raised, brunette hair blowing back—is a dramatic presence in her husband's office and one which Ron nods at when speaking of her.

━━━━━━━━━

Whatever Ron's personal or professional motivation for moving his products upscale, it scored. In a hazardous gamble, he risked $35 million, nearly all of Curtis' stockholder equity, to introduce Finesse shampoo in 1982. Finesse appealed to women who liked its high-class image but who still bought their hair care products while doing their grocery shopping. There are plenty of women who won't walk into an intimidating salon to pay a luxury price for a Paul Mitchell Co. shampoo, but who don't mind putting down some extra change for a top-of-the-line Curtis product.

Finesse was a marketing triumph and pumped sales up so that Gidwitz could expand the line with profitable Finesse hair spray and mousse—all while keeping up that glossy image. "Ron wants to be talked about in the same breath as Vidal Sassoon, and for that, he needs a product like Finesse," observed one industry watcher. Finesse may suit Ron's image, but it is also very successful as the third largest hair care brand in America. Nineteen eighty-six was a year of both near-record earnings and a semiannual dividend, the first since 1964.

In 1987, Salon Selectives was set in motion, propelled by a $40 million marketing budget, and Ron had finally shed the Curtis image of low-priced products. With Finesse and Salon Selectives, he captured the top of the market while still holding onto value-priced Suave. In Curtis' professional line, Quantum remained the best-selling permanent in American salons.

Today, Curtis is considered a growth leader in the personal care products industry, ranking sixth in overall sales, but first in hair conditioners and second in shampoo sales. What's particularly noteworthy, says Diana Temple of Salomon Brothers, is that Curtis has developed two major brands since 1983.

But a few years before that, there had been some questions raised about the launch budget needed for Finesse and Salon Selectives and the long-term debt acquired for the new factory and headquarters sites. "There are always disagreements when you alter your course. What Curtis needed was a new challenge," Ron reflects.

Several new challenges may be in store for Ron as the new deodorant Degree may or may not justify its costs and as Curtis competes against Procter & Gamble's combination shampoo/conditioner with a similar product from the Suave line.

If there have been serious inquiries about Curtis' planned expenditures and strategy, they did not come from family members. "My family has always been supportive of me," Ron says. "We discuss these issues; we talk about these issues."

Currently the Gidwitz family owns one third of Helene Curtis and retains 73 percent of the voting shares, making family agreement all that matters. Helene Curtis has been controlled by the Gidwitz clan for more than 60 years, which accounts for Wall Street's lack of interest in the firm. In 1984, to protect against raiders, a new Delaware holding company was set up to maintain Gidwitz control by instituting staggered terms for directors and by requiring an 80 percent vote of shares outstanding to approve a business combination.

In 1986, the family issued a new class B common stock to put up new securities without weakening the Gidwitz family's voting power while allowing Curtis flexibility to continue expansion. And in the summer of 1988, the Gidwitzes reduced their equity to 33 percent, again to increase Curtis' capital base.

"We have disproportionate control," says Ron in an understatement, "and the possibility of a takeover is not a problem." He continues, "We're better off having more capital to compete with major companies on a larger scale."

The intensity in Ron's voice is also reflected when he talks of his dedication to economic development and his parallel commitment to politics. He describes himself as a moderate Republican, and for Ron Gidwitz, a political future is foreseen. Following in the footsteps of Republicans Donald Rumsfeld and Charles Percy, two Illinois business leaders who went on to hold national political office, Ron has a double-barreled tag: businessman-politician.

Right now, Ron is Republican Committeeman for Chicago's 43rd Ward and also serves as head of Chicago's Economic Development Commission, civic activities that led him to be named *Crain's* Chicago business executive of the year. Ron has demonstrated that he can maneuver adroitly through Byzantine Chicago politics that recall the Middle East rather than the Middle West. His next political campaign may well be for mayor of Chicago, given his current interests and the continued support of his party.

Ron's interest in using political power for change may be typical of his generation but it also may be indirectly attrributable to his father, Gerald Gidwitz. However, Ron points out the difference between father and son. "Dad is interested in political ideas as opposed to political implications," he says. "He was never involved with politics per se."

Life growing up in Highland Park on Chicago's North Shore meant Impressionist paintings on the walls and all the intellectual advantages of having a father who was a University of Chicago graduate. And home life involved talk about politics as well as business; in both areas the senior Gidwitz had, and continues to have, a strong influence on his five children.

"My father wanted all of us to be involved in business," Ron says, referring to his four younger siblings. (Their mother, Jane Gidwitz, however, has never had a direct business role.) Three Gidwitz children are in the family businesses. Besides Ron at Curtis, James is chief executive of Continental Materials Corp., which for many years was headed by Gerald's older brother Joseph L. Gidwitz. Joseph also serves as vice chairman of Curtis, just as Ron is on Continental's board. Burnham Development Corp. is another Gidwitz enterprise, employing Ron's brother Peter. Gerald Gidwitz commented, "I let them run the companies. And they took my jobs away!"

Two Gidwitz children have struck off on their own. Tom is a stringer for a small Massachusetts newspaper while he continues work on what his older brother wryly and affectionately terms "the great American novel." The only Gidwitz daughter, Nancy, works in public relations.

Gerald Gidwitz showed his oldest son the world of Helene Curtis by having Ron work there while on summer breaks from the Hotchkiss School in Connecticut. But Ron minimizes any proselytizing his dad may have done on behalf of the hair-care company. Ron says that at Hotchkiss he knew he wanted to go into business like his father, and by the time he was studying at Brown, he had a clear idea that Curtis would be his destination. However, he served as assistant to the vice president at a former national financial service company for a short time before joining Curtis.

When asked if being at the Curtis helm was his designated family role, Ron replies quickly and sharply, "It was never designated." Then he changes his tone and laughs, "I wish it were, sometimes. I obviously had the inside track, but I earned it."

Ron worked at a variety of positions throughout Curtis, each at a higher level than the previous one. Beginning in 1968 as a trainee, he was later named assistant to the vice president for marketing. Next came corporate planning director, and later executive vice president. In 1979 he was named president (while Gerald was CEO and chairman), and in 1985, CEO. Gerald Gidwitz continued as chairman. Ron has spent nearly his whole career at Curtis but he points out, "Until I became president, I didn't work directly for my father."

Ron credits his parent for giving him latitude as he grew into his new positions. "He let me make my own mistakes. He was, and is, an unusual father to work for because he didn't meddle, he was supportive. Too many fathers with good intentions insulate their kids from learning experiences, from day-to-day management."

Typical of Innovators, Ron wants to stamp Curtis with his own style, and he encourages innovation in Curtis' employees. Curtis involves people in their work to the extent of letting them design the parameters of their jobs, from the top down to the laboratory and bluecollar workers. "We try to get all of our warehouse employees involved and participating in what their job will be."

Using the corporate move from the westside headquarters to the renovated Exhibitors Building as an example, Ron explains how, through involving staff, he minimized what is usually a very threatening experience and perhaps even turned the move into a team-building exercise. "We designed the prototype for most of our furniture and installed it in the new building space. We called employees in to try the chairs and desks to see how they functioned and to make suggestions."

He concludes, "Everyone had a chance to input. Changes were made as a result of their contribution, or each person received a response as to why their idea wasn't accepted. As a result, we have had virtually no complaint."

This idea of contribution is not limited to the progressive infrastructure at Curtis. The company also reaches out to its neighborhood. "We adopted a high school on the west side and hired kids over the summer. After they receive their diplomas, we'll hire them for permanent positions," Ron says. "Curtis has many managers involved with United Way, as well as contributing time and resources to the other civic and charitable groups."

Embodying education and self-help traditions common to many businesss owned by Jewish families, Gerald Gidwitz began offering after-work classes in the '30s and '40s. The programs themselves were generated through employee request and covered a gamut of topics. Gerald Gidwitz remembers, "One year, though, they asked for tap dancing and pastry-making classes. After that, we made it more restrictive."

Today, making sure all Curtis workers can speak English is a greater priority than tap dancing, so Basic English classes for Polish-American and Hispanic employees are offered, along with rudimentary education skills for native Chicago workers. Ron says, "Unfortunately, Chicago's public school system, like most urban school systems, is not performing as well as required for today's environment and for the future, so we find ourselves doing some remedial work."

It was concern about the '50s public schools, suburban as well as urban, that led Ron's father to start the Education for Survival Foundation. The senor Gidwitz believed that the United States might lose the post-Sputnik space race without more focus on technological education, terming the international competition "a battle of the classrooms." Gerald's ardent belief in a free-enterprise system has always molded his philanthropic concerns, and in the

'80s he helped found and served as a director of the Jamestown Foundation, which assists a handful of Soviet defectors with housing and medical needs and with job counseling.

Jamestown's bipartisan board of directors includes Richard Allen, former CIA director; Clayton Yeutter, current U.S. Secretary of Agriculture and past international trade representative; U.S. Senator Sam Nunn (D, Georgia); and former U.S. National Security advisor Zbigniew Brzezinski. Showing interlinking corporate and familial ties, the foundation's start-up was partially financed by a $50,000 contribution from two Gidwitz-owned companies, Curtis and Continental Materials Corp., as well as with $50,000 from James Kemper, Ron's father-in-law.

It's this type of philanthropy, derived from a compelling urge to keep America strong and to foster economic private enterprise, that Ron learned from his father. Gerald needed to make business his priority and relegated politics to the realm of ideas. As part of the next generation of Gidwitzes, more secure in financial background, Ron has gone a step further into the political arena.

His first political venture was in the office of U.S. Senator Paul Douglas (D, Illinois) in 1962, a volunteer activity set in motion by a call from Gerald Gidwitz to Douglas and one that gave Ron a look at Democratic politics. In 1963, while an undergraduate at Brown, Ron worked on the winning gubernatorial campaign of neophyte United States Senator John Chafee (R, Rhode Island), and he's been active in the Republican party ever since. "It's always a nice experience to win your campaign the first time out," he jokes, bemused at the thought that perhaps he wouldn't be involved in politics today if not for that first victorious election in 1963.

As a young man at Brown, Ron Gidwitz was on the outside looking at the social movements of the '60s. Today, many of Ron's generation have caught up with him, also describing themselves as moderate Republicans. Although his father is a conservative Republican who was a major contributor to far-right U.S. Representative Philip Crane's (R, Illinois) election, Ron is more pragmatic as he begins his political career.

Chairman of the Development Commission, Ron acts as the link between the mayor's office and the city's businesses. To politicians, Ron stresses the need to revitalize Chicago's economic base; to business leaders, he emphasizes that political relations are a legitimate and important function of business.

His priority is to create a road map for economic development policy, a strategic business plan for the city of Chicago. Ron wants to put together a long-range tax plan to encourage city business to expand. He'd like to see a competitive real estate policy developed, and industrial incentives put in place to stem the flow of businesses into the suburbs. Chicago is "blessed" with enterprise zones, says Ron, and adds that it is well-positioned to take advantage of the opportunities enterprise zones carry with them. He want to convince out-of-town businesses of Chicago's reliable transportation system to move both goods and services and its stable work force with an accompanying solid work ethic. Ron and the Development Commission also want local industry to stay put.

In an ingenious 1986 strategy, Ron worked together with the Illinois Commerce Department, the local development corporation, and the Teamsters, and successfully impeded a move to Missouri by Chicago's Ekco Housewares, Inc. "There are lower taxes elsewhere," he says, "but without the sound infrastructure to support business." Although Ron was not successful in keeping Sears, Roebuck & Co. in Chicago (although it did stay in the suburban area), he helped orchestrate its mortgage refinancing to avoid the sale of the world's tallest building.

Practicing as he preaches, Ron is seriously pursuing building a new research park facility for Curtis' 130 scientists and having it cosponsored by the city, the state, the University of Illinois, and Presbyterian-St. Luke's Hospital. He's cast his personal vote for the city, too, and abandoned the North Shore of his boyhood for an apartment on Chicago's glittering Gold Coast with his wife and kids.

"There's a certain vitality here," he says of living in Chicago. "There are lunchtime activities, there are after-hours activities, there are breakfasts in the morning—which you just can't get if you're out in Bolingbrook."

This urban vitality fuels his own energy and drives him to work long, diligent hours at Curtis, then go on to attend receptions, meetings, and dinners several evenings a week. When asked how he's able to pack all these events into a day and also maintain a semblance of a family life, he gives the explanation, "I'm a great manager," with apparent seriousness.

Citing his current duties as ward committeeman, head of the Economic Development Commission, and CEO of Curtis, Ron is putting off suggestions of the mayoralty, merely replying that the idea is "interesting." He continues, "It's not all that palatable at the moment because of the two small children I have at home."

If Ron is trying to follow Rumsfeld's and Percy's example by seguing from business to Republican politics, he might find his quest to be an urban mayor, especially of a city like Chicago, a little more difficult. There's something about urbane Ron Gidwitz and his annual salary of slightly less than $500,000 that doesn't immediately call to mind a "boss" image. When asked, he wryly replies, "I must confess I haven't given thought to all the negative baggage I might possibly have in great sufficiency."

Upon reflection, Ron concludes of his image, "I don't think that's a problem." Using the example of Ted and Jack Kennedy—"although I'm not placing myself in the same group"—he points out, "They were very successful even though they had the negative baggage of too much money and good-looking wives and being involved with affairs most people just read about in the social columns. But, who knows? The only way you can really test that is to run a campaign."

But Ron succinctly summarizes his waiting game. "I won't run because I can't win."

Although the chances of a Republican Chicago mayor seem slim, Ron retains a clear vision of how he'd carry out the responsibilities of mayor. "Being a public official, particularly being mayor, is a responsibility of the people's health and safety, of creating a climate where people can live to the fullest. It's helping the criminal justice system and a social service system with so many more clients—battered kids, foster kids—than they have ever had before. It means encouraging jobs and effecting reform. It's a broad social goal ... to help people."

Distant goals are a factor, but Ron Gidwitz knows that his first responsibility is Curtis, and he's looking forward to the upcoming challenge of its new industrial park and distribution and manufacturing center. Ceaselessly the strategic planner, he says, "The measure isn't how well you did last quarter but how well are you going to do five years from now?"

Ron's primary concern is to maintain Curtis' strength. His family founded Curtis, struggled for it, and prospered with it. Then the Gidwitzes made the decision to let Ron lead it while he was still in his thirties, and he made some tough decisions as he took Curtis through troublesome times. Ron says he has never thought of walking away from Curtis, even during the difficult times. And he adds emphatically, "It hasn't been all a bed of roses, you know."

The father's judgment of the son plays a large part in Ron's self-image. He guesses, "My father would be most proud of the performance of the company. We are able to sustain our growth, improve profits, and maintain our position in a world market in which we compete. Helene Curtis is an exceptional performer."

He speculates on what he'd do if, for some reason, he were no longer CEO of Curtis. "Realistically, I'd run something else," says this Innovator. Another business, or perhaps a city? He says, "I'd like to be remembered as having helped a lot of people." That sounds remarkably like Ron's definition of the primary function of the mayor. Now that he's brought Curtis where he wants it, it seems as if Ron Gidwitz is looking for another challenge.

Roger King

Michael King

Roger: "We got into this business with everything going against us. Just a tremendous legacy from our dad, which is the ability to sell."

King World Productions, Inc.
Short Hills, New Jersey

Business:	Syndicated television programs
Best Known Products:	"Wheel of Fortune," "Jeopardy!" and "The Oprah Winfrey Show"
Founded:	1964 by Charlie King
Family Executives:	Roger King, Chairman Michael King, President, CEO, Director Diana King, Vice President, Secretary of Company Richard King, Director
Family History:	Second generation
Family Ownership:	About 34 percent
Family Board Membership:	4 family members of 8 directors
Traded:	NYSE, KWP
Net Revenues:	$475,909,000 1991 453,749,000 1990 396,448,000 1989
Net Earnings:	$ 90,591,000 1991 84,100,000 1990 73,212,000 1989

KING WORLD PRODUCTIONS, INC.

Will the Wheel of Fortune Turn?

Roger King, Chairman
Michael King, President and CEO

Possession of cocaine, auto theft, strong-arm robbery—mixed with a drinking problem—make up a list of disasters that could be recited by a woeful guest on "The Oprah Winfrey Show." Or it could be an exposé of a top entertainment executive on "Inside Edition."

Chances are, you won't hear anything on these television shows about the person whose past dilemmas are described above because that man is Roger King, 48, who heads the number one syndication company in the United States. King World brings such hit programs as "Oprah," "Inside Edition," "Jeopardy!," "Wheel of Fortune," and "Candid Camera" to local broadcasting.

Roger has survived the problems that led to his arrest in 1986, the night he went out of control and fought with a Fort Lauderdale taxi driver, making off with his cab. Roger was given two years probation (the strong-arm robbery charge was dropped) and entered a rehabilitation program.

A few years later, Roger explained what happened to an industry publication. "I was drinking too much. I dealt with it and it's over. In a lot of ways it was a godsend.

"Success is intimidating. It surrounds you. Everyone 'yeses' you, and no one tells you what you're doing wrong. I think I was reaching out for help."

Success has not abandoned the burly King brothers since they began working full time at King World. Roger and his younger brother Michael, 44, along with three of their four siblings, own 37 percent of King World, the first syndicator in broadcasting history with three simultaneous top hits: "Wheel," "Oprah," and "Jeopardy!"

Producer Merv Griffin's "Wheel" was the number one syndicated show for more than a half-dozen years and brought Roger and Michael the kind of easy money you'd associate with, well, game show winnings. Roger earns nearly $2 million in annual compensation, as does Michael. This sum does not include stock options. The brothers' personal worth is estimated at more than one-quarter billion dollars each.

Syndicators like the Kings are middlemen who buy the distribution rights to shows from producers and then lease the programs to independent or network-affiliated television stations. Syndicators can also make money by selling the ads that sponsor these shows. King World's subsidiary, Camelot Entertainment Sales Inc., sells ad time for King shows and other programs.

King World is a second-generation family business that began with Charlie King, a radio man, and his wife, Lucille. Charlie made big money in radio programming and syndication, as much as $85,000 a week in the late '40s. Charlie and Lucille lived in a New Jersey mansion more than large enough for their six children: Robert, Roger, Michael, Diana, Richard, and Karen. Years later, Michael said of his father, "He was the kind of guy who could earn $3 million in a year—and spend $9 million."

Six foot three and 350 pounds, Charlie, wearing a homburg hat and a flower in his lapel, would take young Roger along on sales calls. At dinner, Charlie would recap the deals he'd made that day, explaining strategy to his children. But one day television came in, and radio went out. Charlie was broke.

The family was forced to move out of their estate and rent a winter beach house, eventually moving 19 times as Charlie's fortunes rose and fell. When they were down, Charlie would declare to his family, "Strictly temporary!"

Charlie refused to declare bankruptcy no matter how much money he owed. At first, he tried to scrape together a living by working for a film company. In 1964, he wanted to go into business for himself again to buy distribution rights to "The Little Rascals." He was hampered by the small obstacle of having no cash. He talked the show's owners into giving him 24-hour syndication rights, excused himself from the meeting, went to the next room to call a local station and sold local rights to "Little Rascals" for $50,000.

With this money as a down payment, he went into debt again to buy the full rights to distribute all 110 episodes of "Little Rascals," which became the centerpiece of his newly formed King World Productions.

Syndication gave the family a sense of security, but the business wasn't so lucrative that it could afford to hire the King children as they graduated from college. In the late '60s, Roger went from graduation straight to a Worcester radio station that was in the red. For a piece of the action, he guaranteed he could turn it around. Roger describes his first step toward profitability: "I hired Michael." Within weeks, the station was making money.

As Roger and Michael gained experience in radio, King World took a downward dive. By the early '70s, the stereotyped depiction of African-Americans on "Little Rascals" was recognized as offensive. Stations refused to renew their contracts.

In 1973, while on a sales call in San Antonio, Charlie died of a heart attack at age 59. The family tried to continue distribution of "Little Rascals"—this time, out of eldest son Bob's kitchen. Bob re-edited the shows, removing sections that were considered insensitive, while the other Kings worked at jobs outside the family company to help keep the business going.

"We had the focal point of King World to hold us together, something not many other families have," says Michael.

By 1982, King World was benefiting from Roger and Michael's full-time attention. But the company was still an obscure syndicator run by family members in their 30s. Industry bigwigs didn't take King World seriously.

Roger remembers, "We got into this business with everything going against us. No products. No contacts. Just a tremendous legacy from our dad, which is the ability to sell."

The Kings' belief in research rivals their salesmanship. They reviewed 5,000 ratings books covering a decade to determine what shows might profitably be syndicated. They saw that the daytime "Wheel," although no hit, did solidly no matter what its time spot. But even though no other syndicator was interested in "Wheel," Merv wouldn't return the Kings' phone calls.

When Bob King spotted Merv's company president in an hotel bar, he was able to talk the man into giving them an audience with the "Wheel" producer. The Kings have the persuasive banter of carnival barkers and quickly talked Merv into letting them distribute a nighttime version of his show in 1983. Just as their research had indicated, the evening show built an audience and became a smash, enabling the Kings to move it into larger markets. "Wheel" is the foundation of the King empire.

The next season, King World revived Merv's "Jeopardy!" in syndication. Another sleeper became a hit, and it fell into the number two spot after "Wheel." In 1986, "Oprah" surpassed Phil Donahue to land in third place.

"No one's ever had the number one and two shows in syndication," laughed Michael to *Channels*, an industry publication. "You add number three and it's like, 'Geek'!"

In 1984, King World went public to raise capital with one of the best-performing initial public offerings of the '80s, with share price tripling within four months. It remains the only large publicly traded stock dependent on syndication. (Other public Tinseltown powerhouses include Aaron Spelling Productions and dick clark productions.)

Each of the King siblings initially kept a 19.3 percent stake, except for Bob, who had conflicts with Roger over the speed of the company's growth and was bought out for $1.7 million before the public offering. Karen subsequently sold half her shares, which was in conflict with a family agreement and led to a year-long estrangement from Michael, even though they were next-door neighbors. By 1992, the family's stake, by now at 34 percent, was worth about $340 million.

As the company grew, the Kings started to look into diversification through acquisition. But, as Michael said to *Broadcasting*, "after Roger and I looked through bushel baskets of companies, [we saw that] the reason they were for sale was because they diversified."

Instead of diversifying, the Kings concentrated on building up their company. At that point, they had only 11 employees, six of whom were family members, in their Summit, New Jersey office. They hired by raiding the major production and distribution companies and opened offices in New York, Chicago, and Los Angeles. Only then did they diversify into spinoff merchandising and start selling rights internationally through King World International, Inc. King World also moved into developing and supplying programming for commercial and cable networks and in 1991 produced the cable network signature show "Arts & Entertainment Revue" in association with the Arts & Entertainment Network.

The Kings support their programs through some of the heaviest advertising and promotion in the industry. Spending money in order to make it is a cornerstone of the King brothers' philosophy. The early $3 million promotion of "Wheel" was a risk for a company that was struggling to stand on its feet. In 1991, King World broke records with a $10 million launch of "Candid Camera."

Despite their hit shows, the Kings do not inspire devotion or affection from the station managers who must negotiate the distribution contracts. The Kings' syndication fees are among the highest in the business, and they skyrocket with each contract renewal. Managers say the fees they pay can escalate as much as 300 or 400 percent upon renewal. "Intimidation," "shot-gun approach," and "browbeat" are words used to describe Roger's sales tactics. (Michael heads program development.) In addition, station staff may sign a one-year contract only to find Roger at the door three months later to press them into a renewal.

The Kings cackled after they beat Viacom Enterprises, syndicators of the "Cosby Show," to the punch. King World had some openings in small cities where it hadn't yet sold syndication rights to its shows. When the Kings heard that the "Cosby" syndicators were planning to visit small-city stations, they made sure King World insinuated itself into markets it had never before entered to grab the best long-term deals from these station managers. By the time the "Cosby" people arrived, available money had been spent on King World deals. As Michael has said of himself and Roger, "We go with our guts."

But this stylistic difference between the Kings and other industry managers is one that the Kings relish. They don't want to fall into the grey-suit-accountant mentality of most television executives. Certainly they're doing their flamboyant best to live like kings of entertainment.

Luxury-loving Roger, who has houses in New Jersey and Florida, rents a Lear 55 jet for transportation. Flashy Michael tools around L.A. in his white Rolls Royce convertible, commuting to and from his Mediterranean-style Malibu house located near celebrity neighbors like Mel Gibson.

How long their life style will be fueled by King World productions is unclear. Certainly, the company's license fees will take it through 1993 with a guaranteed $1 billion. Their King World stock saw a 46 percent annual growth between 1986 and 1991, and 1991 was its seventh consecutive year of record revenues and profits.

When Roger—who is considered the kingpin of the company—was arrested in 1986, King World stock sold off briefly, garnering a second look from *Forbes'* "Streetwalker" column, which had recently recommended buying shares. Roger's arrest didn't have any long-term effect on the company. At the beginning of 1992, cash flow was strong, and the business had no problem servicing its modest debt. The year earlier, *Forbes* had named King World one of the most efficient companies in the United States, with fewer than 500 employees doing a $475 million business.

However, the company is not yet the entertainment powerhouse the Kings aspire to. The business relies heavily on its top three shows, at one point deriving more than 90 percent of its revenues from them. Yet the slowly eroding shares of "Wheel" and "Jeopardy!" means that these programs are showing signs of age even though many markets have renewed for the 1993-1994 year and "Wheel" remains the most watched television game show in the world.

There also have been flops along the way. "Nightlife" with David Brenner and "Rock 'n' Roll Evening News" never got off the ground. "Monopoly" was a disappointment, even after the show dropped the controversial female midget who ran around the life-size board dressed as the game's Uncle Moneybags.

As the appearance of the midget indicates, sometimes the Kings' "gut" is off. Although the Kings were the first to recognize the ability of a young black woman to galvanize talk show audiences, Arsenio Hall claims that the syndicate told him that America wasn't ready for two black talk-show hosts.

As growth from their hits flattens out, Roger and Michael say they will aggressively seek new television ventures. The brothers are still looking to expand program development and remain interested in acquisitions, including television stations. They're not afraid of risk. If they lose a spin on the wheel, they'll always find the cash to buy a new vowel or two.

"We will maintain our position as the cruise industry leader."

Carnival Cruise Lines, Inc.
Miami, Florida

Business:	Multiple-night cruise lines
Best Known Lines:	Carnival Cruise Lines, Holland America Line, Windstar Cruises
Founded:	1974 by Ted Arison
Family Executives:	Micky Arison, Chairman, CEO Ted Arison, Chairman Emeritus (retired) Shari Arison, Director
Family History:	Second generation
Family Ownership:	70 percent
Family Board Membership:	2 family members of 12 directors
Traded:	NYSE, CCL
Net Sales:	$1,405,000,000 1991 1,254,000,000 1990 1,057,000,000 1989
Net Earnings:	$ 85,000,000 1991 206,000,000 1990 194,000,000 1989

CARNIVAL CRUISE LINES, INC.

Low Rollers Put Wind in Sales

Micky Arison, Chairman and CEO

Until 1974, cruise ships were strictly transocean carriers for the affluent. Then came Ted Arison, now 68, who originated cruises that were also vacation alternatives, offering entertainment on board and frequent stops at land-based resorts and sightseeing destinations. Ted knew that if he wanted to attract customers, these vacations had to be geared to the average budget. By offering shorter trips with lower costs, Ted opened the cruise line industry to younger travelers and Middle America.

Ted and son Micky, 42, built their business from one ship in 1974 into the largest cruise line in the world through low-priced packages hawked by heavy advertising. Now the company has 16 ships operating in the Caribbean, the Mediterranean, the South Pacific and in Alaskan waters. Carnival Cruise has operated at about 106 percent occupancy (by fitting in more than the standard two passengers per cabin) for the past decade, versus the industry average of 90 percent.

Carnival Cruise's market share leads the cruise ship industry at 26 percent. Since 1980, its revenues have grown three times faster than the industry's as a whole, and its earnings have doubled.

Carnival Cruise is also credited with history's most ambitious cruise ship construction program, carried out on Micky's watch. In the '80s, the company took delivery of one super liner each year for three years. Then in 1990 and 1991, it built two 2,600-passenger ships each year.

In addition, Micky bought the prestigious cruise line businesses of Holland America, Westours and Windstar in 1989. These acquisitions have allowed Carnival Cruise to broaden the vacation packages it offers for both higher- and lower-priced trips. In 1992, the company became a part owner of Seabourne, so now it can enter Scandinavian waters with two luxury liners. The company announced a joint venture in 1992 with Club Mediterranee S.A., which will allow it to take advantage of a new European market for popularly priced entertainment cruises.

Carnival Cruise's selling point is its colorful, glamour-packed fun vacation on ships with names like *Ecstasy*, *Fantasy*, and *Mardi Gras*. "The names tell the story," says Ted. Discotheques, night-clubs and casinos are included on board, enabling the company to pitch its cruise trips as entertainment.

More sophisticated guests might opt for the unstructured and unregimented cruises on the Windstar line, computer directed sailing ships that resemble huge luxury yachts. Micky hopes that as the young Carnival Cruise passengers become older and wealthier, their mature tastes will hunger for tours on upscale Windstar or Holland America ships.

Although this company is only two decades old, the Arisons were a shipping family long before the birth of Carnival Cruise. Ted took over the family's shipping business as a young man when his father died unexpectedly. He sold it in the '50s to start a sea-cargo business which he turned into a public company. Ted again sold out and, at age 42, moved to Miami to retire.

Leisure didn't suit him. Ted soon went into business with the founder of Norwegian Caribbean Lines. That partnership even-tually broke up and Ted turned to the chairman of Rapid-American Corporation to bankroll Carnival's 1972 start-up. In its first two years, the company was off to a rocky start, which gave Ted the opportunity to buy the nascent company outright from his partner for $1, as long as he assumed the company's $5 million debt.

Remembering how he'd taken over his family's shipping com-pany while still a young man, in 1979 Ted turned Carnival Cruise over to Micky. His son was 30 when he became president and CEO of the five-year-old company. In 1990, Ted retired as the compa-ny's chairman, again giving his title to Micky.

Micky, like Ted, was Israeli born, but he grew up in New York and Miami, where the company is headquartered. (Carnival

Cruise Line ships are registered in either the Bahamas or Liberia, registrations that have both tax and safety implications for the company.) Micky worked for his father as sales agent and reservations manager, and as vice president in charge of passenger traffic before taking the top position. Micky's sister Shari heads the Arison Foundation and is a company director.

The company went public in 1987. By 1992, the Arison family retained more than 70 percent of the company's stock, valued at slightly under $2 billion. Ted retains all of the company's Class B voting shares.

Although Ted is continually mentioned as one of the world's wealthiest people, the family lives modestly and mixes with a group of friends who are outside the social set of Miami Beach. "Nothing about them brags," says one Miamian. Ted's greatest indulgence is his ownership of Miami's pro basketball team, the Miami Heat.

Micky claims that his father, who was a piano prodigy as a boy, would have preferred a life in the arts to one in business. Now that Ted has retired, he devotes his time and philanthropies to his first love. Through the family foundation, he has endowed many arts scholarship programs, and in 1991 gave Miami's New World Symphony $14 million.

Despite the tremendous growth of the cruise market and its still-untapped potential for vacationers who've never taken a cruise, some rough waves have been felt by the industry. It was affected by the recession of the late '80s and the resultant empty-cabin problems and the deep discounting that cut into profits. But Carnival Cruise was not as badly affected as were its competitors, although the company's resort and casino operations in Nassau decreased in 1991 due to reduced tourism.

However, the Arisons are masters at turning difficulties into advantages. Take that first ship of Ted's, the retired transatlantic liner dubbed "the golden ship of the fleet"—although it wasn't gold and there was no fleet. This ship ran aground in the Port of Miami on its maiden voyage while loaded up with tour agents.

Once the ship got going again, she guzzled so much fuel that Ted decided to slow speed and cut some of the scheduled port visits. To substitute for the traditional sightseeing, Ted provided less expensive on-board entertainment, including movie theaters and nightclubs. The cruise became the destination itself. Adversity stimulated the Arisons' creativity and spurred the creation of a multibillion dollar industry.

"You can't delegate turning a company around."

Playboy Enterprises, Inc.
Chicago, Illinois

Business:	Publishing, Product Marketing, and Entertainment
Best Known Products:	*Playboy*, "Playboy At Night" and "After Hours"
Founded:	1953 by Hugh Hefner
Family Executives:	Christie Hefner, Chairman and CEO Hugh Hefner, Editor-in-Chief and Chairman Emeritus
Family History:	Second generation
Family Ownership:	72 percent
Family Board Membership:	1 family member of 6 directors
Traded:	NYSE, PLA
Net Revenues:	$174,042,000 1991 167,697,000 1990 166,174,000 1989
Net Earnings:	$4,510,000 1991 6,228,000 1990 (3,830,000) 1989

PLAYBOY ENTERPRISES

Shaping up the Figures at Playboy

Christie Hefner, Chairman and CEO

As a girl, she earnestly considered a career in law or politics—until she realized that America may not be ready to elect Hugh Hefner's daughter to public office. Now a 40-year-old woman, her mission is just as sober. Christie Hefner must send the Playboy empire into the twenty-first century and continue the recent profitability that is attributed to her good business management and her innovative marketing of what had become a tired corporate image.

The company's main product, as we all know, is *Playboy* magazine. It's the biggest seller in the men's magazine market and, with a circulation of 3.5 million, ranked number 14 of all U.S. magazines in 1990. The magazine also has 15 foreign editions that feature such pictorials as the German *Playboy's* "Girls of Friedrichstadtpalast." The latest foreign *Playboy* was launched in 1991 in Czechoslovakia. While the vital signs of many other magazines weakened in 1991, *Playboy* performed robustly, reporting a 17 percent increase in earnings and an increase in the number of advertising pages and subscriptions.

Newsstand specials, calendars, and art reproductions are also part of the publishing line, which entered a joint-venture agreement in 1991 to publish *SV Entertainment*, an in-hotel television and entertainment guide. Playboy's catalog business, which sells videos, back issues of the magazines, and other merchandise, grew 44 percent over 1990's revenues.

The company's entertainment operations include video production and the syndicated television show "After Hours." It has a new pay-per-view service, "Playboy At Night," and the videos and the European television show "Playboy Late Night" are especially popular in overseas markets. Sales in the television and video area "couldn't be hotter," reported the Wall Street column of *Money* magazine in 1992.

An important unit of the company stems from the recognition of its image. *Playboy* is the world's only magazine that had the name strength and marketability to become an international brand. Through its licensing program, it receives revenues on men's and women's apparel, accessories, and other products. Here also, international sales in 60 countries are very strong.

Playboy Enterprises in 1992 was far healthier than it had been a decade earlier when Christie became president. Although then only 30, she was given the responsibility of reversing the company's dizzying free-fall. The company had a shopworn image, no cash, and a $20 million debt.

Not only did Christie stop the firm's dive, but she pulled the company up to a second year of profitability in 1991. Her infamous father says Christie is carrying out his own evolutionary plans for the company. If that's what he believes, fine. It's apparent that the entrepreneur in the black pajamas stepped down from the company's leadership role just in time.

But to give Hef, 66, credit, he's also the man who brought Christie into his business. After receiving a literature degree from Brandeis University in 1974, Christie was working on a Boston underground newspaper when her father suggested she try Playboy Enterprises. Prior to Hef's proposal, Christie had no thought of a career that involved intimate knowledge of *Playboy's* balance sheet.

When Christie entered the company, she started off in legal and financial operations, partly because she realized that she could never top her father's editorial vision. Hef remains editor-in-chief of *Playboy* and has firm control over the magazine pages. But even as a young manager, Christie forced others in the organization to make their own decisions rather than send ideas from the Chicago headquarters westward to Los Angeles' exclusive Holmby Hills for Hef's blessings.

Hef further loosened his control over the business operation when Christie became president in 1982. (She was elected chairman in 1988.) That year, the company lost $52 million in the first negative balance sheet since it had gone public in 1971—when it issued the country's only stock certificate decorated with a naked woman. By the early '80s, Playboy Enterprises was in a crisis.

Red ink streamed through each of the company's core businesses, both domestic and international. The party was over.

Recent events that had hurt the company included its forfeiting of profitable British gambling operations and its Atlantic City casino. The magazine was considered passé and had lost its younger, demographically desirable subscribers. Also, its book-publishing venture was unprofitable.

These problems would have daunted other young executives. But Christie has her father's midwestern optimism and conviction that anything is possible. She knew she had to unleash her assertiveness and make necessary but painful changes. "You can't delegate turning a company around," she pointed out. One of her early decisions was to eliminate some of the management layers.

And as loyal as Christie is to her father and his chosen way of life, she told him the excessive luxuries had to go. Sold were the black DC-9 jetliner, the limousine, the 69-room Chicago mansion, and even the treasured $4.5 million Jackson Pollock painting. To set an example, she got rid of her own Porsche, in favor of a Toyota, and flew business class.

It took the analytic Christie a longer time to convince Hef that the Playboy Clubs should be dumped, but in 1986 the firm shuttered its last Bunny hutch. Christie is also credited with the decision to sell the company's resort hotels.

In addition, she pulled licenses for such tacky Playboy-branded products as air fresheners for automobiles and slashed at other merchandise inconsistent with the magazine's preferred upscale images. She bought a mail order jewelry company and a stake in the auto magazine *duPont Registry*.

Christie revamped the video line by changing the videos' X-rating to R and refigured the former Playboy Channel pay-cable service to the more profitable pay-per-view. The company became the third-largest nontheatrical video distributor in an odd triumvirate of Walt Disney, Jane Fonda, and Playboy Enterprises.

After the 1986 Meese Commission frightened such vendors as Southland's 7-Eleven stores, *Playboy* was dropped from thousands of newsstands throughout the country. This renewed the importance of subscribers to Christie, who courted them aggressively. By the end of 1991, nearly two-thirds of the magazine's circulation derived from subscriptions, twice what it had been five years earlier. And Christie profitably sells this new subscription list to other marketers.

By 1990, she had brought the company into the black and had shaped the company into its current three operations—publishing, entertainment and licensing—and had improved each of them. At the beginning of 1992, Playboy Enterprises had little debt, $30 million in cash, and an improved balance sheet.

Christie hopes to diversify into different media outlets and add another publication, a lifestyle magazine for young men. But so far, such reality-based magazines do not appeal to Hef's fantasies. She does want to take advantage of the tremendous global possibilities in a world where in logo recognition, the Playboy Bunny takes second place only to Coca-Cola.

In 1990, the company completed a recapitalization plan to finance these new ventures in stock rather than cash. The plan also forced those of Playboy Enterprises' 14,000 shareholders with only one share to sell their shares back to the company. This move reduced mailing costs to such single shareholders, who would keep a Playboy Enterprises stock certificate as a collector's item. (The new certificate pictures a clothed Bunny, to avoid arousing the interest of inexperienced investors.)

More important, the recapitalization, which converted common stock into voting and non-voting classes, allowed it to raise money without diluting Hef's 71 percent voting stake, valued at about $35 million at the time.

Surprisingly, Christie owns less than one percent of the company's shares, although she could gain more nonvoting shares through the company's new stock option incentives. Hef wants to hold on to his own stake even though he acknowledges that he will never return as chairman or CEO. Although Hef is still Playboy Enterprises' creative force, he is delighted to leave its business performance to Christie.

Of course, now that Hef has remarried and has a new family, the issue of which child will inherit controlling interest is undecided. On the other hand, it looks as if Hef planned his two families well: By the time his son by former Playmate Kimberley Conrad graduates from college, Christie will be entering her 60s.

Christie, so far, is unmarried and has no children. And for her part, Christie says she will run Playboy Enterprises for the rest of her life.

Gene Pressman   Robert L. Pressman

Gene: "We have no debt, we have great partners, and our marketing and
merchandising strategy is for the long term."

Barneys New York
New York, New York

Business:	Specialty retail stores for men, women and home
Best Known Departments:	Men's international and traditional clothing and accessories; Women's designer, private label and contemporary clothing and accessories; Chelsea Passage (home and gifts)
Founded:	1923 by Barney and Bertha Pressman
Family Executives:	Fred Pressman, Chairman Gene Pressman, Co-President and Co-CEO Robert L. Pressman, Co-President and Co-CEO Phyllis Pressman, General Merchandise Manager, Chelsea Passage Bonnie Pressman, General Merchandise Manager, Women's Accessories and Shoes Holly Pressman, Corporate Program and Investment Director Liz Pressman Neubardt, Buyer, Baby Nancy Pressman-Dressler, Buyer, Women's Contemporary
Family History:	Third generation
Family Ownership:	Barneys Inc.: 100 percent Barneys America, Inc.: 75 percent
Family Board Membership:	Substantial majority
Traded:	Privately held
Net Sales:	$210,000,000 1991-1992 160,000,000 1990-1991 130,000,000 1989-1990
Net Earnings:	Will not disclose

BARNEYS NEW YORK

Innovation By Generation

Gene Pressman
Robert L. Pressman
Co-Presidents and Co-CEOs

It's 1923. A trepidatious 28-year-old Barney Pressman pawns his wife's engagement ring for $500 and uses half the money for the downpayment on a 500-square-foot rental space in lower Manhattan. With the remaining $250, he pays for the 400 cut-rate men's suits that will constitute his merchandise. He calls the off-price retail store on East 17th Street "Barney's."

Fast forward to 1992. Barney's grandsons, Gene (41) and Bob (37), are using their in-air jet time to Japan to talk over developments at the company's approximately 680,000 square feet of retail space, which spreads from Manhattan to Beverly Hills and jumps the ocean to Japan and Southeast Asia. Now it's "Barneys New York," the apostrophe having been dropped in 1983 to lessen its identification with one person and the "New York" added to emphasize the cosmopolitan merchandise.

It's a long way from New York's Lower East Side to Tokyo's Shinjuku district. Three generations of Pressman men—and Pressman women—have traveled on this journey since Barney's wife, Bertha, insisted on his pawning her ring to open the shop laid the foundation for this global retail empire. For 65 years the company remained solely at that first site at 17th Street and Seventh Avenue. The out-of-the-way location meant an uphill battle to attract customers (despite free parking), but the store's service, quality of merchandise, and selection brought in shoppers from the metropolitan area.

Early customers saw Barney on the floor, Bertha ringing up sales, and son Fred, appropriately born the year the store opened, sweeping up sales tickets. (Barney and Bertha also had another son who did not enter the business.) Later, as the business expanded and its reputation spread, shoppers were asked to take a seat (on a user-unfriendly plastic chair) and were assigned a salesperson by Bertha.

Fred's adult debut at the store was in 1946. If there's a man who could be said to have retailing in his blood, it's Fred Pressman. Maintaining his parents' focus on service, quality, and price, Fred trained himself to become the preeminent men's apparel shopkeeper. It was Fred who told his father that the store couldn't sustain growth because bankruptcy sales weren't providing enough of the quality goods he wanted to sell. As Fred started to buy directly from manufacturers in the late '50s, the image of the store shifted. By 1964, Barney's was no longer a discount retailer. And Barney himself "was wonderful" about the change, says Fred. "He listened to me."

No sooner had Fred reshaped the business as a full-priced specialty store than he started to stock European designs. There'd long been Burberrys available at the store, and Daks, but by the mid-'60s the hot stuff was the Carnaby Street merchandise in the boys' department. Soon European apparel was represented in menswear, with Fred spending more and more time in Europe working with designers and manufacturers to meet American tastes.

In the '60s, Fred brought Pierre Cardin designs to the United States, and in 1968 he opened the pace-setting International House within the store. He sewed up his reputation as an innovator in merchandising with the American debut of Georgio Armani in 1974. The store now had the rare ability to carry off a mix of traditional suits for Wall Street and designer merchandise.

Additionally, Fred's wife Phyllis augmented the merchandise selection to include the gift and antique shop she heads, called Chelsea Passage. This line of fine items for the home expanded the Barneys merchandise from apparel to lifestyle.

While Fred and Phyllis were making second-generation changes at the store, at home their four children were showing varying interest in the family business. Bob, who heads the financial and operations side of the company, says it was his curiosity in math that lead him, as a nine-year-old boy waiting for his dad one Saturday afternoon, to pick up the day's sales receipts to add and to check against the accountant's figures. And re-add and re-check, for the accountant had made a $15,000 error. Bob's career was clinched when he showed Fred the adding machine tapes.

Bob's older brother, Gene, on the other hand, showed scant curiosity about the family's clothing store as a boy and feels his attitude is typical of that of most children. When told of other business heirs who report their life-long interest in a family business, he laughs. "Without meaning to be rude, unless their dads were baseball players, I think they're full of bullshit. Give me a break."

Nonetheless, Gene fell into the family business in 1972 after college graduation and an unsuccessful try at filmmaking. Gene's focus is on merchandising and marketing, and one of his first contributions was, in 1976, to push his father into adding a glitzy Women's Duplex to what was the largest men's clothing store in the world. (The original store had been expanded a number of times and by 1986 had grown to its current 170,000 square feet.)

The volatile world of women's wear appeals to Gene, whose creativity and good eye for design led him in 1978 to launch BASCO All-American Sportswear, a men's and women's clothing line that earned the *Prix de Cachet* and the Cutty Sark award for the most promising U.S. designer. Gene has two partners in BASCO, brother Bob and designer Lance Karesh. The BASCO line is also sold in such prestigious department stores as Neiman-Marcus, and it was the first U.S. designer line to have an independent store in Japan.

Bob began at the store in 1976 after graduation and worked nights and weekends on his MBA. With Gene, he helped push for an in-house advertising agency. The company's advertising was noticeable in its early years ("Calling all men to Barney's!") and has been notable of late (a stark Annie Leibowitz photo of Sarah Bernhardt attired in a man's suit). Partly to have better creative control over the ads, in 1985 the Pressmans formed BNY Advertising. BNY Advertising also takes on other accounts and does *pro bono* work—for example, for Art Against AIDS.

Also attracting attention to the business have been the hip, celebrity-oriented window displays. Don't look at the Barneys

New York windows for traditional Christmas tableaux of family ice-skating in Central Park. Instead, displays have included Tammy Faye Bakker with a Christmas tree shaped like a mascara brush; George Hamilton tanning under a revolving Imelda Marcus sun; and a bathrobed, cigar-smoking Jesse Helms gazing at a Robert Mapplethorpe photo book, with the message "Merry Christmas to All, and to All a Far Right!"

The success of the women's duplex led to the opening of a 70,000-square-foot women's store on 17th Street in 1986. An annex to the flagship store, its atrium features a spiral staircase under a 25-foot skylight. The addition of women's apparel added significantly to the company's rise in revenues during the late '80s.

A satellite men's store opened in 1988 in the World Financial Center. The expansion to the Wall Street area was the company's first away from its original site.

In 1989, the Pressmans formed a new retail company called Barneys America Inc., which operates Barneys New York stores in swank areas throughout the country. The smaller Barneys New York stores feature what the Pressmans call "the best of Barneys" and are located in the New York City suburbs of Manhasset, Short Hills, and Westport; in Chestnut Hill, Massachusetts; Troy, Michigan; Costa Mesa, California; Seattle; Dallas; Houston; and Chicago. (The Chicago store is a full-line Barneys New York at 50,000 square feet.)

The Pressmans' flexibility allowed them to switch their merchandise mix from their original plan for the new stores, which was to have men's sportswear occupy 20 percent of floorspace and to devote the remaining space to women's high fashion apparel. But most of their male customers turned out to be familiar with the 17th Street store and expected to find a similar merchandise selection in the Barneys New York branch stores. The answer was not to take from the women's selection but to add a full range of dress suits, shoes and ties to the men's by expanding the 6,000-square-foot branch stores to 20,000 feet.

This privately held company can be characterized by flexibility and adaptability. Gene says, "We're not worried about change. We're not worried about mistakes."

All the transformations—the women's store, the World Financial Center site, and the branch stores—seem almost trifling when balanced against the decision to enter a joint venture agreement with a major Japanese retailer.

In 1987 and 1988, the Pressmans were seriously talking about radical expansion. They weren't attracted by leverage, even in the heyday of LBOs. They wanted "to do the opposite," says Bob. "We felt it was more prudent going forward without debt. We'd have more flexibility and could make better long-term decisions if we funded the growth with equity capital rather than with a lot of debt, which would have put us under duress and pressure.

"We hired Goldman, Sachs & Co. and came up with a plan that would accomplish a lot of things: to open stores, both large and small, throughout the United States, and to open stores outside the United States, in Japan."

The Pressmans went to Japan in the fall of 1988 to look for a retailer who'd act as a strategic partner. After meeting with Japan's most important retailers, the Pressmans chose the Isetan Company Limited, which is the sixth largest retailer in Japan (with sales of $4 billion in 1991) and which ranks first in profitability in that country. The joint venture agreement was for an initial investment of $250 million, with Isetan putting up more than half.

Part of the attraction is that Isetan is publicly run and managed by the fourth generation of its founding family. "So here we were," says Bob, "family retailers to family retailers, with a president of the company [Kuniyasu Kosuge] in his early 40s—also unusual for Japan—who speaks English very well and who has a global outlook."

It was a good fit. "The nice thing about it was that our viewpoint and theirs was the same: If the concept makes sense, the numbers will come. Everybody else seems to look at the numbers first to see if the concept works. Our outlook is totally opposite," says Bob.

The two companies worked out a joint venture agreement that gives the companies reciprocal investments for Barneys New York in the United States and in Asia. The Pressmans have a majority interest in Barneys America, the smaller branch stores where Isetan has a minority interest. Conversely, the Pressman family has only a minority interest while Isetan holds the majority interest in Barneys Japan Company Limited, which includes the Tokyo Barneys New York—opened in late 1990 as Japan's largest free-standing store associated with an American retailer—and the Yokohama Barneys New York, to open in 1993. Other stores are planned elsewhere in Southeast Asia.

"Through their capitalization, we gained the opportunity to expand even in what is considered not very favorable economic times," says Gene.

In 1992, Barneys New York added the largest specialty store to open in Manhattan in more than 60 years at Madison Avenue between 60th and 61st Streets. The 230,000-square-foot store will be evenly divided between menswear and women's apparel, accessories, and the Chelsea Passage gift area. (The family expects sales of about $150 million in this store's first year.) In 1993, there will be a 110,000-square-foot store in Beverly Hills on Wilshire Boulevard and Camden Drive. The flagship store and the stores located at the World Financial Center, Madison Avenue, and Beverly Hills are wholly owned by the Pressman family.

There's also a joint venture company in which the Pressmans and Isetan have acquired the real estate for the Madison Avenue site (purchased outright for $100 million cash) and the Beverly Hills site to lease back to the Barneys New York company that operates these stores under the Pressman family. (With the Pressmans' interest in real estate, it seemed natural for them to invest in restaurants—they are partners in eight throughout the United States, not including the restaurants and cafés in their stores.)

The Pressmans' unique financial structure allows them to stay aggressive in a fluctuating retail economy because they can focus on the business instead of being distracted by debt as are other retailers. And as those other specialty and department stores have staggered in a bumpy economy, there is less competition for the surviving stores.

This is very much a family that looks out for the long term, by involving many family members. Also involved in decision-making are Gene's and Bob's younger sisters. Liz Pressman Neubardt is the buyer for Chelsea Passage's baby merchandise and Nancy Pressman-Dressler is the buyer for women's contemporary. Neither of the Pressman daughters' husbands works at the store—both of the women married physicians. ("My mother is thrilled," Gene jokes.)

But the brothers' wives are at the company. Gene's wife, Bonnie, a former Ford model, is general merchandise manager for women's accessories and shoes. Holly Pressman, Bob's wife, is director of corporate programs and investments, having been an investment manager at Morgan Stanley and Co., Inc.

Gene points out that even with eight family executives, Barneys New York still offers employees room for upward movement. "We have more than 2,000 employees, with four senior vice presidents, plus more than 20 vice presidents and assistant vice presidents," he says.

The question of balance always arises when two sons take charge of the family business. Luckily for the Pressmans, Gene's and Bob's natural talents complement each other. And if one brother's grooming and sartorial style can rapidly identify him as the creative head and the other brother can immediately be spotted as the financial head, well, that's fine with the Pressmans because it works so well.

Even Fred serves as counterpoint, acting occasionally as a sage during strategy talks. As Gene says of his father, "He's very aggressive, but he's a good failsafe for us. He questions and criticizes—in a good way—and makes us think. It's a good check and balance."

So far, so good. Sales doubled for Barneys New York from 1986 to 1990 and were running nearly 30 percent ahead in 1992 over the previous year. The firm's step-by-step expansion strategy is more than meeting expectations: The spring season of 1992 saw the company running a double-digit increase in sales from 1991. Additionally, the comprehensive style appeal of specialty retailers like fashion-forward Barneys New York continues to increase as corporate consolidations of department stores lead to homogenized merchandise and poor service. Sales run approximately $650 per square foot for this specialty retailer, about three times the national average.

Through its creative capitalization, Barneys New York has positioned itself in major markets, using the same fashion-forward retail strategy in each part of their organization. Gene says, "We're doing this in difficult times so that when times open up, we'll be ahead of our competition, which is vulnerable right now. But we have no debt, we have great partners, and our marketing and merchandising strategy is for the long term."

None of the Pressmans let up an inch. These alert merchants stay ahead by spotting trends and quickly translating them into retail sales. They have a good example in their founder. Until his death at 96 in 1991, Barney would call from Miami Beach each afternoon for the day's receipts.

Dean: "We certainly have dusted [Hammond Maps] off and shaken it up and blown it toward the future."

Hammond, Inc.
Maplewood, New Jersey

Business:	Maps, atlases
Best Known Products:	*Hammond Atlas of The World*
Founded:	1900 by Caleb Stillson Hammond
Family Executives:	C. Dean Hammond III, President, CEO and Director
	Kathleen D. Hammond, COO, Executive Vice President and Director
	Caleb Dean Hammond Jr., Chairman
Family History:	Fourth generation
Family Ownership:	More than 90%
Family Board Members:	7 family members of 12 directors
Traded:	Privately owned
Net Sales:	Will not disclose
Net Earnings:	Will not disclose

HAMMOND INC.

Mapping the Future

C. Dean Hammond III, President and CEO
Kathleen D. Hammond, Executive Vice President and CEO

C. Dean Hammond, 45, and his wife Kathleen, 41, made a decision in the '80s to keep this privately owned company in family hands—specifically, in their own hands. The couple also strove to ensure Hammond's future success by innovating and updating map production. In 1987, the company began development of a high-quality, cartographic production system that has transformed map-making from a mechanical to an automated process.

The company's database system has no maps stored in it; rather, the information has been classified by latitude and longitude coordinates in more than 1,000 categories. This allows a cartographer to configure any section of the world in any projection or scale desired. The company developed its own software to use this data.

This flexibility for a wide range of applications allows Hammond atlases to exceed the detail level found in other commercial atlases and to achieve greater accuracy than ever before. In developing the system, the Hammonds worked with Mitchell J. Feigenbaum, Ph.D., who holds the Toyota Chair at Rockefeller University. (Feigenbaum is recognized for having solved the Theory of Chaos, a study of the predictability of molecular systems.)

Dean explains Feigenbaum's contribution to Hammond mapping: "There are points on a sphere where, if you have to squash the world out flat, you want to do it with a minimum amount of distortion. If you envision taking an orange peel and stepping on it, you're going to have wrinkles in it. The idea is to mathematically minimize those wrinkles. That is what Feigenbaum has done with the creation of the Hammond Optimal Projection software. It mathematically minimizes the distortion of continents and produces the best maps that can be created.

"This gives the consumer a much more accurate map from which to develop trips. If you're measuring distance from city to city on any given map, you can have distortion of up to 20 percent. On the new Hammond maps, distortion has been cut down to one-tenth of one percent."

In addition, having a single data base allows Hammond to make changes quickly. "So we have more accurate maps and the ability to create them much faster," says Dean.

Of course, software and data bases were unknown when Dean's great grandfather Caleb Stillson Hammond, a salesman, founded the company in 1900. (The initial before Dean's first name stands for Caleb.) The original Caleb's motivation came from being turned down for a raise by the business he worked for—Rand McNally & Company.

Starting Hammond with a little capital from his family, he initially sold two products. One was a conventional United States map, but the other was a world map drawn on a new projection. The popularity of the early Hammond maps was due to the development of a system by Caleb's cartographers that gave the best equivalent projections.

Caleb responded quickly to the public's interest in world events, producing a photo book of the San Francisco earthquake in 1906 within a week of the disaster. He planned a polar map book to hit the stores as soon as Perry reached the North Pole in 1908. As countries changed borders and names at the end of World War I, Hammond offered loose-leaf substitute maps.

Road maps became a staple of the company. Hammond maps were included as inserts in *Compton's Encyclopedia*, *Encyclopedia Britannica*, *Funk & Wagnalls*, and other reference books. Wall maps were produced for trade purposes and for schools, and Hammond diversified into table games and puzzles.

In 1950, under the leadership of Dean's father Bud (Caleb Dean Hammond, Jr.), the company left New York for a town in New Jersey where all its facilities could be contained at one site. Although sales were still sound in the '80s, it seemed to some that Hammond could sharpen Caleb's innovative edge. One person who wanted to improve Hammond's position was his great-grand-son Dean.

In 1974, 27-year-old Dean joined Hammond as a salesman, when the company was headed by Stuart Hammond. After college graduation with a business degree, Dean had attended law school but left to co-found a successful bicycle retail store in Florida. He felt drawn back to Hammond, however, and when he arrived, he decided to put his own stamp on the company. One of his first accomplishments was to convince such large circulation magazines as *Time*, *Newsweek*, and *Readers Digest* to use Hammond products as circulation premiums.

Dean's future wife Kathy was initially one of his clients, an advertising sales manager with *The New York Times*. They married in 1978. After four years of persuasion, Dean convinced Kathy to leave her job at the *Times* and join Hammond as director of corporate development. Their mutual ambition was to jointly lead Hammond into the twenty-first century.

However, Dean and Kathy owned only a nine percent stake in the company. In addition, a dozen other family members and a few nonfamily members were shareholders. In this decade of takeovers, the couple worried each time a potential suitor approached Hammond.

The textbook publisher Silver Burdett Company made a serious offer for the company in 1985. Dean's uncle, who was the company's president and who owned 30 percent of Hammond's shares, was thought to have seriously entertained the possibility of selling his shares to Silver Burdett. There was also another director of Hammond who hoped to buy a Hammond relative's 22 percent for the purpose of selling.

"It never occurred to me when I joined that it would ever be anything but a privately owned company," says Dean. "Then it began to look like that could change and we certainly woke up."

After hearing of the behind-the-scenes maneuvers, Dean, Kathy, and Bud, who was a board member and former CEO, approached the relative and offered to buy her 22 percent stake. Because she liked the idea of the company remaining within the family, she agreed to sell to the Hammonds rather than possibly holding out for a higher price. The trio continued buying more shares from other family members until they had a majority stake in the company. Dean's uncle relinquished the presidency to Dean, who reflects on this period, "It was rough. It wasn't fun at all."

As soon as the company was under Dean's leadership, the priority was to create a single database of the world for which all future Hammond products could be drawn. "That you could take a single set of information and make very accurate maps to any scale had never been done before," says Dean.

Conversations with Feigenbaum, a friend for several decades, convinced Dean and Kathy (who had been named executive vice president in 1986) that such an undertaking might possibly be doable—under Feigenbaum's creative direction. Having enlisted a world-renowned physicist to create this single database for the company, Hammond now has ownership of a unique mapping system.

Hammond Atlas of The World, a completely new atlas, was introduced in 1992 and is considered the most sophisticated on the market, reflecting computerized database work on a world scale. It is the first atlas produced entirely from a computer database and has vivid, three-dimensional topographic maps, which are hand-sculpted by a Hammond master cartographer.

And as the Hammonds look to the future, they see many possibilities for their product line to roam the world. With Hammond's automatic type placement, they can create an atlas in any language within five months. Any kind of customized mapping can be done quickly. "Since all our data is electronically sorted and digitized," says Dean, "we can create a map and bounce it off a satellite and send it with whatever colors or information are wanted."

Dean says that Hammond is now firmly managed by people with a controlling interest in the company. "We can decide on the proper direction for the company and drive it there without having endless meetings. We can have a quick headcount and boom, we go. It enables us to respond to opportunities very, very quickly—whether they are world changes or technological advances."

Dean does not seriously consider bringing Hammond public. "We're having too much fun," he responds. Also, Dean and Kathy have two children, age six and ten, whom they'd like to become fifth-generation mapmakers in the twenty-first century.

And Josh Hammond, Dean's 18-year-old son from a first marriage, is already at the company full-time, learning how maps are made—from the base up—as he works the cameras and does drafting work. "He's actually the first Hammond in five generations who has the job of making the maps," reflects his father.

"I'm pleased that he's here and I'm pleased that he's pleased to be here," says Dean. "It's one of those things where you're not quite sure how it's going to work. He came to me after a few months and sat at my desk and said to me, 'I never thought I'd be saying this.'

"I wasn't sure where the conversation was going. Then he continued, 'I'm proud of being here and I love having my name on the Hammond books.'"

Dean reflects, "The company has given Kathy and me a vehicle with which to see our dreams come true—and to do it together. We want this same opportunity to be there for the children as it has been for us."

And to keep the company healthy, Dean says, "We have certainly dusted it off and shaken it up and blown it toward the future."

Keith Crain

Rance Crain

Rance: "I think we'll both run it—together—and we'll just have to work hard at finding the proper elements of agreement. There's no doubt in my mind that we can."

Crain Communications, Inc.
Chicago, Illinois

Business:	Trade publications
Best Known Products:	*Crain's New York (Chicago, Detroit, Cleveland) Business; Advertising Age; Automotive News; Electronic Media*
Founded:	1916 by G.D. Crain
Family Executives:	Gertrude Ramsay Crain, Chairman Rance Crain, President Keith Crain Vice Chairman
Family History:	Second generation
Family Ownership:	90 percent
Family Board Membership:	5 family members of 6 directors
Traded:	Privately held
Net Sales:	$140,000,000 1989 135,000,000 1988
Net Earnings:	Will not disclose

CRAIN COMMUNICATIONS, INC.

Shared Power

Rance Crain, President
Keith Crain, Vice Chairman

The brothers Crain have transformed their parents' small yet influential industrial trade magazine group into a substantial media corporation. Not only have they increased Crain Communication's trade publications from seven periodicals at the time of their father's death in 1973 to 26 periodicals in 1990, but they've also attracted a new readership—the consumer.

Crain Communications, founded in 1916, is one of the largest industry trade publishers in the United States and also one of the fastest growing companies in publishing. Two characteristics of the privately held Crain company are its explosive growth under Rance and Keith and the unusually warm family feeling between the Crains and their employees. As Rance and Keith's mother, Gertrude Crain has modestly said, "We're trying to convey that this is a small family business." Gertrude's "small family business" has catapulted the family onto the Forbes 400 list.

By the time his sons were born, Rance in 1940 and Keith in 1941, G.D. Crain was recognized as dean of the advertising press and one of the founders of the industrial trade publication field. He'd married Gertrude in 1936 when he was 51 years old, following the death of his first wife. Gertrude was only 25, less than half his age.

Thus, Crain Communications had its start well before Rance and Keith arrived on the scene. G.D. had been a business news reporter (with a master's degree in English) who cannily anticipated the growing need for trade publications. During World War I, he began two industry magazines.

In the late '20s, G.D. had another hunch. This time, he saw a market for a hard-news advertising trade journal. In the wake of the stock market crash, G.D., by now an influential publisher, traveled to Washington, D.C. in 1930 to discuss his idea for a new publication called *Advertising Age* with President Herbert Hoover. Hoover gave G.D. his personal assurance of a sound economy.

Years later, Keith asked his dad, "What if Hoover had warned you of the upcoming depression? What if he told you it might last for years?" G.D.'s reply was, "I would've started it anyway." And *Advertising Age*—after a few scary years spent in the red—turned into the cornerstone of the Crain media empire and the family's personal fortune.

Crain seemed like any other prosperous company to the two boys who were growing up in Evanston, Illinois, hearing their parents talk of the family's publications at dinner.

Gertrude was involved in local charities and the children's schools, but she had latent management talents and a strong sense of self esteem. Her belief in herself came from her experience as an executive secretary at NBC before her marriage and from G.D.'s trust in her business instincts.

Gertrude noticed that pensions and investments in G.D.'s growing company were not getting the attention they merited. G.D. listened to his wife's suggestions on aggressive money management and finally told her, "You do it." She did.

Gertrude's early activities in the company (which included serving as the board's treasurer/secretary) left no particular impression on her sons because she matched her work hours to their school day. "She could have been out pumping gas," Keith laughs, for all the attention the children paid to their mother's activities.

As the boys grew, both worked summers in the company's circulation department, although once Keith walked out because he discovered he could make more money somewhere else. Rance stayed and moved on to writing fillers. A career at the company, though, was "left completely up to us," says Keith. G.D. had seen too many men pressure their sons to follow them into their family businesses, with disastrous results for both the companies and the families. "He was very careful, unbelievably careful, to never suggest it to us," says Keith. "And I never grew up assuming I'd take over Crain Communications."

Rance, the more intense older brother, didn't give a future at Crain Communications any real thought, either, until his last year at Northwestern University after he read Allen Drury's bestselling novel, *Advise and Consent*. Eager to work in Washington, he asked the Crain Washington bureau chief to give him a shot as a reporter. Soon he moved to Crain's New York office and for the next ten years, worked either in New York or in the Chicago headquarters. By the time Rance joined *Advertising Age* in Chicago, G.D. was already in his eighties but still working full-time.

Keith reports that when he got out of Northwestern a year after Rance, he asked his parents, "Are there any jobs?" Keith began in sales, and he says both he and Rance got high marks from their supervisors because "we worked cheap and we weren't going to quit."

Rance eventually returned to Chicago in 1971, when his 86-year-old father thought perhaps he'd cut back on his work schedule. On the days G.D. came into the office, he and Rance worked closely together. (Rance officially reported to other people because G.D. wanted to avoid having either of his sons answer directly to him.)

Although G.D. was well past the age when most businessmen want to take new risks, he and his family took a chance on another publication. They bought *Automotive News*, a Detroit-based paper that was losing a lot of money. While Rance stayed in Chicago to work with his parents, Keith shifted to Detroit to steer *Automotive News*. Gertrude increased her time at the firm's offices and soon was working every day. Upon G.D.'s death in 1973, the title of chairman passed to Gertrude, Rance became president, and Keith became vice chairman, titles they retain today.

Rance and Keith split the company's publications list so each had his own group of magazines and newspapers. This strategy continued as they added more publications to their respective piles, through acquisition or development.

Rance made a move in 1978 to develop a business weekly, *Crain's Chicago Business*. Naysayers predicted that it was doomed — but it has since become the fifth largest business publication in the country. Keith started the Detroit regional weekly along with a few Detroit magazines, and Rance's *Crain's Cleveland Business* came next.

Then Rance took a more personal leap of faith. Passionate about everything he does, Rance moved to the New York area with his wife (their two children are grown) to oversee his new weekly, *Crain's New York Business*, and the other publications that are his responsibility, including *Advertising Age*. Rance's enthusiasm for the new magazine ran so high, reported *Madison Avenue* magazine, that he stood on Wall Street in 1985 handing out the weekly to commuters. As usual with a new publication, *Crain's New York Business* bled cash the first few years, but it is now close to breaking even.

Keith is happy in Detroit managing his publications and focusing on the company's sales and financial growth. And while Keith may have a penchant for fast cars, it's not matched by a yen for fast living. Spare time is spent with his wife and three children, who are still at home. His idea of a great vacation is to take the kids on a trip that mixes pleasure with Crain business.

One thing that bothers both brothers is the inability of Crain employees to know each other now that staff are concentrated in Detroit with Keith, in New York with Rance, and in Chicago with Gertrude. Crain Communications also has employees in other U.S. cities and in London, Frankfurt, and Tokyo, for a total of 13 offices.

Keith says, "The people in Akron tend to become very involved with the people in Akron, and they don't interrelate with the people in New York at all. And the people in Chicago tend to become very Chicago-oriented. And *Advertising Age* is so big, it tends to become an entity all in itself. It's much tougher than when we had two or three publications and we were in the same rooms."

If Gertrude is credited with maintaining the warm, personal standard in the company and Keith is relied upon for number crunching, Rance's great talent is his creativity. He describes himself as an idea man. "More than anything else," he says, "I like coming up with new publication ideas—such as *Crain's Chicago Business*, or *Electronic Media*, or *Pensions and Investment Age*."

This doesn't mean that ideas have never fizzled. A second edition of *Advertising Age* failed, as did *Crain's Illinois Business* and a consumer magazine for people who invest in collectibles. Rance let these go within a couple of years rather than cling to duds.

The key component of Crain magazines is their extensive and candid news content. *Electronic Media*, *Advertising Age* and *Automotive News*—all publications of record within their industries—are respected for their editorial independence from the major industry powers. Keith, for example, didn't lose any sleep after General Motors, angered at an *Automotive News* editorial, pulled G.M. staff out of a planned seminar sponsored by the publication.

And Rance's *Electronic Media* was the first trade publication to report on a trend toward "shock" radio—talk shows rife with sexist, racist, and homophobic slurs. When the Federal Communications Commission released new broadcast guidelines for talk radio, this regulatory agency credited *Electronic Media* with bringing the issue to its attention.

Besides their candor, Crain publications are easy to read and are only minimally riddled with industry jargon. "Some of our publications are primarily consumer publications," says Rance as he ticks off the names of the city business magazines, and adds another of Keith's publications, *AutoWeek*, to that list. "But we run our trade publications like consumer publications. We want to serve our reader, first and foremost." To that purpose, each Crain publication assures its readers that a letter to the publisher goes directly to the publisher and receives a response.

Both men say that the company's most important asset is the editorial staff. "Our assets go home at night," Keith points out. "Without them, we're nothing." Although starting salaries are not tops in the field, Crain staff quickly catch up and surpass their colleagues at other magazines. Frequent cash bonuses and one of the first profit-sharing plans in the country, started by Gertrude while Rance and Keith were still school boys, make for what Crain employees jokingly called the golden handcuffs, reported *Family Business* magazine.

Crain reporters and editors appreciate the money, but what's more important in their eyes is the creative freedom and respect they're given. The Crains keep a very loose rein on editors. "Every publication is autonomous," Rance says. "We expect the editor to run the magazine without regard to the top management of the company. They're expected to develop it and keep it profitable. And they have a lot of leeway to do that."

The Crains insist they have no master plan for the company. Instinct and intuition play a heavy part in the family's opportunistic decision-making. Rance says, "We just take advantage of the opportunities as they come along. That leaves us free to pursue whatever avenues we want to pursue. If I want to worry about *Advertising Age* for a while, I can do that. If I want to pull back and think about a new publication idea for a while, I can do that, too." Rance added two new publications of his own in 1989; they operate independently of Crain Communications under the corporate name Turnstile. One is *Golf Week* and another is *Main Events*, an hour-by-hour listing of activities for visitors to different cities. In 1991, *Main Events* was limited to Atlanta, but plans are under way to expand this tourist publication to other cities.

Keith adds, "We have a lot of little projects that kind of float around. Sometimes they become big projects, and sometimes they float away." He notes that Rance's *Electronic Media* began as an insert in *Advertising Age* and is now one of Crain's most important publications.

Following their instincts and doing what seems like fun was a deciding factor, after Rance bought a place in Key Largo, in the company's purchase of *Florida Keys Magazine* and several radio stations. (Rance's secret yen is to be a disc jockey.)

When a company is privately owned and as closely held as Crain Communications—the family accounts for 90 percent of the company's ownership—it's possible to buy a Florida magazine because Rance vacations down there, or to buy *Monthly Detroit* (now called *Detroit Monthly*) because of Keith's civic interests.

Keith says, "Being private gives us an opportunity to react. I remember getting a call from the publisher of *Rubber and Plastic News* about a new opportunity for *European Rubber Journal.* Two days later we bought it. You can't do that if you're public."

Not surprisingly, both Crains define themselves as risktakers. "Definitely," says Rance of himself. "I'm perfectly willing to spend a lot of money to develop a new publication with the idea we can make it very successful. *Crain's New York Business* is a perfect example. It's going to cost us $15 million to get that thing in the black. But it's certainly worth every effort because down the line that's going to be an enormously successful publication."

Keith brings up the balance the company needs to strike between the risks he takes "all the time" and the company's responsibilities to its employees. "We have certain constraints. We're not wildcatters pumping for oil in Oklahoma. These are not just 1,000 employees we're responsible for, but 1,000 families—each with mortgages and kids to educate."

Right now, when one of the brothers finds a market and wants to leap in with a publication, the start-up expenses are paid out of earnings. "If for some reason we want to plow all our profits back into the growth of the company in any one year, that's our prerogative. We've done that on occasion, and we'll probably do it again," says Rance.

If the brothers are offended at the possibility that one day they might need to borrow money for a launch or an acquisition, still they're adamantly against going public. Rance says, "That would just create all kinds of problems that we wouldn't want. Then we'd have to start managing the company for quarterly growth, and that's an awful thing to have over your head all the time."

Additionally, Rance believes that Crain Communications wouldn't be a growth company if it had been public. The company's management would've been too cautious to bring out a new publication that would cut profits in half in a given fiscal year.

It sounds as if Rance and Keith are in accord on just about every issue affecting Crain Communications. But rumors of thunderstorms have hovered over the brothers for 30 years, ever since they both joined the company. Despite these whispers, the brothers themselves are careful to credit each other for the company's achievements. Rance, for example, says that his father would have been most proud of the start-up of *Crain's Chicago Business* and the 60-year success of *Advertising Age*. Then he adds, "And acquisitions like *Automotive News*, which my brother is running. When we got that, it was not doing well. Now it's extremely successful."

Despite their reluctance to discuss that will happen when their mother is no longer there to head the company, Rance says "I don't think there'll be any one designated person. Keith cares about it as much as I do, and he has as much right to try to influence the direction of the company as I do. I'd say that in a family company it doesn't really matter that much. I think we'll both run it—together—and we'll just have to work hard at finding the proper elements of agreement. There's no doubt in my mind that we can." Rance continues, "I think it's important that we're all trying to do the same thing. We're all trying to make our publications as good as they can possibly be." Disagreements are resolved by their agreement not to go ahead with a plan that either brother or Gertrude doesn't fully support.

G.D. exerts a strong presence nearly 20 years after his death. Keith says, "I don't think of him as gone; his ideas still remain with us," and Rance will sometimes slip into the present tense while speaking of his late father.

Helping to continue the Crain tradition are the Crain wives. Merrillee Crain, Rance's wife, serves on the board as executive secretary. Keith's wife, Mary Kay Crain, is executive treasurer. Rance became momentarily confused about which wife served in what board capacity, and at first asserted that Merrillee was treasurer and Mary Kay, secretary. After checking a Crain masthead, he dismissed his confusion with the comment, "In a family-owned business, formal roles don't matter."

Neither of Rance's daughters is at Crain Communications, but the older daughter's husband Ken Hanson is circulation manager for *Crain's New York Business*. Rance's younger daughter is working in advertising. "That's great," says her father. "As long as she's doing something she enjoys doing, that's the important thing so far as I'm concerned." (G.D.'s grandson from his first marriage also works for the company in Chicago.)

Keith's children are too young to be thinking of joining the company, but, Keith has always taken his kids on Crain trips and kept up that Crain tradition of talking about the day's work at the dinner table. Keith, like his father, would never pressure his children to enter the firm. In fact, despite speculation about which brother—singular—will succeed Gertrude, Keith, unlike many family business theorists, thinks succession is easier for the second generation.

Keith frowns. "The third generation is tough." He shakes his head. "Now, that's the time when succession starts getting tough."

"I want to be the Wizard of Oz."

McCaw Cellular Communications, Inc.

Business:	Provider of cellular mobile telephone service
Best Known Products:	Cellular One
Founded:	1937 by J. Elroy McCaw as McCaw Communications; 1969 by Craig O. McCaw as McCaw Communications
Family Executives:	Craig O. McCaw, Chairman and CEO John E. McCaw Jr., Director Bruce McCaw, Director
Family Ownership:	33 percent Class A common stock; 88 percent Class B voting shares
Family Board Membership:	3 family members of 17 directors
Traded:	NASDAQ, MCAWA
Net Sales:	$1,037,453,000 1990 504,138,000 1989 310,826,000 1988
Net Earnings:	$ 48,380,000 1990 (140,222,000) 1989 (154,139,000) 1988

MCCAW CELLULAR COMMUNICATIONS, INC.

Goodbye, Ma Bell; Hello, Craig McCaw

Craig O. McCaw, Chairman and CEO

Craig McCaw, 42, doesn't look like a gambler. A conservative business suit covers his slight frame; a youthful demeanor is set off by studious reading glasses, a quiet voice, and a shy demeanor. Yet this introvert is one of the notable risktakers of his generation. He's aggressive and innovative and operates on the edge. But Craig prefers to remain unseen as he plots strategy to unite the nation via cellular technology.

"I want to be the Wizard of Oz," Craig said at a company retreat in 1988. He was referring to the perception of the Wizard's ability to work great wonders anonymously. Although Craig's photograph has appeared on the cover of all the country's top business magazines, he dislikes the glare of publicity—especially the kind that named him one of America's best-paid CEOs for the decade of the '80s. Much to Craig's chagrin, he was ranked the third best-paid CEO for his 1989 total pay of $53.9 million, including salary, bonus, and stock options.

From his father's legacy of one cable station and lots of debt, Craig has built a communications behemoth. McCaw Cellular Communications is the largest cellular telephone company in the country and the fifth largest radio common carrier. It has more subscribers than any other company—and also more potential subscribers, a vital statistic in this neophyte industry. With its 1990 purchase of LIN Broadcasting, McCaw Cellular gained access to 103 cellular markets, including the cities with the busiest markets, such as New York and Los Angeles.

The cellular system brings phone service to customers— rather than requiring customers to come to the phone—by eliminating conventional telephone wires and using radio waves and transmission sites instead. Craig's vision is of a seamless network of cellular phone systems, a national system linking local and regional networks. "People who call your phone number will be connected to you, wherever you happen to be," he says.

Using wireless technology, a cellular call is transmitted through groups of cells, with each group having a low-power transmitter. These cell-group transmitters cover wide geographic areas. A call is handed off from one transmitter to the next, a technology that is dependent on radio waves. There are occasional glitches, and a call may be cut off or interrupted by static due to system overload or poor environmental conditions.

The system, Cellular One, was created out of a hodgepodge of small independents competing against regional telephone companies. Cellular One still has a long way to go before it is the seamless, national system Craig envisions. Since McCaw Cellular is the main operator under the Cellular One trademark, Craig naturally wants it to be the first truly national cellular carrier in America—in a sense, the country's single telephone company. But bringing this farsighted vision into reality is a capital-intensive venture that has bowed McCaw Cellular under a yoke of debt.

Dreams can be expensive. At the end of 1991, the company's debt was $5.28 billion. Servicing this debt is very costly: its interest payment that year was $578 million. Principal payments aren't due until 1994. It's predicted by some that the company will be in the red well into the '90s. (However, in the late '80s, other analysts mistakenly predicted that the business would be out of debt by 1991.) Craig's risktaking may be the characteristic hazard of being a visionary, but his history suggests that he can pull it off.

When talking of debt, many people in the cable industry remember Craig's father, J. Elroy McCaw, whose unexpected death in 1969, while Craig was at Stanford University, and the debt Elroy had incurred collapsed McCaw Communications. He'd been running the business out of his hat. The family spent eight years struggling out of the financial morass that was Elroy's material bequest. McCaw Communication's holdings of cable systems and television and radio stations had to be sold. The only reason the McCaws could save the one small cable system that gave the company its new life under Craig is that Elroy had placed that outfit in trust for his sons.

The debt changed the life of a family accustomed to its 28-room house, its expensive toys such as sailboats and cars, and its private school tuition for the four boys. (Craig went to Seattle's Lakeside school a few years ahead of Microsoft founders Bill Gates and Paul Allen.) The McCaw sons, of whom Craig is the second oldest, grew up with a great deal of independence in a freewheeling household where their mother was trying to manage the company's headquarters office while her husband was on the road.

Marion Scott, Craig's mother, infused stamina into the company after Elroy's death. As its office manager and accountant, she was able to bring a semblance of professional management to the company. She carried this off even though before Elroy's death she sometimes didn't know what deals he was writing—usually on the back of an envelope.

Craig himself had been a dealmaker since age 16, when he took a summer job in exchange for flying lessons. His summer experience selling cable subscriptions stood him in good stead after Elroy's death, and he worked with his mother and older brother to build up the company's single cable holding while he was still at Stanford. Craig improved programming, cut costs and raised subscription fees during the '70s, all before his thirtieth birthday.

By the '80s, he had seen something more appealing—and farther in the distance—than cable. Craig recognized cellular communications as an industry with intriguing possibilities well before the Federal Communications Commission accepted its first cellular service license applications for large cities in 1982. The first system was switched on in Chicago in 1983.

Craig was ready: He won all six licenses he pursued. Within two years, he was buying the coveted licenses from other companies, often paying hefty prices. At first, people wondered about his judgment; $2,600 car phones were for the extravagant. But Craig believed.

By 1987, he had rid McCaw Cellular of its remaining cable holdings, selling them to Jack Kent Cooke for $755 million. He also brought the company public, offering 12 percent of McCaw

Cellular, and used junk bond financing to grab more licenses from competitors.

He and his three brothers now own 33 percent of the company and control 88 percent of the voting shares, making the McCaw clan one of America's billionaire families. John McCaw is executive vice president for acquisitions, and Bruce and Keith are board directors but not involved with the company's daily operations.

In 1990, McCaw Cellular made one of the largest buys of the year with its $3.38 billion bid for LIN Broadcasting. The purchase gave McCaw Cellular five of the top cellular markets (and seven television stations) and helped stitch together the company's patchwork of markets. With this acquisition, Craig also sewed up his lead, giving him twice as many potential subscribers as his next rival.

McCaw Cellular also bought half of the New York City cellular franchise with its purchase of Metromedia for $1.9 billion in 1990. That same year, McCaw Cellular grabbed Contel for its South-eastern cellular market, paying $1.3 billion. In 1991 it entered a joint venture with Pacific Telesis, which further enlarged its cellular properties.

Craig's goal is to continue linking the company's regions without requiring callers to use roaming access numbers. He wants to reach people rather than places. By 1992 McCaw Cellular had already linked four regional areas into a network that automatically passes on calls. Craig wants to make other independent cellular carriers part of McCaw Cellular's communications network.

McCaw Cellular is also a leader in the development of digital technology that will vastly improve the quality of cellular communication, eliminating its familiar static and disconnections—the snap, crackle, and drop of today's cellular phones. The company has also signed up with Oracle Systems Corporation, a database software supplier, to broadcast data to computers via airwaves rather than telephone lines. This cellular data broadcasting system, which should make running data much less expensive, may become an $8 billion market by the end of the '90s.

Although the costs have been enormous, many believe that McCaw Cellular's debt strategy makes a lot of sense. Leveraging is the only way that McCaw Cellular is going to make a profit. The company needs to build itself up in fast-growing markets and fund its rapid expansion. Debt may be the nature of the franchise in an industry where subscriber growth can accelerate rapidly and pretax profit margins can move just as rapidly from red to black.

But this doesn't mean McCaw Cellular's expansion is worry free. Some of Craig's innovations may end up helping other cellular companies as much as they do McCaw Cellular. In addition, it turns out that many customers in the cellular industry are not the high-volume subscribers the system needs for profitablity, and these same people have a high "churn" rate—25 percent drop out each year. Cellular stocks plunged in value at the beginning of the decade, with McCaw Cellular taking at least as big a hit as the rest of the industry.

At this point, the company isn't able to pay its debt load out of its cash flow, and more expenses are on the horizon. In 1995, McCaw Cellular must buy the 48 percent of LIN that it doesn't own. And if the company wants to develop digital technology, it must continue to pump in capital. No wonder Craig is said to have nerves of steel.

On the other hand, some of his financials are looking healthier. The 1990 purchases enabled the company to increase its market by 42 percent in 1991, so that revenues went up and cash flow increased by 46 percent.

Amazingly, Craig doesn't let his company's debt distract him from long-term goals. He's developed the ability to cut through all the details and focus on what's important, a crucial skill whether he's planning for the future or piloting the company's Learjet and Gulfstream IV. He also flies an amphibious two-seater just large enough for him and his wife Wendy. (They have no children.) Craig also swims and bikes, neither one necessarily a team activity. Craig likes sailing, another solitary sport, nearly as much as flying. He and Wendy left their modest ranch house on Lake Washington to sail the Caribbean for several months in 1986.

These quiet pursuits fit a billionaire who may be the shyest CEO of a major American company. Craig must force himself to chit-chat at business-related social functions and prefers to have a McCaw executive at his side to help smooth any conversational awkwardness. It's these dichotomies—as well as his brilliance in envisioning needs of the future—that led *Fortune* to categorize Craig as one of the 25 "most fascinating business people" of 1989.

Craig craves his silent time on the water and in the air to visualize improved, high-quality communications systems. As an avid amateur historian, he's bound to think about his place in history. In an era when American business is getting static from foreign competitors' talk about its lack of technological innovations, it could be that Craig McCaw will be lauded no matter what the ultimate profitability of McCaw Cellular will be.

On the other hand, having put all his chips on one enormous bet, Craig may be the biggest winner of all.

SECTION II

THE REPLICATORS

Replicators do business much as the parents who proceeded them did. Replicators model behavior after the traits they've observed in their parents rather than being guided by what they've heard of their parents' behavior when the older generations were just starting out. These heirs themselves will point to the close similarities between the generations of yesterday and today. The media identify Leon Tempelsman of Lazare Kaplan diamonds as a financial wizard while characterizing his celebrity father Maurice as a dealmaker and diplomat without portfolio. But Leon says he is involved in many overseas deals—and that his father obviously knows enough about finance to have nurtured a prosperous diamond business. Dan Amos, who heads the insurance business AFLAC, says he closely resembles his father, Paul, who's now chairman, rather than his better-known uncle and AFLAC founder, John Beverly Amos. Paul was primarily a salesman, and Dan, although CEO, sees himself in the same mode.

REPLICATORS USUALLY...

1. see no reason to reorient a business that's already successful and don't feel personally driven to venture into the unknown.
2. say they've always wanted to work with their parents in the family business.
3. have not gained experience working in any other company.
4. have parents who encourage them to take a leading role in the business but who still guide them carefully.
5. model themselves after their parents' management style when their parents' businesses were well established.
6. are second-born children.
7. have parents who are self-educated.
8. surpass their own parents' education level.

To many people, Robert Haft of Crown Books seemed to have been cloned from father Herbert, the founder of this discount dynasty that began with Dart Drugs in 1954. Although Robert and Herbert no longer sell pharmaceuticals, the concept behind the son's off-price retail bookstores is identical to that of the father's drugstores. The son and father also joined together several times in the '80s for hostile takeover bids, displaying a common flair for enriching family coffers while showing little concern for public opinion.

Replicators are usually not known as risktakers. "I think I am conservative," says Tom Bloch of H&R Block. "And I'm not ashamed of it."

Ken Feld of Ringling Bros. and Barnum & Bailey says that when his father died, he stopped concentrating on the administrative side of the business, with which he was most comfortable, to move to what had been his father's focus, selecting new circus acts. Ken even takes on the time-consuming task of personally negotiating every circus performer's contract—just as his father had done.

Hasbro toys heir Alan Hassenfeld is replicating the acquisition strategy taken by his late brother, Stephen, the CEO who proceeded him.

Although some of these Replicators have graduate degrees, not one of them has worked outside the family business. Lack of exposure to the way others do business may be one reason they prefer the known. And Replicators see no reason to change something that has worked well in the past. Their desire to harmonize with their parents can meet their personal needs while still producing a strong company.

"I sleep very well at night, knowing that I sell the best."

Lazare Kaplan International Inc.
New York, New York

Business:	Diamonds
Best Known Products:	Laser inscribed ideal cut diamonds and diamond jewelry, sold through quality retail jewelers
Founded:	1903 by Lazare Kaplan
Family Executives:	Maurice Tempelsman, Chairman Leon Tempelsman, President and Vice Chairman Robert Speisman, Vice President and Director
Family History:	Third generation of Leon Tempelsman & Son
Family Ownership:	66.7 percent
Family Board Membership:	3 Tempelsman family members of 8 directors
Traded:	American Stock Exchange, LKI
Net Sales:	$133,016,000 1991 100,012,000 1990 72,279,000 1989
Net Earnings:	$4,073,000 1991 5,268,000 1990 2,768,000 1989

LAZARE KAPLAN
INTERNATIONAL, INC.

A Family is Forever

Leon Tempelsman, President and Vice Chairman;
Partner, Leon Tempelsman and Son, Inc.

Investors in the 1970s took a joyride on some slippery ice: diamonds. OPEC had thrown the economy into a second oil-price rise nightmare. Inflation and a weak dollar were combining with the oil panic to push up diamond prices. Speculators, tax shelter advisers, and even little old ladies were buying diamonds as a hedge against inflation. The crest of the ride came in March, 1980, when an investment grade, 1-carat, D-fine stone could command an asking price of $62,000.

Then the thin ice shattered. Dumped into the frigid depths were both the heavily leveraged diamond firms and the small investor, who was forced to sell in a recession. That $62,000 diamond was now going for a little over $12,000—if a buyer could be found.

One prominent diamond family had been watching the market carefully, but feeling queasy at what they saw. While others were greedily buying, the privately held firm of Leon Tempelson & Son, with worldwide interests in diamonds and minerals, was liquidating its diamond assets. Maurice Tempelsman—son of founder Leon—and his son, another Leon, favor solid surveying over wildcat prospecting. The Tempelsmans were not about to be dazzled by fool's gold.

Leon is a modest man who, despite a slight stammer, projects a strong sense of who he is and what he believes. Level-browed and firm-mouthed, he's too self-assured to need to hype himself: "It's very easy to make good decisions appear as if they were very neat and calculated, but they usually involve a fair amount of fingernail chewing and an awful lot of rationalization in retrospect."

Leon and Maurice bought Lazare Kaplan International Inc. for $22.9 million in cash and debentures.

Lazare is known for cutting and polishing diamonds in the "ideal" proportion and selling only to quality jewelers throughout the United States. Founded in 1903, it's the sole diamond manufacturer with stock listed in a national exchange and publicly traded. But Lazare declared Chapter 11 bankruptcy in 1983. The floundering of Lazare represented a chance to throw a lifeline to a company whose name was synonymous with quality in the diamond industry.

When a family firm has been private for 45 years, and when its head, Maurice Tempelsman, is a man who keeps the lowest of profiles, the questions that must have arisen when discussing the purchase of the only publicly traded diamond company in the country can't have been easily resolved. But Leon and Maurice went ahead in 1984 and bought 51 percent of Lazare Kaplan, deciding then not to take it private. (They retain options to convert debentures for interest of up to 73 percent, and in October 1990, increased their ownership to 66.7 percent by means of this option.)

"The moment to take the company private was the time of acquisition, if that's what we wanted to do," says Leon. "We still have our interests, which are outside of the diamond business, through Leon Tempelsman & Son, so we still enjoy the benefits of being a private company in that area. I think people have to recognize the business for what it is. Due to the nature of the diamond business, we are still running the business like a private business. You must focus on the development of a long-term business strategy."

However, buying a diamond company in the middle of a bust period was not universally viewed as a wise move. "Frankly, we bought Lazare because we thought that people were excessively pessimistic about the diamond industry," says Leon.

Not everyone at Leon Tempelsman & Son was of the same mind. But the key players in this minerals and diamond company, founded by Leon's late grandfather in 1946 when Maurice was 17, are Maurice and Leon (born in 1956). These two men were in agreement.

"The decision to acquire Lazare was one that both my father and myself reached. It's not surprising that we reached it jointly. That's the way most of our decisions are reached," says Leon.

"We're not looking to build a business that will be able to enjoy the benefits of a rising market and not be able to withstand the inevitable difficulties. Because sooner or later, no markets rise forever. So we are concerned about building the business for that inevitable downturn."

Lately, Lazare hasn't been worrying about a downturn. The firm has done very well in the hands of Leon and brother-in-law Robert Speisman. Leon, in his unassuming way, attributes much of the company's success to its previous owners. At the time of acquisition, Lazare had been owned by the family members of the founder, Lazare Kaplan. Today, the founder's son, George R. Kaplan, is a director of the firm and is very active in the rough diamond end of the business. Leon says, "I must give a lot of credit to my predecessors because most of the focus on this quality product was something that was there long before we arrived on the scene.

"One of the attractions of Lazare Kaplan is its recognition within the trade as being one of the finest quality products. And therefore I sleep very well at night knowing that I sell the best."

Selling a diamond that is recognized for its quality through better independent jewelers is a good move in today's market. Lately, consumers want to purchase highly ranked products with brand recognition. The trend toward high quality, brand recognition goods, and making an educated purchase on large-ticket items fits Lazare as easily as an engagement ring slips on the finger.

Both the quality stone and the ideal cut diamond are characteristic of Lazare. Their stones are cut to maximize brilliance, even if this results in a smaller diamond. "The Lazare diamond," reads the sales copy, "setting the standard for brilliance." This standard setting may mean a premium price for the buyer, but many in the industry agree that the ideal cut is best for showing a diamond's sparkle. (Of course, "cut" is only one of the four important Cs that speak to a diamond's brilliance: the others are clarity, color, and carat size.)

Although other companies' stones may also be ideal cut, Lazare's innovation is laser branding each of its stones with a unique identification number on the perimeter. The marking is invisible to the naked eye but can be seen with magnification.

Lazare hopes buyers will want a diamond that will always be identifiable, protecting the consumer from a possible switch of stones when a ring is reset and making a diamond traceable in case of theft. "Once removed from its mounting, a diamond that is not laser marked is as good as ownerless," says Leon.

Laser branding has its detractors, though. Some industry analysts see it as a contrivance, and a few stores will not purchase a laser-marked stone. The most prestigious of these is Van Cleef & Arpels, Inc. "We don't carry them, and I don't think we ever will" says a spokesperson. "The whole thing is very gimmicky." Tiffany's carries Lazare stones but removes the laser inscription.

Lazare has spent millions of dollars for a media blitz on the advantages of laser branding, so obviously it doesn't see this desire for uniqueness as a passing consumer fad. *Time* magazine acknowledged Lazare's branding: "A girl's best friend may soon be the marking on her stones."

The process of doing business seems to be as important as the business itself at this family firm. "Of course, business is important," says Leon, "but it's nothing to the family, because that's what counts in life."

How the Tempelsmans work together as a business and as a family seems to pervade their lives. Of Maurice's three children—Rena, Leon, and Marcee—Leon and Marcee both work in the family firm. Leon's brother-in-law Robert Speisman (Rena's husband) is vice president for sales and an officer of Lazare, and Marcee designs jewelry.

Being in one firm works out well for these three members of the younger generation. Says Leon, "My brother-in-law is terrific at sales—I'm a disaster. He has a passion for it. My sister has a creative passion, and she is able to bring that together for the creation of jewelry. Frankly, I wouldn't know where to begin. So it works out well."

Leon notes that many family business cave-ins are the result of personal divergences that may have little to do with the business.

"We call that arguing over the pot and the pans, which in reality is not what you're arguing about. In reality, it is a different agenda that is being satisfied. And that unfortunately leads to the downfall of many family businesses. You need to get your priorities straight."

The top priority is so strongly fixed on the family unit that Leon scoffs at the media's attempt to focus on his own strong skills. Leon's own operational duties as president include many of the same activities that his father spent time on as a young man. Constantly out of the country, Leon cements ties with African political leaders and business people so that the third Tempelsman generation will be as well-placed as the earlier generations. Lazare Kaplan's marketing director, Amy Wiener, says of Leon, "He spends considerable time nurturing a long-term relationship with countries producing diamonds," traveling frequently to Africa. Concerned also with distribution, Leon goes to Asia when he feels his presence is needed.

When Leon is back at the office, he is a hands-on manager. "As a general manager, he's involved in every aspect of this business," Wiener says. He pays attention to strategic planning at every level, and Wiener gives him special credit for having initiated the company's brand-name marketing strategy. At the same time, she points out, Leon's management style is "conducive to encouraging people to think for themselves." Wiener notes that he establishes the type of dialogue that ultimately lets managers act autonomously. "It's comforting to have a family business member take responsibility day to day" yet still allow management freedom to act. "He represents a good balance," Wiener concludes.

Some say that Leon understands business operations and finance more astutely than does Maurice. But Leon refuses to receive compliments at the expense of other family members, particularly his father. Refuting the tag "financial mind of the company," this Harvard MBA says, "My father knows how to pay bills, too."

Yet investors give Leon credit for the 36 percent revenue rise to $100 million dollars in 1990, with profits doubling to $5 million.

Yet it has been Maurice's diplomacy and psychological insight—demonstrated first on his taking over the firm when his father died an early death in 1956—which led Leon Tempelsman

& Son to its current status in the industry. Perhaps watching his father being undermined by the turmoils of prewar Europe inspired Maurice's careful and constant testing of political substructures.

In the 1950s, while State Department desk officers were sending frantic cables from Foggy Bottom to embassies in the troubled African capitals of Salisbury and Leopoldville, Maurice already had a man on the scene.

He feared a communist power grab, both hating communism as an ideology and knowing it would destroy his business. Lacking allegiance to the Belgium of his birth (which didn't protect his Jewish parents from Europe's anti-Semitism), Maurice defied Belgian interests and was firmly anticolonial. He aligned with pro-Africa nationalists from the start. Adlai Stevenson was Maurice's legal counsel from 1953 to 1960. The Tempelsman-Stevenson relationship helped identify the Tempelsman family with the Democratic party and its leaders.

Maurice and Stevenson were a potent combination. The politician gave the diamond merchant entree to the nascent political leaders and cliques who soon were to govern new, mineral-rich nations. Also through Stevenson, Maurice gained access to the incoming Kennedy administration. Mining this vein to his advantage, he urged the U.S. government to buy industrial diamonds—with himself as middleman.

Maurice watched as strife turned to war in the Belgian Congo. This civil war saw a quick turnover in leaders, from Lumumba in 1960 to Mobutu in 1965. But whoever came to power would end up needing Maurice. By continuing to form relationships with existing players, Maurice tunneled himself and his firm into the bedrock of these developing African countries.

Maurice was known as one of the closest U.S. business colleague of Zaire President Mobutu Sese Seko. To help his interests in Zaire, Maurice hired CIA agent Lawrence Devlin, who, back in 1965, suggested Mobutu as the most viable candidate for leadership of Zaire and then helped place Mobutu in power through the U.S.-backed coup. After retirement from the CIA as Chief of Station in Zaire, Devlin worked in Zaire for Maurice for more than a dozen years, while retaining his former immediate access to Mobutu.

Today, Maurice's representative is Jerry Funk, former head of the African section of the National Security Council in the Carter administration. Some Africanists say Funk, like Devlin, has CIA ties. Funk had headed the international division of the AFL-CIO in Ethiopia.

One thing is clear. Maurice is a man who likes to hedge all bets, outside this country and within it. He has given strong financial support to Democratic candidates, but also contributes to Republican candidates, giving him access to both Republican and Democratic administrations. Through his support of American leaders, his intelligence links, and political acumen, as well as his position as the senior American businessman in western Africa, he has influenced U.S. policy on African affairs for 30 years.

And Africa means diamonds.

———————

Of course, no assessment of the success of a diamond trader or a retailer is relative without factoring in the influence of the world's dominant diamond-trading syndicate—De Beers and Anglo-American Corporation and its majority owner, the Oppenheimer family. Through their syndicate, 85 percent of the world's uncut diamonds are privately regulated for sale. De Beers holds virtually the world's mother lode of uncut diamonds in its four-story vault in London.

The Oppenheimers set up a formal procedure to sell rough diamonds to the buyers who will cut and resell them. After De Beers chooses the specific stones to be sold to cutters, an invitation is issued to several hundred selected clients throughout the world, including a Tempelsman representative, to attend a "sight." These clients are known as "sight holders."

Each client is walked by armed escorts to a private viewing room outfitted with an electronic scale, a telephone for consultation with partners, a magnifying glass, and natural northern light. A small paper box arrives, and inside are dozens of tiny envelopes holding uncut diamonds varying in quality and size. Which dealer gets what diamonds is determined entirely by the Syndicate's analysis of the number and type of diamonds already on the market. Remember, the entire diamond industry is based on this market of official demand and supply.

If you are a client, you're allowed to request certain types of stones, but this is like burning your Christmas list and hoping the smoke gets to Santa Claus. In the end, you receive only what De Beers wants you to get. You take the whole box of diamonds you're offered, or you get none at all; you are not allowed to compare your diamonds to another client's diamonds; you cannot wrangle over price; you cannot resell these uncut stones to another dealer; you cannot sell the diamonds after they are cut to retailers who are known to discount prices; and when De Beers asks you fill out their lengthy forms disclosing your inventory and future sales projection, you give De Beers all the information it wants. Violate any one of their rules and you are out of the game.

This cartel is patriarchal, causing an unnamed diamond executive to comment to *Forbes*, "It's a father-child relationship. If you do something wrong, they spank you." But, to be fair, a sight holder can also hit pay dirt. Those sight holders favored by De Beers may find a surprise bonanza in the form of a special, high quality gem in one of their envelopes.

Thus does E. Oppenheimer & Son, the private holding company that runs both De Beers and Anglo-American, fortify its control over diamond mining, production, and distribution. Its bulwark against unrestricted trade in rough diamonds accounts for perhaps an 800 percent markup in the price we pay for a diamond. (Twenty years ago, the U.S. Congress held hearings on the diamond monopoly, but saw that it's difficult, if not impossible, to regulate an international monopoly.)

Such a markup translates into big money in any currency. The diamonds De Beers controls are estimated at a low figure of $2.5 billion. Their other company, Anglo-American, is one of the world's largest gold quarries and governs several hundred other gold and mineral companies. Combined assets of Anglo-American are conservatively set at $6 billion. E. Oppenheimer & Son is the richest, most powerful family business in any industry—and the largest cartel in the world.

How entangled is the Tempelsman family in the De Beers Syndicate? It is true that the Tempelsmans have their own diamond sources in Angola; they recently signed a deal to import, process, and market $20 million of high-quality Angolan diamonds each year. They also have such other independent African diamond interests, like their cutting factory in Sierre Leone. Still, Maurice has had many different links to De Beers over the years, and it would be naive to think that he and his business have been operating independently of the world's strongest cartel. Occasionally, the Tempelsmans will buy stones from De Beers. In turn, if there is a diamond abundance, De Beers might by stones from the Tempelsmans to hold them out of the market. Certainly Maurice's drive for self-determination leads him to act as his own broker when he can carry it off. His wish for autonomy led to diversification into minerals (most notably copper), and the family owns the world's largest petroleum drill bit company. He also profits from acting as a middleman for interests needing footholds in Zaire, Angola, Ghana, Sierre Leone, Gabon, and other West African countries. These separate business deals are said to be done with the full knowledge and approval of De Beers.

When De Beers is the source of 85 percent of American diamonds, how could any American company maintain total independence? Leon is asked whether the Tempelsmans' Lazare Kaplan Inc. was less dependent than other companies on De Beers for its stones. He shrugs his shoulders in a "perhaps" motion—possibly mindful of the tape recorder in front of him. He repeats the noncommittal gesture when asked the question a second time, ending by saying "It probably is."

Then he continues, "Our raw material, which is rough diamonds, comes from a variety of sources. The most important player in the rough diamond business is De Beers. So we are influenced by whatever they do. If tomorrow they raise their prices 100 percent, we will not be immune. So I don't want to pretend that we operate in another universe, and that what they do doesn't affect us."

Diamond rings became a symbol of betrothal in the United States only after the Civil War, and through the depression engagement rings were limited to small, poor-quality stones. De Beers needed to create a larger, upscale American market for their product. An advertising campaign was set in motion in 1938 by Harry Oppenheimer, who sailed to New York to brainstorm with the cartel's advertising agency, N.W. Ayer.

Oppenheimer envisioned associating diamonds with royalty in the public view. In the early 1950s, Queen Elizabeth agreed to take a well-publicized trip to South Africa. Amidst popping flashbulbs, she was given a stunning diamond by none other than Oppenheimer himself.

Currently, 82 percent of all first-time brides are given a diamond ring. And while sales of formal white gowns, another modern "tradition," drop dramatically for the second-time bride, the diamond engagement ring holds its place. About 70 percent of women who remarry receive this second diamond ring. Oppenheimer's syndicate looked to Japan as a fertile market before most of the rest of the world saw that nation's purchasing potential. Just as Americans were captured by the image of a British monarch with stunning gems, Oppenheimer decided (with the help of J. Walter Thompson advertising agency) that the Japanese in the late 1960s should be treated to advertising displays of Western women gazing lovingly at diamond engagement rings.

The figures speak for themselves. In 1968, less than 5 percent of engaged Japanese women were being given diamond rings. Now, 70 percent receive them. Thus, a new Japanese "tradition" was born.

Most diamond buyers are, of course, recently engaged couples. Leon humorously points out these couples need a great deal of reassurance about the high-cost purchase they're making because "they're coming to the table somewhat anxious to begin with, due to other life changes." Yet this diamond engagement ring "tradition" is a recent phenomenon and one that has been bolstered primarily through marketing techniques.

Creating tradition and consumer demand through advertising is fitting for the sales of a product that costs hundreds, thousands, tens of thousands, and up to millions of dollars—but relies on consumer demand rather than real need. The interest in diamond engagement rings is as artificial as the supply level of diamonds.

To begin with, there is such an abundance of diamonds under the earth's surface that every person in the world who ever desired a diamond could be satisfied. This is one reason why a middle-class buyer should not purchase a ring primarily for its investment value. Indulging the desire for the brilliant sparkle of a diamond is fine, but the stones that are most assured of keeping their value are those costly ones that are out of reach of all but a few truly wealthy people.

And even if this superfluity of natural, medium-quality diamonds weren't discouraging, gem-quality synthetic diamonds can be produced very cheaply in laboratories. This remains true despite Sir Ernest Oppenheimer's assertion, when he first heard the rumor in the early 1950s of industrial synthetic gems: "Only God can make a diamond."

Sir Ernest was wrong. Here, God has been one-upped by General Electric. Worse still, after GE announced its capacity to manufacture industrial diamonds in 1955, De Beers stock plummeted. The cartel was in a frenzy. Not only was there a cheap and ready supply of these synthetic gems, but artificial stones were free of the natural flaws found in mined diamonds.

Global politics came into play—no doubt after some nudging from the syndicate—when American officials became worried over the capacity of the USSR to countermand GE's experiments. The U.S. Patent Office, through directives from the Eisenhower administration, actually refused patents to GE on GE's own designs. Only after De Beers, working in direct competition with GE in an attempt to reduce the threat, was close to manufacturing industrial diamonds itself did the administration direct the Patent Office to grant GE the patents it deserved. Now synthetic diamonds are a half-billion-dollar-a-year business and will become even more important with GE's recent announcement of a synthetic industrial diamond that is better than a flawless natural diamond: This new diamond is not a heat conductor and will be preferred over natural diamonds for use in silicon chips.   .

The unthinkable happened again in 1970, when GE disclosed it could synthesize gem-quality diamonds. However, GE came to the same conclusion that the cartel had reached nearly a hundred years earlier: When it comes to diamonds, you can have too much of a good thing. Flooding the market with gem-quality stones would result in a total market collapse. What would be the point in manufacturing these stones? GE's top management buried its synthetic gem operation.

The abyss still yawns, though. Sumitomo Electronic Industries of Japan is now producing gem-quality yellow crystals on a large scale. Last year, a gemologist found a quarter-carat diamond from Sumitomo mixed in with a group of natural stones he was testing for a dealer. No one is sure how many of these artificial stones may be on the market, threatening the entire industry.

———

Diamonds destined for the United States travel through the diamond pipeline to arrive on "the Street." The Street is the long block of West 47th Street stretching between Fifth and Sixth Avenues in Manhattan, where cut diamonds are traded.

The offices of Leon Tempelsman & Son and Lazare Kaplan International are a few blocks away. Although the building has a Fifth Avenue address, a visitor enters on 56th Street. The fifth floor is the reception area for both Tempelsman and Lazare, which occupy this floor and the one above. If you take the elevator to five, you're observed through cameras and then buzzed through various doors until you enter a small empty waiting room.

Now you're locked in on all sides. One mirrored wall looks as if it's made of two-way glass, with a guard watching you from behind. The receptionist is facing you, sitting along another wall behind a window of security-strength plexiglass. A third short wall contains the locked door to corporate offices. The fourth wall has the door through which you entered. and you won't be able to leave until the receptionist checks via monitor that no one is standing outside and then buzzes you out.

You also need an escort to get you through security on the sixth floor, where Leon awaits in the tastefully decorated boardroom, ready to talk about family values.

Always, Leon returns to the image of his family's primary interest as being one of values, and not business interests. Leon's father, as the second generation member, surely was taught the business by his father. But Leon takes umbrage at a question that referred to Maurice having "grown up in mining and minerals." He cuts it off flintily.

"I wouldn't say Maurice Tempelsman 'grew up in mining and metals.' I'd say Maurice Tempelsman grew up in a world of great turmoil, and Maurice Tempelsman is a great observer of life… Europe in the second world war, Africa as it gained independence, and in his experiences in the United States as he built the business.

"'Mining and minerals' was the business end of it, but that's not where he 'grew up.' The business is not where I 'grew up,' either." Having bombarded this crude characterization of his family, Leon continues. "We did not sit around the dinner table talking about 'Gee whiz, what a great deal we made today.'

"There are a lot of things in life much more important than business—and business has been very good, it's given us a lot of nice things—but those are not the most important things in life."

Leon is careful to attribute his philosophy to both his parents. However, Leon's progressive humanism seems to follow the direction of his father's beliefs rather than those of his more religiously devout and observant mother. When asked whether his philosophy derives from religion—after all Leon attended Ramez, a Jewish day school—he firmly and immediately shakes his head 'no.' "This stems from humanism," he avers.

Leon says that he was never brought up to feel that he must head the family business and didn't think seriously about it until he was a college senior. "I'm reasonably stubborn," he says. "Had I been forced in a particular direction, chances are I would have revolted. That was never an issue. Where I worked was not preordained."

Maurice whetted Leon's interest by taking his teenage ponytailed son to Africa with him on a number of trips. But Leon says, "It was never, 'This is my son, a potential asset.'"

Consequently, Leon began at Leon Tempelsman & Son directly after college, leaving his full-time position for Harvard Business School but returning during breaks. While in Cambridge, Leon looked at other career options but said to himself, "As long as one is enjoying it and doing reasonably well at it, there's no point in changing: you might as well go on doing it."

The only crevice in the smooth surface of the Tempelsman family landscape is Maurice's romance of more than a dozen years with Jacqueline Bouvier Onassis. By all accounts, the early marriage of Maurice and Lily was a love match, engineered despite parental disapproval. But with the years' attrition, rifts have appeared and the couple seems to have grown apart. Some blame this separation on Maurice's cosmopolitanism when his wife prefers a quieter life.

Evidently, Maurice's social ease appealed to Onassis. The friendship dates to the late 1950s, when Maurice met Senator John F. Kennedy through his relationship with Stevenson. The friendship deepened when the widowed Jackie Onassis turned to him for advice on investing her $25 million bequest from Aristotle Onassis. Slowly, Maurice's financial acumen replaced that of financial wizard Andre Meyer of Lazard Freres, and of her friend John Kenneth Galbraith. Onassis was reportedly impressed by Maurice's wisdom during the crazy fluctuation of silver and gold prices; it was his guidance that allowed her to pump up her principal while so may others lost money through speculation. Reportedly, Maurice has snowballed Onassis' inheritance into several hundred million dollars.

Today, the relationship between the most famous woman in the world and the man who would prefer to keep a low profile has apparently mellowed into a comfortable, mature association. Maurice is a polished escort who speaks French with Onassis when they dine at Manhattan's best restaurants. More important, they share interests in art and history. And, one assumes, in fine gems.

In the summer, Maurice travels down to Onassis' home in the Gay Head section of Martha's Vineyard on his modest schooner (named Relemar, a combination of his three children's names). In the earlier part of their relationship, when Maurice was Onassis' escort at family occasions such as daughter Caroline Schlossberg's law school graduation, Maurice sat apart, waiting to join the Kennedys only after the phalanx of photographers had left the scene. Now, they are more open. Maurice was Onassis' escort at the wedding of Kerry Kennedy (Robert and Ethel's daughter) to Andrew Cuomo, son of New York Governor Mario Cuomo.

Maurice's children are nonjudgmental of his friendship with Onassis, and have socialized with the couple, even visiting them at Onassis' summer home. In turn, Maurice provides support for her children. When John Kennedy was an undergraduate at Brown University, he spent a summer working in a Tempelsman office in Africa. In fact, Maurice initially funded a short-lived group that Kennedy formed called South Africa Group for Education.

Maurice lends support to Onassis' children in more personal areas, as well. When Caroline went into labor with her first child, Rose, she called her mother—who had Maurice's car and driver sent to take the Schlossbergs to New York Hospital where the child was born.

After a scary 1987 illness, Maurice is careful to maintain a walking regimen, leaving Onassis' house to walk through Central Park to the Tempelsmans' midtown offices. Smiling, he has the cherubic look of anyone's balding grandpa. But in repose, his face falls into a few well-defined, downcurved lines—it's the face of a man who doesn't expect any pleasant surprises.

In any case, no divorce seems to be in the works. The liaison is accepted by the key family members, and Lily Tempelsman continues her work with middle- and low-income families—as a marriage counselor.

"My job is risk management and I am a believer in taking risks, calculated risks," says Leon of being president of Lazare. "Sometimes things work out, sometimes they don't. Risk sometimes gets rewarded, but one thing—if you don't take risks, you don't get rewarded."

Leon is referring not only to the acquisition of Lazare but to the family's ventures in exploratory projects. Leon Tempelsman & Son is processing possibilities for business ventures throughout the world. It's a company where creativity, flexibility, and political acumen are at least as important as Lazare's retail sales, and which are less easily discerned by those looking from the outside in.

It was Maurice's fortune, accumulated through years of diamond and mineral mining and production, that gave the family a base from which they could commit themselves to purchasing Lazare. The Tempelsman family used its own money to move into a new area, with some sense of risk and adventure. But the risk the Tempelsmans were taking was appropriate to their means—financial and emotional.

Today, the Tempelsmans are characterized as "a trading family" by the trade journal *Jewelers' Circular-Keystone*. When they spot a possibility to do business, they go for it. In Europe a few years ago, Leon and Maurice met with one country's mining minister. "We began to talk," Leon says. "It was rather simple, really." And in the fall of 1990, Lazare Kaplan entered the European market.

"My father and I are friends. He obviously has my allegiance and loyalty, but we also happen to have fun together. Most of the time it's not focused on whether we work together. When you think in terms of friendship, you don't really think in terms of succession."

Leon is continually examining and reshaping his values. As a new father, he looks to see how beliefs transmute as they move from parent to child. "The ethics and overall morals—and the sense of priorities—that are passed on to the next generation are critical in the formulation of one's set values. These things get modified and shaped by one's own life experience."

He points out, "Life will change, and my priorities will change, but you keep your values and go on. There are no guarantees for success." Again, modestly pointing to luck as a pivotal factor, he says, "We've been very fortunate in that the business has been growing and things are going in the direction we want it to go."

But Leon also adds, "It's always nice when the business goes well, but I don't believe that that's the drive." Now Leon ties the generation before him to the generation that will succeed him when asked what personal accomplishment of his own Maurice would be most proud of.

"My daughters. Without a moment's hesitation. In the end, there's no question but that it's his granddaughters."

"There have only been three owners of the circus: P.T. Barnum, the Ringling family, and the Feld family. That's it since 1870."

Ringling Bros. and Barnum & Bailey Combined Shows, Inc.
Tysons Corner, Virginia

Business:	Live entertainment
Best Known Products:	Ringling Bros. and Barnum & Bailey Circus; Walt Disney's World on Ice; Siegfried & Roy
Founded:	1870; 1967 bought by Irvin Feld
Family Executives:	Kenneth J. Feld, CEO and Chairman
Family History:	Second generation of Feld family
Family Ownership:	80 percent
Family Board Membership:	1 family member
Traded:	Privately held
Net Sales:	$263,000,000 1991 (estimated) 260,000,000 1990 (estimated) 255,000,000 1989 (estimated)
Net Earnings:	Will not disclose

RINGLING BROS. AND BARNUM & BAILEY COMBINED SHOWS, INC.

Flying Without a Net

Kenneth J. Feld, President and CEO

Kenneth Feld, owner, producer, and chief executive officer of the world's largest live entertainment company, leans back in his chair and shakes his head. "No, no," he says, "don't thank me. Julie, in public relations, told me to do the interview." Once more, Ken is following the choreography set out for him, and he's dancing as fast as he can.

With a Feld-owned show performing somewhere in the world each hour of the day, 41-year-old Ken Feld travels everywhere, all the time. He used to watch his father Irvin audition each new act himself. In 1984, when Irvin died unexpectedly of a brain hemorrhage at age 66, Ken was caught short. Although Irvin Feld had trained his son for fourteen years, he'd also always said, "Nobody can teach circus."

So at 35, Ken inherited a chunk of American social history called *The Greatest Show on Earth*, fully aware that its continuance depended on his novice business acumen and untested creative talent. It's no wonder that Ken tries to replicate many of his father's ways of getting things done. Feld Productions owns Ringling Bros. and Barnum & Bailey Combined Shows, Inc., which in turn owns Klowns Publishing Co. (printer of the show programs); concessionaire Sells-Floto; Feld Brothers Management (a personal management service); Walt Disney's World on Ice; and it also produces illusionists Seigfried & Roy. Ken Feld owns 80 percent of the company, with the remaining 20 percent owned by three other executives. This entertainment combine brings in $260 million yearly, with ticket and concession sales alone accounting for cash revenues of more than $500,000 each day. Each year, more than 40 million tickets to Feld shows are sold throughout the world.

Japan is where Ken's been focusing his sights, taking advantage of Japanese affluence as well as the Japanese addiction to Western entertainment. Disneymania, strong since the opening of the theme park in 1983, promoted interest in Ken's 1986 international opening of Disney ice shows there. But bringing an American-style circus to Japan in 1988 was more complicated, and carried a start-up cost of $49 million.

Ken says he's able to maintain his far-flung empire by working six or seven days a week. He finds it hard to relax, even when home in Potomac, Maryland with wife Bonnie. "The only thing I could wish for is three days without any responsibility. Sure, you can take a day off, but what never goes away is the responsibility."

Feld is describing the burden of running a business that has been family-owned for 120 years. Discounting a short term while it was in the hands of Mattel, Inc., Ken says, "There have only been three owners of the circus: P.T. Barnum, the Ringling family, and the Feld family. That's it since 1870."

Two inspirations have shaped the American circus. The first was when P.T. Barnum said to James Bailey, "Why not make it three rings?" The second was when five-year-old Irvin Feld found a dollar on a coal-cellar step in 1923 and declared to his mother, "I'm going to buy a circus."

Young Irvin worked the summer sideshows of traveling circuses, selling nickel bottles of snake oil at two-for-a-dollar. His 90 percent profit induced brother Israel to join him at working the circus during the summers and in selling sundries door-to-door in the winter. It was a relationship that continued throughout the brothers' lives, with Israel subordinate to his younger brother.

Irvin spent only a few years in high school before going to Washington in 1938 to open a novelty store in a primarily black Northeast neighborhood. But Irvin, with his hundred-dollar dreams, was frustrated selling dimestore items. In segregated Washington D.C., his white knight turned out to be the local NAACP, which had been looking to invest in a place where black customers could get their prescriptions filled and be welcomed to refresh themselves at a soda fountain while they waited.

Investing $500 of his own, Irvin opened Super Cut-Rate Drug-store (the first of his "Super" stores) in 1940. There he lured customers in by blasting gospel and popular music through a loudspeaker. It wasn't long before his customers began asking for the records Irvin was piping out to the sidewalk. But no record company would sell to a pharmacy. So Irvin started his own private-label venture, aptly named Super Disc.

Still, Irvin's first love was live entertainment. He wanted to use the record acts he'd signed to promote their recordings by singing before audiences. Driving home one Washington summer night in the late 1940s, he noticed that city residents had brought their radios outside to listen to music while waiting for a breeze. Irvin realized he could gather people who wanted to get out of a warm house on summer evenings, and bring them to outside amphitheaters and arenas. First the residents of ten cities, then before long of eighty cities, were whiling away the steamy nights listening to Feld's gospel and popular music acts.

By the early 1950s, the Feld brothers had worked out a routine: Irvin traveled to promote and drum up acts, while Izzy minded the store. Irvin packaged teen singing idols Chubby Checker, Bill Haley and the Comets, and Fats Domino. In 1956, the company grossed $5 million. "We never had a week when our performers didn't have at least seven of the top ten records, and we had many weeks when we had all ten," Irvin boasted. The man was a profit machine.

He was also, it was rumored, bisexual. It was both Irvin's attraction to other men and his pull towards booking yet a bigger act that kept him constantly out of town away from wife Adele at night.

On a meltdown July night in 1958, with Irvin out of town and children Ken and Karen away at summer camp, Adele shut herself into the garage and left the car running. Her suicide devastated Ken and Karen, but Karen says today that "My mother's death wasn't half as bad as having to live with my father. He was just never there. The business came first." As for Ken, "I never had a lot of friends," he reflects. "I don't today."

Meanwhile, Irvin was having some problems of his own. Real-izing that teenage fans changed their rock 'n roll loyalties faster than they gulped down cherry Cokes, Irvin had been looking for a live entertainment vehicle with a longer history than a few weeks on a Pop 40 chart.

He was anxious for good reason. For those who grew up in the 1950s, the Day the Music Died is a pivotal memory. For Irvin, the crash of a small plane carrying his touring stars Buddy Holly, the Big Dipper, and Ritchie Valens was a personal financial disaster. The sudden deaths of his hottest singers coming after Adele's unexpected suicide reinforced Irvin's belief that it's just as well not to rely on individuals. Irvin wanted his name identified with something permanent.

Three years earlier, he had heard that the Ringling circus was in trouble after 84 successful years. Irvin helpfully wrote majority owner John Ringling North, telling him what he was doing wrong and how Irvin could do it right. Silence from North.

Six months after Irvin's letter, *The Greatest Show on Earth* declared bankruptcy. The phone rang in Irvin's office; it was John Ringling North. "I told my secretary to wait a minute or two," recalled Irvin with glee. "Finally, I answered the phone."

North was not happy at being kept waiting. "Do you know who I am?" he yelled when Irvin finally got around to picking up the line.

"Yeah," was the response. "You're the guy whose circus closed today."

Irvin told North, who'd run his circus the same way for forty years, to get rid of the traditional Big Top. North had 2,000 circus employees on the payroll, yet only seventy-five were performers. By booking the circus into air-conditioned, indoor arenas, North could let go the more than 1,800 roustabouts needed to put up the tent and its massive rigging, slashing costs by $50,000 a week.

Irvin's advice put the circus back in business in thirty days, and put its management in Irvin's pocket in 1956.

He made the management decisions, but he couldn't touch the worn-out circus performance. Cutting costs by $50,000 a week didn't solve the problems caused by an uninterested, long-distance owner. But the more Irvin hammered away at improving the show, the less responsive North became.

Circus attendance rocketed despite the show's flaws, and Irvin wanted to inject his own creativity to turn the show into first-class entertainment. Flying to Europe on New Year's Day, 1967, Irvin told North he wanted to buy the circus. North laughed and asked for $7.5 million. Irvin, reverting to his typical negotiating mode —aggressive but without regard for the personality he was trying to bargain with—countered with $7 million.

Now North laughed harder. He raised the tag to an outrageous $8 million for the antiquated show.

Although the price was 50 to 60 times annual earnings, Feld thought he could repay a loan that size in five years. He set up the circus transfer in 1967 at Rome's Colosseum, home of history's ultimate circus.

After ninety-six years, the circus was being adopted by a new family, with the Ringling patronymic preceded by the Feld name. Reflecting on the first announcement, "Irvin and Israel Feld present Ringling Bros. and Barnum & Bailey Circus," Irvin noted, "It was the happiest moment of my life." While Ken sat restlessly at Boston University and Karen pursued her journalism major at the University of Pittsburgh, Irvin had a real problem: Up close, the accumulated circus props looked more like a junk sale than theatrical properties, and the average age of his circus performers was 46.

Finding a fresh clown supply was Irvin's priority. As P.T. Barnum observed, "Clowns are the peg you hang a circus on," and Irvin needed a fresh set. Half the clowns were older than 70, prompting Irvin to ask, "I know they can fall down, but can they get up?" The clown shortage was hurting Irvin's plans to open a second unit of the circus.

Two units could cover twice as many cities as one, allowing Ringling to double profits and amortize costs over two years. The acts would change at the end of the second year, so no city would get the same show twice.

Ringling's Red and Blue units are accepted without question now, but in 1969 the concept caused a hullaballoo. Naysayers called it unworkable: How could the public accept two *Greatest Show* (singular) *on Earth*? Then the man with formal schooling that ended in high school left his mark on education with the establishment of Clown College, a preparatory school for funny men and women that would make up for the lack of clowning tradition in this country. Doubters scoffed at this concept, too. "Everyone said, 'You're crazy, you can't do it.' Or else they thought it was just a publicity stunt," Ken remembers.

With the circus firmly established twice over, Irvin pulled up a chair for his son. The day after Ken took his last final in 1970, he called his dad to collect on a bribe offered four years earlier: "Graduate from college and I'll let you learn circus by watching me."

Ken jokes that associates must have thought he was both deaf and mute as he sat in on meetings, lunches, and dinners while Irvin talked. He traveled with Irvin, he was by his side on airplanes, at circus shows, during contract negotiations, at auditions. Alone with his dad at night, the questions would begin. "That was my graduate school," Ken says. Carefully and cautiously, Ken learned circus.

Karen, however, wasn't part of the picture. In contrast to her brother's experience, she says that when she graduated, "They didn't want me. I'm one year ahead of Kenny, so when I asked, it was, 'You don't do that. He's got to get the head start, not you.'"

There was another, more significant shift than Karen's departure going on at Ringling. It began when Irvin took the circus public in 1969, offering another first—a multicolored stock certificate. But the circus hadn't come up to profitability in the way Irvin had predicted, and no institution was going to pay a price ratio that was 64 times earnings. In 1971, Irvin and other investors sold to toy manufacturer Mattel for $50 million in stock, with Irvin retaining a long-term contract as head of Mattel's entertainment division.

Irvin's entrepreneurial genius showed itself once again, when he sold Ringling, yet kept their goldmine concessionaire, Sells-Floto.

Plans immediately began to develop Circus World, a Florida amusement theme park sited on 800 acres off Interstates 4 and 27, southwest of Disney World. Richard Evans, now CEO of Madison Square Garden, was brought in from Disney to help mastermind this $75 million venture. But Mattel executives couldn't seem to get a handle on a circus business whose revenues weren't evenly reflected in each quarterly statement for the toy company which was also being badly damaged by fallout from the toy industry's video game collapse.

"The good Lord never meant for a circus to be owned by a big corporation," was how Irvin explained the 1982 flip from Mattel back to the Felds for the very reasonable price of $22.6 million in stock, which included the ice shows Mattel had acquired along the way but not the theme park. But Ken remembers that the leveraged buyout as consummated with trepidation. "Then, interest rates were 19 percent. It was a pretty hairy time." It was worth the risk to Ken. "When I walked into this office the day after we bought Ringling back, it was a whole different feeling. It's a sense of pride."

In 1984, when Irvin was at winter headquarters to greet the year's entrants to Clown College, he died in his sleep. The *New York Times* honored him as "The Man Who Saved the Circus."

Reflecting back, Ken says, "My father was the driving force, but I knew I'd get my chance. It just happened to come sooner than expected, and you never know what you can do until you're in a position to do it."

Ken could see he needed to modernize operations. Speaking of Irvin, his Replicator son says with unconscious irony, "He was unwilling to let up any control of a lot of things. He could only expand so far. But you've got to let the business grow."

Ken admits that he likes to keep busy. He moves mechanically from one meeting to the next, saying, "I don't want any free time." A few associates believe Ken has sacrificed his own individuality, and any hope of leading a normal life, to his entertainment companies. When asked to imagine what he'd be doing if he hadn't inherited Ringling, he's taken aback and refuses to speculate. "No, I don't have to think about that," he responds.

The greatest change made by Ken since Irvin's death has been to turn a production company know primarily in the United States into one as well recognized internationally as Warner Bros. was in the 1950s. Currently, 40 percent of the company revenues come from outside the United States, and Ken is hoping to push beyond the 50 percent mark. And with entertainment the central theme for diversification, Ken's pushing a line of circus videos, producing television network specials, holding Taste Festivals in a half-dozen cities with a tie-in to local restaurants, and developing product licensing and merchandising.

But serious mistakes were made in Japan because of Ringling's necessary reliance on a local promoter. As the Gold Unit—the third, foreign-based, circus division—and the ice shows enter new markets with unfamiliar cultures, there's nervousness over the thought of more logistical and marketing nightmares. With its tremendous daily costs, a capital- and labor-intensive business can quickly eat up profits.

One cost that's accelerating at a faster rate than revenue is insurance. Premiums in 1989 were greater than Feld's 1968 gross. Ken is also dreaming of reviving the romance of The Big Top. Calling it a "possibility for the future," he's got architects designing tents to be used in selected U.S. cities at some point in the 1990s.

Ken says he'd like it if his daughters succeed him, but "they'd have to want it. I don't want to visibly direct them. If you don't want it, you'd better not be in it, because it's a killer." But, he concludes, "It can't stop for any reason. It hasn't in 120 years."

Today, when Americans are asked to identify a circus, 96 percent think of Ringling. Irvin was successful in creating Clown College to help perpetuate his beloved circus, and he was equally successful in molding his son in his image, to keep The Big Show alive. Ken has used his own talents to improve and build on Irvin's legacy—within that mold.

*"The best thing that can happen [to increase business at H&R Block] is when
Congress changes the tax laws."*

H&R Block, Inc.
Kansas City, Missouri

Business: Tax returns for individuals

Best Known Products: Tax Services; Computer Services (CompuServe): Temporary Help Services

Founded: 1955 by Henry and Richard Bloch

Family Executives: Henry W. Bloch, Chairman and CEO
Thomas M. Bloch, President, CEO and Director

Family History: Second generation

Family Ownership: 7 percent

Family Board Membership: 2 family members of 11 directors

Traded: NYSE, HRB

Net Revenues: $1,370,698,000 1992
1,190,767,000 1991
1,052,696,000 1990

Net Earnings: $162,253,000 1992
140,108,000 1991
123,529,000 1990

H&R BLOCK, INC.

New Kid on the Block

Thomas M. Bloch, President and CEO

The professionally planned succession of Tom Bloch, 38, to the presidency of H&R Block, Inc. could stand as a model for other family businesses. All the key procedures of family business succession were followed by this giant tax preparation and computer service company, which dominates its industry: professional advice sought by Henry Bloch, 70, before son Tom began at the company; a formal training program designed for and followed by Tom; mentorship by a key member of the company; consultation with a law firm specializing in family business succession planning; and the resulting succession plan voted on and approved by H&R Block's board of directors.

Nothing is left to chance at H&R Block, a company that provides its office managers with policies-and-procedures manuals, tax code reference books and plan-ahead calendars. The company is institutionalized as America's tax preparer and files about one in nine U.S. returns. Its popularity is reflected in its bottom line: There's been only one down year (1972) since its incorporation in 1955. So it would be unlikely that Henry Bloch would have been lax when it came to launching his son's career.

Precision and service are keywords at H&R Block, a tax preparation business that began in 1955 when Henry and brother Richard took out two small advertisements extolling their low $5 tax preparation fee. (The $5 bought the customer both a federal and a state return.) Actually, the brothers had been in business together doing bookkeeping for small companies since 1946 as United Business Company. As a favor to their clients, they'd prepare tax returns for free. But in 1955, the brothers notified customers that tax preparation was too time consuming to continue. One client, an ad salesman for the *Kansas City Star*, not only talked them into continuing the tax preparation service but also convinced them to specialize in it. On top of that, he sold them the two ads that alerted Kansas City to its new business.

Preparing carefully, the brothers planned that first ad to run the day after most people in Kansas City received their 1040 form. Coincidentally, within the year the IRS began phasing out assistance in preparing returns for taxpayers. The savvy Blochs set up shop across the street from the Kansas City IRS office, ready to take disappointed taxpayers turned away by the government office.

On that first day of business, Henry was picking up office supplies when he was tracked down by Dick, who told him to get back to the office—the waiting room was jammed with hapless taxpayers. Henry's characteristic modesty shows when he attributes the company's beginning success to "luck." Careful planning and managerial follow-through are the more likely reasons for the company's strong takeoff.

The first year, the company—which altered the spelling of the Bloch family name to avoid mispronunciation—grossed $25,000. That year, Henry was found in the waiting room of a local hospital the day before federal returns were due, sitting with his adding machine and filling out tax forms. Tom was born, somewhat inconveniently, the day before the federal tax deadline.

Although Henry never directly encouraged any of his four children to enter his business, he did reinforce Tom's interest by taking him, rotating with the other children, on business trips without mother Marion. And as he grew up, Tom says, "I always felt that this is what I was going to do. Gosh, I didn't seriously consider anything else."

In the company's first decade, there were bumps despite Henry and Dick's careful planning. Although Henry graduated college as a math major, he was neither an accountant nor a lawyer like his own father. His new company had to fight threats of lawsuits from accounting and legal firms that feared competition. And after opening a New York office, the brothers realized that neither wanted to move from Kansas City nor be on the road constantly. As a result, their first franchise—and the first for the tax preparation industry—was sold in 1956.

The New York City territory went for $10,000 and, because the value-conscious Blochs felt that was a steep fee, they threw in Connecticut and New Jersey as an incentive to this first franchisee. When they became unhappy 10 years later with the way the franchisee was running the area offices, they bought the franchise back for $1 million.

Tom attributes the origination of H&R Block franchises to Dick's initiative. "My uncle," says Tom, "was more of the entrepreneur and my father was more of a manager. My uncle was the guy going out and adding offices and finding franchisees and really developing the network around the country."

The company has two types of franchises. A major franchise is a large territorial franchise, like the state of Oklahoma. The other type is what the Blochs call a satellite franchise, which is a small town franchise "where it's better, from a management point of view, to have an independent operator than to try to operate it ourselves," although about half the H&R Block offices throughout the country are owned and operated by the company. The company has 7,793 outlets in the United States and another 1,084 in Canada and 271 in Australia. There are 80 other tax offices throughout the world, located on or near U.S. military bases.

It would be no use trying to buy a lucrative major franchise today. "That's something we don't sell anymore," says Tom. "In fact, we'd like to buy those guys back." The nation is also pretty much saturated with satellite franchises, although a new office might open when there's a population shift.

In addition to the franchise and H&R Block-owned offices, the success of the company rests on two other factors. First and foremost is the reputation of H&R Block as a tax preparer that stands by its customers. This trust factor is a crucial determinant in a service industry characterized by highly anxious clients, and it helps account for the company's 75-percent customer return rate. Everything is done to keep the client happy, including having the regional office double-check each tax return. If a customer is not happy with the way the return is prepared, next year's return is provided free of charge. If the company makes an error, it pays any resulting interest or penalties. And if the unspeakable happens, an H&R Block representative will accompany the customer to the tax audit for no additional fee.

Another determinant of success was Henry's managerial skills. While Dick was making the franchise deals and opening up offices, Henry was strengthening the company's foundation by his hands-on management, which included the step-by-step guidelines provided to each office manager and the multivolume tax code books especially developed for its preparers. He also was responsible for the plan-ahead calendar that suggests the day's activities to office managers, detailing even what supplies to order on a particular day. Henry kept costs low by emphasizing frugality, which apparently includes his and Tom's no-frills offices.

Most important, Henry emphasized specialization. H&R Block knows it surpasses at tax preparation, and the company sticks to that operation rather than trying to become a supermarket of financial services. Their client-oriented spin-offs are related to tax preparation: *H&R Block Income Tax Workbook* (the only best-seller whose cover notes that its cost may be tax deductible); tax preparation videos; and H&R Block Income Tax Schools. The tax school classes are difficult: The basic course requires 75 hours of classroom teaching. About 40 percent of those who successfully complete the basic course with high scores are hired as preparers. Because the work is seasonal, H&R Block has become the nation's largest employer of white-collar, part-time workers—many of them women. Just as the company has a high return rate for customers, it has a similarly high retention rate for seasonal workers.

In 1962, Henry and Dick decided that in order to grow, they had to bring H&R Block public. Today, Tom reflects on the negatives of being publicly owned. "It's much tougher. There's so much pressure from Wall Street, from institutional shareholders who expect continued growth. And I think sometimes you make decisions in order to satisfy those outside concerns that are not always in the best interests of the long-term interests of the company. "I'll give you an example," he says. "Pricing. By increasing prices each year, it helps to increase the bottom line. Now we know that there are some customers who are very sensitive about price increases. [The typical charge is around $50.] There are some who may choose not to come back to use our service because the price has gone up too much. Well, we're very interested in serving as many people as we can. You have to balance that desire and that need with the interest and desire of shareholders to keep those profits going up every year."

Seven years after the decision to go public, Dick decided to leave the business and subsequently sold his shares in the company. Tom says, "I believe—and I've not discussed my uncle's decision with him in any detail—that he just felt, 'I'm no longer actively involved, so I might as well sell my interest in the company.'" By the time Tom joined the business in 1976, there were approximately 7,000 H&R Block offices dotted throughout the country. The name of H&R Block was synonymous with tax preparation. When Tom graduated from Claremont-McKenna with a degree in economics, he came straight to H&R Block, working in the supply department as a paper buyer. "I didn't even consider going to graduate school," he says. "I thought the experience I could gain here would be better than that, and I didn't consider working someplace else, either. I don't regret it."

Tom is the only young Bloch family member working at the company. "I was the only one who said, 'Dad I want to do this,'" says Tom. Neither his two sisters nor his uncle's daughters were interested in entering. Tom's brother, Robert, recently joined the H&R Block Foundation after a short career running a gallery and working at a museum, but he was never interested in the tax business. (Henry—who himself comes from a prosperous family—and Marion have a fine collection of Impressionist works and help support the city's Nelson-Atkins Museum of Art.)

While Tom was still at college, Henry consulted with advisers outside the company and came up with a training program that gave Tom a short exposure to each department in the company, with the long-term goal of being head of tax operations. Henry originally wanted to place Tom in one of the company's acquisition businesses, but Henry's adviser, H&R Block's lawyer, argued that if the company's basic business was tax preparation, that's where Tom should go.

Some of Tom's stints included taking the tax course, working as a tax preparer, and eventually teaching the tax class. "If you don't learn the business from the ground up, you're really putting a lot at risk both for the individual and for the company," he says. "And I don't know how you'd get credibility."

Although Tom was comfortable with his work-related tasks at H&R Block, he was sometimes uneasy at being the founder's son. He's one of the few business inheritors who candidly admits the giant step forward he gained by being The Son. And he also says, "It's a tough position to be in. I don't think that I fully realized that a lot of other people may think that person is there because of his father. You feel like you've got to prove yourself a lot more than you would otherwise. You put it on yourself as much as other people put it on you and that's tough to overcome."

Tom was assigned Jerome Grossman, vice-president of the board and former H&R Block COO, as his mentor. (Although within the company Grossman is not generally thought of as a family member, he actually is Tom's mother's cousin.) "It was very helpful to have a guy like Jerry Grossman in there to talk things over with," says Tom, who never reported directly to his father.

It wasn't always easy working for Henry. "There were some times when it was difficult," says Tom. "That's something we had to work on. Sometimes we'd just talk it out, and sometimes it would take a few days to think it through a little further and try to think about the other's perspective and it always seemed to work out."

In those early days at the company, Tom would also pressure himself to suggest changes in operations. "I'd say, 'Oh, I've got to show that I can come up with good ideas and a better program.'" Now, he reflects, "I shouldn't have put pressure on myself to develop these new ideas and programs and to see that they got implemented. It's just something I had to go through and you learn by your mistakes."

Tom became president of the Tax Operations Division, which accounts for about half the company's revenue, in 1981 and then president of the company in 1989. (Henry remains board chairman and CEO.) Tom's beginning decades, the '70s and '80s, were a time of diversification for H&R Block. By 1970, stock was selling at 100 times earnings. Growth became slower the more deeply the company penetrated its market. H&R Block had virtually run out of new areas in which to open offices and had solid cash at hand. With this cash, the firm diversified in 1972 with a promotional materials business, Consumer Communications Services, Inc.

(CCS), which delivered coupons and newsletters door-to-door. This foray proved to be a misstep, and CCS was sold in 1980.

H&R Block changed its acquisition focus to client-oriented, rather than company-oriented, businesses. The firm bought Personnel Pool of America (PPA) for $22 million in 1978, putting its expertise in part-time workers to good use in this employment agency for medical and traditional temporaries. PPA also has franchise operations. In 1991, the business bought Interim Systems Corporation, which strengthened Personnel Pool's number one spot for temporary help in North America.

In 1980, the firm bought an 80-percent share of Hyatt Legal Services' tangible assets and formed Block Management Co. The concept was to operate a chain offering simple legal services, just as H&R Block offered basic tax preparation. Henry envisioned legal services becoming as important to the company as tax preparation, but the idea of law service clinics didn't appeal to consumers. Another disappointment was the 1985 purchase of a management seminar company, Path Management Industries, Inc., for $35 million. H&R Block eventually sold Path at a loss and sold its legal services back to Joel Hyatt.

Although Hyatt Legal Services and Path Management were losses, they were more than offset by the company's tremendously successful and far-sighted acquisition in 1985, CompuServe, Inc. At the time of its purchase, CompuServe was a computer time-sharing company. Under H&R Block, it expanded to include bulletin boards, support forums, games, and home shopping applications in downloadable software. This computer information service is a leader in the industry, with 800,000 subscribers and revenues of more than $250 million. H&R Block is careful where it puts its money, and although it blipped with Path and Hyatt, CompuServe and PPA look like brilliant acquisitions. As president, Tom oversees the acquisitions as well as running the company's tax division. He considers himself in his father's mode as a professional manager. "I'm a lot like my dad," he says. "I think I am conservative. And I'm not ashamed of it. I hate to take risks that are just really risky. I may be a little skeptical about a hot area if management knows nothing about it."

This chip off the block also says that he's never liked the idea of having a lot of debt. "During the time when everybody was making big acquisitions and doing leveraged buyouts and getting huge amounts of debt, we were criticized because here we were sitting on lots of cash and being very conservative in the acquisition area. Now we're being applauded for not having all that debt. We didn't do anything differently. It's just sort of a change in the mood at Wall Street."

He still meets with Henry—along with mentor Grossman—to go through the weekly agenda. Tom says, "It always helps to have that other person there to keep it on a professional level."

In 1987, Henry called in a succession-planning expert from Sibson & Co. of Princeton, New Jersey, to devise the timetable the company is following. In August 1992, Tom became CEO of the company, adding that title to the one of president. Tom says that it made sense, "looking from a shareholder's view, for a succession plan to be formalized. We thought the best way to do it is to get an expert to help plan. "The board has always recognized that this is a publicly owned company. The family does not control it," says Tom of the Blochs, who own 6.5 percent of the shares. "The board was fully supportive of the development of the succession plan. They thought it should be done the right way."

Shareholders have received a bigger return on their investment every year since Tom has entered the company. The Tax Operations Division showed an increase of nearly 16 percent in 1991, and the company's market share of U.S. taxpayers rose to a record high of 13.7 percent. In 1991, the company surpassed the billion dollar mark in total revenues' including the franchisees for the sixth consecutive year and surpassed that mark for the second consecutive year counting only the company-owned offices. (The business shows a loss for three-quarters of the year due to the seasonal nature of its tax business.) H&R Block has excellent financials: little debt and a nice cash cushion. With all three operations now kicking in—tax operations, PPA, and CompuServe —the company is high-powered on all fronts.

Fueling the tax division revenues is electronic tax filing, which gets a tax refund back to the filer in two to three weeks, versus eight weeks for a mailed return. Because many of H&R Block customers are lower-income wage earners eager to receive their refunds, the Rapid Refund program is popular. It shot from 724,000 returns in 1989 to more than 4 million in 1991.

"That has done more to stimulate growth in our business than anything in at least 20 years," says Tom, referring to H&R Block's capture of a 67-percent market share for electronic filing.

Since the company had wisely geared up for electronic returns when IRS introduced the concept in 1986—1990 was the first year it was available to taxpayers nationwide—operational start-up expenses are over, allowing this revenue to drop straight to the bottom line. In addition, CompuServe provides computer and network resources for the firm's electronic filing program. With the IRS continuing to push electronic filings, the operation will continue to soar.

In Canada, the company's biggest foreign market, the tax refund is essentially advanced by H&R Block. "And then the government sends the actual refund to us," says Tom "So in a sense, we are making a loan to our clients for a fee." In the United States, a taxpayer can choose a Refund Anticipation Loan, which is made by a participating bank and not by H&R Block directly (due to legal restrictions).

Another plus for the company is the frequent changes in the U.S. tax code, which invariably mean more business for a company that now serves 17 million taxpayers. "The best thing that can happen is when Congress changes the tax laws," Tom says. H&R Block's biggest competitors are not the big eight accounting firms or the tax lawyers, who generally work with a more sophisticated return than H&R Block handles. Instead, the company's biggest threat comes from those 50 percent of Americans who file returns themselves. But even these self-preparers will seek a tax specialist whenever the tax code is revamped. Because of the company's $648 million in current assets at the end of 1991, which includes $37 million in cash and $192 million in marketable securities, the possibility of a takeover is sometimes discussed by analysts. The threat is dismissed by Tom, who feels that the neighborly, trustworthy aura of this family business would be ruined by an unfriendly takeover. "We'd be hard to take over in a hostile manner," he points out.

The service-oriented image of H&R Block has been personified by Henry in his two-plus decades of television commercials, which began with the 1970 landmark ad, "17 Reasons Why H&R Block Should Prepare Your Taxes." "My dad is so well recognized today, and he's got a lot of credibility," says Tom, who demurs from sharing the spotlight with Henry.

No matter who represents H&R Block's public persona, the family hopes that with the ascension of Tom to the presidency, there is now one more reason H&R Block should prepare your taxes.

"You'll never have to pay full price again."

Crown Books Corp.
Landover, Maryland

Business:	Specialty retail book stores
Best Known Products:	*The New York Times* best seller list at 40 percent discount
Founded:	1977 by Robert Haft (Dart Drugs founded 1954 by Herbert Haft)
Family Executives:	Robert Haft, CEO and President (also President, Dart Group) Herbert Haft, Chairman, Dart Group Gloria Haft, Vice President, Dart Group
Family History:	Second generation of Dart Group
Family Ownership:	54 percent owned by Dart Group, which is wholly owned by the Haft family
Family Board Membership:	3 family members of 6 directors
Traded:	OTC, CRWN
Net Sales:	$220,304,000 1991 204,447,000 1990 183,821,000 1989
Net Income:	$10,649,000 1991 10,327,000 1990 9,981,000 1989

CROWN BOOKS CORP.

Discount Dynasty

Robert Haft, CEO and President

The Haft family of Washington, D.C. stands out even in a retail industry where generosity is often thought of as a sign of vulnerability. What's best known about the Hafts—father Herbert, oldest son Robert, and Robert's siblings Linda and Ronald—are their takeover attempts of the mid-'80s. That these takeovers conducted by the Hafts' Dart Group Corp. (largely a holding company for two retail chains, including Crown Books Corp.) have failed is no reason to question their savvy. An analyst commented to *The Washington Post*, "They make more profits with failure than most people have made with success."

The sale in 1984 of the original Haft venture, Dart Drug Stores, gave the Hafts a high $161 million with which to play a serious game of takeover. Unsuccessful bids for Supermarkets General Corporation brought the Haft family profits of $32 million; Jack Eckerd Corporation brought them $10 million; May Department Stores, $1 million; Stop & Shop Cos., $17 million; and Safeway Stores Inc., $152 million. Dart Group did suffer a loss of $5 million on Federated Department Stores and dropped close to $100 million on Dayton Hudson Corporation when the market crashed in 1987, but Herbert summarized that last hit as "no big deal" to Washington's *Regardie's* magazine.

The Hafts adamantly deny charges of greenmailing, and justify their profits—more than $148 million for the years 1985–1988—as legitimate. They point out that they've made their money from buying and selling at market price, rather than receiving an above-market price. The Hafts also denounce those who blame them for the layoffs that usually resulted after their takeover attempts. Herbert says of the companies he'd hoped to acquire, "I think it's insane what they are doing. Our plans were not to fire workers and close divisions," he told *The Washington Post.* Herbert's denunciation is unusual in that he rarely speaks to the press, leaving that chore to son Robert. The Hafts have always been a tightly-knit family with a tradition of working together. Gloria Haft was a cosmetologist when she met Herbert and continued working at Dart drugstores well after the Hafts became known for their wealth. (*Forbes* magazine places the family's worth at $450 million.)

Robert is the son who resembles Herbert most closely, especially in his management of the retail bookstore chain, Crown Books. Crown—which was solely Robert's idea—revolutionized bookselling by offering heavily discounted prices on new publications. In this gamble, Robert emulated the earlier success of his father, who'd used price cuts to turn one drugstore in Washington, D.C. into the 73-store Dart Drug chain. (Herbert also used his discount philosophy in 1979 to start Trak Auto, which now has 330 stores. Cabot Morgan Real Estate Corp., the family's real estate firm, owns dozens of shopping centers and is run by Robert's younger brother, Ronald. This is no small job in that real estate is increasingly becoming the basis for the Hafts' wealth. Sister Linda is in charge of Dart Group Financial Corp.)

But it was actually Robert's grandfather, Abraham, who bought the family's first drugstore across the street from the National Zoo shortly after the Depression, while Herbert was in high school. Herbert later earned a pharmacy degree and spent World War II as a supply officer, activities that helped him initially in his career. But he felt his solo drugstore, opened in 1954, put him at a disadvantage compared to the two large competing regional drug chains. "I really can't beat them," Herbert acknowledged in a 1986 speech, quoted in *The Washington Post Magazine.* "If...everybody's rowing upstream, I've got to row downstream." Herbert's method of outselling the competition was to slash prices—the same method Robert uses today at Crown Books.

As Herbert rowed downstream with Dart Drug Stores, he took his son with him. Robert was involved in his parents' business in a way that might make more traditional families shudder. The price gouges Herbert made to stay competitive didn't endear him to drug manufacturers. He refused to charge the manufacturers' assigned retail prices for medication like Benadryl or Chloromycetin. Be-

cause fair trade laws prohibited retailers from the type of discounting that Herbert introduced, he was hit by more than 100 lawsuits
filed by manufacturers and suppliers. Robert recounted to *Fortune*
magazine that it was left to him, as a young child, to tell process
servers knocking on the Haft door, "My father says he's not home."

Although Herbert initially lost many of these cases, his spirit
in fighting fair trade price fixing agreements won the support of
consumers. Senator Estes Kefauver (D, TN) arranged for the
federal Justice Department to grant a hearing and as a result,
Justice charged the giant drug company Parke-Davis (now owned
by Warner-Lambert Company) with price-fixing. The government, and Herbert, initially lost their case, but the Supreme
Court vindicated Herbert in 1960. And the era of discount merchandising began in earnest.

During this time, Robert learned how to buck convention
and ignore retail industry customs. Robert watched his father
with curiosity as he was led to meetings with bankers and suppliers. He recounted to *The Washington Post*, "I went to the convention show when I was three years old, and in the *Philadelphia
Inquirer* there's a picture of it: the youngest convention goer."

His interest in business never abating, Robert went to the
University of Pennsylvania for a business degree, and from there
to Harvard for an M.B.A. It's not surprising that Robert was intrigued by the idea of replicating his father's discount drugstore
nor that he turned to the concept of discount books as something
he wanted to start. He's always been a little more introspective
and intellectually-oriented than his father, as well as being a vo-
racious reader, finishing a book every few days.

Robert presented his idea to some of his Harvard professors
who, in the custom of academia, immediately tried to discourage
him. Convention had it that discounting would never work in
bookselling. But the only other person who needed to believe in
Robert was Herbert. In 1977, they opened the first Crown Books
in a suburb outside Washington. Robert, then 32, served as president of the company, which began as a Dart subsidiary.

Initially, the bookstores looked more like small warehouses
than cozy nooks for book browsing. Decor was strictly utilitarian.
But the prices were right. Robert sold *The New York Times* best-
sellers at a phenomenal 35 percent discount (now 40 percent off)

and gave a smaller discount on paperbacks, magazines, and other merchandise. "You'll never have to pay full price again" became his motto in a heavy budget spent for print, radio, and television advertising. Wherever a Crown Books opened, cries arose from independent booksellers who pointed accusingly at Crown's smaller selection and limited service. Even the chains like B. Dalton Bookseller (owned by BDB Corp.) and Waldenbooks feared losing customers to Crown's deep discounts. Additionally, Crown is located outside of suburban shopping malls. Robert believes that books are a planned purchase, so putting stores in expensive mall rentals just to entertain browsers has no payoff. Here again, Robert bucks conventional bookselling wisdom: nearly every suburban shopping mall contains a Barnes & Noble (also owned by BDB Corp.) or another chain bookstore. And the Hafts smartly purchased strip shopping centers in which they placed both Crown Books and their Trak Auto stores.

Criticism of Crown Books was criticism of Dart Drugs, redux. This new company was going to force its gentlemanly competitors (substitute booksellers for pharmacists) to be price aggressive, with the customer ultimately suffering. And customers, long accustomed to comparison shopping for the best buy in Bufferin, knew that they could pay less for popular books at Crown. According to these critics, Robert's aggressive merchandising techniques were sullying the concept of bookbuying.

As the controversy swirled, Robert kept opening new stores and attracting bookbuyers. Houston, Los Angeles, Seattle, San Diego, San Francisco, and Chicago sported Crown Books, first in their suburbs and then in the urban sections. Clustering in these cities kept Crown's distribution efficient and targeted its heavy advertising. While Robert has created a niche as a discount bookseller, he's lost a great deal of personal privacy in doing so. Although *Advertising Age* quotes a manager at Ferris & Co. calling the Haft family "the Greta Garbo of the corporate world," Robert's anonymity flew out the television screen as he personally pitched his messages in his unmistakable squeaky voice. Now, he can be recognized as he helps customers in the newer stores, having always characterized himself as a hands-on retail manager. No central computer system graces the Crown empire because reordering is done by each manager, who is supposed to understand local interests. "We're trying to keep the business at store level," Robert says.

And there's another concept Robert is trying out. Five Super Crowns were planned to open in the Washington area in the early '90s. Robert calls these larger, upscale bookstores "experimental" and is watching sales carefully before he decides to move his idea west. Pleasing bookbuyers led him to open these Super stores, he told *The Washington Post*: "People seem to want everything these days, all at the same time—price, selection, a nice place to shop—so we decided to do this after listening to our customers." Perhaps those initial Crown stores were too sparse, after all. Robert may have proven that discount bookselling was an idea whose time had arrived—thanks to Robert. Crown Books Corp. is rated by *Forbes* magazine as one of the 200 best companies in the United States as profits rose by 3 percent in 1990, with revenues going up 11 percent. Another sign of its sure success is its low return rate: only around 10 percent of its books, a proportion far behind other bookstores. The chain now operates 259 stores, with the Hafts owning a 54 percent interest (and 100 percent of the voting shares) since they took Crown Books public in 1983.

Robert is amply rewarded for these corporate gains. At age 39, he's number 168 on *Forbes* magazine's list of best-paid executives with a flat salary of $1.3 million and an extra $300,00 in bonuses. Perhaps his response when *Forbes* called him about his generous compensation was meant to sound disingenuous, "Are you sure? I really have no idea what I make."

Has Robert mellowed since his marriage to Mary Haft, an independent television producer, and the birth of his son? That's doubtful. This man models himself after his father and Herbert certainly has never let up as he ages. Robert told *Fortune* that he and his father have "started, redone and renewed businesses." This is certainly true—looking at the drugstores, car supply shops and Crown Books—but both men have paid a personal price by being viewed as outsiders within their various industries. Robert, like Herbert, remains distant and isolated—perhaps a technique to stay out of the seductive culture of the bookselling industry to maintain his competitive advantage. But neither Robert nor his father acts as if he's missing anything, as long as they have each other.

"We don't think anybody can do it cheaper than we do it in Japan."

AFLAC
Columbus, Georgia

Business:	Supplemental health care insurance
Best Known Products:	Japan: Cancer protection; Super Cancer Plan U.S.: Cancer protection; Intensive care; Accident; Medicare supplement; Long-term care; Lifecare; Hospital confinement indemnity policy
Founded:	1955 by John Beverly Amos
Family Executives:	Paul S. Amos, Chairman Daniel P. Amos, Vice Chairman, President and CEO John Shelby Amos II, Alabama State Sales Coordinator and Director William L. Amos, Jr., Director
Family History:	Second generation
Family Ownership:	Approximately 6 percent
Family Board Membership:	4 family members of 23 directors
Traded:	NYSE, AFL
Total Revenue:	$3,282,669,000 1991 2,678,354,000 1990 2,438,172,000 1989
Net Earnings:	$148,684,000 1991 117,186,000 1990 80,806,000 1989

AFLAC
(AMERICAN FAMILY
CORP.)

Insuring the Succession

Daniel P. Amos, CEO

President Jimmy Carter and Roslynn Carter, along with three
U.S. senators and three U.S. representatives, grieved at the 1990
funeral of 66-year-old John Beverly Amos, founder of AFLAC.
Family members included Elena Diaz-Verson Amos, John's widow, who is also the daughter of the late Salvador Diaz-Verson,
Cuba's well-known journalist, former chief of military intelligence, and anti-Castro activist.

By Elena's side was her half-brother, Salvador Diaz-Verson
Jr., at that time president of AFLAC's holding company and its
chief investment officer. Also present were John's brother, Paul
Amos, who became chairman of AFLAC upon John's death, and
Paul's son, Daniel P. Amos, John's nephew and his as-yet un-
proven successor.

John B. Amos was a master builder who forged political ties with
business acumen to construct an insurance company with $3.3
billion in revenues and $10 billion dollars in assets, the world's
largest cancer insurer. The company ranks among the 100 largest
U.S. multinational businesses. While John's creation of AFLAC is
extraordinary in itself, the unique monument to his talents remains
AFLAC's position as the American insurance company that sells
more than 80 percent of Japan's supplemental cancer insurance
policies. By 1992, one out of five Japanese citizens were privately
insured by AFLAC. Because of John's singular penetration of the
Japanese market, in 1988 *Forbes* named him the most innovative
chief executive within the insurance industry.

John's ability to plan for the long term enabled AFLAC to step in and scoop up Japanese business, which in 1991 accounted for 83 percent of the company's net profits. While America's corporate executives and government officials were scratching their heads in 1992 trying to figure out how U.S. business interests can do as well in Japan as the Japanese have done in the United States, this southern entrepreneur entered Japan and created a new, multibillion dollar market 20 years ago. Not that his accomplishment took place overnight. It wasn't until 1958, three years after John founded American Family Life Assurance Company with less than $300,000 in investment capital, that he entered cancer expense insurance with a policy that pays for deductibles, noncovered expenses, copayments, and other supplemental needs. At the time, cancer insurance had a dubious reputation, and few other businesses wanted to enter the field, much less to specialize in it. But John identified supplemental cancer coverage as a potential niche that would allow his firm to compete in an insurance area that had few contenders.

That first year, 5,800 supplemental cancer care policies were sold as John concentrated on building a unique force of independent contractors to cluster-sell policies to payroll groups rather than to individuals. AFLAC's sales territory enlarged to include more southern and midwestern states. In 1969, an expansion program began that spread the firm's market to 42 states by the end of 1979. In its first year on the NYSE in 1974, AFLAC became the industry's leading stock performer.

Six years earlier, in 1968, John had taken a portentous trip to the Osaka World's Fair in Japan. As a man whose curiosity kept him alert to nuances in human behavior, John was immediately struck by the gauze masks he saw stretched over the mouths and noses of the Japanese with head colds. "I concluded that a nation that was so health conscious would certainly buy our cancer insurance," he said years later. John began an intricate courtship of government officials in Tokyo's Ministry of Finance, at one point moving with Elena to Japan for a year. He also maintained a house in Washington D.C., where he sought the influence of former House Ways and Means Chairman Wilbur Mills to keep the Japanese license application moving.

"John's politics played a part in our receiving recognition to be considered for a license [in Japan]," says Paul. John's patience with the complex Japanese system paid off when AFLAC's application to do business was approved in 1974. In his negotiations with bureaucrats and businessmen, he was also able to use skills learned in law school at the University of Florida many years before. AFLAC was the second U.S. insurance company to receive a Japanese license—in a country with its own national health insurance. (The first was American Life Insurance Co.)

Several factors aided AFLAC. First, Japanese companies did not choose to offer cancer policies, mostly for cultural reasons. Ironically, being a cancer victim in a country where cancer is the number one cause of death was considered shameful and unmentionable. "To the Japanese, cancer was a taboo subject," says Paul. "People didn't want to talk about it." (By 1992, there was a handful of Japanese companies offering cancer policies, but the most successful has only a 4 percent market share compared to AFLAC's 80 percent.)

Second, Japanese interests feared a high-powered insurance company like Prudential or MetLife moving into its territory. AFLAC was a relatively small insurer headquartered in a small, antebellum Georgia city. It was headed by a Southerner whose personal style favored cigars and white suits. Perhaps if the Japanese Minister of Finance had possessed the prescience of AFLAC's Georgia founder, the license would have been granted to another insurer.

AFLAC's original investment in the Japanese market was $1.6 million. The company predicted that it would write $3.5 million in premiums that first year. Instead, AFLAC's premiums came in at $25 million—the same premium level that it had taken 16 years to reach in the United States.

Having pioneered cluster-selling in the United States, John structured a sales system for Japan that virtually guaranteed success. He enabled each Japanese company to set up its own sales agency, which then acted as a corporate agent for AFLAC, selling—for a commission—supplemental cancer policies to their employees. This employer sponsorship serves as an endorsement of the AFLAC policy to loyal Japanese workers, who rarely question the automatic payroll deduction. AFLAC was also able to take advantage of another cultural phenomenon. Because the mandatory retirement age for Japanese business executives ranges from 55 to 58 years, AFLAC put these esteemed retirees to work representing its insurance subsidiaries. By 1992, 92 percent of Japan's top 2,000 companies had AFLAC subsidiaries. These agencies also sell AFLAC policies to the employees of their contractors and vendors. Additionally, employee turnover is notoriously low in Japan, leading to a policy renewal rate of 76 percent for a ten-year period, compared with the industry rate of 25 percent in the United States.

Once it granted the exclusive license, the Japanese government took its usual protective role toward the company, giving it an eight-year monopoly so that the company could stabilize its new operations. "When you get a license in Japan, the government does all it can to help you," says Dan, 41. Well before John's 1990 death, AFLAC was entrenched in Japan as an insurance powerhouse.

On the other hand, AFLAC's American operations are steady but not showing the profitability of Japan. Many U.S. health groups have guided consumers away from purchasing single-disease policies such as cancer insurance, which are needed less here than they are in Japan due to basic insurance coverage differences. For this reason and others, AFLAC has been broadening its insurance base by moving into other coverage. This includes accident, Medicare supplement, hospital indemnity, and long-term care insurance. Dan points to this expanded product line as one of his accomplishments. Additionally, AFLAC expects to receive approval for a general supplemental policy offering "senior market" long-term care in Japan in 1992, according to Dan.

Since becoming CEO, Dan has kept a more watchful eye on administrative costs. "We don't think anybody can do it cheaper than we do it in Japan," he notes of the operation established by his late uncle. But in the United States, Dan has cut out the few highly visible expenses that he's noticed, such as company planes, and he plans to eliminate 100 headquarters positions (out of 1,500 in Columbus) as employees leave the company. He's reorganized several of the American operations to increase efficiency, and—in a more controversial move—he's also axed foreign operations in several overseas markets that were not yet profitable. Dan came up through the U.S. operations side of the company, having joined AFLAC immediately after receiving his degree in risk management and insurance from the University of Georgia in 1973. He entered as assistant state manager for Alabama. By 1974, his father had rejoined AFLAC's managerial ranks after an absence of a number of years while he ran his wife's family's Florida variety stores and gas stations. By 1981, Dan was the leading state manager within the United States. In 1983, he became president of the subsidiary, involved with only the American operations. He began to learn AFLAC's Japanese operations in 1987 when it became clear—for the first time—that he would be his uncle's successor. In 1988, he became deputy CEO.

Dan points to Paul as the AFLAC senior manager he most closely resembles. He classifies John as having an entrepreneurial management style and his father as being more of a professional manager. John's law degree, however, and his redesign of cancer insurance to fit a new market—as well as his successful leadership of a global company for 35 years—indicate that he had management skills that went far beyond those of a classic entrepreneur.

One of John's concerns was the direction the company would take beyond his lifetime. As the younger men in the family became adults, he shaped their careers. And when John was diagnosed with lung cancer in 1986, he immediately began planning the succession process. His own son Shelby (John S. Amos, Jr.), 40, chose to remain state manager for Alabama, having opted out of competition for the top position in favor of a less pressured career. John and Elena's daughter Maria Teresa had never been interested in a professional life within her father's company, although her husband was Florida state manager before his 1991 death in a car accident.

The leading contender for John's spot seemed to be Sal Diaz-Verson, 40, John's brother-in-law, who had served under John in the number two job, president of the holding company, for nine years. Years earlier, Sal had considered a career as a lawyer, influenced by the fact that John had earned a law degree and Elena had attended law school for several years. But John convinced Sal to study finance instead, telling him he'd need a good investment manager as his insurance company grew.

It was another good move on John's part. Sal, who had joined the company in 1974, is credited with increasing its assets from

$45 million that year to $6.5 billion in 1991. As AFLAC's chief investment officer, Sal was responsible for *Financial World's* 1991 number two ranking of AFLAC among the nation's top insurers for the quality of its financial base. Sal's conservative fiscal philosophy avoided junk bonds and real estate—investments that brought down other insurance companies.

Sal has always pointed to John Amos as his mentor, and he's reflected this in his business achievements as well as by his immersion in behind-the-scenes politics. Given their similarities, it surprised some that John passed over Sal in favor of Dan. But perhaps John favored Dan's sales experience and recognized that Sal had an entrepreneurial bent—like his own—that caused Sal to leave AFLAC in 1991 to establish a global investment business in Columbus, called Diaz-Verson Capital Investments, Inc.

Dan says the gap Sal left at AFLAC isn't that deep considering that, "to give Sal the highest compliment, I chose his number one man to take the job over. Sal's been gone now six months, and the last six months were exactly alike. We've changed nothing." Dan points to a smooth transition implemented by John's having decided on his successor at the beginning of his four-year illness. While John was living, the board passed a resolution that upon his death, Dan would automatically become CEO and Paul would become chairman. "The day John died," Dan says, "we never had to have a meeting." Paul continues, "When he died, there was no question as to who was going to succeed; it was automatic. And we let the investment community know of our plans."

The Southern entrepreneur with a law degree had once more designed a plan to keep his legacy intact. And while it's easy for some to make superficial judgments about the management ability of an entrepreneur who favors short-sleeved shirts and white suits in favor of a younger man with a button-down look, life is rarely so clear-cut.

It has been a relatively short time since John died of cancer in mid-1990. Dan, by his own admission, must still prove himself.

"It's like playing a poker game. My uncle and my dad had built up so many chips from successful things. I'm in the game now and I haven't gotten many chips. So when I play one, it's got to be right."

"Hasbro will 'stand the test of time.'"

Hasbro, Inc.
Pawtucket, Rhode Island

Business:	Manufacturer and marketer of toys, games, puzzles and infant care products
Best Known Products:	Scrabble; Monopoly; Easy Bake Oven; Nerf toys; My Little Pony; G.I. Joe; Tonka trucks; Play-Doh; Cabbage Patch Kids
Founded:	1923 as Hassenfeld Brothers by Hillel and Henry Hassenfeld
Family Executives:	Alan G. Hassenfeld, Chairman and CEO Sylvia Hassenfeld, Director
Family Ownership:	Approximately 10 percent
Family Board Membership:	2 family members of 11 directors
Traded:	AMEX, HAS
Net Sales:	$2,141,096,000 1991 1,520,032,000 1990 1,409,678,000 1989
Net Earnings:	$81,654,000 1991 (a) 89,182,000 1990 92,194,000 1989

(a) Includes restructuring charge due to Tonka acquisition

HASBRO, INC.

Passing GO and Collecting...

Alan G. Hassenfeld, President, CEO, and Chairman

The succession of Alan Hassenfeld from the presidency to the chairmanship of Hasbro was the end result of a tragedy. Alan's older brother Stephen had died of pneumonia in 1989 at age 47. For several weeks, rumors of a company sale swirled around Wall Street. Then the board of directors elected Alan chairman and CEO of the world's largest—and the country's most profitable—toy company. Alan has replicated his late brother's talent at making toys live on forever. In 1991, the company was ranked 198 of the Fortune 500 largest U.S. industrial business.

Alan has vowed to make Hasbro "stand the test of time." In particular, Alan wants to carry on the business that was begun in 1923 by brothers Hillel and Henry Hassenfeld—his grandfather and great-uncle—as a fabric remnant distribution firm. Within a few years, the company was producing fabric-lined pencil boxes and other school supplies. By the '30s, it was also making pencils.

In the '40s, Alan's father Merrill introduced the firm's first toys: doctor and nurse kits. The initial Hasbro hit in 1952 was Mr. Potato Head, whose popularity increased when it became the first toy to be advertised on television. Other continuing favorites were Candyland, Lincoln Logs, and Tinker Toys.

The '60s were another time of growth for the business, when GI Joe and related figures based on the World War II-era soldier were introduced. (GI Joe went out of style and was dumped by the company in the mid-'70s, but reentered in the late '80s to become the best selling toy in the United States.)

Merrill brought his oldest son, Stephen, into the business in the late '60s. Soon after, Stephen talked younger brother Alan into joining Hasbro after college graduation. The company went public in 1968 and changed its name to Hasbro, an acronym of Hassenfeld Brothers. In 1979, Merrill died and Stephen became CEO. But Stephen's uncle, Harold Hassenfeld, had argued with Merrill five years earlier when he appointed Stephen president. Now, Harold refused to acknowledge his young nephew as head of the company. These bitter feelings led to Empire Pencil, the nation's largest pencil manufacturer, splitting off from Hasbro in 1980.

Hasbro was doing poorly in the late '70s due to the drop-off in GI Joe sales. Stephen began an ambitious plan to turn Hasbro into a top toy manufacturer. One way to ensure that the company never again became dependent on one product was to enlarge the business through acquisitions. Purchases included Knickerbocker, Playskool, Milton Bradley, and Child Guidance. Within five years of taking charge of Hasbro, Stephen had pushed the company past Mattel as the country's largest toy manufacturer.

Alan had been working to build up Hasbro's foreign operations, moving from there to marketing and sales. In 1984, Stephen appointed him president. Unlike other siblings working together, these brothers had no conflicts; they were close at work and at home. The bachelors shared both their Rhode Island house and their Manhattan apartment, although they were infrequently in the same place at the same time.

In 1987, Stephen became ill with endocarditis, an infection of the heart lining. It is a painful and debilitating bacterial infection, and Stephen worked from home for 10 weeks. He never fully recovered. Although the extent of his illness was unknown by outsiders, the board took care to institute a poison pill plan. As Stephen became weaker, management was reorganized. The new setup took effect six months before Stephen's death, although the company says that this was a coincidence.

The board considered it unnecessary to disclose Stephen's illness, despite rumors of AIDS—which Stephen denied. The board did not, however, appoint a successor in the case of Stephen's death and this needed to be done as immediately as possible after his death. Alan, who had few shares in Hasbro, also inherited Stephen's 10 percent stake in the company, valued at $100 million.

Alan's first year on the job as CEO and chairman couldn't have been easy. Hasbro, like other toy manufacturers, was hurt by the popularity of video games and sales of competitor Playmate Toys

Inc.'s Teenage Mutant Ninja Turtles. This line ate away at Hasbro's sale of GI Joe and TransFormers, as did the popularity of video games. But the company had also bought Coleco's Cabbage Patch Kids and refreshed the line, once more building up Cabbage Patch popularity from $35 million in 1989 to an anticipated $100 million in 1992 sales. In addition, the company had the license for the hot New Kids on the Block promotional toys.

In 1990, Hasbro bought Tonka Corp. and hoped to update some of its familiar toys as it had done with Coleco. Hasbro's traditional toys helped keep their 53 percent gross margins the best in the industry. The company is also obtaining revenues from many product lines, so it is less vulnerable to cycles in toy popularity. It is expanding internationally, and overseas sales accounted for 40 percent of revenues in 1991. In 1992, Hasbro signed a letter of intent with Nomura Toys Co. of Japan, to enlarge its presence in Japan through buying Nomura's toy and game division.

The Hassenfeld family is also well known for its many contributions to children's charities, to which Alan's mother Sylvia devotes her time. Perhaps the most stunning gift will be the Hasbro Children's Hospital in Providence, Rhode Island, to open in 1994.

The next family members to enter Hasbro will probably be the college-age children of Stephen and Alan's sister, Ellen Block. These young adults have already indicated their interest in perpetuating Hasbro as a family-run business, with Alan's full approval.

In the meantime, Alan may continue to rely on acquisitions to build Hasbro, as did Stephen. If this is his strategy, given the few remaining small independent toymakers, the Block children may eventually find that all the toys in the toy chest are theirs already.

SECTION III

THE CONSERVATORS

Conservators want to maintain their companies in perpetuity. Their business strategies center on this long-term goal. They often elect to head their family companies because they, rather than their siblings, have the strongest sense of identification with the family business.

Conservators run companies that are many years old, dating back to at least the beginning of the century. Levi Strauss & Co., founded during the gold rush of the 1850s, is the company with the greatest longevity to be led by a Conservator. This type of heritage makes today's generation of leaders mindful of the importance of preserving their companies for tomorrow.

CONSERVATORS USUALLY...

1. focus on conserving the business for many generations to come.
2. run businesses that are at least three generations old.
3. Are younger or only children with a strong sense of identification with the family business.

4. have parents who are not involved in daily operations or who are deceased, strengthening the conservators' sense of responsibility to the company.
5. enjoy playing ceremonial roles.
6. are noted for strong employee relations.
7. have worked outside the family business while young.

To this end, some Conservators of businesses that fell out of family hands have been active in bringing the company back again. For example, in 1985 Bob Haas of Levi Strauss & Co. carried off a $1.65 billion leveraged buyout, the largest in American history to that date.

The youngest company to be mangaged by a Conservator, third-generation Kiplinger Washington Editors, uses careful financial structuring to maintain family control. Knight and Todd Kiplinger and their father Austin are carefully maintaining impressive liquidity to keep the company safe from what might otherwise be overwhelming estate taxes that would threaten Kiplinger ownership.

Conservators also recognize that long-term employee commitment has played a major role in building their businesses. Some of their employees are themselves second- or third-generation workers. In recognition of these workers' loyalty, Conservators are patriarchal—sometimes in ways that make employees chafe. This was a problem of the previous generation that led Adolph Coors Co.

But paternalism can mean viewing employees as family members. One reason the Haas family wanted to return Levi Strauss & Co. to family hands was to stop layoffs. And as Ellen Gordon of Tootsie Roll says, "We run the company with the rigor and professionalism of a public company but we also run it with the heart and the vitality of a private company. It's important to perpetuate our succcess and be a home for our many workers."

Conservators see their ceremonial roles as being nearly as important as leadship. As Willie G. Davidson of Harley-Davidson says, "I am the keeper of the flame." He's right: Harley riders look for the popular Willie G. at rallies. And when the company needed to raise funds by going public in 1986, it was Willie G. who led hundreds of Harley-Davidson bikers in a parade down Wall Street. Similarly, Donna Steigerwaldt of Jockey makes it her business to participate in every company-sponsored holiday party and picnic.

Pete Coors shows that being a Conservator does not necessarily mean being conservative. Pete deserves credit for bringing the brewing company to the coveted Number Three spot through his progressive management. He knows that to survive for future generations, his company had to grow—it could not stay the same size. Pete's '80s decision to make Adolph Coors the third largest brewery in America and his '90s strategy to move that company into the Number Two position are driven by his fervor to keep the business in familyhands.

"People think we're antiunion, antigay, anti-, anti-, anti-. It just takes time. Some people will never be convinced that it's changed."

Adolph Coors Company
Golden, Colorado

Business: Beer, aluminum, packaging, biotechnology and ceramics

Best Known Products: Beers: Original Coors, Coors Light, Coors Extra Gold, Coors Dry, Keystone Beer, Keystone Light Beer, Keystone Dry, George Killian's Irish Red, Winterfest

Founded: 1873 by Adolph Coors

Family Executives: William K. Coors, Chairman and President
Joseph Coors, Vice Chairman
Peter H. Coors, Director and President, Coors Brewing Company
Jeffrey H. Coors, Director and President, Coors Technology Companies
Joseph Coors Jr., Director and President, Coors Ceramics Company

Family History: Fourth generation

Family Ownership: 55 percent

Family Board Membership: 5 family members of 9 directors

Traded: OTC, ACCOB

Net Sales: $1,917,000,000 1991
1,863,354,000 1990
1,763,870,000 1989

Net Earnings: $25,500,000 1991
38,900,000 1990
13,132,000 1989

ADOLPH COORS COMPANY

Brewing up a New Culture at Adolph Coors

Peter H. Coors, President, Coors Brewing Company

Men named Coors have learned to be wary of the press. But Pete Coors, 46, president of Coors Brewing Company and rumored future head of its holding company, is by nature a friendly man who says his parents Joe and Holly taught him to live by the Golden Rule. Aware that he is the Coors family member selected for visibility—and probably future leadership as well—he leans his slim, six-foot-five body forward to talk about the company in which his family owns 55 percent of the nonvoting shares (worth approximately $415 million) and all the voting shares. Appropriately framed by the company's emblematic Rocky Mountains at his back, Pete, elbows jutting out to either side, clasps his hands together on a utilitarian conference table in an unpretentious room in the Golden, Colorado brewery. The view is out of this world, although the surroundings are down to earth. Pausing to think before each response, Pete starts to talk about his vision for Coors ˎ Brewing Company, the third largest brewer in the United States.

"I'd like to see us be twice as big as we are. And have twice the market share. Then I think we would be ideal," Pete says, referring to the company's 10 percent market share, behind Miller's 22 percent market share and giant Anheuser-Busch's 44 percent in 1990.

He notes that Coors Brewing Company's current growth will not be simple to maintain. "This market's going to be flat. We think we can grow in it, but it's going to be expensive and not very profitable." Coors won't rely solely on national growth, Pete says. "Our brands have good brand identity throughout the world, so we're pursuing multiple avenues as we launch internationally."

The '90s already look like a growth decade for Coors Brewing. The company moved ahead in 1990 and 1991 through significant volume expansion. Showing its competitive strength, in 1990 Adolph Coors Company led the top 19 publicly held drink makers in net income, with a 196 percent gain. It shoved Stroh Brewing Co. aside that same year when it became the country's third-largest brewer. Coors' shipments jumped nine percent, nearly three times the industry average. The expansion was helped by Coor's Light, the country's fastest-growing premium light beer, which moved ahead at a double-digit rate. And Silver Bullet beer wounded Bud Light in 1990 to become America's third most popular beer and Canada's No. 1 light beer. Adolph Coors Company ranked number 776 in market value of *Business Week's* top 1,000 American companies in 1992, and placed number 220 in *Fortune's* 500 largest U.S. industrial corporations.

The company has undergone a major change since Pete entered in 1973. The clean light taste of Coors beverages had spread by word of mouth rather than by advertising. Coors beer is brewed with Rocky Mountain spring water and is unpasteurized, so it must be shipped refrigerated. The beer's availability had been limited to Western states, giving the brand cachet as the Golden brewery—the world's largest—began to ship cases to East Coast celebrities. Mere mortals were forced to lug their six-packs back on the plane from Denver.

Growth in sales, expansion of product lines, and extension of marketing regions are only a few of the things that've changed about this company. "Just about everything's different," Pete agrees. "When I first started working here full time [after receiving a B.S. in industrial engineering from Cornell University and an M.B.A. from the University of Denver], we were growing faster than we could build capacity. Everything was going well. We were making lots of money and reinvesting all of it back into the business. We were a private company.

"Now we're a publicly owned company. Where once we were in 11 states and ranked fifth in the nation, we're now in all the states plus international and rank third," he says.

Pete refuses to take credit for Coors' incredible two-decade growth. "Everybody wants to focus on the next generation," he says. Speaking of his uncle William K. Coors, 75, chairman and president of the holding company and of his father Joseph, 74, vice chairman, Pete refers to the company's past reputations as being antiunion and right-wing. "They've taken a lot of heat for some of the problems we've had in the last 20 years or so. Some of it justified, and some of it unjustified." Pete smiles at the possibility of an attitudinal flip. "I suspect that after they're gone and my brothers and I are in charge, we'll start getting the heat, and the next generation will be the great saviors of the Coors company."

But he's also angered when he thinks about some of the shortsighted judgments passed on to his father and uncle by the business media. His ruddy outdoorsman complexion flushes deeper red.

"I did not build this company. They built this company. I'm just trying to be the next good steward and take it to another plane. When my uncle started working here [in 1939], we were only doing 180,000 barrels a year. When I was born [in 1946], this place was just a small pile of bricks. Tiny. We didn't hit a million barrels until 1960. Small potatoes.

"They developed incredible technology and have driven a huge period of growth for the company. So over those 50-plus years since my uncle started, he's made an enormous contribution. And so did my father when he was here, particularly in our ceramics end of the business. They deserve much more credit and much more of the recognition than I think they are given."

Pete's uncle Bill and father Joe are the grandsons of Adolph Coors, born in Prussia in 1847. Adolph emigrated to the United States in 1868 after having worked as an apprentice to a German brewer. Eventually migrating to the Denver area, Adolph bought a partnership in a bottling company in 1873 and was soon sole owner. On a leisurely Sunday walk through the town of Golden, Adolph's brewer's instinct was alerted when he spotted the cool springs of Clear Creek valley. He founded a brewery there devoted to making premium beer and turned a profit his first year.

By 1890, the Adolph Coors brewery was firmly established, with an annual output of close to 18,000 barrels. Adolph was by then the father of six children. At the turn of the century, output had increased to 48,000 barrels. In 1912, Adolph named his 28-year old son superintendent of the company. Adolph Jr. developed manufacturing operations as Prohibition threatened. Cement and porcelain facilities, along with sales of near-beer and malted milk, kept the company thriving while half of the country's brewers had failed by the time of Prohibition's repeal. Those that survived were often family businesses that seldom pushed out of their regions.

Even though the company enjoyed continued success, the Coors family was not without personal tragedies. It is suspected that as a result of the stock market crash, founder Adolph Coors committed suicide in 1929. Two generations later, his grandson Adolph III (Bill and Joe's older brother) was kidnapped. After a year of agonizing waiting, the family learned that Adolph was dead, murdered in 1960. Then Bill's first wife died young, having been an alcoholic much of her adult life. Their daughter, Missy, committed suicide in 1983.

But the family ethic is to keep working during tough times. At the insistence of their father, Adolph Jr., Bill and Joe were educated to keep pace with technology. Both men graduated from Cornell with engineering degrees and, having been taught the importance of diversification through their own company's history, pushed brewing technology. Today Coors is often considered the leader in innovative techniques. Some of the company's introductions in the '50s and '60s include the aluminum can, the sterile-fill process, and constant refrigeration.

Says Pete of Bill and Joe, "They get a real joy out of technology. That's what turns them on. Our focus as a company, if you look at the broader Adolph Coors Company, is still highly focused in the technical areas." The separate companies within the holding company of Adolph Coors Company included Coors Brewing Company (with 71.8 percent net sales in 1990); Coors Technology Companies (with 19.4 percent net sales); and Coors Ceramics Company (with 8.8 percent net sales). He says, "We continue to look at ways of light-weighting our cans, of improving our distribution systems from a technology standpoint, of developing environmentally friendly inks. So we still haven't lost the importance of the focus of technology innovation. It's a very important element."

―――――

What the company seemed to lack were the softer skills of communication. In 1978, Adolph Coors Company had one of the country's most bitter labor/management disputes since the end of World War II. Soon 1,472 unionized brewery workers had walked off the job and were replaced by non-union workers, leading to a national AFL-CIO boycott of Coors products that lasted 10 years. The well-organized boycott, which was fueled by millions of union dollars, stunted Coors Brewing's attempt to move into the Midwest and the East. Outlets up and down the East coast were heavily unionized, especially in the New York-New Jersey area where 10 percent of the nation's beer is consumed. The college kids who had turned Coors into a cult beer were the same people who'd sympathize with a *cause célèbre* involving fair labor practices. Rival beer manufacturers, newly engaged in aggressive marketing, were able to grab market shares away from Coors; even Coors' share of core Western markets slipped during the boycott.

When the country's largest teacher organization, the National Education Association, joined the boycott, company management realized enough was enough. Two years after Pete was made president of the brewery, in 1987, he represented the company in the first crucial meeting with AFL-CIO representatives. The same year, the boycott ended when the company agreed to let organization attempts proceed at the brewery. Ironically, employees in 1989 rejected Teamster representation by two to one.

But the boycott wasn't the only reason people viewed Adolph Coors Company askance. When the product, company and family name are identical, controversial actions of family members affect sales. In this family, the blow comes from the far right and is usually thrown by Joe. For example, in the '60s, as University of Colorado regent, Joe attempted to rid the campus of Students for a Democratic Society. In 1973, Joe gave a $250,000 seed contribution to found the conservative think tank Heritage Foundation and contributed to anti-ERA groups (although Bill supports the ERA). In the '80s, Joe gave a $65,000 airplane to the Nicaraguan Contras.

Then Bill went to a minority business conference in 1984 and sounded off with what were widely perceived as disparaging comments about black Americans, Africans, and Hispanics. Soon Pete was meeting with the Reverend Jesse Jackson. After a few months of negotiations, Pete signed an agreement binding Adolph Coors Company to stimulate black employment in the company and increase the number of black managers and directors.

"I think our actions politically, although they were private actions, reflected back on the company because of the name," Pete says. He mimics, " 'I'm not going to buy beer from a company that does those things.' So we've been working very hard to change that around. We've taken a little bit lower profile publicly in terms of political things that are controversial.

"People think we're antiunion, antigay, anti-, anti-, anti-." He laughs ruefully. "It just takes time. Some people will never be convinced that it's changed." (Coors-bashing continues. As recently as 1990, the University of Colorado student government voted to reject Coors Brewing Company's sponsorship of activities.)

In previous generations, responsibility at Adolph Coors Company was passed down to the oldest son. But it's Pete—not his two older brothers, Joe Jr. and Jeff—who was selected for the spotlight during these controversies. Joe Jr., the oldest of six sons, was ostracized in 1963 for marrying while in college. After a decade of family rancor, Joe Jr. joined the company in the '70s and is now president of Coors Ceramics Company.

Jeff heads Coors Technology Companies and, for a while, looked like the successor. He was named president of the holding company in 1985, giving the impression that he'd eventually become board chairman. That perception altered after Jeff gave an interview to the *Los Angeles Times* in 1988 in which he discussed his father's extramarital affair. Jeff took a leave of absence for health reasons, citing stress. When he returned, he took back only his position as president of Coors Technology. Bill came out of semi-retirement to fill the presidency of the holding company in 1989.

Of Pete's two younger brothers, W. Grover serves as Vice President of Adolph Coors Company for National Affairs and works to increase the company's U.S. Defense Department contracts, after having been chief of the Coors subsidiary Advanced Electronics Group which makes electronic modules for the military. (Grover, in his '60s hippie days, returned his draft card and was subsequently cut off by Joe for two years.) Pete's youngest brother John is Vice President and Plant Manager of the Memphis brewery.

At its 1992 annual meeting, the company announced a plan to spin off its nonbeer technology companies to shareholders. Rather than being a holding company with several units, Adolph Coors Company would create two different companies: Adolph Coors Company, which would consist of the brewery, and AC Technologies. Reasoning behind the move is attributed to the up-and-down earnings of the energy and aluminum company, which supposedly were responsible for the jam of the Coors stock at about two-thirds of book value. The restructuring also forges a stronger link between the corporate identity of Adolph Coors and the brewery.

The plan keeps Pete as CEO of the brewery and gives him the title of vice chairman. He would relinquish the title of president of the brewery to an outsider. At AC Technologies, Joe Jr. and Jeff would share the office of the president, along with a third Coors official, Harold Smethills, who was CEO of Adolph Coors Company when the plan was announced.

Bill would retain the chairmanship of both companies. Pete's status as the only Coors member of the younger generation to operate with the title of CEO or vice chairman continues to indicate that the bets have been placed on him as the next chairman.

———

In the '70s, Pete and Jeff sketched out a plan for a new beverage, Coors Light—the beer that turned to gold for the company in the late '80s. A few years later, Uncle Bill let off with a comment about bringing in an outsider upon his retirement. Pete and Jeff knew it was time for a powwow.

"We were both a little bit frustrated. The impact [Bill's comment] had on the organization was that people started to line up.

Some were behind Jeff, some were behind me, some took off on their own. It was a very unsettling period of our history when we weren't doing well in the marketplace."

When the brothers met for lunch at their mother's house, their first reaction was, "If that's what they want to do, let them." After more thought, Pete said, "If we are going to be in control of our own destiny, we better say what we'd want to happen." So they came up with a plan.

"We didn't want to offend them by saying, 'We want to run you out.' But if their desire was for Adolph Coors Company to continue to be a family business, then we wanted them to bring us in to the decision-making process in a more significant way while they were still here to advise and counsel us."

Pete realized that at the worst, the older men could have dismissed their request and sent them back to their jobs. Instead, Bill and Joe were receptive and it brought a strengthened role for the younger generation and a sigh of relief to analysts who hoped for a change at what was considered a stodgy company.

When Philip Morris Companies bought Miller Brewing in 1970, the giant tobacco company put its aggressive marketers to work in what had been a sleepy industry. Anheuser-Busch responded in kind with new brands and similar marketing strategies. The beer industry changed dramatically in the next two decades, and it took a while for the Coors company to wake up.

Although Coors Light was introduced in 1978, it got off to a slow start. Relatively little was being spent on advertising at Coors. Comments like Bill's boast in 1975—"We don't need marketing. We know we make the best beer in the world"—inflamed analysts. Again, it was Pete, then senior vice president of sales and marketing, who is credited with having tripled the advertising budget in 1979 to $46 million from $15.5 million two years before. Pete gave the production-driven company a strong customer orientation.

Typically, he demurs. "People say I'm too modest about it. [The new thrust in marketing] is partly my interest, but it's partly that companies go through stages, and I happened to come along at a point in time when the company needed a different focus and a different direction.

"I think my uncle and my father were brilliant marketers. But they chose to take advantage of marketing elements—product and distribution—that were different than ones that have become important in the last few years. We just changed the marketing focus from product and distribution and, without diminishing these elements, we have elevated the advertising and promotion sides of marketing and balanced the elements.

"We've basically come from a regional brewery with almost no dollars invested in marketing to a national brewery where we have to demonstrate our presence through all of our marketing activities." Beginning in 1990, the advertising budget became about $250 million annually, making Coors No. 53 in top national advertisers, still well behind Philip Morris Companies, Inc. at No. 2 and Anheuser-Busch at No. 22. "It was either get engaged in the marketing game or fall by the wayside, like some of our competitors did," Pete says.

Ironically, the success of Coors marketing campaign uncovered another problem. Sales skyrocketed when the boycott ended—and more than doubled by the end of '80s—but the company was hitting the wall of capacity limitations. The capacity of the single-site Golden brewery was limited to 20 million barrels, and the company was shipping 19 million.

Pete says, "We've been sitting here running out of capacity just about the time when we'd get a new product fired up and going well." As an example, Pete says, "Our keystone product was going great and then we had to tell our distributors last summer [1991], 'No promotions.' "

A variety of alternatives had been weighed for a number of years. Coors' Elkton, Virginia packaging site was purchased in 1987 and eventually will be used to brew. The company considered buying Stroh's brewery a few years later. The buyout would have given it greater capacity and increased their market share to the 20 percent Pete says he wants. But the $425 million price tag was deemed too high. Instead, company leadership was considering buying pieces of Stroh or even parts of G. Heileman Brewing Co. (Stroh dropped 12 market shares in 1990 and Heileman dropped 6 shares.) In 1990, it bought Stroh's Memphis facility, which will eventually increase capacity by several million barrels. Additionally, the Golden facility is being renovated.

So capacity, once a major stumbling block, is no longer an issue. "Being able to have the brewing capacity in Memphis will help us get to our next hurdle, which, from the capacity stand-point, is somewhere around the 27–28 million barrel level. [The company produced 19.3 million barrels in 1990.] So we think we've got three to five years before we need to make that next critical jump to a new brewing facility," Pete says.

Living with debt was another hurdle for Adolph Coors Company. In the late '80s, Pete was still chanting the Coors mantra: "Leverage is not in the vocabulary." By 1990, the company was willing to offer up to $300 million in unsecured debt to aid its expansion. Pete is asked whether he'd put the word "debt" into the Coors dictionary. He laughs and says, "The answer to that is, yes, we have. We've taken debt—not in terms of a permanent, long-term tool—but as a relatively short-term financing project tool necessary for us to do some of the things we want to do and grow as fast as we want to grow." Projects the money will be spent on include an aluminum rolling mill and brewery acquisitions.

Now awake and alert, Coors is moving quickly. The brewing company went from two major brands in 1980 to nine brands in 1991—plus Coors Cutter (a near-beer) and Coors Rocky Mountain Sparkling Water. Its aluminum technology (including recycling) includes the world's largest aluminum can manufacturing facility. Although Adolph Coors Company has been criticized for lack of diversification, Pete says this would have to come through internal development. Outside of the beer business, "We don't see much sense in acquiring existing businesses."

The brewing company plans to have entered 20 markets worldwide by 1995. It's now in the United States and British Virgin Islands, Cayman Islands, Bermuda, Puerto Rico, and Greece and has licensing agreements with Molson Beer of Canada Ltd. and Asahi Breweries Ltd. of Japan. In their first attempt to brew outside the United States, the company entered a joint brewing venture in South Korea with Jinro Ltd. in 1991. Later that year, the company entered a joint venture and license agreement with Scottish & Newcastle of Scotland to brew Coors Extra Gold for the U.K. market.

Pete's vision for Coors includes professional growth for em-ployees as well as growth in sales and profitability. The company's vision statement is teaching the word "empowerment" to this brewery with Prussian roots as it switches from an authoritarian,

chain-of-command structure to one that's flatter and less hier-
archal. Although shared decision-making is not a new concept, it's
a radical one for the Coors company and is being experienced
company-wide.

Pete says, "We typically do not do things on a modest scale.
We do it in the way we think is meaningful, and that includes
everything from our Coors Literacy—Pass It On campaign to Pure
Water 2000 to the agreements that we've reached with the black
and Hispanic communities. And our programs are not just, 'Let's
do this to look good,' but they're sincere and visionary."

Some of these ideas are tossed around with the elders at lunch.
Every day, Pete and brothers Jeff and Joe Jr. meet at the founder's
22-room Queen Anne residence with Bill and Joe Sr. (when he's in
town). "It used to be the joke around here that lunch is where all
the board decisions were made," Pete jokes. "But yesterday, we
talked about sailing."

When Grover and John were working in Golden, these two
younger brothers apparently made do with deli take-out at their
desks. Don't ask Pete why they weren't invited to lunch. "That's
something that I just let my dad and uncle worry about. It's not
something I want to take on yet."

Pete thinks the company avoids falling prey to the pitfalls of
competition among the brothers because of its size, although he
notes that the 1989 reorganization that put Bill back in the driver's
seat, was prompted partly by the fact that "we were in each others'
businesses a little bit too much."

Pete gets riled when he hears it said that he, not one of his
other brothers, will become head of the holding company. "Is it the
board that's saying that?" he asks. "When the board of directors
start saying that, then I'll listen. There's no predetermined path."

He adds, "I don't have any burning, passionate, competitive
desire to step up to the front and take over. It's just not in my
nature. But if the board or the family were to say, 'We want you to
do that,' or if I thought it was appropriate for me to suggest that I
was the best person to do that, then I wouldn't shirk.

"But at this point, we don't have to worry about that problem.
We've got great leadership. Until that changes, I've got my hands
full at the brewing company."

Unlike some other family businesses, there's no succession plan in place at Adolph Coors. (That's a little odd, considering that it was Adolph Jr.'s lack of estate planning that forced the company to go public in 1975 to pay the $120 million tax.) But Pete doesn't think succession plans are viable.

"I don't think you can program it." He says if he'd been told when he was younger that he'd take over the brewing company, "I wouldn't have had anywhere near as much appreciation if I hadn't come to the conclusion with Jeff that we needed to step up to the plate." However, given the Coors sons' ability to fall in and out of grace, the absence of a firm succession plan is noted with displeasure by analysts. (It should also be recognized that Pete is the brother who hasn't stumbled.)

Pete hopes to reduce the brewery's vulnerability to its competition by generating a 15 or 20 percent market share. "Our challenge is those monoliths," he says, referring to Anheuser-Busch and Miller, with its sugar daddy, Philip Morris. "They have the capability of weathering the storm whereas we are sitting here basically on our own in a small position. We also expect they will be very aggressive, and we usually aren't disappointed.

"So we will use every device that we're capable of—acquisition, new brands, new marketing techniques, joint ventures—to be competitive."

It's a time of risk for Coors Brewing. The combination of the thrusts Pete identifies will—or will not—propel the company ahead in the next decade. Coors may not be able to leapfrog over No. 2 Miller, but it could very well position itself to breathe down Miller's neck. And it's the success of Coors Brewing that will determine whether Pete is the son who rises at Adolph Coors Company.

"I'm a symbol because I'm an avid rider."

Harley-Davidson, Inc.
Milwaukee, Wisconsin

Business:	Superheavyweight motorcycles (850 cc +) and related products; Holiday Rambler recreational vehicles; Harley-Davidson MotorClothes; Ultimaster Corporation commercial vehicles
Best Known Products:	Motorcycles: Sportster series; Low Rider series; Softail series; Electra Glide series
Founded:	1903 by brothers William, Walter, and Arthur Davidson, and William Harley
Family Executives:	William G. Davidson, Vice President
Family History:	Third generation
Family Ownership:	Several percent
Family Board Membership:	No family members of 9 directors
Employees:	5,000
Traded:	NYSE, HDI
Net Sales:	$939,900,000 1991 864,600,000 1990 790,967,000 1989
Net Earnings:	$37,000,000 1991 37,830,000 1990 32,942,000 1989

HARLEY-DAVIDSON, INC.

The Hog with Attitude

William G. Davidson, Vice President for Styling

Harley-Davidson, Inc. showed that American manufacturers can fight the Japanese—and win. This company, which accounted for a 62.3 percent share of the super-heavyweight motorcycle market in 1990, was only days away from Chapter 11 at the end of 1985. What saved Harley, which remains the sole American motorcycle manufacturer, was the government's agreement to impose a stiff tariff against Japanese heavyweight cycles.

William G. Davidson, 57, played a crucial role in jump-starting the sputtering company. Willie G., as the long-haired and gray-bearded man is called, contributed significant design talents that recaptured the heart and soul of Harley cycles, lost during the days when production was accelerated at the expense of customers. Willie G. summarizes his design contribution to Harley as putting "the sizzle back on the steak." But Willie has a more profound value, too: As the last senior family member to remain with the company, he also admits that he's viewed as keeper of the flame.

Willie G. is the grandson of founder William A. Davidson who, with the Harley brothers—William, Walter, and Arthur—formed the first motorcycle company in this country. Initially, in 1903, they put together what was basically a bicycle with a motor. The men could scarcely keep up with demand as they worked from a 10 x 15 shed in the Davidson's Milwaukee backyard. By 1907, the company had manufactured a police bike, still an important segment of their sales today. In 1909, the company's trademark two-cylinder, V-twin engine was introduced. World War I proved that the military would also play a pivotal role in Harley sales. World War I newsreels show the first American soldier entering Germany after the Armistice—riding on a Harley.

The standard for motorcycles throughout the world was set in the '20s when Harley introduced a newly designed gas tank that looked like a silver teardrop suspended outside the bike. But Americans were dropping motorcycles in favor of cars, and the company entered a short-term slump. Sales eventually picked up, only to plummet with the Depression. Then World War II escalated production as the armed forces devoured Harley's entire output. Americans salivated over these cycles during their war-imposed diet. When it ended, they gorged on Harleys.

Then in the '50s, American popular culture was permanently colored by a new group of strangers called teenagers. The interests of these teens and their coming-of-age woes were reflected in movies, books, and songs. Just as James Dean, Marlon Brando, and their followers turned a white cotton undershirt (see JOCKEY INTERNATIONAL) and a pair of jeans (see LEVI-STRAUSS) into the uniform for an entire generation, so did their vehicle of choice—a Harley-Davidson motorcycle—become a symbol of rebellion. The beauty of the powerful bike was that it equated style with speed. "Hogs," as these insolent heavyweight cycles are nicknamed, gained a mystique that continues for the generations that followed. On a Harley, masculine merges into macho.

Harley felt secure in its heavyweight market. New models were introduced, and the company expanded manufacturing sites to Italy and Switzerland. No one saw the small, inexpensive motorcycles introduced in this country in 1959 by the unknown Honda Motor Company of Japan as a threat. Harley believed its niche was untouchable, ignoring the possibility that Honda might move into the heavyweight cycle market.

Fortunately, president William H. Davidson foresaw the need for continued design innovation. He called on his son Willie G., who was working for a general industrial designer in Milwaukee, to join the company in 1963. Willie was ecstatic. After having done some moonlighting for Harley, he knew that, given the chance, he could update the Harley image in an evolutionary sense.

The company needed cash for expansion, with sales spiraling up as Harley's all-important image kept pace with the times, moving from adolescent Wild Ones to slightly older Easy Riders.

In 1969, American Machine & Foundry (AMF) bought Harley-Davidson. After leading the motorcycle industry in the heavyweight category for half a century and capturing as much as 90 percent of the market share for these cycles, Harley didn't recognize the trouble ahead. As AMF's Harley division focused on churning out 75,000 units a year—up from 15,000 units only a few years before—quality lost out to quantity.

Harley's design and production systems weren't able to adapt to the increased manufacturing pace. Customers and dealers alike were unhappy, but AMF kept pumping out oil-leaking, unstable cycles that vibrated so badly they rattled teeth. The joke was, if you ride a Harley you'd better own a pickup truck to haul it back for repairs. But no one in Milwaukee headquarters was laughing. Additionally, Harley's product development was being neglected in favor of quarterly profits. Then AMF—a company that was best known for its bowling balls—imposed their own logo on the cycles, losing sight of a good part of why the customer was buying a Harley-Davidson.

At the same time, interest in cycle riding was escalating. Such Japanese megaconglomerates as Honda, Suzuki, and Yamaha were easily getting their high-tech, lighter cycles out onto America's highways. And these bikes weren't leaking oil all over the roadway.

Though the founding families had lost control of their own company, William G.'s brother, John A. Davidson, took over the presidency from their father William H. in 1971. AMF had as little feeling for the essence of Harley-Davidson as Mattel had for Ringling Bros. circus after buying it from the Feld family (see RINGLING BROS.). But AMF did recognize that Harley was in trouble and headhunted for an experienced CEO, choosing Vaughn L. Beals in 1975. Beals made quality control his priority. He ordered more testing, asked plant workers for their ideas, and instituted inspection of every bike coming off the production line.

Luckily, Beals also had Willie G., who seemingly has the ability to design a cycle that both appeals to Harley customers and is manageable to produce. Willie designed the Super Glide, basically a combination of the popular Sportster and an Electra Glide, in 1971. The Low Rider came in 1977, awakening riders' desire to sling low to the pavement. "These worked very well and became an important part of our lineup," says Willie.

Beals needed more than Willie's design talents, though. He needed $80 million to develop an improved engine. With all its other commitments, AMF refused to allocate this type of money to the Harley division. Learning of this decision, Harley management felt that AMF was giving up. Believing that Harley could be turned around, Willie G., Beals, and ten other Harley officers bought the division from AMF in an LBO of $81.5 million in 1981. These men believed that owner/managers would be more successful than short-term, transient managers in dedicating themselves to Harley's survival.

"It was a very emotional time," says Willie. "The day of the buyout was one of the happiest days of my life. There was no feeling of being a division of a division of a division." The executive owners spent a week on the road in a ride-back celebration, traveling on Harleys from their York, Pennsylvania factory to the Milwaukee headquarters and stopping at dealerships along the way. "I'll always remember pulling into a dealership in Pittsburgh," says Willie, "and seeing a mechanic with a big paint brush painting out the letters 'AMF' as we pulled in."

But the renewed commitment didn't end problems with quality or productivity. The Japanese were cutting deeper into Harley's share. Seemingly unbeatable after their conquest of the light bike market, they now were discounting their larger bikes in America and even sending them overseas to compete with Harley's foreign sales. "We were extremely fragile," Willie remembers. Reflecting an overall drop in industry sales, Harley lost $25 million in 1981 in addition to the $70 million buyout debt. Its market share of the super-heavyweights dropped to below that of Honda. Overseas sales were plummeting. In 1982, the company's losses increased to $32 million. Up against the wall, management went to Washington to ask for a stiff 49 percent import tariff against Japanese large bikes. It was granted, extending from 1983 to 1988. "That was the starting point" to recovery, says Willie.

The tariff helped, but management realized they needed to look inward, too, to solve their problems. Beals told *The New York Times*, "For years we tried to figure out why the Japanese were beating us so badly. First we thought it was their culture. Then we thought it was automation. Then we thought it was dumping. Finally we realized the problem was us, not them."

Trying to learn from their opponents, a 1982 visit to an Ohio Honda plant turned top Harley staff into true believers in many of

the Japanese methods. Old manufacturing and inventory procedures were scrapped as the company identified new methods
long adopted by the Japanese that worked more efficiently. Parts
were put into cycles as they came off the line, resulting in an
immediate quality test and a dramatic inventory reduction. Production increased 50 percent as production time was slashed.
Workers initiated manufacturing changes and took pay cuts while
increasing their hours; suppliers agreed to wait for payments; and
the state of Wisconsin invested money in the company. The V-twin
engine was improved, reducing vibration.

In the meantime, Harley benefitted from its strongly loyal
customer base and its very patient dealers. Luckily, the Harley-
Davidson mystique was selling cycles to its colorful and dedicated
customers whose tee-shirts proclaimed, "I'd rather see my sister in
a whorehouse than my brother on a Honda." An early sign that
times were changing was the happy announcement by the California Highway Patrol in 1984 that it was once more buying Harleys,
absent from their fleet for a decade.

The tariffs had their intended impact, so the company asked
to have them removed in 1987, six months ahead of schedule—the
first time any company requested shortening a tariff. Much hoopla
ensued as the federal government chose to use Harley-Davidson as
an example of how American companies can recover with the
imposition of short-term tariffs. President Ronald Reagan helicop-
tered to Harley's York manufacturing site, dropping down to deliver a red, white, and blue speech.

But the company was controlled by its debt. The deal cut by
the new owners was one of the most highly leveraged, a buyout of a
$300 million company for little more than $1 million equity. Realiz-
ing again that Harley's goals couldn't be met without cash infusion,
in 1986 management brought the company public on the American
Stock Exchange and moved to the New York Stock Exchange one
year later. (The Davidson family members own no more than a
small percent of the company.) Beals told *The New York Times*,
"Going public was a hard decision, but we had such difficult
financial problems it was the only decision." Additionally, the
owners wanted to pay off the LBO. The increase in cash fueled
manufacturing innovations already identified by this progressive
management team.

Additionally, Harley learned not to compete with the Japanese in what the Japanese did best. The company refocused on super heavyweight cycles, retreating to the niche it had created many years before. Willie pushed that niche's borders by generating mininiches within the super heavyweight category. The sales of these new tour, street, and customized motorcycles accelerated profits.

The company also paid more attention to dealer and customer needs as it revamped its marketing to appeal to a new Yuppie rider—typically a man in his mid-thirties, working as a professional or manager, with an income of about $45,000. The proliferation of stockbrokers and art directors buying the fat '50s-looking Heritage Softail were noticed by the media and dubbed RUBS, or Rich Urban Bikers. Malcolm Forbes' adoration of Harley cycles promoted their uniquely American "Look," especially after Forbes commissioned a giant hot-air balloon shaped like the Heritage Softail. And when a Harley adorns the cover of the upscale *Sharper Image* catalog, as it did in 1990, the metamorphosis from redneck to white collar is complete.

The company has successfully dispelled any remnant of a Hell's Angels image as it revamps its dealerships, brightening showrooms and selling a new line of upscale MotorClothes. Retail shops and catalog sales were added as part of this attempt, and field sales staff increased by 50 percent. Adapting a close-to-the-customer philosophy, Harley started a Harley Owners Group with its own newsletter and town meetings, where owners can express their thoughts.

This, again, is where Willie G. enters. "I attend many, many rallies and weekend rides, overseas as well as here," he says. (In a typical two-week period, Willie participated in the Sacramento Mile, a ceremonial POW/MIA flag raising at the York plant, and a grand opening of a huge new Harley dealership in Chicago.) "Because of that exposure, I'm kind of a good-will ambassador. I talk to literally hundreds of riders at each rally about their bikes and their style interests.

"By being accessible to a lot of our riders, you come home with a feeling of what they want." (Like the family members of Crain Communications, Willie has a direct-dial telephone number at his headquarters office.) This close-to-the-customer approach has paid off: In 1990, 94 percent of Harley cycle customers stated they would again purchase a Harley.

Other members of Willie's family make strong contributions to the company, too. "My good wife Nancy rides with me to almost all of these rallies. She's an important part of my job. A lot of our customers are with their wives or girlfriends at these events, and she's been a tremendous support and an important part of this whole thing."

Daughter Karen, 32, is the creative director of the entire clothing lineup. "She's enjoying her activities," Willie points out, "which I see as ever-expanding because of our licensed products and our European market, where we've just scratched the surface."

Willie's son, Bill (William J.), is manager of events and entertainment marketing. "While Bill has the sensitivity in creative areas, he has more to do with budgets and managing and things that put him in a little different category than Karen," says Willie. Is Bill, 30, ambitious for the top job at Harley? Willie replies enigmatically, "I think he's doing fine and has a great future here at the company." (Another son, Michael, is an artist living in New York and is also an avid rider.)

Harley has vroomed back to its majority market share in super-heavyweight cycles and has virtually forced Honda to abandon this market. In 1990, Harley hit its fifth consecutive year at the top in this category, with a 62.3 percent share, compared to Honda, its nearest competitor, lagging at 16.2 percent. "We actually cannot make enough products," says Willie. "Our dealer inventories are as low as they've ever been in recent years. There are waiting lists, and there's money being put down for new models that aren't there yet."

Harley also profits from the renewed interest in American products and themes throughout the world. Judging from sales, their American image has a universal appeal. Exports to Japan and Europe are increasing and accounted for 31 percent of motorcycles manufactured in 1990. Most likely, the company's future growth will come from these markets. "We just have to be careful and do it right and maintain our quality" as production increases, cautions Willie.

The company showed solid growth as revenues increased to 9.3 percent in 1990 over 1989 and income to 14.8 percent. In 1986, the company took its cash balance to diversify to a closely related industry—Holiday Rambler Corp., a top-line recreational vehicle company. However, by 1990 this division was having problems in the industry's soft market and was dragging at Harley's bottom line. Harley-Davidson also is a contract manufacturer for various industries and manufacturer of casings and engines for the U.S. Department of Defense.

Harley-Davidson, having learned its lesson the hard way, is being run for the long term. With Willie G. as its grizzled guru, it's selling the authentic motorcycle, a vehicle that equates to a lifestyle. Although Willie's midwestern modesty compels him to share credit for Harley's turnaround with his colleagues—"I'm a cog in the big wheel"—he also knows his own value. "I'm a symbol because my last name is on the gas tank. I'm a symbol because I'm an avid rider. I'm a symbol because I attend these rallies on a motorcycle the same as the customers. I'm a symbol because I'm accessible, whether you want to call me up or whether you want to see me at any of our rallies."

With Willie as the symbol, his wife at his side and the fourth-generation son and daughter riding behind them, it looks as though Harley's continuity remains safe. Harley-Davidson can teach a lesson to America's businesses: Through innovation, hard work, and meeting problems head-on, a sleek silver-and-chrome machine has risen from the Rust Belt and left its Japanese competitors behind in a cloud of dust.

"If you want to have an impact on your society, you should be where it [power] is."

Levi Strauss & Co.
San Francisco, California

Business:	Apparel for men, women and children
Best Known Products:	Levi's brand jeans; Dockers branded casual wear products; Brittania branded Sportswear, Ltd.
Founded:	Dry goods business originated in 1850 by David Stern; brother-in-law Levi Strauss joined in 1853
Family Executives:	Robert D. Haas, Chairman and CEO Walter A. Haas Jr., Honorary Chairman Peter E. Haas, Director and Chairman of Executive Committee
Family History:	Fifth generation
Family Ownership:	Approximately 90 percent
Traded:	Privately held; Parent company, Levi Strauss Associates Inc.
Net Sales:	$4,247,000,000 1990 3,628,000,000 1989 3,117,000,000 1988
Net Earnings:	$265,000,000 1990 272,000,000 1989 85,000,000 1988

LEVI STRAUSS & CO.

Fitting Ideals to Profits

Robert D. Haas, Chairman and CEO

"When your [family's] name is on the door, you take what you do very personally," said Robert D. (Bob) Haas, 50, fifth-generation CEO of Levi Strauss & Co., to *Industry Week* magazine. LS&CO. is the world's largest apparel maker and jeans maker (V.F. Corp., with Wrangler, Lee, and Rustler brands, ranks close in blue jeans but has seen its market share for Lee jeans slip in the past few years). LS&CO. manufactures casual wear for people of both sexes and all ages living in more than 70 countries, capturing the largest market share worldwide for casual wear.

LS&CO. does more than one-third of its business outside the United States, leading *Business Week* magazine to term it "the only U.S. apparel maker that honestly can be called global." In fact, the name "Levi's" ranked No. 6 by Soviets and other eastern bloc citizens on a product recognition poll, below only two other American products, Pepsi and Coca-Cola.

The company was privately owned by the Strauss, Stern, and Haas families until it went public in 1971 and then was brought private again (except for its Japanese subsidiary, Levi Strauss Japan K.K.) in 1985. In order to bring LS&CO. back to family ownership, Bob Haas carried off the largest leveraged buyout in American history to that date—$1.65 billion. Bob was only 43 at the time. The company is ranked twenty-sixth in the 1991 *Forbes* list of largest American private companies.

LS&CO. is as closely linked to our American heritage as any company. Its corporate history is woven from the story of European immigration and westward expansion, and scattered throughout with the romance of gold miners, ranch hands, and cowboys. It was 1853 when Bob's great-great-granduncle Levi Strauss followed the gold rush to San Francisco after emigrating from Germany. He was sent from New York by his brother-in-law David Stern not to pan for gold but to sell a grubstake of dry goods. Levi had sold everything before his boat had docked in San Francisco except some tent canvas. Figuring that men needed pants made of durable material, he ordered pants to be stitched up from the canvas. Soon after, he used the same pants pattern on a denim material. The prospectors repaired "those pants of Levi" after the pockets ripped when they stored the gold-veined rocks there. One miner brought his Levi's brand jeans to a Carson City tailor for a pocket repair. The tailor wrote Levi Strauss disclosing his long-lasting repair: "The secratt of them Pents is the Rivits that I put in those Pockets." Thus was a $4.2 billion business born.

When Levi died a wealthy bachelor in 1902, he left his eponymous company to his four nephews. (Well in anticipation of modern business involvement in education, Levi also funded 28 scholarships at the University of California.) Under Jacob Stern, the oldest nephew, LS&CO. continued to grow, and its owners made paternalism for employees and philanthropy for the community their leitmotif. After the great San Francisco earthquake and fire in 1906 decimated the company's buildings, the company kept the workers on at full salary. Most remarkable is that this gesture was made within an industry better known at that time for its sweatshops.

The company passed from Jacob to his younger brother Sigmund, and then down to another generation. Employee security and altruism increased over the years, and LS&CO. was one of the first apparel companies to hire garment workers on a year-round basis. Walter A. Haas, Sr., Bob's grandfather, and Bob's uncle Daniel Koshland worked together as they modernized the company and dropped its wholesaling, concentrating instead on manufacturing. With this third generation, the company again moved laterally, from brother to brother before moving down another generation to a son or son-in-law.

In the '30s, the basic blue jean continued to be a solid seller to men who worked outdoors or at blue collar jobs. Then Walter Haas made a significant design change on the traditional Levi's brand jeans. An avid outdoorsman, Haas once crouched too closely over a campfire, heating the copper rivet that reinforced the crotch stitching. His exact words were not recorded, but an executive order went forth to remove those crotch rivets.

The post-World War II decades were golden for the company. The company moved from its modest size in the hands of the first three generations to legendary success. Credit the baby boomers with the success of Levi brand jeans. Their youth culture, exemplified by Marlon Brando and James Dean, decreed blue jeans to be its uniform. LS&CO. was transformed from a medium-size family business serving outdoor workers to a global enterprise. In charge during the company's transitional period were Bob's father, Walter Haas Jr., and then his uncle, Peter Haas.

The family has always placed emphasis on accommodating all the men in the family interested in serving in management. Because the men take their turns in quick succession, they've established a pattern of passing on command. For example, Bob's father Walter A. Haas Jr. served as CEO from 1970 to 1976, and then released the top spot to his younger brother Peter. Peter later complimented his predecessors, saying "The greatest thing they ever did was letting go in an evolutionary way."

The company continued to expand in the boom times of the '70s. To get the capital needed for new plants and development, LS&CO. went public in 1971. Family members retained 40 percent of the shares. For a while, it looked like a smart move. More manufacturing plants went up to meet what seemed to be an endless demand for jeans. Sales went to $1 billion in 1975 and to $2 billion by the end of the decade. The company diversified and entered into a myriad of licensing agreements. When Peter Haas left the presidency in 1981 (giving that job in this now-public company to the first nonfamily member, Robert T. Grohman), LS&CO. had become the world's largest apparel company, with sales of more than $2.5 billion.

But LS&CO. had serious problems, some of which began as early as 1973, when the cash-flush company expanded too quickly into the European market. The company had accelerated its product line, going from one product in 1945—men's denim jeans—to 120,000 items in the '70s. This forced it to make dramatic inventory markdowns.

As LS&CO. grew bloated, its service to retailers declined. When the company turned to mass merchandisers like Sears,

Roebuck & Co. and J.C. Penney Company, Inc., some small retailers were angry. A number of alienated buyers dropped the entire line from their stores. And the farther the company moved from the industry retailers who are first to spot upcoming fashion trends, the more it distanced itself from the changing styles. By the time LS&CO. noticed fashion changes, it was too late for such a corpulent company to react.

The company had been looking internally for too long. For 30 years, its main challenge had been to manufacture as many jeans as it could to meet the demand. Now, misdirected management decisions, coupled with the changing demographics of aging baby boomers, meant a shrinking jeans market. Having estranged some retailers, the company no longer had a base to fall back on when sales dropped. Additionally, designer jeans companies like Guess, Inc. and Jordache Enterprises Inc. (each owned by two brothers) were taking a small portion of market shares from LS&CO.

Some immediate cost cutting measures were tried in the '80s. Factories were shut down and employment was cut, a particularly painful measure for this paternalistic company. As Eric Johnson (see JOHNSON PRODUCTS) found, though, changes like these are only a stop-gap measure. Operations need to refocus, too.

Bob had joined LS&CO. after it went public and was strongly affected by what he was seeing. The family business was not Bob's immediate choice, though. He'd graduated from Berkeley in the '60s and served in Africa for two years as a Peace Corps volunteer. When he returned, he earned a Harvard MBA, then became a White House fellow. Following that, in 1969 he began several years at management consultants McKinsey & Company.

Bob says he finally went over to LS&CO. in 1973 because "I wanted to build something myself" rather than work for other companies. Not many of his college friends approved of his choice, he told *Forbes* in 1973. "My friends thought I was selling out" he says, "but if you look where the leverage is in this world, it is in the elected and appointed levels of government and in the upper areas of corporate management. If you want to have an impact on your society, you should be where it [power] is."

As Bob moved through LS&CO., the company's problems didn't ease off. More people were let go, and more distribution centers and plants were closed. Something needed to be done.

Bob became president and CEO in 1984. He immediately paid attention to the mistakes made by the company in the recent past, and LS&CO. became a more responsive vendor. Marginally profitable businesses not related to the company's core were axed. But the overexpanded foreign operations were still losing money.

The company showed a loss of $19 million in 1985 with $2.6 billion in sales. A dramatic change needed to be made to restore LS&CO.'s luster. The family had had enough and were displeased with the effects of public ownership on their company. Bob was concerned that it would be more difficult to turn the company around if he had to worry about shareholder reaction and quarterly profits. And the perception was that it was time to reinsert the family values. The best way the family saw of doing this was to take the company private.

Bob oversaw a leveraged buyout of $1.65 billion (twice the book value per share), even though he was only 43 and felt "stark terror" at leading the company through this period. He thought the LBO would work, but the thought of the debt was frightening. Alhough the family remained supportive, many questions were asked during this critical time period when the family fortune was at risk. As Bob later characterized this period to *Harvard Business Review*, "We were a family in crisis."

The Haas family had to put little money of their own into the buyout. A group led by San Francisco's Wells Fargo Bank lent $1.45 billion. The same investment banker firm that had brought LS&CO. public now took it private in 1985. (The parent company's name is Levi Strauss Associates Inc.) The firm, Hellman and Friedman, was led by Warren Hellman, a distant cousin of Bob's. Some relatives questioned the fee being paid Hellman. The $7 million he received ended up as only part of the deal. Hellman was also allowed to purchase for $42,500 stock that is now worth about $42 million.

Bob was also criticized by some of his relatives as he continued the LB&CO. cutbacks. Bob replied that not to cut staff would jeopardize the welfare of all the workers. LS&CO. finished its reductions and the restructuring, and by 1990, 16 percent of the workers and 26 plants were gone.

There's little family questioning of Bob now that the LBO has gone so well. *Fortune*, speaking of LBOs, said that LS&CO. showed "how to do one right" by making changes such as developing new products and emphasizing technology and better marketing techniques—all expensive steps that couldn't have been taken if the company were focused on short-term results.

In its product lines, the company made a natural evolution from jeans to casual wear. Its relaxed Dockers brand, for example, appeals to customers who want casual wear but not blue jeans and who are not concerned about the current fashion fads of the day.

And to help support retailers, the company splurged heavily on advertising, spending $100 million in 1990. Bob says that now he thinks with a retailer's mind and no longer see things first as a manufacturer. As further evidence of Bob's retail mindset, the company opened three test market specialty stores in 1991 to try out the concept of an Original Levi's Store and a Dockers Shop.

Foreign managers are allowed more initiative, although LS&CO. is maintaining tighter control of their valuable name through their operation of overseas operations as subsidiaries rather than as licensees. Instead of being the drag that they were before restructuring, foreign sales, which surpassed domestic by 1989, account for much of LS.&CO.'s fast growth.

Bob has put a great deal of thinking into the "aspiration statement" of the company, which talks about cooperative work, diversity, recognition, empowerment, ethical management practices, and communication. The business statement says where the company wants to go, and the aspiration statement tells how it wants to get there. A good portion of managers' evaluations are tied to how well they manage aspirationally, "no matter how many pants that got out the door," as Bob puts it. What he is doing is creating a common culture that help binds the staff in this huge, global enterprise. Bob says that he wanted the company to be family-owned once again to reinfuse it with family values, and he's done that. Still, he acknowledges, "The family feeling is harder to maintain as the company grows bigger." However large the company, it was named the best big company in employee benefits by *Money* magazine in 1992.

Bob also is continuing Levi's Community Involvement Team, a program his father began in 1970. It involves one quarter of all staff throughout the world, gives them time off from work, and provides the resources of the company to aid projects staff feel are worthwhile. The volunteer program also exemplifies Bob's belief in employee empowerment. Rather than allowing the top members to target money to their own favorite philanthropies, LS&CO. lets its entire staff decide on the projects they and the company should help. This is very similar to the grass-roots philosophy of alternative philanthropists as characterized by George Pillsbury (see the FUNDING EXCHANGE). (For a while, Bob's brother Wally directed the company's community affairs office, but after their father bought the Oakland Athletics professional baseball club, Wally left LS&CO. and is now president and CEO of the ball club.) Bob says proudly, "This company tells people that ideals are okay."

Under the leadership of Bob Haas, LS&CO. has once again returned to its earlier success story. In 1989, Bob was made chairman of the board, and Thomas W. Tushner replaced him as president. In 1990, sales were at $4.2 billion, representing the fourth consecutive year of record sales. Additionally, LS&CO. has pared down its buyout debt well ahead of schedule, having paid back more than two thirds of its $1.5 billion debt seven years ahead of its repayment schedule. Of the LBO period, he remarked to *Fortune*, "Overall, I think the family has grown closer, although part of it, of course, is the glow of a risky venture." One of Bob's cousins may sum up the family reaction best: "Everyone is extremely pleased, but then every story is wonderful that ends so well." By 1991, the Haas family had a fortune of more than $2 billion, according to the *Forbes* 400 listing. Of that wealth, $280 million belonged to Bob.

It's too soon to tell if Bob's teenage daughter Elise will be interested in joining the family business. It's definite, though, that there will be a strong global company for her to join. But if she enters LS&CO., it will still be a family-owned company. Bob told *Fortune* that LS&CO. has no intention of returning to public ownership. "I don't see any glimmer of a reason why we would want to."

Austin and Knight Kiplinger

Knight: "It is apparently [my father's] intent to divide that voting control between his two sons. Fortunately, my brother and I are very close; we get along very well."

The Kiplinger Washington Editors, Inc.
Washington, D.C.

Business:	Publishing and communications: newsletters, magazine, books, videos and television feature spots
Best Known Products:	The Kiplinger Washington Letter; *Kiplinger's Personal Finance Magazine*
Founded:	By W.M. Kiplinger in 1923
Family Executives:	Austin H. Kiplinger, President and Chairman
	Knight A. Kiplinger, Executive Vice President and Director
	Todd L. Kiplinger, Vice President for Investments and Director
Family History:	Third generation
Family Ownership:	Approximately 67 percent non-voting shares; 100 percent voting shares
Family Board Membership:	4 family members of 12 directors
Traded:	Privately held
Revenues:	$100,000,000 1991 (estimated)
Earnings:	Will not disclose

THE KIPLINGER WASHINGTON EDITORS, INC.

Financing the Future

Knight A. Kiplinger, Executive Vice President
Todd Kiplinger, Vice President for Investments

Sitting before his typewriter one night in 1923, a 32-year-old financial reporter wrote a letter that appropriately began "Dear Client" and ended, "Yours Very Truly, W.M. Kiplinger." He had just invented the newsletter.

W.M.'s vision wasn't limited to the birth of the modern newsletter. The journalist who established The Kiplinger Washington Editors consciously made a decision to favor company stability over family wealth. This firm is one of those rare, privately held family businesses established for family control but not for family accumulation of great riches. Founder W.M. Kiplinger ensured longevity when he started this business, which is best known for its five business-forecasting newsletters and *Kiplinger's Personal Finance Magazine* (formerly *Changing Times*). The company also publishes personal finance and business titles through Kiplinger Books.

The Kiplinger Washington Letter was—and is—a working tool for business owners and executives who need to make decisions based on economic and political forecasting. This flagship Kiplinger publication had, in 1992, a circulation of 360,000 and is the most widely read business newsletter in the world.

The Letter is a succinct statement of the Kiplinger editors' analysis of what might impact business. "Not whether we like it or whether we want it to happen," says W.M.'s son Austin H. Kiplinger, 73, "but what—in our best judgment—is most likely to happen." The 1800-word newsletter begins each concise, single-thought statement on a new line, with the topic underscored. To save time for readers, the Letter places the conclusion at the beginning of the line.

Every Monday morning, Kiplinger editors gather in Austin's office to talk over political and economic issues that might be included in that week's Letter. This is not a feet-propped-on-the-coffee-table brainstorming session; rather, it is a meeting tightly controlled by Austin, who asks questions and calls upon his conservatively dressed news editors for answers. Austin sets the pace and direction of the week's assignments. The editors then hit their Rolodexes or walk the halls of federal agencies to talk with sources, usually middle-level government or business leaders.

Kiplinger editors also rely on experts throughout the country because they don't want the Letter to reflect a solely Washington outlook. The format of the Letter means that no Kiplinger sources are ever quoted or identified, allowing them to speak more freely. This no-attribution practice is accepted today but was another first for the Letter.

Because Kiplinger readers are not given names of sources, they must trust the judgement of the Letter's editors. Access and accountability are key words at this company. A subscriber who questions an item in the Letter may phone or write. One of the editors will go through the appropriate files to document the item or answer more questions on the subject. It's as if readers have their own research service. Although taking these queries is time consuming for editors, it gives them a feel for their subscribers' interests.

The first deadline for the Letter comes every Wednesday morning, when copy goes to the editorial director. On Friday, the Letter goes to Austin or, if he's out of the office, to his son Knight, 44, for a final polish. It's then printed and shipped out, to be in the reader's mailbox on Monday, just as Austin and the editors are meeting again for a new week's Letter.

This procedure has been in place for years. Kiplinger Washington Editors is not a place where people break tradition just for the sake of change. Instead, the company is heavily influenced by both the editorial and organizational influences of its founder.

W.M. came to Washington D.C. in 1916 as an Associated Press reporter during the Taft presidency. He covered the Treasury, the Federal Reserve Board, and the Justice Department, and he became known as a specialized economic reporter in a period when such creatures were rare. In his spare time, W.M. also reported to New York's National Bank of Commerce on any matters that he thought would have an impact on the bank's operations. It was actually the demands of this bank that led to the format of the unique Letter. W.M. wrote, "They wanted to know what was going to happen. And if I replied that I didn't know, their answer was, 'Give us your best judgment, advise us, guide us.'"

In 1920, the post-World War I boom had faltered, and banks closed. When W.M.'s by now only employer notified him of financial cutbacks, W.M. suggested an alternative: Why not cut his salary by half but allow him the freedom to add other clients?

At first, he signed up only other banks. By 1923, W.M. realized there was a wider circulation for his letter. With the permission of his banking clients, he began the Kiplinger Washington Letter. Two years later, he started the Kiplinger Tax Letter, a biweekly. In 1920, he added the Kiplinger Agriculture Letter.

W.M. was a top-flight editor, but he was less skillful in working with people, a drawback that impeded both his personal and his professional relationships. He married three times; Austin is the oldest child of the first marriage.

Austin majored in political science and economics at Cornell University and set out to establish a journalism career outside the family business. He was hired by the *San Francisco Chronicle* shortly before the start of World War II, when he joined the navy and served as an aviator in the South Pacific.

W.M. waited out the war. He had already conceived of a new kind of magazine, a publication advising people on how to manage their own money. The magazine would be called *Changing Times*, and it would originate the specialty called the "personal finance" publication.

Austin returned to Washington in 1945 with his wife and infant son Todd to join the business, and he soon become executive editor of the magazine. It was a stressful period for the new magazine and for its editor and his father. Austin quit the magazine in 1948, one year after the magazine was begun, severing the professional relationship between father and son but, in the end, saving their personal relationship.

At first, Austin worked in Chicago as a print journalist writing the daily front-page column of the *Chicago Journal of Commerce*. He added part-time work as a radio newscaster at WGN, then moved to television full time while it was in its infancy. By 1952, Austin was a pioneer newscaster at ABC, working with fellow network correspondents Martin Agronsky and Pauline Frederick as part of the 1952 presidential election team that won a Peabody. He rose as a newscaster, moving to NBC in 1954.

During these years, there was little communication between Austin and W.M. The Letters were doing well, and the circulation of the magazine was strong, but W.M. was mercurial in dealings with his staff and was a poor business manager. When W.M. asked Austin to come back to the family business in 1956, Austin did so—this time, from a position of strength. He entered as executive editor of the Kiplinger Washington Letter.

For the next nine years, until W.M.'s death at age 76 in 1967, father and son worked together. Kiplinger subscribers would intermittently see different signatures on the fourth page of the Letter and would write or call with the question, "Who's Austin Kiplinger?" Austin's signature appeared sporadically at first, then later alternated with W.M's. This way, a transition between the generations took place. (The same transition in the Letter's editorship has been taking place with Austin and son Knight since 1983.)

Austin also loosened his father's entrepreneurial control and moved the company to a more professional style of management. By adding more staff, he and W.M. were able to begin two more letters: the Kiplinger Florida Letter, established in 1956, and the Kiplinger California Letter, established in 1965. Together the five Letters have a circulation of 555,000.

While Austin was taking charge of the Kiplinger publishing business, he was also raising a family with his wife Gogo. A second son, Knight, was born in 1948. He and Todd grew up on their parents' farm in the Maryland countryside.

Austin never asked them to work summers or part time at the 10-story Kiplinger Editors building near the White House. Still, when Todd left college he immediately joined Kiplinger Editors—but not the editorial operations with his father. Instead,

Todd worked on the business side of the company, in circulation and marketing. At 46, Todd settled into the management of the company's nonoperating divisions and assets.

Knight appreciates Todd's accomplishments. "The importance of the nonoperating assets of the company are that our stock and real estate portfolio give us the liquidity for estate planning, which will keep this business in the family," he says. "The market value of the company is less visible to the outer world because the outer world is aware of revenue growth—circulation, ad pages—all the public indices. But that's not where the value of the company lies. It lies in the growth of shareholder equity, in the non-operating assets, which my brother manages. So much of our retainer is in non-operating assets."

The company keeps a high reserve of cash and cash equivalents, a conservative fiscal approach in anticipation of eventual estate taxation. The company's liquid investments can represent up to 40 percent of annual earnings, if it's a soft year for the publications.

Knight, 44, took a different path than Todd. First, he is more interested in the editorial function of the company. After following in his father's and older brother's footsteps at Cornell, Knight went to work at a small chain of 22 daily papers, Ottaway Newspapers, Inc., owned by Dow Jones. He became Washington bureau chief in 1978 and left Ottaway in 1983 because this family man thought it was time to join his brother and father, for financial reasons as well as for job security. (Both he and Todd are married and have young children.)

He entered the firm as vice president of publications, with broad editorial responsibilities. His first project was *Changing Times*, which was then the least financially robust Kiplinger publication. In 1991, the magazine was renamed *Kiplinger's Personal Finance Magazine*, with a circulation of 1.1 million. The magazine is the only Kiplinger publication that accepts advertising.

After strengthening the magazine, Knight moved to the nascent book division. It has become one of the company's most successful activities, with 10 titles by the end of 1992, including *Lew Altfest Answers (Almost) All Your Questions About Money* and *Take Charge of Your Career*.

Around 1990, the company under Knight's direction became an editorial provider to Prodigy database and is now its largest supplier of personal financial and investment material. Next came personal finance video tapes. In 1992, "Kiplinger's Personal Finance Report" debuted on several dozen television stations. All of these venues—newspaper syndication, books, videos, computer databases, and television—bring the Kiplinger name to a larger market.

Additionally, the company has two subsidiaries: Editorial Press, a full-color lithographer that relies on outside, non-Kiplinger printing for most of its annual $30 million business; and Kiplinger Computer & Mailing Services, one of the largest direct mailing service houses in the United States.

Despite this strong profitability and conservative investments, and as well as the company does, its owners do not believe that the most important things in life carry price tags. W.M. believed, according to grandson Knight, "Great wealth corrupts greatly."

W.M. was also concerned about estate taxes, which can wipe out a family business by forcing a sale if sufficient liquidity hasn't been conserved. Lack of preparedness for estate taxes can push the family into debt or, at best, into public ownership as a means of raising tax money (see ADOLPH COORS).

W.M. took a number of steps to protect the business for his heirs. Knight elaborates: "He created two classes of stock, voting and non-voting, which both pay the same dividend. The number of voting shares is relatively small, which was his way of ensuring family control even if beneficial interest of the dividend was widely dispersed."

Austin controls 100 percent of the company's voting shares and will presumably retain this control until his death. Knight says of his father, "It is apparently his intent to divide that voting control between his two sons. Fortunately, my brother and I are very close; we get along very well. We are sensible, mature people."

Although it makes some sense to pass leadership on to the brother heading the editorial operation, Austin says that "the hand out of the grave" will not make this decision. After his death, his sons will continue to collaborate or will mutually decide on a leader.

Grandfather W.M. also established the Kiplinger Foundation, which has assets valued at about $15 million, and he gave a large chunk of nonvoting stock to an Employee Profits Sharing Trust. Its largest single asset is the Kiplinger stock, which invests its earnings in other interests.

Today, the trust owns about one-third of the company—giving it more than three times the ownership interest of the largest Kiplinger family shareholder. After three generations, there are about a dozen shareholders who collectively own 67 percent of the nonvoting shares. "No individual member of the Kiplinger family owns more than 10 percent of this company," says Knight. Additionally, all Kiplinger board directors except for one family member are employees of the company.

The gifts W.M. left to his employees and foundation greatly exceeded the inheritances that he left to his descendants. Although W.M. minimized his family's financial inheritance, the split of voting and nonvoting shares has maintained family control. The bulk of earnings are retained within the company and are used to help build liquidity. By deferring gratification and sacrificing their current level of wealth, the Kiplingers have stabilized their company. Their scheme of investing earnings in other interests and keeping their nonoperating assets liquid safeguards the business for the next generation. The Kiplingers are in it for the long term.

Now Knight laughs and acknowledges his grandfather's talent at both starting a new form of journalism and anticipating modern inheritance problems inherent in family businesses. "But there's also a purpose here. You have to save enough money to pay Uncle Sam when the tax bill is presented."

Knight continues, "W.M. left more of his fortune to people other than family members. I think that was appropriate. There's no resentment in this family. We agree that people don't need vast riches."

Ellen: "We built a solid working relationship long before we comanaged a company."

Tootsie Roll Industries, Inc.
Chicago, Illinois

Business:	Confectionary
Best Known Products:	Tootsie Rolls, Charms, Mason Dots
Founded:	1896 by Leo Hirschfield
Family Executives:	Ellen Rubin Gordon, President and COO Melvin J. Gordon, Chairman and CEO
Family History:	Second generation
Family Ownership:	50 percent
Family Board Membership:	2 family members of six directors
Traded:	NYSE, TR
Net Sales:	$207,875,000 1991 194,299,000 1990 179,293,000 1989
Net Earnings:	$25,495,000 1991 22,556,000 1990 20,212,000 1989

TOOTSIE ROLL INDUSTRIES, INC.

Family Sweet

Ellen Rubin Gordon, President and COO
Melvin J. Gordon, Chairman and CEO

Under the capable and firm hand of Ellen Rubin Gordon and her husband Melvin, Tootsie Roll Industries entered the '90s as a highly profitable company that has earned a spot of *Forbes'* honor roll of the country's best 200 small companies. The company's most profitable product line, Tootsie Rolls, from which the company derives its name, accounts for nearly half of the company's total sales.

The company began in 1886 in a small shop in New York City when Leo Hirschfield hand-rolled chocolate confection from a recipe he'd brought from Europe. Looking at the candy, Hirschfield thought how much his little girl would enjoy it and promptly dubbed it with her nickname, "Tootsie." Hirschfield's popular product was soon bought by a larger candy company, and in 1922 the company was listed as the Sweets Company of America on the New York Stock Exchange. In 1966, the name was changed to Tootsie Roll Industries to reflect the company's best-known product.

The Rubin family's involvement with Tootsie came in 1931, the year Ellen, their only child, was born. Ellen's mother, Cele Rubin, liked the chocolaty candy so much that she bought the family's first Tootsie share around the same time Ellen's father, William Rubin, a packaging manufacturer, began supplying Tootsie Roll with paper boxes. The relationship between the two companies developed. Ellen's uncle Bert Rubin joined Tootsie Roll as president in the '40s, and William served on Tootsie's board. William then followed Bert as Tootsie's president in 1948. When William took over management of the company, he and Cele began increasing their shares until the family gained control. Now, Ellen Rubin Gordon's family owns 37 percent of Tootsie Roll Industries' nonvoting shares and 67 percent of the voting shares.

Ellen was in high school, keeping her interest in business a secret to avoid her teachers' derision when her father took over Tootsie Roll. As a math major at Vassar College, she met Melvin Gordon, a Harvard College graduate 12 years her senior. After their marriage, Ellen relocated to Boston and enrolled as a sophomore at nearby Wellesley College. Pregnant with the first of her children, she was told it wasn't "seemly" to appear on campus while pregnant. Luckily for her, the new university in the area, Brandeis, was happy to enroll her, pregnant or not. By the time Ellen graduated from Brandeis University, she'd given birth to three of her four daughters.

Melvin was asked by Ellen's parents to join the Tootsie board in the '50s. He was named chairman and CEO of Tootsie in 1962.

In 1968 Ellen, who had earned a master's degree in linguistics from Harvard, joined management to work on pension plans and investments and was appointed to the board of directors. Ellen also started looking at Tootsie Roll's quality control. (Today it wins high marks within the industry for purity of product.)

That first decade of Gordon management found Ellen and Melvin building a solid base at Tootsie. Ellen attributes their strong team to their 18-year marriage: "We built a solid working relationship long before we co-managed a company." The Gordons prefer to make decisions through consensus whenever possible and won't go through with an idea if one of them disagrees.

Ellen was elected Tootsie president in 1978, after having served as vice president for product development in 1974 and then as senior vice president in 1977. The Gordons consolidated New Jersey and Los Angeles operations in Chicago's southwest, and set up adjoining offices decorated by a wall unit jammed with Tootsie Rolls and other candies.

In their second decade of leadership, the Gordons began the practices that characterize Tootsie today. In 1972, Tootsie Roll Industries bought the Mason Division of Candy Corporation of America, which makes Mason Dots and Bonomo Turkish Taffy, products particularly popular at movie theaters. Mason was Tootsie's first major acquisition and was accomplished without heavy leverage—the Gordon's preferred procedure. Cella Confectioners, best known for its chocolate-covered cherries, was Tootsie's next acquisition, in 1985.

The greatest competitor of Tootsie Roll Pops (the hard lollipop with a soft-center filling) was Charms Co., the country's number one lollipop manufacturer. In 1988, the Gordons decided it was worth the risk to use their accumulated cash and to take on some short-term borrowing to acquire Charms for $65 million. At 3 billion pops a year, Tootsie is now the world's largest lollipop manufacturer. Giving Tootsie a stronger position in the hard candy market and more shelf space was worth the debt, says Ellen. Immediately, Tootsie made gains with Charms by incorporating some of its procedures into Tootsie's ongoing purchasing, accounting, and traffic operations. Higher net profits in 1989 and 1990 reflected the results of the Charms purchase.

Tootsie concentrates on its own market niche as a traditional, popular product, because 70 percent of the candy market is controlled by just two companies, Hershey Foods Corporation and Mars, Inc. There are other family candy businesses that enjoy niches similar to Tootsie's, most notably the fourth generation confectioner Henry Heide, Inc., making traditional candies like Jujyfruits, Mexican Hats, and Jujubes.

There's also a need for Tootsie to diversify through line extension, partly because there are 150 new candy products introduced nationally each year. Some of this new candy is produced by huge food corporations, which are better able to bear the costs of a new product. Herculean competitors reinforced Tootsie's need to extend their popular brands.

Line extensions began at Tootsie in the '30s, when it developed the Tootsie Pop, the first soft-centered lollipop. Recent extensions continued with a Cella chocolate-covered peanut butter candy, the Charms Sweet and Sour Blow Pop, and for aging baby boomers, a softer version of the classic Tootsie Roll called Tootsie Bar.

Ellen says she brings her early corporate work in quality control to bear along with the lessons she's learned from watching the disintegration of the car and steel industries. "We have a very sophisticated manufacturing operation with state-of-the-art equipment [and] a very sophisticated information system with the highest technology in computers."

To bring Tootsie's manufacturing up to this level was costly, Ellen says, and was paid for out of profits. "We spent maybe $30 million in the last years on new equipment. That's a lot of money. There were risks involved. In some cases, we developed our own machinery, very expensive to do but very necessary, because our products are unique." Now the candy is mixed, cut, sorted, and wrapped by machines monitored by employees. Tootsie's technical upgrades have allowed the company to bring out their candies at margin and efficiency gains, resulting in a mouth-watering bottom line. The company maintains a strong capital structure and plans to continue making new equipment one of their priorities.

Capital upgrades have also been made at Tootsie's Mexican plant (it's "Tutsi" there), and their candies are popular throughout the Caribbean countries and in Canada.

Another part of the strategy Ellen and Melvin put into place at Tootsie has been to maintain vertical integration. The company makes its own lollipop sticks, it has a truck subsidiary and its own in-house ad agency, and it's one of the few confectionery companies to have its own sugar refinery.

A rise in the price of sugar can mean sugar shock for a company using millions of pounds annually. Luckily for Tootsie, even when material costs vary, candy consumption does not. Candy sells well, even in a recession.

Analysts had been advising the Gordons to leverage their company to buy others. Ellen and Melvin have always been uncomfortable with this concept, believing it unwise for long-term survival. For a while, Tootsie—with its equity equal to about 70 percent of its assets—seemed old-fashioned and out-of-step. Now analysts see just how smart Tootsie is. The Gordons want not merely to survive, but to lead the industry—partly for the success of their own family.

The next phase for Ellen, 59, and Melvin, 71, may be the addition of another family member to the Tootsie management. The four Gordon children cover an age span of nearly 20 years, an efficient way to start the older daughters off in the company while the younger ones continue their education and outside training.

Again, this family believes in a solid education in any area, followed by work in different fields.

The oldest daughter Virginia is an electrical engineer; Karen is a partner is an investment firm; Wendy is a physician; and the fourth girl, Lisa, is an undergraduate at Harvard. Despite the differences in background, Ellen says of her children, "They're all geared for joining [the company]."

The Gordons want to keep control of Tootsie Roll within the family, no doubt about that. "We sometimes say that we run the company with the rigor and professionalism of a public company, but we also run it with the heart and the vitality of a private company. We think that this family interest in the company helps make it as successful as it is," Ellen says.

Confident in their leadership at Tootsie and secure in their controlling share in the company, the Gordons use any opportunity to announce that they don't wish to be swallowed by a larger firm. What would happen if there were a takeover attempt on the company? *Forbes* magazine asks.

"We'd kill them," replies Ellen Gordon.

"Most of the companies that make women's underwear are run by men, so why shouldn't a woman run a men's underwear company?"

Jockey International, Inc.
Kenosha, Wisconsin

Business:	Men's, women's and children's underwear; men's and women's hosiery; men's sleepwear
Best Known Products:	Jockey brief; Jockey For Her underwear
Founded:	1876 as Cooper Company, 1967 name changed by Harry Wolf to Jockey International
Family Executives:	Donna Wolf Steigerwaldt, Chairman
Family History:	Third generation
Family Ownership:	Virtually 100 percent
Family Board Membership:	2 family members of 7 directors
Traded:	Privately held
Net Sales:	$450,000,000 (estimated) 1991
Net Earnings:	Will not disclose

JOCKEY INTERNATIONAL, INC.

Holding the Reins

Donna Wolf Steigerwaldt, Chairman

There is only one underwear trademark that is in use throughout the world: Jockey. It was introduced in 1934 by the company that now bears its name. Inspired by the new men's swimwear worn on the French Riviera, Jockey was the first elastic top brief underwear for men and remains the world's most popular. In 1992, the company had an approximate 30 percent share of the men's underwear market.

The company that originated the best-selling men's brief was founded in 1876 as Cooper Company. By 1895, it was Cooper's Underwear Company. But it wasn't until 1929 that Harry Wolf became a partner in the firm in which he served first as a financial consultant, then as CFO and, beginning in the early '40s, as chairman.

The introduction of the Jockey brief ushered in a growth period for the company. For many years, it was the only brief available to men. By 1959, Harry had bought out his partners and owned virtually all the stock. The company saw another growth period in the mid-'60s, when it introduced fashion underwear for men in a variety of colors and styles. Harry's son Harry Wolf Jr. had been a manager in the business and served briefly as its chairman upon Harry's death in 1978.

Although no one had planned for Harry's daughter to take over, Donna had grown up "talking about Jockey at the dinner table," says Howard Cooley, Jockey's president. Donna, now 63, inherited her father's skill at figures and worked at an insurance company before becoming a homemaker. (Donna is married to

Chicago contractor William Steigerwaldt.) While she was raising her children, she attended Jockey's national meetings with her father and became familiar with the company and its employees.

After Harry died and Harry Jr. subsequently decided to retire, Donna realized that she did not want to see the company sold. Nor did she want it to become public. Although she had never worked at the company before, she stepped in at 51 to fill the chairmanship and to plan for an even stronger company.

"Everything we do is for the long term," says Cooley. Donna took steps to preserve that outlook, which includes nourishing and protecting the Jockey brand, the firm's biggest asset. She also believes in reinvestment in the business, high standards of business ethics, an open management style, and continued growth. Her major interest is in seeing that the managers hired for Jockey's key positions subscribe to these objectives.

"We don't pay much attention to quarterly results except as to see how we're doing against budget," says Cooley. "Never are we looking for a quick buck."

Jockey's growth has been phenomenal since Donna's entrance in 1979. The company introduced Jockey for Her in 1983 with the eye-catching ad, "Look Who's Wearing Jockey Now!" The company also pitched the underwear via letters with coupons to 25,000 gynecologists, who, it was surmised, might be interested in having patients wear the 100 percent cotton garment.

Jockey For Girls was launched in 1985, and Jockey Pantyhose in 1988. The company also began a significant advertising and marketing campaign for the men's line. Under license, men's sleepwear was offered, and then a hosiery line for men and women. During the '80s, domestic employment went up from 2,500 to 5,000 as domestic sales and exports increased. In 1992, Jockey was ranked the fifth largest woman-owned business in *Working Woman.*

A complicated network of resources and marketing establishes the Jockey brand throughout the world. In 1936, Jockey was one of the first American companies to license outside the United States. By 1992, it had business units in 32 countries, which market into about 100 countries.

Although the company's current management can take credit for strengthening marketing and advertising, its well-known celebrity spokesmen and women are nothing new to Jockey. After all, Babe Ruth and Red Grange were featured in Jockey ads in the '20s. Jim Palmer may be better recognized today as the Jockey man than as a pitcher, having appeared in its ads since 1980. He also acts as company spokesman—fully clothed—at department stores. Bart Conner, a gold Olympic winner in gymnastics, also appears in Jockey ads.

Nancy Hogshead, winner of three swimming golds in the 1984 Olympic Games, appears on behalf of Jockey For Her. In 1992, Jockey signed a contract with Olympic gold-medal gymnast Nadia Comaneci to represent the women's underwear line. Other campaigns include such everyday people as a doctor, a lawyer, and a married couple who are construction workers. Even a young Rockefeller has appeared to advertise a Jockey tee-shirt and boxers.

Donna's forward-looking ads capture the spirit of a company that sees nothing surprising about the leading maker of men's underwear being headed by a woman. As Donna has said, "Most of the companies that make women's underwear are run by men, so why shouldn't a woman run a men's underwear company?"

Donna's family is in the process of buying out even the few minority shareholders. Although both of Donna's daughters, who are in their 30s, have worked in the company, no succession plans are discussed by the company that believes in strong, professional management.

One daughter, Linda, is now raising young children. Deborah is a merchandiser in the Jockey For Her underwear group. "Ever since she came here," Cooley observes, "she has been just another junior person with a junior salary and junior responsibilities." But in 1992, ten years after entering the company, Deborah began directing the Jockey for Her division.

Never would a hasty decision be made about the company's future. Says Cooley, "Our plan is to keep Jockey a successful, privately owned company for another 100 years."

SECTION IV

THE BENCHWARMERS

Benchwarmers are heirs whose parents still play the dominant role in the company's daily operations. The company, in fact, is more closely identified with the older generation than it is with the younger. Leonard Lauder—and not his son William—serves as lead manager of Esteé Lauder, just as Bill Marriott is the head of his company—and not sons Steve or John.

There are two companies in this section, Georgette Klinger Salons and Lillian Vernon, that have benchwarmers ready to step up to bat. These heirs—Kathryn Klinger, and Fred and David Hochberg of Lillian Vernon—are the on-deck players. Although Georgette Klinger and Lillian Vernon themselves are still intrinsic to the company's daily operations, both of these chairmen have children who, for the past decade, performed a leading management role. However, if there's a disagreement between generations, even the young company presidents in the on-deck circle ultimately yield to their parents' judgment. As Kathryn Klinger says, "I feel that it's her business, and she created it, and that I just bow to her, basically."

BENCHWARMERS USUALLY...

1. have parents who hold key leadership positions as well as highly visible roles within the business.
2. defer to their parents' decisions, but—
3. are eager to see the business diversify and expand.
4. represent professional management skills as compared with their parents' entrepreneurial talents.
5. are second- or third-generation members.
6. are still in their 30s.
7. work with siblings in the business.

Not surprisingly, the Benchwarmers are the youngest group of heirs in this book. Most have barely reached their 30s, while the oldest is only 42. The majority of these Benchwarmers are second-generation business heirs and work with parents who are entrepreneurs. Katie and Bill Ford's parents Eileen and Jerry founded Ford Models in the mid-'40s, which is also when Georgette Klinger established her skin care salons. Wendy Thomas' father Dave founded the famous quick-service restaurant chain in the '50s and Lillian Vernon founded her eponymous mail order catalog during the same decade.

In contrast to these parents' entrepreneurial talents, many Benchwarmers perceive themselves as bringing professional management skills to their family companies. Katie Ford, Fred Hochberg, Steve Marriott, and David Crane of Crane Paper have M.B.A.s, and the other two Benchwarmers at Crane Paper hold graduate degrees. These professional managers put their skills to work immediately upon joining the family business. Katie Ford's first contribution to her parents' modeling agency was to renegotiate deals with Ford's bankers, who, she thought, were overpricing their services to a valued client.

Some Benchwarmers carve out a section of the company to call their own. Emily Cinader Woods is the guiding light behind the clothing catalog and retail chain J. Crew, while her father oversees the holding company that includes several other apparel and household catalog businesses. William Lauder is vice president and general manager of Origins, the newest line of Estée Lauder cosmetics, while Leonard is CEO of the enormous cosmetics company.

There's something else that Benchwarmers share. As many of their parents have become comfortable with prosperity, this older generation is less willing to take risks. Benchwarmer children, on the other hand, are eager for new ventures and would like to see their businesses branch out and diversify. Members of the on-deck circle have already brought about many changes: Kathryn Klinger has extended Georgette Klinger salons across the country, and Fred and David Hochberg oversaw Lillian Vernon company's state-of-the-art distribution operations.

Less experienced Benchwarmers must realize that they need to prove themselves before their parents allow them to try new ventures. As Bill Ford says, "And that's why you've got to wait. Because the business is still theirs."

David: "I think the key to the success of the three of us working together is that we all have our own distinct areas of expertise."

Lillian Vernon Corporation
Mount Vernon, New York

Business:	Specialty catalog company
Best Known Products:	Gifts, household, gardening, decorative and children's products
Founded:	1951 by Lillian Vernon
Family Executives:	Lillian Vernon, Chairman and CEO Fred P. Hochberg, President and COO David Hochberg, Vice President
Family History:	Second generation
Family Ownership:	55 percent
Family Board Membership:	3 family members of 6 directors
Traded:	American Stock Exchange, LVC
Revenue:	$162,400,000 1992 160,300,000 1991 154,700,000 1990
Net Earnings:	$ 9,493,000 1992 9,270,000 1991 10,806,000 1990

LILLIAN VERNON CORPORATION

"Mother Is A Genius"

Lillian Vernon, CEO and Chairman
Fred P. Hochberg, President and COO
David C. Hochberg, Vice President/Public Relations

"My brother, Fred Hochberg, very clearly wants to take over the company," says David Hochberg, 35, vice president of Lillian Vernon Corp. and spokesman for the company. "He knows that, she knows that, and I know that."

David Hochberg is describing the clear succession plan upon the retirement of Lillian Vernon, 64, founder and CEO of a speciality catalog firm that ranks in the top ten of more than 10,000 specialty catalogs in the United States. The Lillian Vernon Corporation markets personal and home accessories, children's and gardening products, and gift items through the 148 million catalogs it mails annually. There are four separate catalogs: the core *Lillian Vernon Catalog, Lilly's Kids, Lillian Vernon At Home*, and the *Sale Catalog*. In these catalogs, the cost-conscious customer will find items like a dozen pastel napkins in a natural willow basket for less than $20 or a plush cotton terry children's shower robe monogrammed for a personal touch.

The company adheres to selling basic items, skipping rapidly obsolescent products like electronics and sports apparel. Product personalization is the company's hallmark, with streamlined operations designed to customize items both quickly and cost effectively. The company processed 4.3 million merchandise orders in its 1991 fiscal year.

These millions of orders were launched by a woman whose success is based on her epitomization of the company's customer.

"I know my customer," says Lillian, "because I *am* my customer." She recognizes that successful items must be both attractive and practical and makes sure the company continually offers unique new products to reflect trends in color and style. Additionally, Lillian Vernon catalog items are priced within the range of middle-class budgets and come with a satisfaction guarantee. In a time when postage and paper costs are soaring, the Lillian Vernon company still manages to offer many basic items at a lower price than retail stores charge.

Lillian points out that the company is unusual for a direct marketing firm of its size because "most of the major catalog companies in America are no longer run by their founders." David adds that in most cases, family members are not even involved anymore. "They either retired, passed away, or sold the company." Lillian has no intention of letting go of her business. "For me it is important to stay involved with the company that I love, and I also like working with my children and would like them to take over the business in the future." When a company is strongly identified with a family and boasts a 19 percent compounded growth rate in revenue over the past ten years, that company is offering the founder's offspring an enviable future.

The company's solid financial status began with the marketing instincts and ambition of one woman, born Lillian Menasche in Leipzig, Germany in 1927. In the 1930s, Lillian's family escaped Hitler by traveling to Holland and from there moved to the United States in 1937. The Menasches became Americanized quickly, so much so that in World War II, Lillian's older brother Fred was killed fighting in the American armed forces. Lillian's father, Herman, continued his career as a manufacturer, switching from zippers to leather goods by the war's end. "My mother, Erna, also worked with him in the business, so as you can see," says Lillian, "a family business is something I am very accustomed to."

Lillian was still in high school in New York City when she took her first job ushering in a local movie theatre. Typical of Lillian's quest for self-improvement, she used the screenplay dialogue to

improve her English skills. Shortly after, Lillian began her stunning retailing career with an inauspicious start as a Barton's Candy
Shop clerk. After two years at New York University and marriage to
Sam Hochberg, she took a secretarial job but left because of the
impending birth of Fred, named after her late brother. Lillian's
drive wasn't appeased by socializing with the neighborhood wives,
and she also worried about the adequacy of husband Sam's $75-
a-week salary, earned working in his parents' ladies clothing shop.

A strong believer in self-sufficiency, in 1951 Lillian took $2000
she and Sam had garnered in wedding money and invested in her
own business. Of this, $495 went to *Seventeen* to pay for an adver-
tisement of a personalized leather purse and belt, designed by
Lillian and manufactured by her father. "He acted as a typical
supplier, giving me the same terms that he gave his other
customers," she says. This businesslike attitude is natural to
Lillian, who thinks adult children should earn their own way.

When Lillian decided to start her own mail-order business,
this 24-year-old homemaker couldn't count on extensive market
research to help her make business decisions. She says her feelings
for merchandising are "self-taught." "I always enjoyed fashion and
design, but it was an area that I was never formally schooled in."
But she had a good eye for what women would find attractive,
parents who gave her solid business advice, and a lot of drive. Still,
she says, "I never dreamed that my company would become as
large as it has."

Signs of Lillian's merchandising brilliance shone early. The
monogrammed belt and handbag indicated that Lillian instinctively
understood women's desire for personalized items. Although
Lillian's business has moved from a kitchen table in a cramped
apartment to a 52-acre distribution center in Virginia Beach, personalization is still her emblem: in 1991, 2.3 million catalog items were
personalized. "No one can start a mail-order business the way I did
in 1951, but if I had to start over now, I'd definitely begin with
monogrammed merchandise again," she says.

And that initial set of personalized purses and belts showed
her how well these reasonably priced items would sell. Orders of
$32,000 poured in from the first magazine advertisement, and
her entrepreneurial company was launched. Still, Lillian was reluctant to leave Fred, and later David, in the sole care of a house-

keeper. Her desire to be at home with her children, coupled with Sam's tendency to treat Lillian's business as a hobby, slowed the growth of the company in the 1950s. Social disapproval of working mothers and career women was also a handicap and so Lillian became, in her words, "a closet worker." Luckily, Lillian's father gave her practical feedback. "And," Lillian points out, "since he was a businessman, that obviously influenced my interest in the business world." Her own ambition and the example of parents who were both self-starters and positive thinkers compelled her to continue her business.

Lillian put her profits back into leather goods and magazine advertisements. By 1954, she'd developed a brochure, which she mailed to those 125,000 customers who'd previously responded to her ads. Only 16 pages long, this black and white flier featured relatively inexpensive items. Savvy Lillian noted that some of the higher-priced giftware sold solidly, and soon she was adding more of these products to her catalog. By 1956, the year of David's birth, Vernon Specialties (so named because of her residence in Mount Vernon, New York) was able to rent office and warehouse space in nearby buildings, with two additional structures providing separate monogramming and shipping areas. The company also began manufacturing custom product containers for personal care and cosmetic companies like Revlon, Avon, and Elizabeth Arden.

Despite having this much office space, Lillian maintained a home office in her den, which was shared by her television-watching sons when they came home from school. "She always made sure to be accessible when we were in the house," remembers David. And Lillian continued to rely on her parents, sometimes as caregivers. "The mail-order business is seasonally oriented," says David, "and if Lilly was overwhelmed with orders coming in the last three weeks before Christmas, my grandparents would come up and take care of us."

By 1965, Lillian's identification with her company was nearly a perfect fit, and she personalized the company with her given name just as she monograms her products. The newly dubbed

Lillian Vernon Corporation was by now solidly profitable although Lillian was not yet a household name. But with her sons' departure for school and her recognition that marriage to Sam wasn't the relationship she wanted, Lillian filed for divorce and devoted herself fulltime to merchandising.

In 1970, the company achieved its first annual million dollars in sales, and for the first time Lillian began traveling to European trade shows. Ironically, her initial show was in the Germany she'd fled as a child. Upon her arrival in Frankfurt, Lillian broke out in a psychosomatic rash. (Although now many of her suppliers are German, Lillian refuses to go back to Leipzig itself out of respect for her father's memory.)

The early 1970s saw Lillian building her business through canny merchandising. Her confidence allows her to know precisely what shade or style will sell, and she seeks out manufacturers who will meet these specifications. She's continually "sourcing" (looking for new suppliers) to keep ahead of the competition. A tough negotiator, Lillian will walk away from a deal if not completely satisfied. She's delighted that she can offer customers merchandise from around the world, but as an American businesswoman she laments that the majority of her items are imported, something she attributes to the willingness of foreign manufacturers to alter their product to fit her requirements. She believes American manufacturers are less creative, and she criticizes them for this: "I don't think they're aggressive enough to go out for the business. They should. They'd get it."

Two events in the 1970s helped propel the Lillian Vernon Corporation into high gear. The first was the great influx of working women with little leisure time to shop. More than 90 percent of the company's customers are women, with an average household income that approaches $50,000. The majority of these customers are women holding jobs. "Working women are the base on which we built our current success," says David.

The Arab oil embargo in 1973, which discouraged consumers from driving to stores, also had a positive impact on the catalog business, pushing it up to a $150 billion industry. Lillian now began to realize that her company was becoming nationally recognized, and with this 1970s success, she began treating herself to luxuries for the first time. No longer did she feel compelled to plow all of her profits back into the business.

This decade also saw the introduction of Fred, now 40, and David to the work world. They'd help out in the warehouse or the office when they were free on school breaks. David recognizes that his mother probably always wanted her sons to follow her into the company. But working for Lillian was never considered a family duty. "For me," David says, "it was just kind of fun and social and different. It certainly was never forced down my throat."

Lillian concurs, "I never pressured or forced my children to join the business. I certainly hoped they would and encouraged them, but I felt that was something they had to want from within."

Both sons made an early decision to share in the business, and soon after they finished their schooling, they joined the company. Fred, who graduated from the University of Rochester and received an M.B.A. from Columbia University, joined the company in 1975. David graduated from George Washington University and entered Lillian Vernon Corp. in 1978. Fred worked at the Mount Vernon headquarters office with Lillian and specialized in marketing, moving up to Chief Operating Officer in 1986 and, in 1989, adding the title of president.

David started at the new wholesale showroom on Fifth Avenue in Manhattan. Soon the company realized that its efforts would be better targeted if it remained focused on cataloging, so the wholesaling business was scaled back. At the same time that David's energies were no longer needed in the showroom, there was a public relations opening in headquarters. As the growth of the company jumped in scale in the 1970s and 1980s, the communication function increased in importance. So David, with his college degree in journalism, stepped in. Additionally, Lillian needed someone close to her, someone she trusted to speak as her alter ego, to handle her increasing interview and speaking requests. After all, Lillian is not just a CEO, she's also a symbol, a real-life Betty Crocker of the catalog business. It soon became clear that David's expanded functions entitled him to move into a new spot, vice president for public relations. (When he was asked his exact title, David, like many other family business heirs, was not certain until he checked on it.)

"I think the key to the success of the three of us working together is that we all have our own distinct areas of expertise," says David. "Lillian's the expert on merchandising, Fred's the expert on marketing and on some of operations, and I'm the expert on communications. And while there is, of course, interaction, it's very much distinctly separate responsibilities and areas that we're involved with."

Lillian concurs. "The three of us each have our own distinct areas of responsibilities. This has been the key to our successfully working together. There is very little overlap."

━━━━━━━

In some ways, the tremendous growth of the company just as Fred and David were entering may have smoothed potential conflicts. There was just too much to get done and too much that was new to each of these players (including Lillian) for them to have time to try to look over each others' shoulders.

A real crisis faced them in the early 1980s as the company underwent quick growth. Sales tripled to $89 million between 1980 and 1983, and the company lacked an adequate infrastructure to support this magnitude of expansion. Inventory was overbalanced and expenses were high. Lillian took aggressive steps, freezing inventory and reducing staff. These first steps pulled the company out of trouble and also convinced the family that they needed to improve their communications center, which received the catalog's telephone orders from customers.

Necessary believers in the potential of technology, they opened a state-of-the-art communications center in 1984 in New Rochelle, New York, which achieved honors from *Newsweek* as an office of the future. A year later, the first of the Lillian Vernon Outlet Stores also opened in New Rochelle in recognition of the need to reduce overstock inventory. 1983's inventory surplus showed Lillian the possibilities for a discount store, her solution to ridding the warehouse of "the cats and dogs"—Lillian's term for slow sellers. Now there are three outlet stores, including one in Virginia Beach and the newest in suburban Washington's Potomac Mills. Being able to rid themselves of excess products allows the company to be "very bold marketers," says David.

He continues, "Lillian and Laura Zambano (senior vice president and general merchandise manager) and the whole merchandising group are very innovative and aggressive in their pursuit of new merchandise." Lillian travels with her team of merchandisers most of the year across America and the world looking for new products. Her team members log an average of 150,000 miles annually on their quest; Lillian says it's an ongoing search. "We cover all the major trade fairs around the world. We custom design and have manufactured to our specifications many of our products. Exclusivity is very important to our company." In fact, what sets this company apart from others is their merchandising strength.

Unlike many catalog companies, this one conducts market research only on categories of products, and not on specific products. "So if Lillian and her merchandising group like a product, they're not going to do focus groups and surveys, they're going to just put it in the catalog," says David.

"And the advantage we have is, if we put it in and it sells well, we've got a winner. If it doesn't sell well, we've got sale catalogs and outlet stores," David says. "That allows us to take risks in terms of specific product offerings."

David also notes that the company stays with what it does best: catalog sales. David points out that many of the retail companies in this tighter economy "have financial problems because they've diverged from what they're known for. They've diverged from what they're good at. But, for us, mail order is going to remain the main thrust of the business."

Fred concurs. "We have always felt that traditional retailing is a very different business than direct marketing. I feel it's important that we stay focused in our growth and concentrate on the areas we know best."

And it's no longer Lillian's merchandising instincts that solely direct product selection. Now, says Fred, "We are a data-base-driven company." With a proprietary customer data base of more than 12 million names it's possible to segment the data and focus on which consumers need what products and then serve that niche.

"Ten years ago," says David, "if Lillian wanted to launch a new catalog, we didn't have a large marketing department, and we couldn't afford extensive market research. So therefore her instincts were key because we couldn't afford to do surveys and focus groups. It had to be based on instinct for obviously pure economics. Now a lot of that instinct can be supplemented by market research.

"Who ordered children's products, which ones ordered gardening products, how often do they order from us, what is their average purchase? Those are very crucial pieces of data in deciding who gets what book."

A tangible example of the company's successful use of this data is its upscale *At Home* catalog, developed in 1989 and featuring home decor and accessories that are both decorative and functional. This new catalog is bringing in the highest average dollar order expended by Lillian Vernon customers.

Another new catalog, *Lilly's Kids*, was launched the following year to take advantage of the recent high birthrate. Not that Lillian herself needs to follow demographics: she sensed that the pregnancy of Diana, the Princess of Wales, was indicative of an upcoming birth trend. And as children's products became a best-selling category for the company, it seemed logical to spin off a separate catalog and fill another niche. (However, there is some product overlap between the catalogs.)

"Say we decide in the future we want to do a gardening catalog, which we've never done yet," says David. "Well, in our data base we have millions of names of people who have bought gardening products from us. So in that sense we've got a very good, strong, solid foundation to build on for future growth. And we'll continue to go into an area we've covered. Our philosophy is you build on your success. That's been our corporate strategy."

In our era of ever-increasing postal cost, one asset of spin-off catalogs is lighter weight, which results in economy of scale. "This niche marketing," David says, "is a cheaper way for us to reach the customer because we can mail, say, *Lilly's Kids* to all the parents and grandparents on our list. It's a smaller, lighter catalog that costs less to mail." David also notes that catalog retailers are exploring alternatives to the U.S. postal service: third-class mail can be delivered by private carriers and there's the possibility of increasing magazine ads. But still, including the catalog mail costs and the subsequent shipping of products, direct marketers face an expensive distribution system.

By 1986, the idea of going public (which had been tossed around by the three of them for a few years) was becoming more attractive. The company needed updated technology and a larger, more efficient warehouse. And it needed these programs quickly. Their proposed 454,156 square foot warehouse and the IBM 3090-170S computer system—crucial to the company's continued growth—were capital intensive.

To raise funds, Lillian Vernon Corporation went public in 1987. Luckily, the offering was made in August, before the market crashed. The family sold about 30 percent of its shares and retained 70 percent of the company's stock. By 1991, Lillian and her two sons had reduced their ownership to about 55 percent of shares.

Lillian didn't rush into the decision to go public, giving it careful thought and consulting with experts. Although few direct marketing companies are publicly owned, Lillian and her sons were enthusiastic and felt going public was the best way to raise the kind of sum they needed. At the same time, the company set up its first ESOP (employee stock option program). The family sees ESOPs as good motivators and, as Lillian says, to give employees "a personal stake and commitment" to the company.

Lillian is noted for standing behind her women employees and promoting them from within the company. "I have always felt it is important to give the women who work for us a chance to reach their full potential," Lillian says. "I realize that many corporations hold women back, and I would never do that." Always practical, she told *Working Woman* magazine "I believe in doing it at a grass-roots level rather than joining NOW. You hire an hourly worker and then strive to make her a supervisor. We had a party last night for our operations people, and there they were in silk dresses and high heels. That's not the way they walked *into* this company."

The company reinforces other social responsibility values throughout the company, too. David lists some of their decisions: "We don't sell fur in the catalog, we don't sell ivory in the catalog, we don't buy parts from South Africa." The company links their products to several philanthropic programs, and it gave stuffed bears to 7,000 hospitalized children in 1990 and donates blankets and towels to the homeless. Although Chesebrough-Pond honored Lillian as a business hero for the company's product donations to more than 500 charities, David deserves recognition for promoting causes within the company. "I think I was the one who'd been pushing the social issues probably the most aggressively," he notes.

━━━━━━━━━━━

In the late 1980s, after a second short marriage, Lillian went full circle and changed her surname to Vernon. In an era when Americans search for their roots, she found hers in her own business. After all, that first *Seventeen* ad showed a purse and belt monogrammed with their designer's initials: L.H. Even today, a customer can see that the brass card holder shown for purchase in the core *Lillian Vernon Catalog* displays the business cards of Fred and David Hochberg.

Lillian's own image adorns the inside left-hand page of each catalog, positioned above her traditional letter to customers. That column is important to Lillian because its her direct message to the company's shoppers. Her familiar face—with the chestnut hair arranged in a sensible yet flattering style and the brown eyes brought out through understated makeup—evokes trust. Her look projects her values, and her closeness to those who receive the catalog is seen by her selection of photograph. For the first issue of *Lilly's Kids*, the picture illustrating her message shows Lillian, one year old, posed on a favorite wooden rocking horse.

According to a recent Gallup poll, 26 million people recognize the Lillian Vernon name. When this level of recognition is accorded to the company's founder, who calls the final shot in a disagreement between Lillian, Fred, and David? "We have a discussion and reach a consensus, but obviously," says Lillian, "I am the CEO and if I feel that strongly about an issue, I usually prevail."

Again, the separation of powers into merchandising, marketing, and communication works well for this family. Since Fred is being groomed to take over the company, it's natural that long range planning is his responsibility in addition to marketing. He also sets the agenda for the biannual meetings of the vice presidents and board members. Although Lillian and Fred work closely together on the bottom-line issues confronting the business, David's asset is that he's the family member most aware of what may be important to the company outside of the merchandising and marketing issues. When the company went public, David added the responsibility of investor relations to his duties, discussing the company with potential or actual investors and using these talks to bring investors' comments back to his frenetic mother and brother. Additionally, it's David who keeps them conscious of social issues like the needs of the homeless or including the crafts of Third World artisans in a special catalog selection.

Having worked together for about 15 years, the triumvirate of Lillian, Fred, and David have settled into a comfortable groove. This doesn't mean that Lillian has mellowed a great deal as she entered her sixties. Her self-confidence occasionally segues into self-assertion, but again, this is a trait typical of both entrepreneurs and gifted merchandisers who must project their own image onto their products. And like most people who are quicker than others, she's said to be a tad short-tempered if staff aren't measuring up to her standards. But, as Lillian told *Nation's Business*, "The buck stops with me and, well, sometimes the buck gets very hot." She adds, "It's okay for a man to lose his temper, but it's not okay for a woman?"

Despite her exhausting travel schedule, Lillian still wants to be kept in touch with the details of the business. In this way, Lillian resembles other entrepreneurs. (Because this canny woman was at first intimidated by financial reports, she asked one of her controllers for a tutorial. Now she's proficient at reading a balance sheet and other important financial information.) It's guaranteed that the catalog layout will always get Lillian's total attention. What should go in the upper right page corner? (That's the location that sells the most items.) Which color shade photographs the best? Should the products be shown in every color selection?

Fortunately for the company, Fred has talents that are different from, yet complement his mother's considerable capabilities. Lillian has a tactical approach to problems, always asking "Will it work?" This style is rooted in the present. Fred is geared toward the future and asks the question, "What will we need five years from now?" As a professional manager, his style is strategic. Additionally, Fred works closely with the daily operations of the company, whereas Lillian focuses on the merchandising. His instincts are to share decision-making with team members, whereas Lillian operates a little closer to the chest, an attitude that is, again, typical of an entrepreneur.

"Lillian and Fred complement each other perfectly—one is a classic entrepreneur, the other a professional manager," says Gordon Muckler, vice president of marketing. "The business benefits from the synergies of these two approaches."

Fred's solo abilities can be judged by the Virginia Beach operation. In 1988, under Fred's oversight, the company opened its National Distribution Center. The Virginia location was chosen partly because Westchester was getting to be an increasingly tough labor environment, Fred told *Crain's New York Business*, even with the company subsidizing transportation and paying cash incentives to employees for bringing in other workers. The center's 52 acres give it vast warehouse and shipping capability. In 1989, the company opened its new computer center at the site. Electronic scanners move over product items, providing inventory information and routing packages, saving substantially on labor costs. A new customer service center opened the next year, stationing the company in a good spot to weather the rough economic period ahead.

The company's 1991 fiscal year was a trying period for all retail and catalog companies due to the continuation of the recession and the Persian Gulf war, but Lillian Vernon Corporation continues as one of the best-positioned catalogers. Earnings fell short of the previous fiscal year but despite this slight drop the company is comparatively well-off. Lillian's "pay as you go" philosophy gives the business a conservative debt load of 21 percent ($14 million) of equity ($65.8 million). While many smaller catalog companies are in trouble from operating in an industry that's been flat since 1984, the company's nearly $36 million in cash means it can protect its margins and, if something attractive appears, still acquire one of these shaky catalogers. 1991's poor economic climate also means that the well-capitalized Lillian Vernon Corporation will face fewer new competitors in the next couple of years.

Other smart decision-making is paying off for the business, too. An increased number of core catalogs, raising the company's circulation by 23 percent, were mailed to new households in 1990 in the hopes of gathering additional customers before the postal rise occurred in early 1991. (However, these mailing costs were one factor temporarily hurting earnings in their 1991 fiscal year.) More importantly, the Virginia Beach operation was a very smart strategy. Fred told *Crain's New York Business*, "Probably by luck we moved at the right time and were able to cut costs just as the business got tougher." Higher freight and postal costs for this catalog company will need to be offset in the future by continued reduction in expenses made possible through their new operations site and through the decision to mail fewer catalogs and raise shipping fees.

But it was the family's ability to work together and Lillian's adeptness at giving up control that allowed them to go public, enabling the development of the cost-efficient Virginia Beach complex, which has become crucial to the company's competitive position and which nearly guarantees its ability for continued growth. The Virginia Beach facilities have excess capacity, allowing the business to grow—either through acquisitions or through increased sales—without burdensome capital expenditures.

Succession is another one of those issues where this family has reached a consensus. "My son David has no desire to run the company, yet my son Fred would definitely like to do so," says Lillian of her two sons, who have different personalities and skills. David admits, "I think if we both wanted the top spot, there would be a tremendous conflict here. But what's made it a very harmonious progression is that I have *zero* desire to take over the company. Therefore, there's no conflict. It's pretty much decided on. And that's very good because in a lot of family businesses there's a lot of tremendous conflict and friction over that subject. We're fortunate that it doesn't exist here.

"The problem with most children of entrepreneurs is that they want to compete with their parents. They want to be richer, have bigger businesses, do it quicker. I can speak for myself. I have absolutely no desire to do that. I mean, my mother's a genius. There's no other way to describe her.

"And in terms of my trying to outdistance her or exceed what she's accomplished, I don't think it's necessarily possible, and I don't want to do that. I think a lot of what happens is that these kids of entrepreneurs feel they've got to prove themselves, that they're as good or better than their parents, and I think that's an unhealthy competition. In my case, it's self-defeating because, like I said, my mother's a genius."

Katie: "I could start my own business after 35 years [and] get to where they were at the time, or I could join them."

Ford Models, Inc.
New York, New York

Business:	Model agency
Best Known Models:	Cheryl Tiegs, Christie Brinkley, Lauren Hutton, Kim Basinger, Brooke Shields, Elle MacPherson, Christy Turlington, Rachel Williams, Rachel Hunter, Vendela
Founded:	1946 by Eileen Ford and Jerry Ford
Family Executives:	Jerry Ford, CEO and Director Eileen Ford, President and Director Bill Ford, Vice President Katie Ford, Vice President
Family History:	Second generation
Family Ownership:	100 percent
Family Board Membership:	No formal board; Eileen and Jerry are the decision-makers
Traded:	Privately held
Net Billings:	$40,000,000 1991 40,000,000 1990 40,000,000 1989
Net Earnings:	Will not disclose

FORD MODELS, INC.

Children, Meet Your New Roommate
Kim Basinger

Bill Ford, Vice-President
Katie Ford, Vice-President and Creative Director
Eileen Ford, President
Jerry Ford, Chief Executive Officer

Ford Models, Inc. has been number one since Eileen and Jerry Ford co-founded it in 1946 in New York City. The family-controlled and closely held firm is the only major U.S. modeling agency with two generations of family members. Today, son Bill and daughter Katie serve as vice-presidents of Ford Models. The agency represents about 600 models with annual billings of $42 million, more than twice that of their nearest rival, Elite Model Management.

There were only two names in modeling at the close of World War II: John Robert Powers and Harry Conover, who subsequently landed in jail because he stole his models' earnings. Eileen Ford says the modeling industry was in a shambles when she and Jerry opened their agency

With no background in the business, Jerry stepped in and demanded that Ford models get paid even for a shoot cancelled because of bad weather, developed a voucher system so that the models could get paid weekly, and applied the concept of subsidiary fees to the industry. All of these practices, which are now standard, began with Jerry Ford's professionalization of the modeling business.

Sitting in her unpretentious office in the four-story brownstone that houses Ford Models, delicate-featured, blue-eyed Eileen talks about her business and her family.

Early on, the Fords worked out a division of labor that remains in place today, even with the addition of their children as executives in the company. Eileen, as president, heads the model searches and development of new talent. Jerry, who's CEO, has always attended to the business and administrative functions of the agency. Eileen jokingly states of her more visible role, "I'm the mouth and he's the brains." She also claims that Jerry makes all the business decisions but leaves the communication of them to her, so critics characterize Eileen as a tough businesswoman who calls the shots.

The Ford agency and the Ford's first child, Jamie, both got their start in 1946. Jamie was followed by Bill in 1952, Lacey in 1955; and Katie in 1957. To make room for this growing family, the Fords moved from Park Avenue to a townhouse on East 78th Street. "My life was taken up by the agency and my children," says Eileen. "I believe in the family."

She also believes in running a strong company, a trait fostered by her parents, who ran the family business of R & W Otte, a credit-rating company now owned by Dun & Bradstreet Corporation. (One of Eileen's brothers is still with the business.) "My mother worked," she says. "I knew from day one I'd have to work," despite the comfortable wealth of her childhood on Long Island.

No business head could mesh familywork more closely than through the Fords' technique: They invited a handful of models to live with the family. Usually, these were European girls who didn't speak English, or American girls who were judged by Eileen and Jerry to be too inexperienced to live on their own in Manhattan. Nurturing the models and enveloping them within the Ford fold was a necessity. "The models were our friends," she says. Models like Suzy Parker, Dina Merrill, and Capucine. "So we all saw each other religiously in the beginning."

With four children, and a governess and cook, life was full but it also was a little crowded. So the kids—including young Bill—shared their bedrooms with the models. Jerry Hall, Kim Basinger and a throng of beauties moved in and out of the Ford household.

It was a vibrant household: Katie remembers 40 guests for lunch at her parents' country house in Connecticut, and maybe 20 at dinner every weekend. The four children certainly were aware of their parents' agency. Bill was the first of the Ford children to join—in 1976—because older sister Jamie preferred a career in interior design. (Now Jamie is with Benjamin Flowers, Inc. in Washington, D.C.) As it turned out, Bill was also the only second-generation Ford at the agency for nine years.

Bill was invited to step in and pump up business in whatever division he thought he could have the most effect. Eventually he decided to move into Ford's sports department, working with Chris Evert and Pam Shriver.

Bill's parents encouraged him to pinpoint the areas where he saw Ford falling behind the times. When Bill started booking models and doing scouting, however, there were some real disagreements over the type of models Ford was booking. Eileen Ford has always been known to prefer a fair-skinned, blonde, and blue-eyed face. "How many truly unforgettable brunettes can you remember?" she asks. It's recognized in the industry that she initiated the California Look, best represented by Ford models Christie Brinkley and Cheryl Tiegs. "Blondes have greater longevity," Eileen says.

But Bill wanted to draw a different kind of image. "Not as classically pretty, a much different type of girl. More interesting, more intelligent as opposed to the cosmetic girls my mother likes." Bill's viewpoint on beauty was that of his generation, not of his parents, so it was not unlikely that there'd be a generational clash at Ford Models.

"We had great battles over that," Bill now says with amusement. Eileen concurs, "I have a quick tongue." Bill says the talks with his parents "came down to, 'Okay, goddamit, you want to do it—you do it!' "

In this case, Bill points out, "That was the best thing that could have happened because the girls did work and they did well." Hot new faces like Elle McPherson and Christy Turlington were signed up, along with Ford's well-recognized California beauties. In addition, Hispanic and Asian-American models are also part of Ford's roster.

While Bill was learning about scouting, his younger sister Katie was a great success as a management consultant, doing strategic planning for corporations, after receiving her M.B.A.

from Columbia University. Katie is clear-cut about the things she wanted, which she feared management consulting could never give her: work where she had control, work that was connected to an art form, work that involved people more than it did number-crunching, and work with a fast pace in fun cities. "I came up with a bunch of design businesses I could start, then I realized I had just described my parents' business," says Katie. Even though Eileen was begging Katie to come over—"dying for me to come" says Katie—it took Katie a while to realize she could have what she was looking for in the family business.

Katie noted that her sister Lacey Ford had successfully joined the business to run the Super Model competition, working well with Bill and their parents. (The demands of Lacey's husband's career and those of her young children ultimately became too time consuming for her to be able to continue. Lacey left the agency in 1989, five years after she began.)

Bill pointed out to Katie, "We might as well have an equity interest and have something that will be ours instead of working for somebody else." Katie realized, "I could start my own business and after 35 years get to where they were at the time, or I could join them."

Katie saw some difficulties ahead when she entered Ford in 1981. She's direct when she remembers her qualms: "I thought about my mother, who is a very domineering person, and whether I could work with her. She's used to telling people she wants it her way. She doesn't work by democracy. So I thought about it and decided I was old enough to fight the battles—not that there are many that we fight."

Jerry surprised her, though, when she came in for an interview after she told her parents she was considering a career switch. "My father said, 'If you expect a job description, you're not going to get it.'"

Entering Ford fresh from a consulting job on banking strategy, Katie headed into the accounts department and took a hard look at Ford's banking practices. She didn't like what she saw. "My father had kept the same perspective from when Ford was a struggling company," she says. The agency was paying way too much interest for a company with their credit history, so Katie set that straight. She continued to get accounting in shape and started work on divisional profits, something Jerry never had time to do. Immediately, Katie felt she was making a difference—one that showed on the ledger books.

Katie also brings models home to live with her and her husband (entrepreneur André Balazs), but with a difference. "In my parents' house, the models were like children. In our house, they're more like friends." Having been raised in a crowd, Katie says she finds her five-story, 1830s Greenwich Village townhouse lonely and quiet without the girls.

Katie says her houseguest models are the next Christy Turlingtons, but not all gain such success. Many of Ford's models are in television or the men's division and remain relatively anonymous, booked for their physical characteristics rather than for their notoriety. Ford's top models do not get placed in any one division but rather are booked by name and reputation. Elle MacPherson, Christy Turlington, Rachel Williams, and Celia Forner are today's Ford stars, earning thousands of dollars for a day's work.

Katie, as she gains experience at Ford, continues to move through the company like an in-house consultant, working in areas where she sees a need she can fill. "And to this day, I still don't have one role. I go home, and I can't imagine at the end of the day what I did, but I was so busy doing it!" (The ability of Katie and Bill to move in and out of their roles and not be tied down to a job description is reflected in Bill's refusal to state specifically what arena his vice presidency covers.)

One thing Katie and her family agree on is keeping Ford's dominant position in the modeling field. Ford is to models what RINGLING BROS. (see Replicators) is to circus performers: the most prestigious booking—and with guaranteed payment. Even today, there are agencies that give only partial payment up front or make the models wait days before they collect any fee. But Ford has pockets deep enough to pay fees on time to the models it represents. The agency's income comes from the 15 percent commission it charges models for representation and the additional 20 percent fee it takes from the client agency.

They've resisted one easy source of income: opening a modeling school. In the past, John Robert Powers and, more recently, John Casablancas of Elite opened their doors to hopefuls, using their name to legitimize the quality of their schools. The Fords do not plan to succumb to this cushy form of income. Katie says, "I think modeling schools are fine to teach a girl poise and makeup, but they're not going to lead to a career in modeling. That's the part I don't like, that they may tell them they're going to be models."

Maintaining these scruples is characteristic of this family business. Certainly the extra income from tuition charged to young hopefuls could go a long way to cushion the risk any agency takes to develop new talent. Ford is known within the industry for taking the greatest amount of time with novices, teaching them the business step by step before sending them to the less-competitive atmosphere of Europe to build a portfolio of tear sheets to bring back to New York. Developing a model with potential takes time. Additionally, only one percent of the 10,000 girls the Fords look at each year become supermodels.

That Ford Models has remained at the top is in no small part due to Eileen's notoriously good eye for finding the girl who can shoot up in an industry that will give a multimillion-dollar contract to a top model for exclusive work. Eileen spotted Karen Graham (who represented Estée Lauder) in the stairwell of Lord & Taylor. Although girls walk every day into the Ford Agency hoping for a contract, the agency's Super Model of the World contest brings many hopefuls directly to Ford scouts traveling throughout the world. The televised contest also brings name recognition to the agency, as do the four beauty books Eileen has published, which are widely read by future models as well as by women wanting self-improvement tips. In an industry of faces, not names, Eileen is now a celebrity with both face and name recognition.

But the Super Model contest and the Fords' extensive scouting has its price. Both Eileen and Bill Ford travel several months of the year. Each April, all the Fords but Jerry will be on the road. Eileen will cover the Orient and northern Europe, and cities throughout the United States. Katie will be in Europe, as always taking toddler Alessandra with her in her travels. Bill will be in South America.

It is a wearing business to be in, says Bill, and to be successful you need "endurance, pure endurance." Besides its Miami office, opened as a service to Ford models who are there from November to April shooting magazine spreads, the agency has opened offices in Tokyo and San Paulo. And they've just opened an office in Paris, making them the first American agency in Europe. "You've got to go out and know what's there," says Bill. "You've got to be there far ahead of the planning. It's not good to know that somebody's getting a contract, you need to know that somebody's losing a contract."

Eileen confides that she'd like to retire from the agency she cofounded. "I keep telling them I've got to retire, and they keep finding more things for me to do." When this message is repeated to Katie, she treats Eileen's statement with a strong dose of disbelief. "I think one day she'll do less, but I don't think she'll ever retire." Bill concurs with a snort, "I'm not quite sure she'd know what to do."

Katie would like to move in new directions. Speaking of her parents, she says, "They've built one thing over 40 years, and I don't want to keep it just the way it is. For me, it's just not interesting to keep it the same way."

Bill would like to represent Ford models as they move into acting careers. As soon as a model takes her first movie or television role, she signs with an acting agency, and Ford loses that portion of her representation. As more models turn to acting, it makes sense that Bill is thinking of moving Ford toward incorporating a screen actors' agency.

But Bill points to the heart of the problem: Parents are less open to risk than the upcoming generation. "And that's why you've got to wait. Because the business is still theirs. And I agree with them. I think I would do the exact same thing."

John and Stephen Marriott

John: "It's important that the perception is there of Marriott being a family business."

Marriott Corporation
Washington, D.C.

Business:	Lodging; food and facilities management; airport terminals and toll-road restaurants and gift shops, retirement communities
Best Known Products:	Marriott Hotels, Resorts, and Suites; Courtyard Hotels; Residence Inn; Fairfield Inn; Marriott Management Services
Founded:	1927 by J. Willard and Alice S. Marriott
Family Executives:	J.W. Marriott Jr., President and Chairman Richard E. Marriott, Executive Vice President and Vice Chairman Alice S. Marriott, Vice President and Director
Family History:	Third generation
Family Ownership:	Approximately 25 percent
Family Board Membership:	3 family members of 8 directors
Traded:	NYSE, MHS
Net Sales:	$8,331,000,000 1991 7,646,000,000 1990 7,536,000,000 1989
Net Earnings:	$ 82,000,000 1991 47,000,000 1990 177,000,000 1989

MARRIOTT CORPORATION

Starting at the Bottom

Stephen G. Marriott, General Manager,
Bethesda Marriott Hotel (Bethesda, Maryland)
John W. Marriott III, General Manager,
Crystal City Marriott Hotel (Arlington, Virginia)

The Marriott family became one of the world's leading hoteliers through the simple and humble ideal of service. The company began in 1927 when Alice S. and J. Willard Marriott opened a nine-seat root beer stand called the Hot Shoppe in Washington, D.C. Marriott Corporation has thrived and grown to be an international leader in lodging and in contract services.

Three generations of Marriotts have graced this diversified hospitality company: the founding grandparents, their sons J.W. (Bill) and Richard, and Bill's sons John and Steve. (One of Dick's sons-in-law and Bill's son-in-law also work for the company.) All of these Marriotts share the same devotion to customer service, the ideal that has resulted in the company's inclusion in such books as *Passion for Excellence* and *The Service 100*.

Yet in 1957, 30 years after its start-up, this company, which had gone public in 1953, operated only one hotel. When Bill joined the year before—after having worked part-time and summers at the company—the company's emphasis was still on the food-service business. Under Bill's management (he became president in 1964, CEO in 1972, and board chairman upon the death of his father in 1985), the company grew to be the country's third-largest restaurateur. It included the Hot Shoppe, Roy Rogers, Host, Gino's, and Big Boy chains. The company was also the world leader in airline catering, serving meals since 1937 on 150 airlines.

Bill headed the fledgling hotel division and was named to the vice presidency in 1958. Bill used what he'd already learned in the company's food service facilities to assist him in running hotels. Intrinsic to that was the notion of being a hands-on manager, one who left the headquarters office to get involved in operations.

There was considerable discussion between Bill and his father over using debt to build the company, with the older man being the more cautious. Through an aggressive and creative financial strategy, this transaction-oriented company continued to build (and acquire) hotels. It would then sell them to investors at a profit, and enter into a long-term management contract to operate the facility. The company's revenues quadrupled, and the number of hotels managed by Marriott Corporation shot up to more than 500 by the late '80s. In 1992, it operated more than 720 hotels.

This growth in the '60s, '70s and '80s served as a powerful allure to Bill's sons, Steve, 33 and John, 31, although neither of them thought as children about going into the company. John says, "Like most teenagers, if my parents had said, 'This is what you're going to do,' I would have replied, 'No, it's not.'" Both John and Steve began working part time at the company's restaurants when they were 16.

The Marriott philosophy is to start at the bottom. John's first tasks were to wash lettuce and bread onion rings. Steve flipped hamburgers. The brothers held these jobs after school and during summer vacations. As they matured, they were given increased responsibilities in different areas of the company. They were required to work incredibly long hours: On three or four weekdays, the boys reported from 2:00 pm until 6:00 pm, and 4:00 pm to 11:00 pm for one day over the weekend, in addition to full-time high school schedules.

Both brothers graduated from Brigham Young University and spent two years in missionary work for the Mormon church. John had majored in accounting and was working full time in the accounting office at the company's international headquarters in 1989 when his father had a heart attack and subsequent bypass surgery.

Bill's frightening illness presented a tremendous opportunity for John because his father asked him to help by going through his daily in-box, delegating tasks to staff and summarizing any situation where John thought his father alone should make recommendations.

The heart attack gave John a chance "to really spend some time with my father," he says, "because over the years, I haven't seen him as much as I'd have liked to. It also gave me the opportunity to let him teach me some things and find out what he looked for in people and in the operations."

From that headquarters position, John moved to director of marketing at one of the Marriott hotels. "I always felt it was important to move back and forth between staff and line positions. You learn a lot by getting the different perspectives."

In 1992, John was general manager of the Crystal City Marriott while Steve is general manager of the Bethesda Marriott. One characteristic all the Marriott men have in common is their allegiance to hard work—with the resultant sighs heard from wives who often wish that hotel work didn't require such long hours.

One problem can be having the Marriott last name. These heirs to a fortune (estimated in early 1992 at $450 million) say they're eager to take the extra effort to break down barriers between themselves and their associates, and to become part of the team by never appearing too proud to get their hands dirty by helping out in the kitchen or bussing tables.

Both men have also been strongly influenced by their grandfather, although John admits that he's always thought that grandmother Alice was "the brighter of the two. She really did get the company off the ground." Their grandfather's founding principle was that if you take care of the employees, they'll take care of the customers.

John sees this attitude reflected in Marriott's several hundred thousand employees, who make Marriott Corporation one of the largest employers in the United States. "It's important that the perception is there of Marriott being a family business."

John also feels the family business appeals to customers. He argues that a family atmosphere helps customers identify with the personalities of the owners and feel that they're a part of the family.

"Caring, hard work, pride, integrity, and hard work to do the best job you can were all values that were taught at home," says John. "I see strong evidence throughout the company that those are part of our culture."

Both brothers gained experience in the company's hotel operations, which have been the trickiest part of the company since the real estate bubble burst in the late '80s. The company had already sold its airline catering operations (see GORDON GETTY) and was in the process of selling its family restaurant business, such as Roy Rogers. The founding father's warnings about debt echoed throughout the headquarters building.

Although corporate profits dropped in 1990, the company reported a 74 percent increase in earnings for 1991. The results reflected increased cash flow from continuing operations, the sale of assets, and a reduction in capital spending and administrative costs. Strategy in 1992 continued to focus on reducing the company's long-term debt selling assets. Marriott will minimize building from the ground up and instead will grow through conversion and franchise opportunities. By the end of that year, Marriott planned to double its international hotels in Europe, as well as increase the number of hotels in the Pacific Rim, the Middle East, and the Caribbean.

The brothers are confident of their future and of the company's. They would eventually like to run one of the businesses. In this, they have their father's concurrence: Bill would also like to see his sons continue in the company. John is interested in one of the company's core businesses, the hotel division or one of the contract service businesses. Referring to the company's 23 hotels outside North America (in early 1992), he says, "If we really want to continue to grow as a lodging company, our greatest opportunities are international."

Steve, too, finds the hotel division an appealing place. He divulges his choice with some reluctance, "I would probably like to be president of the lodging division, but I've got a long way to go."

Although it doesn't appear that their sister will ever work at the company, the brothers can't discount their 16-year-old brother David. This youngest third-generation Marriott works in the kitchen cooking hamburgers at Steve's Bethesda hotel. When asked if David appreciates working for his older brother, Steve laughs and gives an example of delegated authority: "The chef can supervise him."

GEORGE WILLIAM SULLIVAN
CLARENCE GORDON WADGE
ROWLINSON DAVID WALTERMIRE
DAVID BRAYMAN WARD
EDWIN ASA WOLCOTT

IN MEMORY OF

ORMES, KILLED IN ACTION, JULY 18, 1918
SANTE, KILLED IN ACTION, OCTOBER 16, 1918
JAKSONS NICHOLS, DIED AT QUANTICO, VA., AUGUST 22, 191
NATHAN SMITH, DIED IN FRANCE, FEBRUARY 11, 1919

Mark Ferri Photography

David Crane and John Kittredge

*David: "People are communicating a lot more, and when you put
your Crane letter against the faxes and cheap paper, our paper stands
out even more."*

Crane & Co., Inc.
Dalton, Massachusetts

Business: Fine social and business papers; Currency and security papers; Drafting papers; Ledger papers; Converting, engraving, and printing

Best Known Products: Crane's stationery; U.S. paper currency

Founded: 1801 by Zenas Crane

Family Executives: John Kittredge, Vice President and Division Manager, Security Papers; Christopher M. Crane, Manager, Sales and Marketing, Security Papers Division

Family History: Seventh generation

Family Ownership: 100 percent

Family Board Membership: 7 family members of 10 directors

Traded: Privately owned

Net Sales: $143,000,000 1990 (estimated)

Net Earnings: Will not disclose

CRANE & COMPANY, INC.

Worth the Paper It's Written on

David Crane, President, Excelsior Printing Co.
Douglas Crane, Manufacturing Superintendent,
Security Papers Division
Timothy T. Crane, Project Manager, New Product Development

The Crane family has been supplying America with paper along a timeline that stretches from colonists to astronauts. Crane, the oldest paper company in the country to remain within one family, is best known as purveyors of fine paper to retailers. But this unassuming company also happens to be responsible for manufacturing the paper for each greenback that you've ever put into your wallet. It's been the sole supplier of U.S. currency paper since 1879 and was one of the country's major suppliers for years before, when notes were issued by a hodgepodge of various banks and insurance companies. It was Stephen Crane who, in 1775, first placed the family smack into America's cashflow by selling paper for colonial bank notes to Paul Revere. More recently, Arnold Schwarzenegger could be seen in "Kindergarten Cop" snooping through a woman's desk drawer and peering at her box of Crane stationery.

From revolutionary patriot to terminator, there's no doubt that this company is in it for the long haul. Crane's emphasis on quality and tradition accounts for its attraction for the newest Crane generation—David, 32, Douglas, 31 and Timothy, 36. David Crane, spokesman for the trio, tells why the men were lured back to the Dalton, Massachusetts company: "The three of us had a discussion about that one time. There were variations on the same theme, but we all felt that the company had traditions that were worth carrying on."

The company plays a major role as the largest employer in Dalton, a community where citizens still gather for town meetings. Nor does Crane let its responsibilities stop on payday. Crane & Co. is noted for its philanthropy toward the New England community where Zenas Crane, Stephen's son, built his one-vat frame mill in 1801.

Not that these seventh (brothers David and Doug) and sixth (cousin Tim) generations hadn't seen life outside the Berkshire Hills. All of them earned graduate degrees and worked outside the company in jobs unrelated to papermaking before coming back to Crane & Co. David was in banking, Doug worked at Baxter Travenol, and Timothy in forest management. Besides having a sense of obligation to the family firm, the young men note that their future opportunities at Crane, which must be linked to increased responsibilities, are attractive. Yet the company's custom of starting Crane men and other future managers in the mills and letting them work their way up can seem a slow process when you're in your 30s. "Our contemporaries from college and graduate school are hopping from company to company or are moving up in a fast-growing company, and they've outpaced us in terms of salary," David notes wryly. "It is ironic, but I think we're all aware that in the long run, we'll be better off."

Each of the men have slightly different backgrounds, and they believe their areas of expertise will help them avoid power struggles as they work their way through the company. To date, none of the Crane women have indicated an interest in the family company, other than holding board positions to look after their financial interests.

The men had all had a taste of the company working at summer jobs while in school, but Crane's training program moved them through the mills over to engineering and then into a stint at research. "It's definitely the right way to do it. The time you're in the mills is a special part of your life. The people treated us pretty well, and they like the fact that there's another generation coming around," says David, whose father is Christopher M. Crane, sales manager of security papers. (Tim's father is Frederick G. Crane, Jr., who was the firm's vice president in charge of research and development before retirement in 1986.) Often, the mill staff may themselves be third or fourth generation Crane workers.

In a company that's seen so many generations of families, the Crane cousins never felt they were getting special treatment at work, as happened to Eric Johnson (JOHNSON PRODUCTS). "All the jobs are well-defined and in categories. We got the same benefits, we're on the same pay scale," says David. "We didn't get any special perks. Obviously, being a Crane at Crane & Co., people treat you a little differently," he says, although he thinks the main advantage to having the Crane surname is in speaking to customers. (In a business like Crane & Co., which may seem slightly old-fashioned to today's telemarketers, personal visits by sales staff to retailers are still the norm.)

The American consumer is most familiar with Crane's social writing paper, cards, and invitations, which are 100 percent cotton rag and sold through prestigious retailers such as Gump's, Tiffany & Co., Neiman Marcus, and Marshall Field's. This is the paper used by the White House and by the State Department for important functions. Crane also manufactures 100 percent cotton commercial business papers, aimed at such image-conscious business people and professionals as corporate officers and lawyers.

This company is the only one in the world that focuses on 100 percent cotton rag paper (rather than wood pulp or 25 percent cotton rag) for both social and business use. This specialization makes Crane the largest buyer of cotton waste in the world.

Additionally, Crane produces drafting vellum (the technical paper used by designers and architects) and ledger paper. Under the brand name Byron Weston, it also produces a small quantity of 25 percent cotton business papers.

David's not nervous about the prospect of a paperless society: "I think the jury is still out on that." Paper is a mature product and certain specialties—ledger paper or library index paper, for example—are fading in an electronic era. On the other hand, the emphasis on quality in the corporate image design business accounts for strong growth in the commercial business paper line. "People are communicating a lot more, and when you put your Crane letter against the faxes and cheap paper, our paper stands out even more," David says.

Crane & Co. may feel recessions less than other companies in the paper industry. "We definitely get hurt in the social, business, and drafting papers. Construction affects how many people are using our drafting papers. But since we're at the high quality level, we're shielded, somewhat," says David.

The basis for Crane's most recent growth is its "converting" functions of printing and engraving, begun on a large scale in the last decade. David explains, "Converting just means taking paper and turning it into a type of a product—for example, an envelope or printed invitation." Converting began as a service to Crane's retailers, who found the cost of doing their own engraving prohibitive. Now Crane handles production for specialty and department stores, using the best of pigments for their dye and ink borders. The company owns three engraving facilities and one commercial printing plant.

Although Crane's fine paper distinguishes this company from other paper businesses, it is the firm's currency paper that truly separates Crane from the competition. The Cranes have been reaping the benefit of Zenas Marshall Crane's 1844 idea—frustrate counterfeiters by including a specified number of red and blue silk threads in the paper. Variations on this theme have been patented by Crane men over the years. In 1988, four generations after Zenas's invention, Timothy Crane received patent approval for a process that places a hidden message, printed on a 1/16th-inch plastic strip, within currency paper. The message is not visible under usual reflected light, but it can be read if light passes through the bill. This sophisticated security measure was designed to thwart counterfeiters using high-resolution color copiers.

In 1991, $100 bills (which account for 62 percent of counterfeits) began to be printed on this new Crane currency paper. These bills have a polyester thread reading "USA 100" running vertically next to the Federal Reserve Seal. In late 1991 and early 1992, $50 bills (which account for an additional 9 percent of counterfeit money) and $20 bills (25 percent) were manufactured with similar currency paper. Ultimately, $10 and $5 bills will also contain the new security thread. (Together, $1 and $5 bills account for less than one percent of counterfeits.) The gradual phase-in will allow Crane to continue to use its older machinery while starting up the new equipment (for which, *Forbes* reports, the company borrowed $15 million).

The company is indebted to Zenas Marshall Crane for more than the initial anticounterfeiting process. Years before Crane became the sole supplier of paper currency to the U.S. government, Zenas contracted with the American Bank Note company to manufacture paper for foreign currency and for American stocks, bonds, passports, bank checks, and deeds. (The first U.S. social security cards were printed on Crane paper.) Beside being America's currency paper supplier, Crane has also manufactured currency paper for more than 40 other countries.

An old-fashioned emphasis on quality is what keeps Crane products unsurpassed. Pride in their product has been mixed with a strong regional work force and strengthened by Crane's profit-sharing program that disperses 25 percent of the company's pretax profits to all employees. Its nonunion workers, who have rarely seen any layoffs in the company's long history, still supply final touches to paper products by hand.

Quality is one characteristic that won't suffer while the company grows. Crane & Co. saw steady growth in the '70s and '80s and may pick up some speed during the '90s as it expands overseas. Although the company has long done business throughout the world in security papers, its social and business retailing was limited to the United States and Canada. In early 1991, Crane opened an office in England for distribution of social papers there and in Europe, adding to the European distribution centers put in place a year earlier for Crane's business and letterhead papers. Crane's social papers have been sold in Japan since the early '80s and the company is optimistic about its future in Asia and the Pacific Rim. Thomas White, Crane president since 1986, is credited with the ambition of Crane's recent growth plan by *Forbes* magazine, which estimated Crane's pretax earnings to be slightly over $20 million of $143 million revenue in 1990.

Crane remains relatively small compared to the world's largest paper manufacturer, International Paper Company, with $11.4 billion in 1989 net sales. The question of going public to maximize growth potential is often raised by outsiders, partly because some of Crane's 70-plus shareholders no longer have frequent contact with the company. But any one shareholder who's interested in selling knows that stock will be bought back by the company. Going public most likely will be an issue discussed with more interest by the younger Crane generation than it has been previously. But, as David points out, the qualities that have led to Crane's steady success—independence, long-term decision making, staying in Dalton, and remaining responsive to community needs—may continue to prove to be as valuable and long-lasting as the paper on which your money is printed.

Kathryn: "I feel that it's her business, and she created it, and that I just bow to her, basically."

Georgette Klinger Salons, Inc.
New York, New York

Business:	Customized skin care
Best Known Products:	Salon facials; 300+ skin care items and cosmetics
Founded:	1941 by Georgette Klinger
Family Executives:	Georgette Klinger, CEO and Chairman Kathryn Klinger, President and Director
Family History:	Second generation
Family Board Membership:	2 family members of 3 directors
Traded:	Privately owned
Net Sales:	$20,000,000 1990 19,000,000 1989 18,200,000 1988
Net Earnings:	Will not disclose

GEORGETTE KLINGER SALONS, INC.

Monday's Child

Kathryn Klinger, President

Not all family businesses move from father to son. It's fitting that
Georgette Klinger Salons, a privately owned company dedicated to
personal beauty with $20 million in yearly revenue, has progressed
from mother to daughter. Georgette Klinger skin care salons
provide facials and other personal care services and from the
Klinger skin care and makeup products purchased either at the
salons or by mail order. The business, founded more than 50 years
ago, is guided by the well-manicured yet firm hand of Georgette
Klinger, now in her 70s.

   Kathryn, her only child, joined the firm immediately after
college graduation. Despite her lack of business courses or work
experience at other companies, Kathryn made an immediate contribution to her mother's company in her first few years. She
strengthened the image of the Klinger salons as family owned,
with the personal touch so important to upscale clients, and she
instituted a profitable mail order division. Through Kathryn's
enterprises, the company grew 20 to 25 percent in the first few
years after Kathryn joined in 1973, with never a down year since
then. It's Kathryn who deserves credit for this growth, claims
Georgette, her mother and CEO. But despite her ability to carry
long-range plans through to success, Kathryn prefers to defer to
her mother in any major decision, perhaps reflecting the tradi-
tionalsim of the family's European background.

   To compete in a 1930s beauty contest, Czech-born Georgette
Klinger slathered foundation on her skin. She won first prize but
also found herself with an unanticipated case of acne. Georgette

has never done anything in half steps, neither as today's CEO nor as a young woman determined to retain a fine complexion. To get rid of the acne, she set out to study the interaction between creams and the complextion, earning a cosmetology degree in the process. And what she learned, she wanted to teach. She opened her first salon in Brno. She thought that convincing an obstinate mother-in-law of the propriety of her work would be her only obstacle, but in 1939, Hitler's approaching army convinced her and her husband to leave the salon and flee Europe. She was careful to take her skin care formulations with her. After a short stay in London, she arrived in New York and set up her first American salon in 1941. The company was incorporated in 1943.

Despite difficulty in obtaining raw materials to produce her jars and the need to make the cleansing and creaming formulations herself, her business took off. She proclaimed, "American women have the worst skin in the world!" and clients rushed to her Madison Avenue salon. She tested new products by trying them out on herself. "I'm a constant guinea pig," she reassured her clients. Georgette and her individually trained cosmetologists provided a haven from the stress-filled lives of Klinger clients, whether they were ladies who lunch or women executives. All customers were treated equally in Klinger's immaculate and serene salon by unpretentious cosmetologists and sales staff. No special privileges were allowed, even for those who expected them. To the demanding Duchess of Windsor, Georgette said, "If a working girl can come in on her lunch hour, why not a duchess? No exceptions!"

As her business grew, Georgette concentrated on the decor and design of her Manhattan salon and paid close attention to the formulation of her product as she competed with Elizabeth Arden's popular Red Door salons. Another threat to Klinger was the full-service salon Elysee, also imported from Europe and opened in New York one year before Klinger's.

Kathryn, only child of Georgette and second husband Jacobo Eisenberg, was born in 1950. In the Manhattan world of the Upper East Side, Kathryn was a child with a working mother—an exotic entity.

Kathryn recognized that the full luxury of her life—including the Park Avenue co-op, the houseboy, and the car and driver—was due part to her mother's entrepreneurial acumen. But Georgette stood back when it came to her daughter's ambitions. "I was never pressured to join the business or given direct advice about whether or not I should work," says Kathryn. "But I was not brought up to think that one did nothing. My mother set an example. I was always around my mother's business. I used to go to the salon (on Madison Avenue) after school let out and wait for her, if I didn't have a play date or lesson, and sometimes I'd help in the stockroom."

Despite her frequent visits and the small jobs she was given at the salon, Kathryn still didn't give a serious thought to joining either parent's business. After high school, Kathryn first attended Pine Manor Junior College and then transferred to Kenyon College, where whe was a cum laude journalism graduate. She was busy scheduling job interviews in 1973 when her phone rang. It was her mother. "Can you please come and help me today because we're very short of staff?" According to Kathryn, "That was the beginning of the end of my journalism career."

Georgette sent Kathryn back to Europe for training not available in the United States. European standards set Klinger's staff above the "aestheticians," as they are called, of other salons in the industry such as Adrienne Arpel. Georgette's criticism of American training is harsh. "European skin care training is so stringent it would send your average American-trained facialist whimpering off to secretarial school!"

Kathryn implemented her own ideas for the company immediately after coming back from her schooling. Georgette had always concentrated on the aesthetic aspects of her salons and the quality of her products but was less comfortable with setting long-range goals. Kathryn harbored a few quiet ambitions for the Klinger salons, including expansion from two salons (by then in both Manhattan and Beverly Hills) to many more. In order to establish Klinger as the premiere skin care salon in women's minds throughout the nation, she knew that Georgette's credo of "service, service, and service" needed to be better known.

Kathryn instinctively understood one of the company's greatest assets: The service it offered was backed up by a family—two women who were easily identified by the public as representing Georgette Klinger Salons. It wasn't long before striking mother/ daughter advertisements began appearing in *Town and Country*, *Vogue*, and *Harper's Bazaar*. It was Kathryn's idea to run this unusual series of glossy black-and-white photos. Both women are blonde, luminous, and fair-skinned, and they look like a million dollars. As Kathryn explains, "We want to let people know that there are real people behind Georgette Klinger."

Today, many other business in the skin care and cosmetics industry have lost their founder's personal touch, so important to the upscale customer. And the image of a female founder has proven crucial, helping the company inspire the trust necessary for a women to put her face in their hands. Already, the Klinger Salons enjoy an unusually high return rate of satisfied clients.

Kathryn believes being a family-owned firm helps personnel management, too. "I think our employees like knowing who they're working for. We're a face, not just a company with somebody who's a manager and who represents somebody who represents somebody who represents some stockholders down the road."

Strong employee relations are crucial to the Klingers because they must impress on their staff that they are working in a service business. Kathryn often hires European staff for the salons because American workers tend to put their own comforts before those of the customer.

At the same time that the public is being shown the two women who personify Georgette Klinger Salons, they are being offered the opportunity to buy the more than 300 Klinger products through the mail. This allows customers who have never visited the Klinger salons to sample their products and lets regular customers replenish their supplies without treking to a salon. The catalog order is responsible for a strong share of the company's increasing revenue. This innovation is also Kathryn's idea.

She is a strategic planner in the Klinger family, believing that Georgette is "basically very creative, and I'm basically very organizational."

Kathryn's impact on the firm was immediate, and revenues rose nearly 30 percent that first year. Part of the quick growth can be attributed to her decision to increase advertising (now at nearly $1 million a year) and spotlight the mother/daughter aspect. Soon after joining her mother in 1973, Kathryn moved to Beverly Hills to manage that salon and plant Klinger roots on both coasts.

It's possible that the move was partly due to tensions resulting from working closely together in a relatively small company. Each of the women has a definite point of view, and each states her opinion firmly. Even when they are separated by the width of a continent, there are phone calls in which differences of opinion are concluded when one woman or the other slams down the phone —only to call back shortly after. This communication mode is apparently understood by both and is is not interpreted as confrontational or ill-intended. Both women have striven for a mother/daughter business relationship that works. Kathryn strongly believes that their separation is an asset both for their own relationship and for the company.

One reported management problem caused by Kathryn's move to Beverly Hills was her displacement of a Klinger manager from his projected career path—to head of the company after Georgette's retirement. Although Kathryn today maintains that keeping good managers in family-owned business where they can't get to the very top is no more difficult than keeping executives in professionally managed firms, trade journals at the time focused on tensions at the Beverly Hills salon that were only resolved when this manager left.

Family business have always had to grapple with this issue. In firms larger than Klinger, the greater number of executive positions alleviates some of the problem. However, being blocked from the CEO position—or being displaced from a lower-level management spot by a less seasoned family member—makes some executives avoid family-owned firms. At Klinger, Kathryn looks at the talent that has remained and notes that no executive ever offered a position at Klinger has refused it because Kathryn will inherit the top spot.

With Kathryn's help, Georgette expanded the company in the 1970s and early 1980s. Besides the salons in Beverly Hills and the Manhattan salon at Madison Avenue and 53rd Street, the Klingers opened a second Manhattan salon at 76th Street as well as salons in Bal Harbour, Palm Beach, Chicago (at Water Tower Place), Washington D.C. (at Chevy Chase Pavillion), and in Dallas (at the Galleria), bringing the total from two to eight salons. "There's just more territory that can be covered with two people," Kathryn explains.

Georgette might have successfully expanded Klinger earlier if she had concentrated less on the atmosphere of the Manhattan salon. Yet Kathryn might not have had a successful product base and an impeccable reputation from which to expand revenues through the additional salons or mail order catalog if it had not been for the integrity of the service and products begun by her mother.

One aspect of the Klinger growth that makes both women happy is that they were able to expand solely from reinvestment of their own profits, which account for slightly more than 15 percent of their sales. "We've never had to go to outside sources," says Kathryn.

Kathryn possessed the foresight to relocate the profitable Beverly Hills salon—which attracts influential movie and television people—from Wilshire Boulevard to North Rodeo Drive in 1977. That year, at age 26, Kathryn was appointed a director of Klinger. She became president in 1982 at age 31. Georgette remains chairman and CEO of the company. In 1983, a few years after the opening of the Beverly Hills salon, Kathryn tackled the planning of the Dallas salon.

Kathryn continues as director of both the Dallas and Beverly Hills salons, in addition to her responsibilities as an officer of the company. Georgette hires professional managers to help out with the remaining five salons and travels throughout the country to lure experienced staff from competitors' salons to her company.

Anchoring Klinger salons on the West Coast is important, but what keeps Kathryn in Beverly Hills is her marriage to real estate lawyer and developer Rudy Belton, whom she met while she was getting started in the Beverly Hills salon. Their young son is in elementary school.

In 1984, Kathryn finally used her writing skills to author *Kathryn Klinger's First Book of Beauty*. In contrast, her mother's earlier book, *Georgette Klinger's Skincare*, was a collaborative effort with a professional writer. In addition to advising women through their writing and when they make in-person visits to out-of-town salons, both women continue to work with their chemists to deliver the purest and most effective products. "We're always testing," says Kathryn. "You need to do that. It's a constant effort."

Georgette's research in the field of dermatology is well recognized by her peers and earned her the Albert Einstein College of

Medicine 1983 Spirit of Achievement award, given for outstanding achievement in the field of skin care. However, it is notable that the Klingers' own labs do not test their products on animals. Kathryn is active in animal rights and contributes time to friend Cleveland Amory's Fund for Animals.

Kathryn's Beverly Hills salon has helped strengthen sales to men. Men's skin care accounts for about a fifth of Klinger revenues since the Klinger For Men line was established in 1972. Another plus for Klinger sales is that skin care items—the bread and butter of the Klinger salons—are always a more profitable line than makeup within the industry.

First, products that cleanse and protect the face don't have to vary with seasonal fashion, as makeup does. More important, skin care is a relatively new concept to men and women in this country, causing sales to accelerate over the past decade, while makeup sales have barely risen. Georgette's European emphasis on correction rather than coverup is paying off.

Like Maurice and Leon Tempelsman's diamond business (see LAZARE KAPLAN INTERNATIONAL, inc.), the Klinger Salons have profited from the consumer movement to the high end of the market.

Although there have been many buyout offers, there is no thought in this family of selling the firm. "I don't think so," says Kathryn. Year after year, the Klingers turn down overtures made by larger companies. "Not having to answer to other people is what it boils down to. You're your own authority, and you have your own integrity. You don't have to worry about what someone else thinks," says Kathryn.

There is also the thought that Kathryn may want to have a business to leave her son. Clearly pleased with the idea of a third generation of Klingers in the salons, she says, "Mmmm...you never know!"

In meetings Kathryn addresses her mother as "Miss Klinger" and shows surprise that other adults who work with parents often address them by their first names. "Why do I call her Miss Klinger? That's what she's referred to. Nobody calls her by her first name. It's not appropriate, really." Kathryn laughs. "We're very old fashioned here."

As well as in address, this Benchwarmer defers to her mother in more important ways. It is Georgette who set the Klinger salons on the road of service and ensured the company's success by her insistence on purity of product and her attention to aesthetics. Kathryn is a strategic planner who will pull back if she senses that her mother is not enthusiastic about her ideas. "I feel that it's her business, and she created it, and that I just bow to her, basically."

Wendy: "Dad wanted a name that was easy to remember and he wanted an all-American mug. I was red-headed and had freckles and buckteeth, so I got elected."

Wendy's International, Inc.
Dublin, Ohio

Business:	Quick-Service Restaurants—Wendy's Old Fashioned Hamburgers
Best Known Menu Items:	Dave's Deluxe Hamburger; Grilled Chicken Sandwich; Wendy's Big Classic; SuperBar; Taco Salad; Hot Stuffed Baked Potatoes; Frosty
Founded:	1969 by Dave Thomas
Family Executives:	Dave Thomas, Senior Chairman
Family History:	Second generation (Wendy Thomas and her husband Paul* are Wendy's Franchise Owners and Managers in Texas)
Family Ownership:	7.6 percent
Family Board Membership:	1 family member of 13 directors
Traded:	NYSE, WEN
Systemwide Sales:	$3,223,593,000 1991 3,070,250,000 1990 3,036,054,000 1989
Net Sales:	$1,060,381,000 1991 1,010,877,000 1990 1,069,697,000 1989
Net Earnings:	$51,305,000 1991 39,280,000 1990 30,423,000 1989

The family does not wish to disclose its last name

WENDY'S
INTERNATIONAL, INC.

Dave's Deluxe Daughter

Wendy Thomas, Franchise Owner

For more than twenty years, people throughout America have recognized her nickname and sketched likeness, but few have known that there is a real person after whom the quick service restaurant chain is named. Her name is Melinda Lou Thomas—nicknamed Wendy as a baby—and she's the 31-year-old daughter of Dave Thomas, 60, founder of Wendy's International.

Wendy's International owns, operates, and franchises Wendy's Old Fashioned Hamburgers restaurants, the third largest chain of hamburger restaurants in the United States. Wendy's was the first chain to exceed $1 billion in sales in its first ten years. By its twentieth anniversary in 1989, sales in about 3,800 restaurants had reached $3 billion.

Wendy's success comes from the quality of its service and food. Wendy's meals are quick service, not fast food. Each hamburger is made with fresh (not frozen) meat and cooked to order. To ensure quality of service and individualized meal production, Wendy's requires that only one person may take customer orders. Compare this system to a McDonald's restaurant, where there may be as many as a half-dozen counter workers waiting on customers and serving the precooked hamburgers (made from frozen meat) that sit under a heat lamp.

It was eating in a restaurant of this type that led Dave Thomas to originate a quick-service restaurant serving high quality meals. "I felt the public longed for the kind of fresh-off-the-grill hamburgers I grew up with. With a goal to make a better hamburger, I opened our first restaurant in downtown Columbus [Ohio] and named it for one of my daughters, Wendy."

The superior quality of Wendy's food led to the food industry's *Restaurants & Institutions* ranking the chain's hamburger as number one every year since 1982. Its first menu in 1969 was limited, including only made-to-order hamburgers, french fries, chili, soft drinks, and the Frosty Dairy Dessert. Today, it aggressively pursues food innovations and has introduced the SuperBar, a self-service buffet that focuses on healthy, nutritious food that reflects the ethnic food craze. American's new interest in low-cholestrol chicken is reflected in Wendy's Chicken Sandwich and in the variety of chicken sandwich entrees. Nutrition trends are also reflected in Wendy's Hot Stuffed Baked Potatoes, which began the "meal-in-a-potato" craze. Wendy's secret recipe chili is also one of its top sellers and is made cost-effective by utilizing the 100 percent ground beef that isn't needed for hamburgers.

It's poignant that Dave Thomas started an internationally known family business using a daughter's image as its trademark because, as a baby, Dave was given up for adoption. His hard luck continued when, at age five, his adoptive mother died. His father remarried a series of women and moved from state to state. Worse still were his father's beatings, although Dave told a Columbus magazine that he doesn't like to go "overboard on this abuse stuff."

The high points of Dave's childhood were at dinner when his father was between wives. Then father and son would eat their evening meal in restaurants. Dave's father was always silent during the meal, allowing Dave to watch the other adults—mothers and fathers who would talk and joke with their children during the meal. This experience taught Dave what families should be and kindled his interest in restaurant work.

Dave learned he was adopted when he was 13. Although he was angry at having been deceived, the knowledge liberated him emotionally from his abusive father. But he was still deeply saddened by his past. "I wasn't proud that I'd been born out of wedlock. I'm still not proud of it," he has said.

Dave dropped out of school in tenth grade to work as a waiter. The idea of raising a family became especially important to him as he bounced between various restaurant jobs. In 1954, Dave married Lorraine, and they soon had five children.

Dave met an unknown white-suited eccentric, Colonel Harland Sanders, in the mid-'50s when Colonel Sanders was distributing his fried chicken to Ohio restaurants. In 1956, over Colonel Sanders' reservations, Dave and a partner opened a restaurant that served only Colonel Sanders Kentucky Fried Chicken. The restaurant became the first Kentucky Fried Chicken franchise and originated take-out chicken in a bucket. By 1968, Dave was a millionaire, boasting the only house in Ohio with a swimming pool shaped like a chicken. But after a disagreement with Colonel Sanders' headquarters staff, Dave sold his interest and joined Arthur Treacher's Fish and Chips chain.

But serving a fresh, grilled, quick-service hamburger was still Dave's goal. He opened the first Wendy's restaurant in Columbus in 1969. (That year, McDonald's already had 1,200 restaurants.) In star attendance was eight-year-old freckled Wendy, wearing a long blue and white pinafore dress, with her hair styled in pigtails sticking out above each ear and tied with blue ribbons kept in place by pipe cleaners. "Dad wanted a name that was easy to remember," Wendy told *People* magazine, "and he wanted an all-American mug. I was red-headed and had freckles and buckteeth, so I got elected."

Dave expanded slowly and didn't leave his position with Arthur Treacher's until 1972, when he opened his first out-of-state Wendy's. Franchising started in 1973, with Wendy's pioneering regional—rather than individual—restaurant franchising. By 1992, two-thirds of the restaurants were franchises and the remainder were company owned.

Although Dave was building a financial foundation for his family, he wasn't home too often. Wendy says, "I used to wish that, as a family, we could have gone on a picnic." The children missed him and then, when he did come home, they disliked his strict discipline. (When Dave left the company's daily operations in 1982, he and his adult children began spending more time together, and the earlier strained relations healed.)

Wendy was more fortunate than some of her siblings because Dave often took her to Wendy's restaurant openings and annual conventions. When she was only 16, she gave a speech to 1,500 franchisees at one of these meetings. She was always proud to be the mainstay of the chain's image, despite the frequent teasing she received from acquaintances, and she looked forward to working at the firm's corporate office during summers.

In 1975, Dave took the company public while remaining its largest shareholder. (In 1992, his shares were worth close to $7 million.) Wendy's first national network ad was televised in 1977. In 1979, the company entered Europe. Five years later, the famous "Where's the Beef?" spot premiered.

However, although Dave remains on the company's board, his move out of management occurred shortly before the firm's mid-'80s downward spiral. Also, Dave Thomas returned in 1989 to appear in Wendy's advertising. Consumers show a higher recognition of these ads than any other in the firm's history. By 1991, its fortunes had turned around while other competitive chains were experiencing a slump.

Wendy Thomas has an entrepreneurial bent that appears to have been inspired by her father. Continuing her interest in her namesake company, Wendy wrote her senior paper at the University of Florida on the influence of children-directed advertising on Wendy's adult market. Wendy used her business major when she joined her husband in managing a country club.

Wendy decided in the early '90s that her true vocation lay with the company her father had founded. She and her husband purchased a Wendy's franchise, which consists of several Wendy's restaurants in Dallas, Texas. She enjoys this entrepreneurial challenge. For the moment, she believes it unlikely that she and her husband will uproot their two young children to work in the company's Dublin, Ohio headquarters.

Few Dallas customers recognize their restaurant's namesake when Wendy stops off at one of her franchises. And although the pigtails have been abandoned for a more sophisticated, dress-for-success hairstyle, it's reassuring to see that Wendy still has freckles.

Dave comments, "I know there were times when she wished her name wasn't Wendy. When you name something after someone, that's a lot of responsibility."

It's a burden that Wendy gladly shoulders. Even while at college and working elsewhere, Wendy continued her role, with Dave, as the company's good-will ambassador. After all, this woman—who hasn't walked into a McDonald's restaurant in more than 20 years—continues as the voice on many Wendy's television commercials that feature her dad.

Leonard Lauder

"Our goal is for Origins to be one of the five largest cosmetics companies in the United States by the year 2000."

Estée Lauder, Inc.
New York, New York

Business:	Makeup, skin care, toiletries and fragrance sold through department stores
Best Known Product Lines:	Estée Lauder; Clinique Laboratories Inc.; Aramis Inc.; Prescriptives Inc.; Origins Natural Resources Inc.
Founded:	Incorporated in 1946 by Estée and Joseph Lauder
Family Executives:	Estée Lauder, Chairman; Leonard A. Lauder, President and CEO; Evelyn H. Lauder, Senior Corporate Vice President; William Lauder, Vice President and General Manager, Origins
Family History:	Third generation
Family Ownership:	100 percent
Family Board Membership:	No formal board, operates with finance committee
Traded:	Privately held
Net Sales:	$2,200,000,000 1991 (estimated) 2,093,000,000 1990 (estimated) 1,900,000,000 1989 (estimated)
Net Earnings:	Will not disclose

ESTEE LAUDER, INC.

Will Green Turn to Gold?

William Lauder, General Manager and Vice President,
Origins Natural Resources, Inc.

It would be premature, according to an Estée Lauder Inc. spokeswoman, for William Lauder—grandson of Estée and son of Leonard and Evelyn Lauder—to speak about the company's newest line, Origins Natural Resources, Inc. This is surprising, because William, 32, has been running the Origins unit since it was started in 1990. But if this Benchwarmer is presented by his own company as a little green, at least his image is in keeping with the natural and environmentally conscious nature of Origins products.

East meets West in the Origins approach. The line combines the use of essential oils from flowers and plants to cleanse, protect, and nourish the skin, with the latest skin-care technology of moisture binders and free-radical neutralizers. In keeping with the company's philosophy, Origins uses recycled paper for its minimalist packing and its brochures; the products do not use petroleum-derived ingredients or aerosols; the company recycles containers; and products are not tested on animals. As William described Origins to *New York* magazine, "Our mantra is 'respect for the consumer, the environment, and animals.' "

After six years of development at a reputed cost of $20 million, Origins was added to the other Estée Lauder companies: Estée Lauder USA (the flagship line), Estée Lauder International, Clinique Laboratories, Prescriptives, and Aramis. The Estée Lauder companies occupy an enviable position as the number one cosmetic firm, racking up an estimated 38.5 percent market share in 1991 of all business at U.S. department store cosmetic counters. It is the largest privately owned cosmetic company in the world and ranked number 58 on the 1991 *Forbes* list of America's largest private companies. Estimated worldwide sales for that year were $2.2 billion.

A handful of names come to mind when speaking of great American skin care and cosmetic firms. Helena Rubenstein, Elizabeth Arden, Georgette Klinger (see GEORGETTE KLINGER SALONS), and Esteé Lauder will be remembered as the empresses of American beauty. But it was Estée who founded the world's largest family-owned skin care and cosmetic company.

Estée was born Josephine Esther Mentzer around 1908 (the exact year of her birth is a secret as closely guarded as the formula for Youth Dew). Nicknamed "Esty," she grew up in Queens, the daughter of Eastern Europe immigrants. In the '30s, she experimented with skin care products developed from the formulas of her Hungarian chemist uncle, eventually selling the skin creams in a Manhattan hair salon.

Estée's drive to succeed was blocked, she felt at one point, by her 1930 marriage to the relatively easygoing Joseph Lauder. Even the birth of their son Leonard in 1933 couldn't prevent their divorce in 1939. But Joe was more a part of Estée than she'd realized. The couple remarried in 1942 with the understanding that he would give up his job and join Estée's skin-cream-and-lipstick venture. In 1944, Ronald was born, and in 1946, the Estée Lauder company was incorporated.

On vacations and at parties, Estée would suggest providing makeovers for guests, an offer usually accepted. The well-dressed, hazel-eyed blonde with the impeccable complexion inspired confidence in the women she sought to make her customers. Estée instituted the industry practice of a gift with a purchase by pressing free samples of lipstick or powder upon her customers and by providing table favors at charity functions. (The late Princess Grace of Monaco once remarked to an interviewer, "Mrs. Lauder is such a nice person. I don't know her very well, but she keeps sending all these things.")

Once women began to recognize the Estée Lauder name, the next hurdle was convincing managers at Saks Fifth Avenue that this mom-and-pop operation could produce the necessary volume. Taking an incredible risk, Estée and Joe stopped selling to salons in order to focus on department stores. Using an approach that the company continues, even now with its 10,000 employees,

Estée says the family pitched in with "four hands: Joe's and mine" to fill the Saks order.

Leonard, their oldest son, remembers that during his adolescence his mother once traveled 25 weeks of the year. During her absence, he was kept busy making deliveries to Saks on his bike before school. Teenage Leonard's duties included attending Estée and Joe's business meetings with their accountant-lawyer. When Leonard was 16, his parents planned to make him temporary plant manager while they were on vacation. Estée wrote in her autobiography, "It was a risk, yes, but one has to risk to succeed." Alas, the vacation plans were scratched when the "plant manager" came down with chicken pox.

Profits boomed in 1953 with Youth Dew, a bath oil with a sweet intense presence that can substitute for perfume. It's a strong seller even today, with sales greater than $100 million. In 1960, Estée Lauder International was launched at a Harrods counter in London. Within a dozen years, the company was selling products in more than 70 countries, and in 1989, Estée received worldwide attention when she opened Estée Lauder boutiques in Budapest and in Moscow, two blocks from the Kremlin.

If Estée will be remembered as the founder of a global cosmetics company, then her son Leonard will be recognized as the builder. Leonard graduated from the Wharton School at the University of Pennsylvania and went into the Navy, serving as a supply officer on an aircraft carrier. He joined the company in 1958, when sales were a relatively modest $800,000. Starting a trend, the company introduced men's grooming products with the Aramis line in 1964.

"I believe only a privately owned company could consider risking a large amount of money on a new, untried product like a men's toiletries line," Estée wrote in her autobiography. "If shareholders were involved, we'd have to show a steady, inexorably upward rise in profit if offering prices were not to be affected."

The Lauders consult only each other when it comes to making important decisions. Leonard says their accountants and lawyers are "great accountants and lawyers. We need them, but we make the business decisions." Estée says she avoids committee votes, preferring to rely on her instinct: "When I knew something was right, I ran with it." The family has no formal board of directors because they do not want outsiders to have authority. In an interview with *Family Business* magazine, Leonard said, "Just to have a board and have them be powerless doesn't make any sense." (The company does have outside members on its finance committee.)

One decision the Lauders made was to launch hypoallergenic Clinique in 1968. Trying to arrive on the international market before Revlon Inc.'s hypoallergenic Eltherea line, family members met in Vienna to spread out to the world's major department stores. With no advance notice, the Lauders arrived at stores to set up counters. Clinique beat Eltherea by one week. "As a family-run business, we could move fast!" said Estée.

Still, both the Clinique and Aramis lines were in the red for years: Clinique had lost $20 million before breaking even in 1972, and Aramis was withdrawn and reintroduced in 1967 before becoming the best-selling group of men's toiletries in department stores. Leonard told one writer sometime after Clinique's introduction, "If we had been public, I would never have launched Clinique. We took a bath before it started paying off."

Ronald took over the Clinique line as general manager but appeared to be biding his time at the company. After all, the age difference between him and Leonard meant that the older brother had a good solid jump on him at the company. Talking of Ronald's entrance, Leonard admitted to *Business Week*, "I had already hired everybody. It was my show."

Although Ronald had become vice president of marketing and sales for all of Estée Lauder, Inc. (and had also headed the company's international operations), he left in 1983 to take a political appointment under President Reagan as Deputy Assistant Secretary for Defense. In 1985 he was appointed ambassador to Austria. Ronald was a New York City mayoral candidate in 1989, stirring up controversy over the amount of money he spent on the race. In 1990, he founded Central European Development Corp. with about $40 million of his own money (around 40 percent of the company's capital). Referring to the length of time it takes to build an Eastern bloc investment, Ronald, who learned the value of patience from his family's business, told *Forbes*, "It's a five-to-ten year call." Estée would rather he'd stayed in the family business.

No matter how much Estée misses Ronald, it's Leonard who has been credited with reorganizing the company and turning the new product lines into subsidiary companies. It may have been Estée's decision to refuse to dilute product prestige by selling to drugstores, but it was Leonard who insisted that different product lines could maintain consistent brand images and still protect the integrity of the flagship Estée Lauder line. (Each line has its own marketing and sales department.) For all of Estée's considerable talents, it is second-generation Leonard who has all the markings of a true entrepreneur.

Additionally , the short- and long-term goal-setting that pushed the company's growth are attributed to Leonard's management skills. According to Lee Israel's unauthorized biography of Estée, Leonard accelerated volume growth by working with store heads to plan yearly goals with detailed tactical strategies. When department store managers achieved Leonard's high-volume predictions, they were convinced. The company uses the same approach in the '90s: Representatives meet with store buyers and specify plans for six-month periods.

Leonard succeeded Estée as president in 1973. By the late '70s, he'd significantly increased the skin treatment development budget, again foreseeing a new interest in skin care. Facial treatment products accounted for about 30 percent of the company's revenues in 1991.

In 1979 the company introduced Prescriptives, a line founded on the idea that makeup should be based on individual skintones. This unique "Colorprinting" appeals to the young professionals at whom it's targeted. *Business Week* reported that by 1989, Prescriptives was the fastest growing Estée Lauder line (although it took an investment of nearly $40 million before it turned a profit). In 1982, Leonard became CEO and said that Estée will remain chairman as long as she lives. It's thought that Leonard's wife Evelyn, who is senior vice president, will become the company's symbol when Estée can no perform her figurehead duties.

Joe's death in 1983 began an unhappy tax battle between the Lauder family and the IRS. The family bought his stock for $28 million and paid taxes on that value. The IRS stated the stock value was underestimated and set the worth at $90 million. The tax issue pivots on the stockholder agreements that the Lauders put into place in 1976. Was the purpose to retain family control or to reduce estate taxes? Despite the Lauders' request for an early favorable ruling, the Tax Court case will eventually go to trial.

Although Estée will remain at the helm "whether she works one day a year or 365 days a year," Leonard told his sons that they weren't welcome at the company until they'd gained experience—and self-respect—elsewhere. "Once you know that you can succeed on your own, then it's okay to come into the family business, but not before," he told *Family Business*.

William, the oldest son, went into an executive training program at R. H. Macy & Company, eventually becoming an assistant buyer and then divisional merchandiser in Macy's Dallas store. (Earlier, during college, he had worked for a summer in the Department of Treasury for Assistant Secretary Marc Leland, later financial adviser to Gordon Getty [see GORDON GETTY].) William joined his parents' company in 1986 as regional marketing director of Clinique U.S.

The original plan was for William to start at another division, but Leonard considered its lead manager too insecure to supervise a family member. "There are people who are terrified that they will end up being replaced by family members," but the Clinique division head "was delighted to have him," according to Leonard in his *Family Business* interview.

William moved over to manage the Eastern Field Sales division of Prescriptives before the 1990 announcement of his appointment as vice president and general manager of Origins. Younger brother Gary received a graduate degree from Stanford University and is now a venture capitalist like his uncle. Gary may eventually be interested in joining the company. Ronald's two daughters Aerin and Jane are still in school, but Aerin has announced her intention to start at the company in the fall of 1992, after college graduation. (Apparently the young women in the family are not expected to begin their careers elsewhere, as are the young men.)

It was serendipitous that the company was talking about a new line just when it was William's turn to step up to bat. "The best thing [children going into the family business] can do is to find a bit of turf that they can handle themselves, one that the father and mother haven't dealt with before," expounded Leonard to *Family Business*.

What better person to run Origins, the product line Leonard characterized as "an expression of the '90s," than the newest business member of the Lauder family? A line that hypes "skin re-training" and "Sensory Therapy" (products that supposedly lessen tension), as well as the upcoming "No Makeup Makeup," appeals most to younger people. Some of the Origins statements seem to be written with an eye toward political correctness. The ad for pressed powder reads, "One touch of nature makes the whole world kin."

If this approach seems a tad mystical, the botanical line with herbal ingredients has been purposely designed for youthful customers. These new shoppers are needed. A dual threat to the company comes from what *The Wall Street Journal* in 1990 characterized as the "somewhat stuffy image" of the Estée Lauder companies and from the decline of department store sales.

To counteract these negative forces, the plan is to gear Origins prices to starter salaries to attract women who can't easily afford Prescriptives and Clinique and to phase in the sale of Origins through company-owned, free-standing retail stores. Retail stores will also help Origins compete against such similar lines as the hip Body Shop International PLC of the United Kingdom, which sells products through its own Body Shops. Origins stores will open at a slow pace while the line continues to be sold in department stores like Nordstrom's and Neiman-Marcus. The first independent Origins store opened in mid-1991 in Harvard Square, Cambridge, Massachusetts.

The questions remains whether Estée Lauder Inc. can continue to grow at the rate established by Leonard. In unit terms, the cosmetic industry is stagnant, and the women's fragrance market is flat. Fewer customers shop at department stores, whose future causes Leonard to lose sleep. The masthead Estée Lauder brand is graying. Although it is still the country's best-selling line in department stores, its first market share decline in many years occurred in 1991.

Perhaps only a company like Estée Lauder Inc.—which prides itself on quick and decisive responses—can continue to be a leader in this environment. Looking toward the challenges of the '90s, in 1989 the flag ship line's advertising dropped the traditional American look to promote a sophisticated European look. With the new advertising, international growth of the line (already about 50 percent of revenues) shot upward. In 1990, 37-year-old Robin Burns, who had successfully launched Obsession and Eternity fragrances as former head of Calvin Klein Cosmetics, was appointed president of Estée Lauder USA. And the company continued its practice of introducing a new line each decade with the addition of Origins, which may add coveted market shares by taking them from companies like upstart Body Shop.

On the other hand, even the new line carries questions. The planned introduction of Origins' Honey Elixirs and essential-oil capsules, intended to be swallowed as an internal beauty aid, was hampered by the Federal Drug Administration's announcement that the agency would regulate these capsules. "We have our hands tied by the FDA to stay out from under the drug umbrella," William told Condée Nast's *Allure* magazine in late 1991. (The FDA does not allow cosmetic companies to claim internal benefits.) Similarly, the concern for health has led potential Origins customers to question purchasing a makeup foundation that does not contain a sunscreen.

The Lauder family's sound instinct and quick decision-making will probably help the company retain its place in the industry. After all, this is one company that sees the race as a marathon, not a sprint. Speaking of Origins, William said in 1991, "We're thinking in decades, not quarterly." He reiterated, "Our goal is for Origins to be one of the five largest cosmetics companies in the United States by the year 2000."

Leonard Lauder touted the advantages of an entrepreneurial, privately held family business in competition with public companies to *Business Week*: "There is little that a professional manager can do to fight off a well-financed, well-educated, aggressive entrepreneur."

But given flat industry sales and the decline of department stores, the Lauders may end up their own best customers for the Origins Sensory Therapy tension-releasing product, "Peace of Mind."

"We have tried to create idealized situations that people fantasize about."

J. Crew Group, Inc.
New York, New York

Business:	Women and men's clothing sold through mail-order and retail outlets; direct selling of women's clothes and furnishings
Best Known Products:	J. Crew; Clifford & Wills; Popular Club Plan
Founded:	Popular Club Plan founded 1947 by Mitchell Cinader
Family Executives:	Arthur Cinader, Chairman, J. Crew Group Inc. Emily Cinader Woods, President, J. Crew Inc.
Family History:	Third generation
Family Board Membership:	3 family members of 6 directors
Family Ownership:	100 percent
Traded:	Privately held
Net Sales:	$460,000,000 1991 (estimated) 400,000,000 1990 (estimated) 320,000,000 1989 (estimated)
Net Earnings:	Will not disclose

J. CREW GROUP, INC.

Merchant of Lifestyle

Emily Cinader Woods
President, J. Crew, Inc. and
J. Crew Group, Inc.

J. Crew's clothing epitomizes a clean-cut and scrubbed look: comfortable cotton and other natural fibers in well-bred earth tones. It's updated tradition with a bit of a fashion twist. The company's customers are upper-middle class, young, and professional (or perhaps this is what they aspire to be). They want honest clothing for weekend wear—nothing that's obvious, and nothing that shouts. The J. Crew image is a small step up from The Gap and a big step down from pricey Calvin Klein.

The company's young president, Emily Cinader Woods, 31, is similarly square-jawed and direct. She heads a privately held company whose revenues in 1991 accounted for more than half the parent company's estimated $460 million in sales. Emily recognizes that for many of her customers, J. Crew clothes express a coveted lifestyle, a way of living that Emily's own family embodies.

The J. Crew story starts with Emily's grandfather, Mitchell Cinader, who founded the Popular Club Plan in 1947. The Cinader family still owns Popular Club Plan, a direct-selling operation that offers moderately priced women's clothing and furnishings. Emily's father, Arthur Cinader, 65, joined Popular Club Plan in 1954 when the business was only a few years old, and soon took charge of the company whose parent corporation was named Popular Merchandise Inc.

Arthur's success with Popular Club Plan enabled his wife and five children to summer at Nantucket and winter at Vail. "My father lived the life Ralph Lauren would *like* to have lived," Emily pointed out to the magazine *Manhattan, inc.*

The oldest child, Emily grew up in suburban New Jersey and in Albuquerque, New Mexico. She went to prep school in Michigan, then chose the University of Denver, as much for its skiing possibilities as for its academics. Emily didn't seem to be personally ambitious beyond marriage and children.

In the late '70s and early '80s, while Emily was away at college, her father noted the growth of clothing catalogs like L.L. Bean and Talbots. In early 1983, he set out to capture a piece of the rapidly expanding market for women's classic clothing. He called the new company J. Crew, a name suggesting casual, collegiate clothing. That first year, sales were an estimated $3 million.

Soon after the first J. Crew catalog appeared, Emily entered the company for what she thought would be an interim period. "I've never planned to work with my father, but I couldn't refuse his offer [of the post of assistant buyer]," she told *Harper's Bazaar*. Her interest and dedication to the company were rewarded with a promotion to chief designer, although she'd had no business or design experience prior to joining J. Crew. (In between semesters studying marketing and finance, Emily had bankrolled her frequent ski trips by waitressing.)

The early catalogs featured a mix of clothing brands, but Emily wanted the company to sell its own brand exclusively, in part so that she could realize her vision for J. Crew apparel. When Emily became chief designer, she decreed that henceforth J. Crew's clothes would never use polyester blends.

The image Emily established is the one that characterizes the merchandise today. "The evolution of J. Crew has been the evolution of Emily," says Arnold Cohen, president and COO of J. Crew Group, Inc. "As the business grew, and as we realized that to be unique we would have to develop our own product, Emily emerged as the leader.

"She has a very clean, crisp, articulate design vision. She believes in simplicity and quality and is very strong on the details," Cohen says.

Promoting the J. Crew look is a priority of Emily's that involves a myriad of details. At the beginning, she supervised each of the catalog's photography locations, knowing that the company sells clothes by representing a lifestyle. In 1988, when Emily was named president (while still in her 20s), younger sister Maud, 26, took over the shoots. Emily, however, still approves the layout for each page.

"We have tried to create idealized situations that people fantasize about," Emily told *Savvy Woman* as she described the biking-and-backgammon catalog scenes. "The idea is to sell to people who say, 'I want to live in the Hamptons, I want that lifestyle, so I will buy that shirt.'"

Indeed, as J. Crew clothes have the look Emily herself prefers, the catalog models bear a strong resemblance to the company's president. (Three-quarters of customers are women.) Emily wears no jewelry; J. Crew models wear no jewelry. Emily appears distant and cool and wears her brown hair short and blunt cut; so do they. Emily is an attractive woman; it's easy to see how J. Crew's unisex clothes would flatter her slim, boyish figure.

For all that this implies about Emily the person, Emily the businesswoman has moved J. Crew from its imitative origins to a company known for its individualized look. When sales from J. Crew grew to about half the parent company's revenue, Arthur changed the parent company's name to J. Crew Group, Inc., a move that reflected the new status of the company Emily headed. Also in the J. Crew Group, besides Popular Club Plan, is another catalog business offering moderate-priced women's career apparel, Clifford & Wills.

Only a few blips have appeared on the horizon to mar this idyllic situation. The first came in 1987, when two J. Crew executives—Ted Pamperin and Jeff Aschkenes—walked out to found Tweeds, their own classic, yet more cosmopolitan, women's clothing catalog. A dozen or so J. Crew employees subsequently defected to Tweeds.

Additionally, the entire catalog industry is threatened by costs that have risen above the inflation rate. (See LILLIAN VERNON INC.) Mail order still feels the effect of the 1989 postal increases and suffers from the general economic downturn. Additionally, new catalog companies have glutted the market. Hurt by these changes in the industry, J. Crew's catalog heyday appears to have taken place in the mid-'80s. When nationwide catalog sales were increasing by 15 percent each year, J. Crew saw an explosive annual growth of up to 30 percent. When mail order increased by only four to eight percent in 1991, J. Crew's growth was 15 percent, only half its usual rate.

Part of the problem may be that J. Crew's market is approaching saturation—the company seems to have fewer new shoppers to recruit. Arthur used his own Manhattan apartment house as an example to *The New York Times*: of the Park Avenue building's 130 families, he said 30 are already regular customers of the 14-issue-a-year J. Crew catalog.

"How much more penetration can you get?" he asked.

One way to get around the marketing overload is to increase sales and revenue from each of the already loyal J. Crew customers. Emily has therefore added a more expensive, work-oriented line of jackets and skirts called Collection to the $18 tee-shirts and $54 cotton sweaters already available. The expanded offerings should increase the number of items customers purchase from J. Crew and raise the total dollar expenditure.

The company is also planning an extension into children's clothes and home merchandise. Additionally, the company's order form asks college students for their home address, ensuring that the students will never miss a catalog and that the company will never miss a potential sale.

An alternative to augmenting catalog sales is to turn to retail outlets. J. Crew opened its first 4000-square-foot store in 1989 in Manhattan's tourist spot, South Street Seaport. By the beginning of 1992, the company had added eight more stores in upscale malls, and by the end of that year, it expected to have 15 stores. A total of 45 company-owned stores is envisioned by 1995. The concern also has 23 factory stores for end-of-season clothing and overstock. By 1993, the company will be international, with Japan its first overseas location.

The J. Crew stores offer a different mix from their catalog. The retail shops allow the company a better opportunity to sell their higher-priced office clothes. Who would want to buy a $260 jacket through a catalog without trying it on? Eventually, about half the merchandise in the stores will differ from what's offered in the catalog.

The initial nail-biting during the transition from catalog to a catalog-retail mix eased off when the company had its strongest year in 1991. So far, store sales haven't cannibalized catalog sales.

Although J. Crew has been extraordinarily successful, there's not much room for mistakes in a company that's not as well-capitalized as some of its competitors, like the king of sportswear catalogs, L.L. Bean, and the encroaching Lands' End. (In what has been interpreted as an attempt to fund the J. Crew expansion, Arthur Cinader nearly sold Popular Club Plan to International Epicure, but the agreement fell through in 1989.)

Still, the attempts to raise capital and continue the retail expansion are signs that the Cinaders meet challenges head-on. Arthur is the real driving business practitioner of the company; he brought in managers like Arnold Cohen—who'd gained experience in marketing and merchandising at Bloomingdale's and Gucci America—to develop the J. Crew stores. This was a smart move. Fewer than half the catalogers who open stores survive because the skills necessary for mail-order sales don't translate to the retail world.

Being in a privately held, family-run business doesn't bother Cohen, who sees substantial benefits to this environment. "The lines of communication are fairly direct, the decision-making process is fast, and often decisions are made on the long-term objectives vs. the quarterly result," he says. "There's no question that you're an outsider and not a family member. But in large part, Arthur has made me feel like a member of the family."

So far, so good. Although growth was slower in 1991 as the year closed, J. Crew saw a solid double-digit rise in sales. With more than 50,000 orders coming in each week from the three million people who receive the catalog, it doesn't look as if the retail outlets are hurting the mail-order operation. "The consumer is moving back to traditional value, and our product line represents that," says Cohen.

And millions of American women mirror the personal style of Emily Cinader. Emily herself benefits from the backup of both a closely held family business and its professional management. Appropriately for this purveyor of fantasy, in 1991 Emily married Cary Woods, a Hollywood agent.

SECTION V

THE STEWARDS

Stewards have stepped one or two feet away from the family business and are not involved in management positions. The members of the younger generation of these families maintain an equity position in its business, but they do not hold jobs there.

Many Stewards hold board directorships. As their name implies, Stewards' primary responsibility is to exercise responsible care of their family businesses.

Stewards may work in other companies, or they may just sit back and reap the benefits of inherited wealth, or they may devote most of their time to philanthropy. Marshall Field V is a stunning example of an heir who does good works: As board chairman, Marshall spends each weekday morning at Chicago's famed Art Institute, which his forebears helped found. One of the daughters of Ewing Kauffman, founder of pharmaceutical giant Marion Merrell Dow, serves part time as an officer of a Kauffman family foundation.

STEWARDS USUALLY...

1. have inherited great wealth.
2. do not work for the family business but own a significant stake in the publicly owned company.
3. hold a board directorship to look out for family interests.
4. inherited shares in an older family business of which the founder is no longer alive.

Except for Marshall's own Field Corporation business, which exists primarily to invest his vast wealth, all the other Steward companies are publicly owned.

Some of these Steward board directors may have chosen not to work in the family business because they have different interests. One example is poet and novelist Dan Gerber, director of Gerber baby foods.

Occasionally, the parents of Stewards can be benevolent curmudgeons who actually prevent their children from taking an active role in the business or who block them from inheriting a huge share of the company. Ewing Kauffman doesn't believe that his children or grandchildren should inherit his great fortune. Although he was worth close to a billion dollars just a few years ago, he and his wife have been giving huge chunks of money to philanthropies. The Kauffman children will get only four or five million dollars because "they don't need any more," says Ewing. Nor do they work in the company Ewing helped to found.

Larry Phillips, chairman of shirtmaker Phillips-Van Heusen, told his son and daughter that they should not aspire to make their living in the company founded by their great-great-grandfather. Larry has strong opinions about sons and daughters who work for their parents. "Nepotism is not good for the company, not good for the recipient, and not good for the other executives in the company," he says.

With the April 1992 death of Sam Walton, the Walton family moved into a stewardship position. Brother Rob is a board member who resisted leading Wal-Mart's daily operations, which are instead managed by a nonmember of the family. Two of the other Walton children have businesses of their own, while one of the siblings works within the family's holding company.

Stewards are members of some of America's wealthiest families. Marshall V has a half-billion dollar fortune as does the Kauffman family, even after giving away hundreds of millions. And the four Walton children are worth $4.4 billion—each.

*"The only real tradition is that each succeeding generation
shouldn't blow it."*

Field Corporation
Chicago, Illinois

Business:	Retail, real estate, media
Businesses Founded by Family:	Marshall Field & Co., founded 1881 by great-great-grandfather Marshall Field Chicago *Sun-Times*, founded 1941 by grandfather Marshall Field III (Businesses no longer owned by Field family)
Family History:	Fifth generation; youngest generation is the Steward
Approximate Worth:	$450 million, 1991 *Forbes* 400

FIELD CORPORATION

Fields of Conquest

Marshall Field V

"They all started out with nothing in those days, and the biggest crooks won. I was just lucky to come from a line of successful crooks," jokes Marshall Field V, 50, fifth generation to follow the eponymous founder of a Chicago dry goods empire.

The preeminence of the Marshall Field department store chain means that even today, Marshall Field V and his half-brother Frederick E. (Ted) Field (see TED FIELD) are often identified as the heirs to Marshall Field & Co. department store. In reality, the family has had only tenuous ties to Marshall Field & Co. since 1917 and no financial connection at all since 1956.

Yet people still think Marshall V is the department store heir. "But that's beginning to go away. There's been so much publicity with Dayton Hudson [recent owners of Marshall Field & Co.] that I don't get asked that more than once a month now," laughs Marshall V.

But one thing is certain: "As long as you have the name Marshall Field, everyone figures you ought to pick up the dinner tab."

The Field fortune was kicked off by the retail store kingdom along with the real estate investment fiefdom that accrued to it. And the third generation of Field men added a media empire. It's these three legacies—retail, real estate, and communications—that have provided both the heritage and the finances upon which Marshall V and his step-brother Ted base their separate operations.

The first Marshall Field arrived in Chicago in 1856, hoping to continue work as a dry goods clerk in a city younger than he. (Marshall I was 22 years old while the city, incorporated in 1837, was only 19.) By 1860, he was a full partner in the largest dry-goods store in Chicago that was rapidly changing from a town of muddy, unpaved streets and wooden buildings to a city that would be the second largest in the country. The urban metamorphosis took shape under the firm hand of the leading Chicago businessmen of the day: Potter Palmer, Cyrus McCormick, George Pullman, and Philip Armour.

With men like these as his contemporaries, no wonder Marshall I resolutely shouted instructions to the employees and firemen attempting to save his building from the Great Chicago Fire that long night in 1871. Marshall I was able to rescue his business records and the store's most expensive goods. More important, he was one of the few merchants who'd bothered to cover their businesses with fire insurance, a relative rarity in the United States. While Marshall I tried to decide where to rebuild his department store, planning first on the city's east side, then on the west, then finally back east at Wabash and State Street, he was also amassing the real estate fortune that eventually rivaled his merchandising empire.

With all its other partners bought out by 1881, the business now named Marshall Field & Co. had profits of more than $2 million annually and a sales philosophy that stemmed from Field's edict, "Give the lady what she wants!" This success rested on the company's dual position as a retail store and as a midwestern wholesaler.

The network established by the Field company was interwoven with the eventual fortunes of other businesses and their heirs. Its mills, for example, ultimately led to the formation of Fieldcrest Cannon, Inc., the fifth largest textile manufacturer in the United States. And some of Marshall I's real estate investments included the property on which Chicago's Merchandise Mart stands; that venture is, of course, a cornerstone of the Joseph P. Kennedy family fortune.

Although Marshall I was an astute businessman, some of his characteristics were not those important to a happy marriage. His wife Nannie lived abroad most of her life with the couple's son and daughter and, it was rumored, was dependent on popular ladies' remedies containing alcohol and opium. One time a friend bluntly remarked, "Marshall, you have no home, no family...nothing but money."

His son Marshall II never worked in the Field stores, choosing as an adult to remain in Europe. (In a sense, a nephew of Marshall I, Stanley Field [1875–1964], took the place of a son by serving as an executive with Marshall Field & Co. for most of his life.)

Marshall II's son, Marshall III, received more attention from his doting grandfather than his father ever had. Marshall I visited his grandson frequently, despite the length of time it took to make an ocean voyage in the 1890s and the burden on him as director or major shareholder of more than 30 American companies. As the most influential Chicagoan in a decade when the city's population doubled, Marshall I stepped in with advice and guidance for other Chicago business interests. Marshall I saved the Pullman company after its labor strike and was influential in having Charles Schwab locate United States Steel (now USX) outside Chicago in Gary, Indiana rather than in Pennsylvania.

Marshall I was also a Democrat, a political allegiance unusual for a leading businessman and one that has influenced the family to this day. However, he feared that immigrants streaming into Chicago were anarchists and Red sympathizers. Occasionally, he lent his Field delivery trucks to the Chicago police when they needed extra vehicles to control labor protests. He also pushed for the establishment of Fort Sheridan on Chicago's North Shore, firm in his belief that soldiers would be needed nearby to quell riots. (Not surprisingly, he ordered union organizers thrown out of the Marshall Field department stores.)

Although distrustful of the immigrants whose labor would turn Chicago into a great city, Marshall I saw philanthropy as a stimulant to Chicago's growth. His serious philanthropic contributions began in his 40s—and he helped found the Chicago Art Institute and the

University of Chicago (although the university is more closely associated with the Rockefeller family). He was also the biggest backer of the 1890 Chicago Exhibition, which led to his founding the Field Museum of Natural History for permanent storage of the Exhibition's artifacts.

The great tragedy of Marshall I's life was the gunshot suicide of his son Marshall II in 1905. Rumors persisted that the suicide was murder and that the location was not the Field home but rather the notorious Everleigh sisters' brothel. But Marshall III, the 12-year-old son, attested that he'd heard the shot while playing at home.

Soon after the death of his son, Marshall I engaged in a New Year's suburban golf game. The players, who included the late president's son, Robert Todd Lincoln, defeated the snow covering the course by using red golf balls. Following the game, the Field magnate developed a head cold and subsequently died.

Seven weeks after losing his father, Marshall III found himself grandfatherless as well—and heir to a $120 million legacy, including the world's largest department store. (A much smaller inheritance went to Marshall I's granddaughter.)

This fortune did not make Marshall III the world's richest boy, as claimed by many newspapers of the day, but it did mean that when he finished his education in England he could take his business training very casually. Marshall III's lack of interest in the family department store was apparent, and by the time he was 24, he and his family had sold all but 10 percent of Marshall Field & Co.

With part of his proceeds, Marshall III built a considerable art collection. He also became a bond salesman and an investment banker and then turned to publishing, which would serve as his new political voice. With his first wife, he had three children (including Marshall IV, father of the contemporary half-brothers Marshall V and Ted.)

Marshall III showed a burgeoning interest in the newspaper business and in 1940 started (with publisher Ralph Ingersoll) the New York daily *PM Magazine*, which ardently supported Roosevelt's New Deal. Marshall III also intended to establish a Chicago newspaper as a mainstream countervoice to the conservative Chicago *Tribune*, whose publisher was the elderly isolationist, Colonel Robert McCormick. In 1941, the Chicago *Sun* was born.

For years, the progressive *Sun* fought the political influence of the more powerful *Tribune* as well as that paper's personal aspersions against the Field family. For example, during World War II a *Tribune* editorial called 49-year-old Marshall III a "slacker" for not fighting in the armed forces, conveniently ignoring both his age and his previous World War I front-line battle duty. The *Sun's* editorial replied in kind: "You are getting addled, Colonel McCormick."

Marshall III came into the balance of his inheritance in 1943 and continued to pour his own money into *PM Magazine*, and deducted the personal losses from his income tax. However, his conservative foes pushed Congress for what was to be called "the Marshall Field amendment," which limited the number of years an individual could deduct losses from a particular operation on a personal return. Marshall III quickly incorporated as Field Enterprises, Inc. and founded a communications empire with his inherited fortune.

In addition to Marshall III's newspaper collection, Field Enterprises bought Simon & Schuster, the publishing house, in 1944. In 1945 it acquired an enormously profitable business, the World Book Encyclopedia and Childcraft Company. Even though *PM Magazine* was sold in 1948 and soon ceased publication altogether, its supplement, *Parade* magazine, was retained by Field Enterprises and continued to be one of its money-making publications. Radio, then television stations, were added to the company. (This was before the Federal Communication Commission's regulations prohibited mutual ownership of newspapers, radio, and television stations.)

To strengthen his hand against the *Tribune*, Marshall III also bought the Chicago *Times*. In 1947, he merged his papers into a morning newspaper, the Chicago *Sun-Times*.

Marshall III, like his grandfather, believed in philanthropy and established the Field Foundation for social justice and civil rights causes. Although he continued his financial support of conventional institutions, he also focused on aid to black and disadvantaged children and contributed heavily to higher education through Roosevelt University, expressly set up for Chicago's working-class students.

By the end of World War II, his son Marshall IV had returned from the war and happily entered Field Enterprises. Marshall IV had already married Joanne Bass, daughter of the governor of New Hampshire and a member of the wealthy Texas Bass family. The couple had two children, including Marshall V, born in Charlottesville, Virginia in 1941.

By 1950, when Marshall IV became publisher a few years after his entrance into Field Enterprises, the *Sun-Times* was no longer losing money. But a number of readers were caught off balance when they realized that Marshall IV was not as enamored of the Democratic party as his father had been. Although Marshall III found Marshall IV's identification with the liberal wing of the Republican party distasteful, he had to admit that his son was also responsible for the sound financial operations and dedication to quality that gave rise to the *Sun-Times'* steady increase in circulation.

To the surprise of those who watched for political fireworks between father and son, Marshall III displayed grudging admiration of his son. He wrote to him after the *Sun-Times* came out for Dwight Eisenhower in the 1952 presidential race: "When the editorial leadership of the paper was turned over to you, I was certain that you would assume an independent and direct attitude, and this you have done."

Marshall III died in late 1956, having outlived Colonel McCormick by one year. Field Enterprises was left to Marshall IV with a trust for the two grandsons, Marshall V (by Joanne Bass) and Ted (by second wife Katherine Woodruff, who had married Marshall IV in 1950 following his divorce from Joanne). Just as Marshall III had enjoyed the lion's share of his grandfather's estate at the expense of his sister, so did he also leave his son and two grandsons a vast fortune in comparison with the inheritance of his five daughters and his granddaughters.

Marshall IV continued the family quest to beat the Chicago *Tribune* in circulation, selling *Parade* for the cash ($24 million) to buy the afternoon Chicago *Daily News* in 1959. (He also sold the last of the family's preferred stock in Marshall Field & Co. to help settle estate taxes.) Shortly before the *Daily News* purchase, Field Enterprises built a new building, overlooking the Chicago River and Michigan Avenue, to house the editorial staff and the printing press for both newspapers.

Unfortunately, the stress of the business transactions following his father's death was too much for a fragile Marshall IV.

Hospitalized for six months, he suffered from symptoms now believed to indicate manic depression. For Field Enterprises, his illness meant that professional managers gained control; for the Field family, the outcome was that Field trustees came into more power. The impact on the two newspapers was to emphasize cost-cutting over quality, and the papers never gained the circulation nor the prestige that Marshall IV had sought. His death in 1965 at age 49 was a shock to the family and the city.

Marshall IV's personal estate, estimated at $25 million, went to his widow and six children: the two (including Marshall V, then 24) from his first marriage; the three (including Ted, then 13) from his second marriage; and the infant daughter from his third marriage. Additionally, 80 percent of the stock in Field Enterprises was to be split between his two sons, Marshall V and Ted, when they reached the age of 25. Compared to the share of 40 percent to each son, the four daughters received a scant five percent each. The legacy followed the pattern of the trust established by Marshall III nearly two decades earlier.

Marshall V dutifully moved to Chicago upon receiving his inheritance in Field Enterprises. He'd lived on the East Coast most of his life, first in New Hampshire and then, after his mother's remarriage to a CIA official, in suburban Washington D.C. Marshall V graduated from Deerfield Academy and from Harvard University with a degree in fine arts. When he entered Field Enterprises he gave up both the possibility of a career in the art world and his new interest in retailing—he has said that the short time he spent selling men's suits in Bloomingdale's was the most satisfying of his career. (Marshall V also enjoyed his short stints hawking World Book Encyclopedias door-to-door to families who never suspected the identity of their salesman.)

When he returned to Chicago, he'd spent so little time there he "didn't know where State Street was." The advantage to being raised outside his family's seat of power, he said, was that growing up away from Chicago kept him from feeling pressured about ultimately going into the family business.

In a carefully devised five-year plan, Marshall V began to train in each of the Field Enterprises operations. But he tired of the training program after four years and cut it short to become, at age 28, the youngest newspaper publisher in the country. (Half-brother Ted, 19, was just beginning college.)

Marshall V was head of both the family and its business: he was in control of a privately owned company with more than $200 million in annual revenue and $10 million in estimated profits. He was also the family's titular head as its only member on the four-person Field Foundation board and the individual designated to be its tie-breaker.

With all these activities—plus his personal philanthropies—to monitor, it's no wonder that Marshall V preferred his role of chairman (gained in 1972 at age 31) and delegated the daily running of Field Enterprises to professional managers. (Not that he didn't keep his eye on operations: Marshall V had a hand in the hiring—and firing—of many top staff at the newspapers.)

A key direction both for the company and, ultimately, for Marshall V himself, was the decision to enter the real estate market. In 1979, he acquired the Boston-based firm Cabot, Cabot & Forbes, a venture made possible by the $120 million raised from the sale of World Book and Childcraft and through leverage. To protect the money Marshall V had put into the sale, some of CC&F's assets were immediately sold to repay his investment. Marshall also made the difficult decision to close down the Chicago *Daily News* because of its increasingly poor circulation figures.

He had married Jan Best Connelly in the '60s while still in his 20s. The couple had a son, Marshall VI, but they divorced a few years later. Young Marshall VI would visit for extended periods of time from his home in Pennsylvania. Marshall V recounts the time he brought his son to the *Sun-Times* office and let him remain during a meeting. Marshall VI was rowdy and was soon asked to leave the room, which he did, switching off the lights and leaving the executives in darkness. "Will the vice-president closest to retirement please go out and kick his ass?" Marshall V requested.

Marshall V, family members, Field Enterprises employees, and a goodly part of Chicago awaited the events of June 1, 1977:

the twenty-fifth birthday of half-brother Ted Field. Ted, who was perceived as a family renegade, came into his inheritance on this birthday and now had equity in Field Enterprises on a par with Marshall V. Although Marshall V couldn't have been more pleased to see that amateur race-car driver Ted was uninterested in running the company, he wasn't delighted when he realized that Ted planned to take as much money as he could out of the company and its traditional business interests in order to foster his own risky enterprises.

Ted, however, was the wild card in Marshall's financial game plan. In 1983, Field Enterprises sold its various television stations and reaped $280 million, yet this closely held company had only two shareholders at this point—Marshall V and Ted. To avoid paying double taxes (at the corporate level and then again at the personal level), Field Enterprises was redesigned into a partnership between the half-brothers.

The concept of these radically dissimilar men as partners was ludicrous. Besides, Ted wanted out of the partnership so he could put his share of the money into producing movies. To accomplish this, the brothers took the Field family out of the newspaper business (after three generations) by selling the Chicago *Sun-Times* in 1983 for about $100 million cash to the controversial Rupert Murdoch.

Sun-Times journalists, who were aghast at the thought of working for the tabloid king, tried to match Murdoch's offer but fell a few million dollars short. Ted allegedly held out for the best price, although Marshall V said to *The New York Times* in 1983, "Had this decision been mine alone, I probably would not have taken this action."

There were, of course, other options open to Marshall V. He might have used his stake to rebuy the *Sun-Times*. Instead, he used it to buy Ted out of CC&F in 1984 for $30 million, thus eliminating the partnership. He could see the partnership wouldn't work and, looking to the future, realized it was better for each family to control its own individual inheritance. Marshall V says that he learned "not just from our family but from all of those that I watched, that when you try to keep the next generation together, it's a loser.

"You pick it—the Gettys (see GORDON GETTY), the Binghams of Kentucky—I don't want my kids to have that pressure." And so the trust was split.

Marshall V was now CC&F's sole owner. Like Marshall I, he bet that real estate would be "stimulating and challenging"—certainly more so than the financially-bumpy newspaper of which he had tired. Once more he sold some of the company's assets in order to recoup his payment, and organized CC&F as a partnership separate from the Field Corporation for tax reasons.

There were considerable tax advantages to having one of his businesses show a negative balance sheet, and, after all, he couldn't afford both the *Sun-Times* and CC&F. The real estate firm allowed Marshall V a foothold in business, and, as he said, "After 20 years in the newspaper business, I personally found that looking for interesting properties and building them up on a leveraged basis was an interesting challenge."

In addition, Marshall V pointed to the Fields' considerable experience in real estate. "The Field family has a long history of involvement in real estate development going as far back as my great-great grandfather Marshall Field I," Marshall V said to a reporter, indicating some of Chicago's most famous buildings as Field developments: the Merchandise Mart, the Field building, and the Chicago Sun-Times building.

When he talks of the Field men who went before him, Marshall V designates Marshall III as the man he most closely resembles. Like his grandfather, Marshall V has a number of interests and a fine art collection. Also, "He inherited a lot of money when he was young, as did my half-brother and myself.

"Like me, he was more interested in projects than one career. He saw things that interested him, and he did them, and then when he'd done it, on to the next thing." (Additionally, both Marshall V and Marshall III had fathers who died prematurely.)

Marshall V continued to keep active with his approximately $130 million cash-in-hand. He reentered the newspaper business one year after the breakup of Field Enterprises. (Ted, of course, walked away from the partnership also, having pocketed about $130 million.) With a cautious buy of 30 suburban weekly newspapers, Marshall V took Pioneer Press Inc. off Time Inc.'s hands for about $30 million. The price paid was slightly more than twice the revenue; the move by Marshall V and his newly formed Field Corporation, set up to acquire media properties, was considered an astute purchase.

Soon Barrington Press Inc. expanded the news holdings, bringing the Field weeklies to 40. By 1985, the company had formed another company, Field Publications, and purchased *My Weekly Reader* (with 9 million school-age readers) and Muzak, the largest company in the canned-music industry. Field Publications also acquired Funk & Wagnalls, a line of reference books including encyclopedias.

Marshall V, however, still focused on his Boston real estate company, which was by now one of the top 25 developers in the United States with $157 million in new construction in 1989. He served as chairman of both CC&F and the Field Corporation.

Prior to Marshall V's ownership, CC&F had enjoyed a reputation as an innovator in real estate development. For years, the company, founded in 1897, did only Boston area projects, widening its scope only in 1954 after the opening of Route 128. Its regional suburban industrial parks—then a new concept—received so much attention that CC&F was able to expand nationally. By the mid-'60s the company was building the first downtown high rises in Boston and putting up striking urban towers in other cities—for example, Chicago's Water Tower Place.

Marshall redirected the company back to a play-it-safe philosophy. It continued its prototype two- and three-story suburban office parks, but Marshall pronounced downtown urban projects too risky.

Marshall equated real estate with commodities in 1987 and continued to take a conservative approach to development. Critics dubbed the work of CC&F "the Muzak of real estate." However, by 1989 Marshall's ownership had pumped up growth to nearly six times what CC&F had been doing one decade earlier when Field Enterprises bought the company. Trade publications estimated the company's growth to be from $300 million to $1.6 billion in assets.

In 1989, Marshall V abandoned his low profile and took over as CEO to pursue a more cautious path for CC&F. He reacted to the late '80s slowdown in the real estate market by cutting the company's workforce, eliminating offices in two states, restructuring the operations into regional centers, eliminating two program offices, and reassigning top executives. Through this streamlining of operations and redirection to traditional real estate development opportunities, Marshall V announced CC&F would improve its position.

Marshall began generating fresh capital by selling off some of CC&F's assets. Employees inside the company coined their own jargon for these sales: "StayCo" indicated the property continuing with CC&F, and "GoCo" was the property to be sold. Unfortunately, as many as half of the company's employees were also designated in the "Go" category. In a move reminiscent of Marshall I, Marshall V sent private security guards into CC&F's headquarters office during the firings. Not that Marshall took this step lightly: "I never had to do this in my life. I hope I never have to do that again."

But the unpleasantness continued. Court suits were filed by former employees who charged that CC&F had reneged on severance agreements, and a limited partner sued as he saw the pie from which his equity derived getting smaller as Marshall sold off one slice at a time.

As the slump in commercial real estate continued, Marshall was receiving and turning down offers to sell the company. There were rumors that the family saw a need to diversify some of their holdings out of real estate. There was serious discussion of selling CC&F's entire West Coast operations to Trammel Crow Co., one of the country's two largest developers. In a dispute over pricing of real estate, the deal fell through, but CC&F was able to sell properties in Seattle, San Diego, and Los Angeles.

By the middle of 1990, the soft real estate market, worsened by the specific downturn in the northeast corridor and by banks' own liquidity problems, caused the company to try desperately to restructure its debts. CC&F announced to some creditors that they would not be paid, and worked with Kenneth Leventhal & Co. to restructure its debt. The company could not keep up payments to lenders but was not in any immediate crisis. Their strategy was to restructure debts and postpone those payments that were already due. CC&F was at this point allegedly worth about $1 billion, although it continued dropping in worth as various properties were sold off. The investment banking firm of Morgan Stanley tried to recapitalize CC&F but wasn't able to find a partner.

Feeling the financial pressure, Marshall V had Field Publications sell *My Weekly Reader* and Funk & Wagnalls, Inc. through Morgan Stanley. The aim was to increase Field's liquidity, and the sale was profitable for Marshall V; *Weekly-Reader* revenue had doubled in the five years of the company's ownership, circulation increased to 10 million schoolchildren, and sales for 1990 were about $300 million. In 1990, the suburban newspapers were also sold.

However, the downturn of CC&F was not adding to Marshall's fortune. It is speculated that its sale may not return his paper investment of about $76 million. (The belief is that the family took out its original investment in tax benefits by property sales.) Nonchalant over losses that would give nightmares to most, Marshall concluded to an industry paper, "I look at this as playing with the house money."

In October 1990, CC&F Realty Advisors was sold to its former CEO. The company, which focuses on property investment and management, administers about $500 million of real estate for pension fund clients. Sounding less than happy, a Field Corporation spokesman called it "an arm's length deal" and told the Boston *Globe*: "He wanted to buy it, we wanted to sell it. He knew how to value it, and we were able to go through with it."

In 1992, Marshall contested the valuation given CC&F in past years. "It wasn't worth a billion dollars, ever. It was probably worth, at its peak, about $150 million, net. Because most of that [billion-dollar valuation] we borrowed, that's how we went under with it. We borrowed 80 percent of the money to build this thing. But when the banks quit lending, the house of cards collapsed."

Although Marshall still owns what's left of CC&F, he says the company is "just a shell of its former self, like all the big development companies."

Looking back in early 1992, Marshall says, "To be perfectly honest, we had a feeling [the recession] was coming. I got caught in the big real estate slide, so that was just a loser.

"The companies we've been attempting to sell off, to get into cash, we've done that in most cases.

"Now I'm sitting on a pile of money and we hope maybe to make some investments, but I have no idea where those investments will be made. I haven't thought that far yet because I'm concentrating on the museum. As long as the stock market is doing as well as it is, why spoil a good thing?"

Like his namesakes, Marshall V takes his philanthropic duties very seriously, devoting more time in the '90s to charitable organizations than some wealthy men spend on their own business affairs. "I decided that I didn't want to work full time making money. The family had plenty of money, and I'd set up all kinds of trusts for my kiddies and grandchildren. Money didn't remain as a goal for me, and I wanted to give up to half my life doing something that didn't necessarily pay me anything but would maybe leave the world a little better off than when I came into it."

Marshall V is active in traditional Field philanthropies, pitching in when needed. For example, he wrote a personal check to make the Field Museum of Natural History accessible to the physically disabled. He increased his time at Chicago's famed Art Institute, where he can put his Harvard fine arts degree into play. He also selected the Art Institute as the beneficiary of his time because he believes it is a nationally ranked institution.

After nearly three decades of service on the Art Institute's board, which included chairing its $40 million fundraising drive, Marshall V is experienced in raising money for philanthropy. He must have had luck getting funds from Chicago's old-money families, because he told author Vance Packard, "I think that with inherited wealth there is time to teach the children they are going to get money. With people who are self-made, it's very unusual to see these qualities in the first generation. So I don't expect from new money what I expect from second- or third-generation."

Marshall V is now chairman of the Art Institute's board. Every weekday he travels on the Chicago and North Western train from his home in Lake Forest to the Art Institute, where he spends his mornings in a cramped, windowless office with his "Marshall Field V" photo ID dangling from a metal chain around his neck.

Marshall V's own contemporary office on State Street contrasts dramatically with his Art Institute space. A visitor walks down what looks like a 100-foot expanse toward corner windows overlooking Chicago and Lake Michigan to reach the desk where Marshall V oversees his domain.

As a serious art collector, Marshall V focuses on American furniture and paintings. He lives with his second wife Jamee and their three daughters in a 25-room neo-Georgian house on 16 acres. The family takes low-key vacations, which often find Marshall V fishing in Florida or salmon-catching in Canada or Iceland. (Although the vacations may be simple, Marshall V estimates his family's living expenses at more than $1 million annually.)

Marshall V's son married Clea Newman, daughter of Joanne Woodward and Paul Newman, in 1989. Two years later, the young man started a retail career with a store in North Salem, New York called Sporting Fields, which sells sporting guns. Marshall VI, 26, made a profit his first year.

"So maybe he has some of his great-great-great-grandfather's retailing ability," jokes his father.

At some point, Marshall VI may join his father in his business activities. But, as Marshall V points out, "He's got to figure out what they are, first. So do I. I do different things, and I told him when he gets tired [of Sporting Fields] and he's interested, let's see what I'm doing at the time."

There's been a Field tradition that's left the lion's share of each generation's fortune to the male next in line. "There was a big Anglophile history in our family, and if that's the way they did it in England, by God that's the way they were going to do it here," says Marshall V. "I watched what happened. It made a lot of bitter people out of the ladies in the family. Although needless to say, as a boy, it inured to my benefit.

"It's broken now. We took all four kids and said they all will be treated the same."

Marshall Field V is the only representative of old Chicago money on the *Forbes* 400 list. In less than 150 years, the Swifts are gone, the Armours are gone, and so are the Pullmans. Perhaps cognizant of fleeting fortunes, Marshall V said, "The only real tradition is that each succeeding generation shouldn't blow it. If you can leave the family fortune a little bigger than you found it, that's what counts."

"There is no dynastic motivation on my part, no psychological reason to be interested in having a fifth-generation dynasty."

Phillips-Van Heusen Corporation
New York, New York

Business:	Men's and women's shirts and sweaters and men's, women's, and children's shoes
Best Known Products:	Van Heusen Company: Additions, 417, Hennessy, Custom Club G.H. Bass & Co.: Bass, Weejun, Compass, Geoffrey Beene Menswear
Founded:	1881 by Endel and Moses Phillips
Family Executives:	Lawrence S. Phillips, Chairman and CEO
Family History:	Fourth generation; members of the youngest generation are Stewards
Family Ownership:	Approximately 11 percent
Family Board Membership:	1 family member of 11 directors
Traded:	NYSE, PVH
Net Sales:	$904,000,000 1991 806,315,000 1990 732,936,000 1989
Net Earnings:	$31,137,000 1991 26,384,000 1990 24,192,000 1989

PHILLIPS-VAN HEUSEN CORPORATION

No Heart on His Sleeve

Family of Lawrence S. Phillips, Chairman and CEO

"Nepotism is not good for the company, not good for the recipient, and not good for the other executives in the company," says Lawrence (Larry) S. Phillips, 65, chairman of Phillips-Van Heusen, the fourth—and presumably the last—Phillips family member to manage the apparel manufacturing and retail company that was founded by his great-grandfather in 1881. (The "Van Heusen" in the company's name derives from a patent—bought from a Dutch inventor—of the process that allowed collars to be woven on a curve to fit the contours of the neck.) Larry says, "There is no dynastic motivation on my part, no psychological reason to be interested in having a fifth-generation dynasty."

In counterpoint to his own predecessor, he says, "My father had the classic dynastic ambitions for the company and for his son, and I was not a party to that decision. I grew up knowing that [joining Phillips-Van Heusen] was the preordained path. It was not a subject open for debate, nor was it the subject that one questioned in those days." That Larry's only sibling is female increased pressure on him to enter the company.

Immediately upon graduation from Princeton University in 1948, Larry started working on the original manufacturing site's shipping floor in Pottsville, Pennsylvania. But he only stayed about six months before moving into executive ranks. He notes dryly, "I had a rapid upward mobility" that he had not requested. "It was all planned by my father."

The awkwardness of being the son of a successful father has led Larry, in large part, to eliminate possible leadership of

Phillips-Van Heusen for either of his children. "I spent a number of years with a desk right outside of my father's office, and I had the uncomfortable feeling that all the other executives were watching and counting. I felt I was being overpaid; it wasn't until 15 years later that I thought I was worth what I was being paid."

Larry continued to work with his father, company chairman Seymour Phillips, until Seymour's death in 1987. Seymour had been with the company since college graduation, 66 years earlier. Seymour had initially worked with his father Issac, just as Isaac had earlier worked with his own father, founder Moses Phillips.

Moses and wife Endel had fled the Czarist oppression in Suwalki, now located in northwest Poland, and settled in America's gateway to anthracite coal. Pottsville was filled with miners who were eager to buy the collarless, button-front work shirts sewn the night before by Endel in the one-room flat she shared with her husband. The next day, Moses would hawk Endel's just-in-time inventory, consisting of two or three workshirts, from his pushcart.

By the end of that first year, Endel and Moses had earned $250. They continued to produce dry goods and, soon, children to sell these goods. As they prospered, they invested in a horse and buggy that allowed them to sell to nearby mining hamlets. Eventually they added outside workers to their homegrown labor force. As the business prospered at the turn of the century, Moses built the company's first factory. Soon after, the couple's son Isaac moved the firm's sales and merchandising operations to New York City.

Growth was slow for this company, which by now was manufacturing dress shirts. In 1922, Phillips-Van Heusen went public to raise capital, initially selling stock over the counter. For decades the firm struggled against its major competitor, Arrow Shirts. However, there were several peaks for the company that coincided with fashion changes in men's dress shirts.

Phillips-Van Heusen transcended its normal growth in the early '50s during the advent of colors (called the "bold look" within the industry), in the late '50s with the introduction of the permanent press shirt, and soon after with the popularity of pink shirts. However, during that period Arrow still had as much as a

25-percent market share, which compared to Phillip-Van Heusen's two percent.

In 1960 Seymour assumed the company's chairmanship, and Larry became president of Phillips-Van Heusen. Larry's greatest challenge, and what he considers his most significant accomplishment, came in 1987 when Rosewood Financial, which belonged to the Hunt family of Texas, raided Phillips-Van Heusen in an attempted takeover. Larry was offended by Rosewood, whose staff and owners he describes as "arrogant Texans," lacking the ability to run Phillips-Van Heusen or any other company.

This was the turning point in the firm's history. Rather than lie down when Rosewood staked its position to 19.7 percent of Phillips-Van Heusen shares (as compared to the Phillipses' 11.1 percent), Larry maneuvered adroitly around Rosewood. First, he had Phillips-Van Heusen repurchase $145 million of its stock. Then he restructured the company by selling a number of divisions to management and buying G.H. Bass Shoe Company for $79 million from Chesebrough-Pond. The company borrowed $150 million from Prudential Insurance to keep it independent. (It retained a long-term debt of $142 million at the beginning of 1992.)

Larry recognized the need to reduce his corporation's dependency on department stores as merchandise outlets, so he refocused on the company's own third-party wholesale business and originated its own retail division. Phillips-Van Heusen now boasts a dual system that distributes both through traditional department stores and through specialty stores that sell Phillips-Van Heusen brand apparel and private-label brands, which have been expanded. Some of the Van Heusen and Bass specialty stores offer hot-line phones for consumers who don't find their sizes in stock. Using these phones, they can order merchandise to be sent to their homes.

There is also a Phillips-Van Heusen chain of factory outlets, which disposes of surplus inventory. The significant cash that comes in from these stores is helpful in servicing the company's heavy debt load. The outlet stores are purposely placed in out-of-the-way locations so as not to alienate the company's retail accounts.

Larry is also turning around Bass shoes, which had a terrible track record, having lost $47 million the year before Phillips-Van Heusen purchased it. The Bass product line was upgraded by Phillips-Van Heusen, which also increased Bass advertising. In 1991, shoe sales accounted for 34 percent of the company's sales and 41 percent of its profits.

Additionally, a contract with J.C. Penney to supply the store with shirts and sweaters meant shipments went up, despite the industry-wide downturn in department store sales. And Larry has the price range covered by offering customers shirts ranging from medium to higher priced.

Looking back on the period from 1987 to the beginning of 1992, Larry says, "We took the company from a volume of $500 million to what will be a volume that will exceed $1 billion in 1992. We have shown an average annual growth of 17 percent in sales and an increase in earnings per share of 22 percent."

In March 1992 the company reached an historic milestone as it passed Arrow Shirt in market share. "For the first time, we achieved leadership with the number one brand in the country at 9.9 percent of market, while Arrow [Biderman Industries] dropped to 9.2."

It's not market share or earnings in themselves that make Larry most proud, however. "Most importantly, much more important than the numbers, we have provided security for the jobs of some 11,000 people, and that was particularly important and noteworthy in a recession, when most of our competitors have been downsizing their facilities or going bankrupt."

Executive turnover is also virtually nil at this lean company, where the head of advertising also serves, when necessary, as public relations head. A significant stock option program is in place for all 130 key executives. Larry believes that his antinepotism policy attracts and keeps the best managers. "The healthiest thing in the world is for a group of upcoming young executives to know that there are no limitations on their own upward potential and mobility. If a company is permeated with family, there are limitations."

In one sense, Larry seems as firmly committed to keeping his kids out of the company as his father was to making sure that Larry joined. Larry says that his son and daughter "were brought up knowing that [automatic membership in Phillips-Van Heusen] was not an option. They could do anything they wanted in life, but they were not going into the company."

However, Larry softened his edict with the proviso that "if they wanted to work in a related industry for five or ten years, with an employer other than the family, and if they did that successfully, they would then be considered candidates for executive positions in the company.

"But neither of them elected to do so," he says. His daughter Laura is a script reader at 20th Century Fox, and his son David is executive director of Congressional Human Rights Foundation, which investigates human rights abuses throughout the world. "They're both doing very well and I assume and hope when it's all over that they will realize that I made the best decision for them and their happiness."

David Phillips, 32, indicates that he believes his father had more free choice about entering Phillips-Van Heusen than Larry acknowleges. David says, "The decisions that one makes in life are his own. He certainly made his."

David contradicts his father's lack of faith in family dynasties in several ways. "I feel that I have very much carried on the dynasty," he says. "But I've taken it to a different level, devoting myself full time to the kinds of values that were a part of my household." Like George Pillsbury (see GEORGE PILLSBURY), David mentions his parents' work in the civil rights and peace movements as having influenced his values, along with his grandparents' more traditional philanthropies.

"Our generational worlds overlap in many ways, and my father and I have found projects—humanitarian endeavors—to work on together." David is also proud of his father's enlightened management of Phillips-Van Heusen. "He's taken an environmental initiative, and the company takes extra efforts with employee relations...I think they're an example of enlightened corporate America and, at the same time, very profitable.

"It's a case where doing good business and doing good work are reciprocal."

David, the only male grandchild, thinks that his grandfather would have preferred him to follow Larry into the company. "But being the good soul that he was, he encouraged me to do my thing."

Again in contrast to Larry's statements, David leaves open the possibility of joining the Phillips-Van Heusen board when Larry steps down. "That's something we'd have to look at and make a decision at that time."

Larry, however, firmly rejects any assumption that one of his children will follow him as a company director. "I know of no reason they should come on the board. People should be on the board only if they make a significant contribution to the future of the company."

When reminded that many family inheritors insist on holding board seats to protect their equity positions, this untraditional patriarch emphatically disagrees. "I don't believe in that. They can make a judgment when I die as to whether they want to keep or sell the stock they inherit, and that will be their call.

"It will not be required that they keep it." Larry spells it out, "Even regarding ownership, I have no dynastic ambitions."

Larry lightens up slightly as he compares his own philosophy to that of most other long-term generational family business members and wryly understates: "It is an unpopular position."

Rob: "Dad was the founder of the company, the leading philosopher and guiding light for us always. I'm not any of those things, and I probably wouldn't be effective if I tried."

Wal-Mart Stores, Inc.
Bentonville, Arkansas

Business:	Discount department stores
Best Known Stores:	Wal-Mart; Sam's Club
Founded:	1962 as Wal-Mart Store by Sam M. Walton
Family Executives:	S. Robson Walton, Chairman James L. Walton, Senior Vice President John T. Walton, Director
Family History:	Second generation; members of youngest generation are Stewards
Family Ownership:	About 38 percent
Family Board Membership:	3 family members of 17 directors
Traded:	NYSE, WMT
Net Sales:	$32,601,594,000 1991 25,810,656,000 1990 20,649,001,000 1989
Net Earnings:	$1,291,024,000 1991 1,075,900,000 1990 837,221,000 1989

WAL-MART STORES, INC.

Caretakers of $22 Billion

The Walton Family

After Sam Walton's leukemia diagnosis at 64 in 1982, he did what he needed to do: prepared for succession. Sam hand-picked David Glass in 1988 to lead Wal-Mart as president and CEO through the '80s and '90s. Glass, 56, immediately assumed all of Sam's responsibilities except those of chairman and inspirational leader. When Sam eventually succumbed in 1992 to multiple myeloma, a form of bone cancer, his oldest son, S. Robson (Rob), 47, ascended from vice-chairman to chairman of the company with nearly $33 billion in 1991 sales. Wal-Mart is one of the *Forbes* super 50 companies, one of the largest U.S. businesses.

The oldest of Sam's four children, Rob joined the Wal-Mart board in 1978. (Until early 1992, Rob served on the board with Hillary Rodham Clinton, when she resigned to assist in her husband's presidential election campaign.) After receiving a law degree from Columbia University in 1969, Rob joined a Tulsa, Oklahoma law firm. In 1976, he left Wal-Mart as general counsel and secretary until 1982 when he moved to the vice chairman position.

As vice chairman, Rob has been particularly interested in furthering Wal-Mart's real estate development, and he played a heavy role in the early '90s decision to open stores in the northeast corridor. However, Rob has never wanted responsibility for the company's daily operations. In fact, Rob took a leave of absence from Wal-Mart in 1983 in order to train for the 1985 Ironman Triathalon in Hawaii. (He finished 510th out of 1,039 entrants.)

Upon Sam's death, Wal-Mart issued a statement that reiterated that Glass would continue to run the business. "The company has no plans to change its policies or direction and will continue to look for operational guidance from its current management team," said the Wal-Mart release.

None of Sam's offspring work at Wal-Mart, and Rob was the only one to serve on the board, until shortly after Sam's death, when the second of his sons, John, was added to the board. Sam's widow Helen has never been a board member although she's always called herself Sam's partner during their 49 years of marriage. While the children were young, Helen was a familiar neighborhood sight, carting them in the rain so they could finish their paper routes. When they left home, Helen stepped up her community work, driving in an old beige Chrysler New Yorker to the day care sites she's established for Wal-Mart employees and area workers. Helen also set up a program that teaches welfare mothers to be day care workers.

Sam said that early in his career he had wanted to settle in St. Louis, but Helen refused to live anywhere where there were more than 10,000 people. They returned to Sam's childhood home of Bentonville, Arkansas (1992 population remains at 9,500), which is located near the four state borders of Arkansas, Missouri, Oklahoma, and Kansas, but is 45 miles away from the nearest interstate highway. When the Walton's modest brick and wood ranch house in Bentonville burned down, they rebuilt it with fewer rooms, noting that their children were grown and out of the house. And the couple located it on the same site, four blocks from the first Wal-Mart.

The Walton's modest lifestyle includes Sam's 10-year-old Ford pickup truck, with its missing hubcaps and his bird dogs riding in the back. Occasionally, the dogs were permitted in Sam's beat-up Chevy sedan where the steering wheel was punctured by the dogs' teeth marks. When Sam was named America's wealthiest man in the 1985 *Forbes* 400, he wrote the magazine in a letter that was duly printed: "I could kick your butt for ever running that list."

Letter to the contrary, Sam retained that lead spot for four consecutive years. The couple's aversion to being dubbed wealthy may have led them to give Wal-Mart shares to their children through a 1990 trust. As a consequence, the couple dropped in rank to number three on *Forbes* 1991 list. The children occupied the places after them, numbers four through seven.

The Walton shareholdings were valued at $4.44 billion for the parents, and $4.44 billion for each of the four children. The total $22.2 billion represents an approximate 38 percent stake in Wal-Mart. The dividends from these shares paid the family $93.5 million in 1991. In addition, Sam's brother, James L. (Bud), who serves as Wal-Mart's senior vice president and as a board member, has shareholdings valued at $300 million. Helen will also receive Sam's modest $350,000 annual salary through 1993.

Rob's brother James C. (Jim) and sister Alice are not directly involved in Wal-Mart. The siblings and their mother control a family holding company called Walton Enterprises Inc., which is headed by Jim and includes six area banks, newspapers, and other local businesses. The kids are not quite as down-home as their father and use private planes—in addition to their pickup trucks—when they travel. John, recently added to the Wal-Mart board, is the only sibling living outside the area, preferring California, where his business is sailboat building.

Alice, 41, might be the most individualistic of all the Walton offspring. After a short stint following college as a Wal-Mart buyer, she left to work as a money manager at national firms, including E.F. Hutton. Then she returned home to head investments for the family's banks while raising cattle and horses on her 900-acre ranch in Rogers, Arkansas.

Alice decided to go into business for herself in 1988. She jokes that she named her new investment business Llama Co. in order to turn her pet llama LaRoy into a tax write-off. But her business is anything but whimsical. It had start-up capital of $25 million, with 75 percent put up by the family holding company. Alice owns 55 percent of the company, which underwrites public and corporate bonds and manages investments for pension funds.

But even with her propensity for numbers, Alice, too, dislikes the *Forbes* 400 ranking. "If we had our way, we wouldn't be on this list," she said to *USA Today* in 1989, disclosing that her father was "very glad" when he dropped in rank after the generous gift to his children.

The children are now middle-aged, just as their father was when he founded the country's largest retail store at 44. Although Sam had hoped to attend business school after his graduation from the University of Missouri, there was no money for it. So in 1940 he settled for a monthly salary of $85 a month at an Iowa J.C. Penney store. A visit to the store from James Cash Penney taught Sam not only how to wrap a package with a minimum of paper and twine, but also the importance of visits by a store's founder. (Sam made one change when he imitated Penney's tours—Sam would swoop down, piloting his own Cessna, for a surprise visit to his Wal-Mart stores.)

After three years in Army intelligence during the war, Sam's next pivotal experience was owning a Ben Franklin variety-store franchise in Newport, Arkansas, which he quickly made the company's most successful. When Sam lost his lease and sold the franchise to his landlord's son, he learned never again to be dependent on one particular store or area.

While still running a handful of Ben Franklin stores, Sam opened the first Walton's 5&10 in 1950. At the end of the decade, Sam and his brother Bud had 16 independent variety stores in the United States. By 1962, Sam was also the country's largest Ben Franklin franchisee, with 15 stores. But when he took his idea of opening discount stores in small communities to Ben Franklin headquarters, the company rejected it. After visiting other discount stores, Sam decided to open his first Wal-Mart that same year in Rogers, Arkansas. Soon young Alice was crying to her friends, "I don't know what we're going to do. My daddy owes so much money, and he won't quit opening stores."

His strategy was to keep costs as low as possible, serve the customer, and work directly with suppliers. In addition, in the '80s Wal-Mart became one of the most technologically sophisticated retailers. Although Sam gave the green light to these computer and satellite communication linkages, he did not originate them but relied on his highly sophisticated headquarters staff, including CEO Glass. Sam always stressed the value of learning from others —and was sometimes ejected from competitors' stores in the process.

Wal-Mart became a public company in 1970, with 18 stores and sales of $44 million. Its associates, as employees were called, were given strong incentives in stock options, bonuses, salary, and other benefits. A Wal-Mart manager, for example, could earn a six-figure income—which would go especially far in, say, small-town Mississippi.

Sam insisted on being addressed by his first name by Wal-Mart associates, although many added the Southern sign of respect and called him "Mr. Sam."

Despite the sobriety that comes from being publicly accountable, Sam never lost his sense of humor. He made good on his promise to Wal-Mart associates and when Wal-Mart hit record earnings in 1984, the discount dynamo who resembled his favored bird dogs donned a grass skirt to hula down Wall Street.

In building the country's largest retail chain, primarily in the sun-, farm- and oil-belt states, Sam's methods have not pleased everyone. Manufacturers found him a hard bargainer. Manufacturers' representatives disliked him for his close relationship to his vendors, which often meant Wal-Mart skipped over the middle-man reps. Some union leaders say he exaggerated with his "Buy American" slogan, feeling that Wal-Mart itself could have lowered its level of imported goods.

The other side of the discount retailing coin was felt by small businesses. Sometimes the opening of a Wal-Mart on the outskirts of town was followed by the death of the community's downtown business area. These small-town, general merchandisers couldn't compete with Sam's low prices and wide offerings. Unable to adjust by finding an appropriate niche for themselves—by specializing, adding rental equipment, or teaching craft and handyman classes—they hammered plywood over their large glass windows and walked away from vacant buildings.

In fact, that's just what happened in Newport. Years after losing his Ben Franklin lease to the landlord's son, Sam built a Wal-Mart in the area. It wasn't long before the Ben Franklin store went out of business. In fact, the Ben Franklin chain, whose managers had scoffed at Sam's discount proposal, was bought by Household International Inc. in 1965, and in 1991 had sales of about $2 billion a year, just a fraction of Wal-Mart revenues.

Sam lived to see Wal-Mart grow to 1,735 stores in 42 states, replacing Sears in 1991 as the country's largest retailer. The chain is multiplying more rapidly each year as the country's fastest-growing retailer. Although it took Wal-Mart seven years to open its first 18 stores, in 1992 it hoped to open 160 additional stores throughout the country, many in the northeast. And Wal-Mart is no longer committed to building only in the kind of small community you see only when you have to turn off the interstate. Wal-Mart is now encroaching on towns within the reach of metropolitan areas. In addition, it announced plans to operate more than 30 stores in Mexico by the end of 1993.

Wal-Mart has committed itself to an ambitious sales goal of $100 million by the end of the '90s. Analysts believe that by the beginning of the next century, Wal-Mart will be the largest corporation in the United States.

As for the possibility of a takeover, CEO Glass said to *The Wall Street Journal* immediately after Sam's death that the Walton's 38 percent stake "will never leave the family." Sam emphasized to *USA Today* one year before his death the importance of maintaining the Walton philosophy after he was gone, a common concern of family business founders. "I worry about keeping our culture, keeping the things we believe in," he said. If the Walton children—the company's largest shareholders who are represented on the board by two of their own—stay committed to the same values, then the Wal-Mart culture remains safe.

"Union organizers knew just to walk on past Marion."

Marion Merrell Dow, Inc.
Kansas City, Missouri

Business: Producer of prescription and over-the-counter pharmaceuticals

Best Known Products: Cardizem cardiovascular medication; Seldane antihistamine; Carafate antiulcer medication; Nicoret and Nicoderm smoking-cessation aids

Founded: In 1950 by Ewing M. Kauffman as Marion Laboratories, Inc.; merged in 1989 with Merrell Dow

Family Executives: Ewing M. Kauffman, Director and Chairman Emeritus

Family History: Second generation; members of the youngest generation are Stewards

Family Ownership: Less than one percent

Family Board Membership: 1 family member of 12 directors

Traded: NYSE, MKD

Net Sales: $2,851,000,000 1991
2,462,000,000 1990
930,000,000 1989 (a)

Net Earnings: $585,000,000 1991
487,000,000 1990
227,000 1989 (a)

(a) The company's year-end changed in 1989 from June 30 to Dec. 31

MARION MERRELL DOW, INC.

You Gotta Have Heart

Ewing M. Kauffman Family

Billionaires Ewing and Muriel Kauffman value hard work and philanthropy. What they don't hold in high esteem is great wealth—especially vast inherited wealth. Each of their children—Larry, Sue and Julia—has been given four or five million dollars, Ewing estimated off the top of his head in the late '80s, "and they don't need any more." The grandchildren will eventually receive about a million dollars each, which the Kauffmans feel is sufficient.

The couple is devoted instead to the education ideals and health programs of the Ewing M. Kauffman Foundation. The foundation's programs include Project STAR, which began in 1984 in Kansas City to teach inner-city high school students to avoid alcohol and drug use. The program was founded after the Kauffmans were hit by the epidemic of substance abuse among young people when four players on the baseball club they owned, the Kansas City Royals, were convicted on drug charges. By 1992, Project STAR had reached more than 100,000 students.

Four years later, they started Project Choice, which guarantees some of these same students a paid college education. "It's worth every penny," said Ewing, 76, of the costly deal which might cost him $10 million.

In an interesting flip, the Kauffmans' own oldest granddaughter paid her own way through the University of California because her grandparents believed she'd value an education she had paid for herself.

As billionaires, the Kauffmans could live a great deal more grandly than they do, although their Mission Hills 28-room mansion, with towers, sweeping steps, fountains, and a massive black metal filigree fence would suffice for most couples. The Italian Florentine house, restored by Italian craftsmen when the Kauffmans purchased it, includes a massive organ, a pistol range, a steam room, and an Olympic-size pool. Although proud of their residence, they put up the fence and gate when passersby started driving up to the door for a better look. (Since Ewing has started swimming in the buff, that fence is probably a good idea.)

The money supporting this residence originally derived from Marion Laboratories, Inc., the pharmaceutical firm Ewing founded in 1950. (Marion is Ewing's middle name.) Ewing had been a top drug salesman in his former job. When he was criticized by company management for earning more money in commissions than the company president made in salary, he went into business for himself.

Ewing's first product as an entrepreneur was a calcium pill made from crushed oysters. He named the product Os-Cal. (Don't laugh: These calcium supplements eventually commanded as much as a 40 percent share of a $100 million market.)

The company's aggressive marketing techniques in the '50s and '60s helped compensate for its lack of research in new drugs. The company excelled at reformulating compounds and selling them. The sales staff was one of the best in the industry, and its members were treated well by a generous Ewing, who called them "associates" rather than employees. For example, the Ewing Kauffman Foundation bankrolled a share of college costs for children of all associates.

"Union organizers knew to just walk on past Marion," says Ewing.

The company went public in 1965, with Ewing and his wife owning a 35 percent stake, worth about $17 million. By the early '70s, the company had become a diversified health-care giant, and the Kauffmans' shares had escalated in value to $150 million.

Some of Marion's most successful drugs were the market leader Cardizem, which treats heart problems; Cardizem-SR, for hypertension; and Carafate, an ulcer medication. These three drugs quadrupled the firm's revenues by the early '80s.

But the company had a few weak spots. For one, it hadn't built up a strong research staff and had been relying on line extensions that were losing patent protection. Because this aspect of the company had been underdeveloped, pumping up research muscle would have been costly. Marion was too small to remain independent.

At the same time, Dow Chemical was looking for a partner in the drug industry. In 1989, it merged its pharmaceutical subsidiary Merrell Dow with Marion Labs. The marriage immediately resulted in a healthy offspring, christened Marion Merrell Dow, which grew up to be the ninth largest company in the drug industry.

Dow Chemical holds two-thirds of the company's stock and began making payments to Marion's shareholders. Since everyone who worked at Marion Labs was a shareholder, nearly 10 percent of the company's then 3,600 associates saw their stake in the new company valued at more than $1 million. The Kauffmans' shares were estimated at $1.3 billion—even after they sold 43 percent of their stock in Marion for $675 million.

In early 1992, the Kauffmans announced their plan to sell the majority of Marion Merrell Dow stock that they controlled through family trusts and the Ewing Kauffman Foundation. Immediately before making this announcement, the couple had given 12.2 million Marion shares—valued at more than $445 million—to their charitable trusts and to their foundations. After selling more shares, Ewing owned approximately one million shares in mid-'92.

These philanthropic values extend to the current generation, too. Daughter Julia serves as a board officer of the Muriel McBrien Kauffman Foundation and has contributed generously to it. The foundation supports dance and the arts as well as health programs.

The Kauffman children seem to reflect their parents' values. Anybody who makes money and doesn't give it away, Ewing thinks, doesn't really know how to enjoy life.

Al Piergallin, CEO, and Dan Gerber

Dan's thoughts on his first day at work: "I've got to get out of here."

Gerber Products Company
Freemont, Michigan

Business:	Baby and toddler food; children's apparel; children's life insurance
Best Known Products:	First Foods; Gerber Graduates; Buster Brown Apparel; Gerber Childrenswear
Founded:	By Frank Gerber as Freemont Canning Co. in 1901
Family Executives:	Daniel F. Gerber, Director Harrington M. Cummings, Director
Family History:	Third generation; members of the youngest generation are Stewards
Family Ownership:	20 percent
Family Board Membership:	2 family members of 13 directors
Traded:	NYSE, GEB
Net Sales:	$1,178,942,000 1991 1,136,436,000 1990 1,033,319,000 1989
Net Earnings:	$112,818,000 1991 94,075,000 1990 85,639,000 1989

GERBER PRODUCTS COMPANY

Finding Board Work Easily Digestible

The Gerber Family

Dan Gerber, 52, uses a family business as the fictional backdrop for his novel *A Voice From the River*. Ambivalence and regret are the themes its protagonist Nick Wheeler struggles with, as he decides to remain with his father's company.

For Dan Gerber—novelist, poet, and journalist—life should not be characterized by regret. When Dan was in college, he told his father Daniel F. Gerber Sr. that he would not enter Gerber Foods. His father talked him into trying the family business before beginning a teaching career.

Unfortunately, Dan was taken under the wing of the company's well-meaning comptroller, who gave the new successor tips on how he should dress (formally) and what hours (long ones) he needed to work. The strictures were unappealing to someone who later was to be active in the protest against the war in Viet Nam. Dan afterward told an interviewer that as the comptroller lectured, Dan had "a fantasy of standing up and tipping the desk over on top of him."

His next thought was, "I've got to get out of here."

Dan's weekend escape was racing sports cars, usually his Shelby-American Cobra, his Mustang, or his Austin-Healey. But even the thrill of racing couldn't compensate for his weekday duties of processing claims from the firm's insurance subsidiary, and he spent many days reading novels hidden within volumes of actuary tables. He quit Gerber and continued to race.

One weekend in 1966, the Mustang ran into a pit wall. Dan's car was thrown back onto the track and hit by three other race cars before bursting into flames.

Dan survived, but with nearly every bone in his body broken. From the wheelchair he used temporarily, he taught English at the local high school. Eventually he began a writing career, and when his father resigned as president of the company, Dan—then 27—joined the board of directors solely because he didn't want to hurt his father. (The husband of one of his three sisters is also on the board.)

It was Dan's mother who was the originator of the company's venture into strained baby food. Dorothy Gerber had progressive ideas about rearing children, and as she began feeding strained fruits and vegetables to her two oldest children (Dan's sisters), she discovered that none were available commercially. She asked her husband to strain some food for their children at the family's Freemont Canning Company.

After experimentation and much discussion, company officials gave baby food a commercial go-ahead in 1928. This adaptability was not surprising for a family business that had changed from a tanning business to a wholesale grocery company to a canning business in response to changes in the region's resources. (The company changed its name from Freemont Cannery to Gerber Products in 1941.)

Within six months, the five varieties of baby food were offered in all major cities. Mothers were liberated from the three-times-a-day chore of pushing vegetables, fruits, and meats through a strainer.

Helping to promote the baby foods was the charcoal sketch drawn by artist Dorothy Hope Smith. It was adopted as the company's trademark in 1931, making the little girl who was its model the world's most recognized baby. Her image helped Gerber Products become the world's largest baby food manufacturer by 1973, with sales of more than $1 billion in 1992.

Not that the company's progress has been as smooth as its puréed vegetables. Dan's toughest period as a board member lasted nearly 10 years and began in the late '70s. The first battle, a 1977 tender offer, was fought successfully by the board. Then in 1984, there were rumors of broken glass in Gerber baby food. Two years later, the same talk surfaced. On the second occasion, Gerber's stock price went down by 20 percent in two days. Market share dropped 17 percentage points, to 52 percent.

At first, the company didn't fight a product recall. Then, when it became clear that copycat reports were being made, the Gerber crisis team resisted a state recall. The company was backed up by the FDA, which vouched for the safety of Gerber products. Subsequently, there were several arrests of people who made false accusations.

By proving the rumors untrue and by boosting advertising, the company's market share rose again. But this time, troubles stemmed from unprofitable diversifications into children's furniture, apparel, and child-care centers. The board recruited a new CEO, Australian-born David Johnson, who showed his sense of humor when he sent top managers a sketch of a skull and crossbones with the caption, "The floggings will continue until morale improves."

Johnson rid the company of its unprofitable units—furnishings, toys, trucking and farming—and refocused on basics by developing from the core Gerber food products. By the time Campbell was recruited away from Gerber in 1990 by the Dorrance family (see CAMPBELL SOUP), Gerber's share of the U.S. baby food market had risen to 73 percent; earnings had tripled; the stock price had doubled; and revenue had shot above $1 billion. In 1992, the company was ranked by *Business Week* at number 298 of the 1,000 most valuable U.S. companies.

In addition, Gerber will market food to toddlers in 1992. The Gerber Graduate line is aimed at young children who have outgrown baby food, and its sales will help the company grow even while the birth rate in the United States remains flat.

Dan is now free of major board worries, although he works on some aspect of board business part of each week. He's used his remaining time to author three novels, four volumes of poetry, many magazine articles, and a volume of short stories.

He also put in time raising three children, all of whom have decided against entering Gerber management. Dan's son Frank is a salesman for Knight-Ridder. Daughter Wendy is a professional chef, and Tamara is studying to be a veterinarian.

Dan values his board membership as a sign that the company will remain a Michigan business. And at 52, he has no regrets over the path he has chosen, as a writer and as a Steward of the family business that bears his name.

Tom Cabot says there's no "eager beaver" in the youngest generation.

Cabot Corporation
Boston, Massachusetts

Business:	Specialty chemicals and materials, and energy
Best Known Products:	Carbon black, fumed silica
Founded:	1882 by Godfrey Cabot
Family Executives:	Thomas D. Cabot, Director Emeritus, Honorary Chairman John G.L. Cabot, Vice Chairman John M. Bradley, Director
Family History:	Fifth generation; members of the youngest generation are Stewards
Family Ownership:	About 35 percent
Family Board Membership:	2 family members of 15 directors
Traded:	NYSE, CBT
Net Revenue:	$1,482,089,000 1991 1,547,910,000 1990 1,803,544,000 1989
Net Earnings:	$127,260,000 1991 71,030,000 1990 18,057,000 1989

CABOT CORPORATION

Ink Black Profits Color This Family

Cabot Family

A mosaic of thousands of satellite images, photographed from far above the planet, show the earth at a glance in the picture on the company's annual report. Superimposed on this photo collage of the world are Cabot Corporation's 96 facilities located in North America, Latin America, Europe, and the Pacific Rim. Make no mistake, Cabot Corporation is a global company.

Cabot is the world's largest producer of carbon black, a powder used in tires and most other rubber products to color and strengthen, and in cables, coatings, inks, and plastics. The business produces more than 200 varieties of carbon black.

Carbon black has been used since the Stone Age, when artists picked up the smutty substance from the ground and used it to draw on cave walls. Today, carbon black must be refined for use by heating a mist of oil sludge to 3,000°F. This plain cousin to the diamond has tens of thousands of applications—for example, it is a component of the ink on this page. Its major use, though, is as an oil-based hardening agent in plastic and rubber goods. Look around: Any manufactured item that is black probably contains carbon black.

Cabot is the only company that can supply this essential powder quickly to clients throughout the world. Its foreign operations accounted for more than one-third of its sales and about half of its profits in 1991. Cabot leads in global market share for carbon black.

Since 1991, Cabot has been composed of four chemical businesses that share similar technologies and markets. Besides carbon black, Cabot also is the leading U.S. manufacturer of fumed silica, a thickening agent in caulking material and toothpaste; the leading manufacturer of plastics concentrates in Europe; and the world's leading producer of tantalum powders and mill products used in defense applications and chemical process equipment. The company also has several nonchemical enterprises that make safety eyewear and earplugs, and it owns the only liquified natural gas terminal in the energy-poor northeast United States. Usually, Cabot's products are used directly by other industries and only indirectly by private consumers.

The founder of this company, Godfrey Cabot, was descended from a respected New England family that made its first several fortunes from the opium and slave trades. When Godfrey founded Cabot Corporation in 1882, the carbon black he sold was used to color inks and pigments. After World War I and the rise in popularity of automobiles needing rubber tires, uses for carbon black skyrocketed.

Today's patriarch of the company is Thomas D. Cabot, 95, who started at the company in 1922, working under his father Godfrey. In 1992, Tom serves as director emeritus of the board, having given interviews to *Fortune* and *Business Week* well into his 90s on the state of the chemical and energy industries.

Tom led Cabot's thrust into global markets in the '40s, when it was discovered that carbon black could be produced more cheaply from oil byproducts than from other sources. By the end of the '50s, the company was the top producer of carbon black for literally every industry that used the substance. Tom's son Louis Wellington Cabot, now 71, joined the company in 1948, after graduation from Harvard University with a business degree, and retired from the company's board in 1992.

Louis, who was president of Cabot from 1960 to 1969, brought modern management principles to the business. Implementing these principles, he hired the company's first outsider—a nuclear physicist—to head the firm when he himself stepped upstairs to chair Cabot's board in 1969.

John Godfrey Lowell Cabot II, 58, Louis's cousin and Tom's nephew, entered the company in 1960 after he received his undergraduate degree and his M.B.A. from Harvard. He, too, recognized that a global company like Cabot could no longer rely solely on family members for top management. John, who is now a board officer, rose to become executive vice president of the company in 1986.

The '70s and '80s were gritty times for the company. Demand for carbon black slackened with the energy crisis; consumers preferred long-lasting radial tires; natural gas went into a slump; and the firm's various diversifications slipped. Another outsider was recruited to head the company in 1986.

Cabot's new CEO, Samuel W. Bodman, was a former M.I.T. chemistry professor who had left academe to start a venture capital fund. Bodman strengthened Cabot's R&D and its marketing efforts. He sold the company's energy assets because the industry's standard of valuation depressed the company's net earnings. In 1991 the company's divestiture of Cabot Gas & Oil was completed. Bodman also oversaw the construction of three new carbon black plants in Asia.

Tom Cabot continues to serve as Cabot's board member emeritus and reports to the office several times a week. He is credited with making Cabot a global corporation. He is also considered one of the Cabot family's flintiest members. While he was skiing in his 80s, he poked out an eye but refused an eye patch, considering a coverup too sissified.

The youngest two generations of Cabots are not interested in working in their family business. They include the two sons and three daughters of Louis, the two sons of John, and the men's grandchildren. Like the Dorrances (see CAMPBELL SOUP), the younger Cabots are into horse breeding. Tom told *Fortune* that there isn't "an eager beaver" among them.

The family owns about 35 percent of this company. At the beginning of 1992, their shares were valued at $190 million. The Cabot board has put a tough poison-pill provision in place to ward off possible takeovers. And there's no thought of selling family shares in Cabot—not, at least, while patriarch Tom is living. He says he'd be "mad as hell" if they did.

He continues, "I don't want the company bought by somebody who's going to hurt the Cabot name."

"Fashions may change, but sex appeal is always in style."

Frederick's of Hollywood
Los Angeles, California

Business:	Women's intimate apparel, leisurewear, sportswear, dresses, and specialty menswear through retail and mail order
Best Known Products:	Lingerie, bras, foundations, hosiery
Founded:	1946 by Frederick N. Mellinger
Family Executives:	Harriett Mellinger, Director
Family History:	Second generation; members of the youngest generation are the Stewards
Family Ownership:	59 percent
Family Board Membership:	1 family member of 7 directors
Traded:	ASE, FHO
Net Sales:	$114,134,000 1991 98,573,000 1990 80,073,000 1989
Net Earnings:	$5,197,000 1991 4,242,000 1990 3,043,000 1989

FREDERICK'S OF HOLLYWOOD

Naughty to Nice

Mellinger Family

Frederick's of Hollywood has changed its image from racy to respectable. The firm that was once best known for X-rated merchandise is now the happy subject of Wall Street's heavy breathing: *Forbes* included the firm in its list of the 200 best small companies in both 1990 and 1991, and *Fortune* listed it in 1990 as one of America's 25 best stocks.

This respectability is welcome to the business, established soon after the end of World War II, that reflected the postwar culture of the United States. Frederick Mellinger realized New York was too sophisticated for his peekaboo bras and wisely moved his mail-order business west to Los Angeles. Eventually he entered retailing, moving into a four-story, glitzy, purple Art Deco edifice on Hollywood Boulevard—overlooking the Walk of Fame—that still stands as a literal monument to the man who originated edible panties.

Frederick's of Hollywood merchandise is not to everyone's taste. When Fred told his former boss of his new idea for a mail order firm, the man called him an "oversexed punk." Fred's own father called the business "shameful." Even *Playboy* in the '50s refused to advertise his merchandise. ("Too competitive," sniffed Fred.)

But Fred knew that he was fulfilling American women's need to mix fantasy with everyday items. "Fashions may change, but sex appeal is always in style," he responded to his critics.

The company's first hit was black lace panties, a difficult item to find in '40s-era department stores stocked with white girdles. In the '50s, the company's growth was attributed to its cone-shaped bras. The L.A. location also made merchandise popular with movie wardrobers, who used Frederick's lingerie to outfit such female stars as Lana Turner—and such male stars as the cross-dressing character played by Tony Curtis in *Some Like It Hot*. The Beat generation was an inspiration for Frederick's black leather bra, and the women's liberation movement must have inspired the early '70s Bird Cage bra, which advertised "How He'll Long to Set You Free." In fact, Frederick considered himself supportive of wo-men's issues. He said, "I've been out for the women's cause longer than any designer. I'm one of the few that wants to make a woman look and feel comfortable as a woman."

In the late '80s, Madonna wore Frederick's black bustier on her "Like A Virgin" tour. Her purple bustier with gold tassels, also from Frederick's, was stolen from the company's Lingerie Muse-um in the flagship store during the May 1992 Los Angeles riots. A reward was offered for its return, because of its value to the company.

The business went public in the '70s with Fred, his wife Harriett, and adult children David and Susan retaining a controll-ing interest in the company. But as Fred became older, the styles and accessories sold by Frederick's of Hollywood slipped a level into sleaze. At its nadir, the company's catalog sold X-rated videos and bondage items.

At the same time, lingerie with sex appeal was becoming respectable. Victoria's Secret mail order and retail stores attracted middle-class customers in their 30s who were turned off by Fre-derick's offerings. To regenerate the company, in 1985 Fred hired George Towson away from the mail-order division of Carter Hawley Hale Stores, Inc.

Towson dropped Frederick's fringe customers and brought in fashions that appealed to a more conventional shopper. He re-vamped the retail stores, making them romantic rather than garish, and located them in shopping centers and mini-malls. By the end of 1991, the company had 194 stores in 37 states, with the retail stores accounting for about 80 percent of the company's profits. Sales increased nearly 70 percent from 1987 and 1990 and, more impressively, earnings jumped 320 percent. As a result, *Forbes* in

1991 identified Frederick's as one of the best small companies in America for investment.

At the beginning of 1992, the family's stake in the company was valued at about $45 million. While benefiting from family ownership, neither David nor Susan (or their young children) has any plans to enter the company, although their mother serves as a board director. Nor will either child enter the fashion industry—the industry that honored their father at his death in 1990, when apparel executives eulogized "Mr. Frederick" and the impact that the sex appeal he introduced to merchandising had on what has become the $8 billion-a-year intimate apparel industry. But through their financial interest in Frederick's of Hollywood, David and Susan will serve as Stewards of the company and retain the Mellinger family presence.

SECTION VI

THE FAMILY FEUDERS

Family Feuders are characterized by strife that sometimes lasts for years. Money and control are the issues behind these conflicts. And when people with great sums of money fight, the inevitable result is protracted litigation. Then everybody loses but the lawyers.

Family Feuders are found in both private and publicly held companies. In private firms such as U-Haul, Koch Industries, or Milliken & Co., damage to outsiders is minimal. But when Family Feuders head such public companies as ethnic hair care Johnson Products, family members who aim their fire at each other often turn shareholders into casualties. Stock prices can drop with news of family brawls, while managers who remain after the dust settles find that their energies are diverted from production as they try to work within the latest power shifts.

FAMILY FEUDERS USUALLY...

1. battle over money or control of the business, with little concern for the impact on the family.
2. argue among siblings, cousins, and parents.
3. have a history of animosities with each other that began in childhood.
4. litigate.
5. take years to resolve contested issues.
6. are not interested in conciliating or mediating their differences because of their "winner take all" attitude.

One feuding family that has argued over company control rather than over money is the Brown family of Brown-Forman spirits and wines. In this case, the losing brother was forced out of the company by his victorious older brother.

Power struggles can involve both siblings and parents, as they did at Johnson Products, U-Haul, and pantsmaker Farah Inc. At Johnson, chairman Joan—who herself had won majority control of the company from her ex-husband in a divorce settlement—sided with daughter Joan Jr. over son Eric, despite his successful turnaround of the floundering company as its CEO. In early 1992, Eric was ousted in favor of Joan Jr.

At Farah, father Willie Farah lost control of the family business partly due to the board votes of his own children. Farah Inc. is now professionally managed. Of Willie's four children, only his daughter remains on the board.

Leonard Shoen was thrown out of U-Haul, the company he himself founded, by a coalition of his 12 children. Also on the losing side was a group of Shoen sons who were ousted along with their father.

The battle that took place at Koch oil was over both money and company control. Although founder Fred Koch died before the litigation between his sons began, he inadvertently facilitated the next-generation feud when he left son Frederick a smaller share of the company than he gave his other sons. Naturally, when Bill Koch—now best known as the owner of the America's Cup sailboat America[3]—needed a confederate to side with him against his other brothers, he turned to Frederick as a natural ally.

The arguments at Campbell Soup and textile giant Milliken & Co. have primarily been over money. But these families, who represent old money, have been better mannered than the other Feuders. Few have talked on the record about family matters; only unattributed comments and SEC filings give a clue to motivation.

But the same refined aura—old money—that makes these relatives shun the spotlight is what caused the enmity to begin with. These families are so old and have spread so far afield since the companies were founded—Milliken in 1865 and Campbell four years later—that many members no longer feel a close allegiance to the company. Their aim is to take the money and run.

Family feuds are a constant threat to family-run businesses, whether private or public. Although dynasties may have some admirable characteristics, the longer they last, the more inevitable are family feuds.

These Feuders quickly adopt all-or-nothing positions that are rarely conciliated. Instead, the sad result of family feuds is that one segment of the family is completely excluded from the business —and from each other. Several Family Feuders, for example, have lamented that Christmases are no longer the same.

Don B. Stevenson

Jim, Joe, Mark, and Joe Shoen

Joe Shoen: "I didn't just fall off a turnip truck."

U-Haul International, Inc.
Phoenix, Arizona

Business:	Truck and trailer rental; self-storage
Best Known Products:	Utility trailer rentals
Founded:	1945 by Anna Mary and Leonard Samuel Shoen
Family Executives:	E.J. (Joe) Shoen, Chairman and President Mark Shoen, Director James Shoen, Director
Family History:	Second generation
Family Ownership:	Approximately 80 percent
Family Board Membership:	3 family members of 8 directors
Traded:	Privately held
Net Sales:	$887,000,000 1991 (estimated)
Net Earnings:	Will not disclose

U-HAUL
INTERNATIONAL, INC.

"Mr. Chairman, I Am Your Father!"

Shoen Family

U-Haul is the move-it-yourself market leader. It leases more trailers to individuals than any other American company. U-Haul is also one of America's highest valued private businesses, estimated at approximately $1 billion. (U-Haul is a subsidiary of Amerco Business Consultants, Inc.) But what could have been the American dream turned into a nightmare.

This truck and trailer rental empire was begun in true entrepreneurial style by Leonard Samuel Shoen (L.S.), now 76, who gave away a portion of his kingdom to each of his 12 children (by three of his four wives) as they were born. That was fine when the children were young. But inevitably, when the sons and daughters reached adulthood, they demanded what was legally theirs. Now some of these heirs—who were the premature recipients of their father's beneficence—have taken control of the principality and crowned themselves king and princes. And L.S. has been banished.

L.S. began his life as the son of Depression-era farmers in Washington state. As a boy, he hated being poor and was always looking for a way to make a dollar, earning the nickname "Slick" from his classmates. Always eager to get ahead, L.S. graduated from college and even attended medical school before a disciplinary infraction caused his expulsion.

While a Navy officer in World War II, L.S. had watched a moving trailer haul a family's goods to its new household. L.S. recognized that Americans move frequently and that they are also avid do-it-yourselfers. He was intrigued by the potential of a one-way rental company.

At that time, moving rentals required a round trip. No rental agency wanted to deal with trucks and trailers left in different states. But what was a headache to others was an idea with great potential to L.S. With an initial investment of $3,000 and one truck, he started U-Haul in 1945. L.S. slowly bought more trucks and wooden trailers and hired a few blue-collar workers to piece them together. U-Haul trailers could be rented from any gas station owner willing to keep them on his lot.

U-Haul was headquartered in Portland, but L.S. was rarely in the central office. By day, he could be found traveling to recruit new dealers. By night, he'd drive by gas stations with U-Haul trailers to check out his vehicles. If necessary, he'd make repairs under the streetlights. When he needed to sleep, he'd curl up in his car in the parking lot.

If a customer wanted to rent a trailer and drop it off in an area without a U-Haul rental outlet, L.S. would let him do it—if he'd promise to try to talk a local gas station owner into becoming a *de facto* U-Haul outlet. L.S. lost a few trailers that way, but more often he gained new outlets and expanded U-Haul territory.

No one called the man who slept in his car "Slick" any more; now, using his middle name, they called him "Sam the Trailer Man." His first wife, Anna Mary Carty, signed all the company's checks with her initials and her own last name. People assumed "A.M. Carty" was the company owner.

Anna Mary struggled to keep the company's books and to raise the Shoen children as observant Catholics by herself. L.S. was always on the road, missing nearly all of the children's births. Earlier, when the couple married, they had been told by Anna Mary's physician to avoid having children because of her weak heart. This was advice that L.S. and Anna Mary ignored, with Anna Mary paying the price. She died in 1957 of a heart attack at 35, after 13 years of marriage—and six babies.

Now L.S. had six young children who needed his attention, along with an equally demanding business. The company won his attention: As orange U-Haul trailers became a familiar sight on the nation's highways, the firm became a seductive profit machine with 250,000 annual rentals by the late '50s.

Yet home obligations nagged at L.S. His solution to competing demands was to delegate the children to his new wife, the young daughter of a neighbor. "I just thought I'd find a good Catholic girl, and all my troubles would be over," he said later. L.S. was 41; Suzanne was 22.

His troubles were just starting. Suzanne was only 10 years older than her oldest stepchild. The couple thought they'd solve that problem by sending the oldest boys, Sam and Mike, away to boarding school. They kept younger sons E.J. (Joe) and Mark as well as the baby Mary Anna at home. Joe and Mark disliked having a stepmother, and they showed it. Each time L.S. returned home from the road, the boys would greet him with a litany of their stepmother's shortcomings.

Five more children were born to Suzanne and L.S. in the next years, increasing the animosities among the 11 children. In an abrupt decision that L.S. hoped would unite them, he moved the family from Portland onto a six-acre estate in Phoenix in 1967. The tranquility of the new house's Frank Lloyd Wright design contrasted with the turmoil of its household.

In addition to the rancor between the children and their stepmother, cliques formed among the kids. The two oldest boys, Sam and Mike, pitted themselves against their brothers Joe and Mark. The leaders of the opposing groups were Sam, now 47, and Joe, now 42. Mark's fighting with his stepmother escalated, and when he was 16 he knocked her out during an argument. L.S., who'd interrupted the fight, described Mark: "It was like watching a prizefighter."

Suzanne called the police and filed charges. L.S. wanted Mark out of the house, but rather than forcing Mark to assume responsibility for his actions, L.S. gave his son substantial cash for an apartment, a car, and a checking account to encourage him to move out.

L.S. did try to involve his sons in the company. They painted so many U-Haul trailers that they joked their blood must be orange. As L.S. prospered, his schemes became more grandiose. For example, there was the Phoenix Wild West theme park he bought to teach the kids fundamentals of business. The family management project was soon sold.

In the '70s, both the patched-together family and the solid company began showing fissures. Suzanne divorced L.S. in 1977 after 19 years of marriage. The last straw had been the child (number 12) born to his girlfriend. As soon as the divorce came through, L.S. married the child's mother to legitimize the birth. His good intentions weren't long-lived; he divorced his bride later that day.

L.S. boasted of his fecundity, "The quality can be questioned but the quantity can't be denied." (L.S. has since married a fourth wife. So far, there are no children.)

In addition to the family's dissolution, the oil crisis of 1973 spiraled U-Haul into a downturn. When a substantial share of the 14,000 full-service gas stations that rented U-Hauls closed, so did many of the company's outlets. L.S. was forced to find expensive, independent U-Haul rental locations. As he watched competitors like Jartran and Ryder enter the industry U-Haul once had to itself, he feared for the future. L.S.'s managers, the loyal blue-collar workers who'd helped with the company's start-up, were incapable of providing professional advice.

Despite U-Haul's slump, the company was still valued at about $300 million. But L.S. had given nearly all of it away. His 12 children—seven sons and five daughters—owned 94 percent of the company. When L.S.'s first five children were born, he had given them each about 10 percent of U-Haul stock, citing tax benefits. (At its peak, a 10 percent stake in U-Haul would have been worth $70 million.) The later children received smaller portions of stock. L.S. gave a stake in the company to its employees, and ended up with only two percent for himself.

In 1973, the older children began entering the business that they collectively owned. Like his father, Sam had gone to medical school, but left his medical career after graduation with the implicit promise from L.S. that he would eventually take over U-Haul. This deal riled younger brother Joe, who felt he should also be a contender. The brothers argued at work just as they'd argued at home when they were boys.

But they had one thing in common: They owned a greater stake in the company than their father, and they were tired of his eccentricities. L.S.'s habits—unnecessary penny-pinching, long-winded speeches quoting philosophers and personal heroes, and surprise inspection visits to U-Haul dealers—grated on the brothers, who knew they needed to move the company into professional management if it were to survive.

Despite lagging truck and trailer revenues, L.S. decided to diversify. He decided that if he could rent trailers, he could rent anything. In 1975, L.S. bought nearly 1,000 former Chrysler buildings from dealers who'd gone out of business. He stuffed the huge spaces with general rental merchandise: party trays, kayaks, picnic tables, VCRs, surfboards, floor sanders, and even motor homes. The diversification was financed with long-term debt, which immediately began to eat into profits.

While L.S. was jump-starting the new rental scheme, the company's core business sputtered. No money was being spent on replacing aging trucks, despite the company's aggressive new rival, Ryder, which offered automatic shift air-conditioned trucks. U-Haul's market share dropped to 55 percent of the industry it had originated and once dominated. Sam and Joe were beginning to wonder whether the business would be around much longer.

Due to the stress of seeing both his business and his family totter, L.S. entered the hospital for depression in 1978. When discharged, he came back to U-Haul to find his sons still arguing. He tried for another of his quick-fix solutions and reassigned them to different positions. It didn't work. Next, L.S. set up group therapy sessions with both a psychologist and a family business expert as mediators. That didn't work, either.

Disgusted with their father and their brother Sam, Joe and Mark resigned in 1979 and started a printing business. L.S. gave much of U-Haul's printing business to his sons' new company and continued their U-Haul salaries for two years. Sam became president of U-Haul.

The company's bottom line was fluctuating wildly, but showing a general downturn. Profits were $28 million in 1982, rising to a high of $42 million in 1984, then dropping to $8.6 million in 1986 and further down to $2 million the next year. Long-term debt equaled nearly half of capital as L.S. continued the general merchandise rentals at the expense of truck and trailer upgrades.

In 1986, Joe and Mark warned their siblings that U-Haul's future was dim but that, under proper management, shareholders could be receiving substantial dividends. Entranced, the sibling followers agreed they'd had enough of L.S. and voted him out of the company. They also expelled Sam (still sympathetic to his father's diversification ideas) from the board and installed Joe in his father's place.

L.S. made himself the sacrificial lamb, agreeing to retire in 1987 if the brothers would meet with a mediator to rethink their own positions. An unworkable deal was struck: Sam became president of U-Haul and Joe was made chairman of the parent company. In addition, a four-member board was established that gave Joe two supporters in the persons of his younger brothers.

Trying to suppress talk of family animosity, the children threw a retirement party for their ousted father. It was called a "Celebration of Love and Respect." The company gathering gave L.S. an opportunity to make a lengthy speech about family love. "I do want you all to know," he exhorted the assembled U-Haul workers, "that I trust my sons and daughters—absolutely."

Sam was unable to stomach board meetings, with their shouting, chest-butting, and punching. Outmaneuvered by Joe, Sam quit the business a few months later. L.S. sided with Sam. The two men, along with those siblings who were sympathetic to them, called themselves "the outsiders."

The improvements in the business were not coming along as quickly as had been hoped. Joe began to lose support from siblings. In a defensive move, he declared the firm's first dividend. Within a few months, a magnanimous second dividend of $12.50 was issued, which distributed $1.3 million among family members. Joe also cancelled U-Haul's traditional Christmas bonus to employees, as well as L.S.'s annual $400,000 contract—which had been his pension.

Various siblings shifted loyalties, and in 1988 Sam and L.S. had cornered support from 52 percent of the stockholders (six of the children). L.S.'s lawyers said to writer John Tayman that when Joe was told of the new outsider coalition, he started "screaming like a bishop cornered by Satan."

Then Joe and his supporters got busy, too. In a formal board move, Amerco treasury stock was sold to nonfamily members who were loyal managers. This conveniently shifted voting power back to Joe, and the outsiders' holdings declined to 47 percent. (As an additional slap, Joe lent the managers the downpayments.)

Then the board put in place a poison pill, a voting trust to unite the votes. The directors also voted that only they could call special shareholder meetings. These steps further locked out L.S. and the outsiders.

Several lawsuits were filed, including a suit over the stock sale and a suit accusing Joe and Mark's printing company of overcharging U-Haul. "We're very frustrated," said Sam in an understatement. One of the outsiders—who requested anonymity—bemoaned his status as he attempted to explain the rationale for the lawsuits: "I don't want the door to my future, my fortune, my inheritance slammed in my face."

With the lawsuits in the offing, Amerco's credit rating went down and virtually killed a preferred stock offering. Now it was time for Amerco to sue Sam and his wife Eva for $750 million, charging that they gave confidential information to outsiders. Another suit was filed against Sam, L.S., and sympathizer Mike on the grounds of harassment. Legal fees surpassed $5 million.

This family business was stuck in a nightmare. At its 1989 annual meeting in Reno, Mike brought a tape recorder to record the proceedings. The insiders didn't like the idea. The arguing started, as did name calling, which quickly lapsed into obscenities. And as in the old days, pushing, chest-butting, punching and hitting ensued. Guards were called in to restore peace, or at least a semblance of order.

L.S. tried to get Joe's attention, crying out, "Mr. Chairman, I am your father, I established this company, I have some points to make!" At the meeting's close, Mike posed shirtless for the press to show his bruises. "I created a monster," moaned L.S.

The lawsuits against Joe were dismissed, leaving him and the insiders with majority share. In a burst of creativity, L.S. adopted a nephew and subsequently gained control of the nephew's Amerco stock held in trust. However, L.S. and his supporters still didn't have enough to reinstate the founder.

Joe believes he's capable of running the company and points out that he has both a law degree and a Harvard M.B.A. "I didn't just fall off a turnip truck," he told *Newsweek*. Although he'd criticized his father for keeping old cronies in the company, three of the top positions were given to loyal brothers Mark, Paul, and Jim.

However, Joe has also concentrated on getting U-Haul back on the road with a back-to-basics plan he instituted in 1989. He's been selling the unprofitable rental subsidiaries, replacing aging trucks and restructuring the company's debt.

But the worst was still to come, with an event that has only been rumored to relate to the family feud. Sam and Eva, 44, had fled the turmoil and moved their family to Telluride, a mountain town in Colorado. One night in late summer 1990, when Sam was in Phoenix working on an Amerco lawsuit, the sleeping Eva was shot with a silenced gun in what looked like a professional hit. The two children and seven guard dogs did not awaken. Tragically, Eva's children discovered her dead body, sprawled on the stairs where she died trying to escape her assassin. They ran to a neighbor: "Mommy's dead, Mommy's dead."

No motive could be determined. Because the murder looked like a professional killing, family and company squabbles were mentioned as a possible rationale. "Nobody is a suspect and everybody is a suspect," laconically explained the county sheriff.

Even the murder investigation broke into factions. L.S. contributed $50,000 to the understaffed local police force to help defray expenses and hired a public relations firm to handle the press inquires. Joe was angered by the rumors that implicated those involved in the family fight. He had U-Haul hire its own investigator, who wrote a report critical of the local police investigation. Meanwhile, Sam offered a $250,000 reward to anyone who could help solve his wife's murder.

L.S. now lives in retirement with his young wife. He freely expresses his thoughts. "No man should give away his wealth or power until he dies. No way. No way."

Jack Dorrance (3rd generation) thought that Campbell Soup was his heritage.

Campbell Soup Company
Camden, New Jersey

Business:	Food product producer
Best Known Products:	Campbell's Soup; Prego Spaghetti Sauce; Vlasic; Pepperidge Farm; Swanson; V8 Cocktail Vegetable Juice; Mrs. Paul's Kitchen; Godiva
Founded:	1869 by Joseph Campbell and Abram Anderson
Family Executives:	John T. Dorrance III, Director and Chairman, Vlasic Foods Bennett Dorrance, Director Mary Alice Malone, Director George Strawbridge, Jr., Director Charlotte C. Weber, Director
Family History:	4th generation board members
Family Ownership:	Approximately 55 percent
Family Board Membership:	5 family members of 16 directors
Traded:	NYSE; Philadelphia; London; Swiss: CPB
Net Sales:	$6,204,100,000 1991 6,205,800,000 1990 5,672,100,000 1989
Net Earnings:	$401,500,000 1991 4,400 1990[a] 13,100 1989[b]

[a] *Includes pretax divestiture and restructuring charges of $301,600,000 (after taxes)*
[b] *Includes pretax restructuring charges of $260,800,000 (after taxes)*

CAMPBELL SOUP COMPANY

Simmering the Family Stock at Campbell Soup

Dorrance Family

The tale of the Dorrance family shows what can happen to a family fortune closely tied to ownership of one of America's best-known companies, Campbell Soup Company. Campbell is ranked 74th in the 1992 *Business Week* list of the 1,000 most valuable U.S. companies, and is the nation's leader in sales of soups, pickles, and olives, ranking second in canned pasta and spaghetti sauce. The Dorrance family shows that it may not be possible to continue a fourth-generation family connection to a business that has made the Dorrances—all nine branches of the family, scattered throughout the United States—enormously wealthy.

The Dorrance link to Campbell Soup Company began in 1876, seven years after the founding of the company. In 1869, fruit merchant Joseph Campbell and icebox manufacturer Abram Anderson had formed a partnership to can and sell vegetables, tomatoes, jellies, pickles, and mincemeat. They opened their first plant in Camden, New Jersey, still headquarters for giant Campbell. This partnership was dissolved in 1876 with the departure of Abram Anderson, who was replaced that same year by Arthur Dorrance, a chemist.

Condensed soup was originated by Arthur's nephew, Dr. J.T. Dorrance, who'd earned a Ph.D. in chemistry from a German university. It allowed the consumer to add water at home, a step that cut in half the can's size and weight and reduced its cost to 10 cents from the 30 cents charged by Campbell's competitors. The Campbell company cleared nearly a penny on every can.

The company's familiar red-and-white labels were introduced in 1898. (The colors were a nod to the Dorrances' alma mater, Cornell University, which also uses red and white.) In 1900, the soup won the gold medallion for excellence at the Paris Exposition, and the medallion's replica was placed on the red-and-white labels (still to be seen there today).

The firm changed its name to the more succinct Campbell Soup Company in 1922. Arthur C. Dorrance, J.T.'s brother, succeeded as president upon J.T.'s death at 57 in 1930, the same year the company formed its first international subsidiary in Canada. (J.T., as sole owner of the company, left an estate valued at $115 million, the third largest recorded in the United States to that date.) J.T.'s son, J.T. "Jack" Dorrance Jr., was only 11.

In 1936, the company began manufacturing its own cans. By 1942, sales exceeded $100 million and four years later, at the death of Arthur in 1946, nonfamily members began to run the company that was still owned by the Dorrance family. Campbell Soup Company went public in 1954 with one class of common stock. (Jack and his sisters sold 42 percent of their shares to the public, retained a few percent for executive stock options, and kept the majority stake for the family.) By 1958, sales had topped $500 million and the company entered continental Europe after a 25-year presence in the United Kingdom.

In 1962, Jack Dorrance joined the board of directors at age 43, having been active at the company since 1946 with a boyhood stint sweeping floors. Jack was one of the last patricians, living a life on Philadelphia's Main Line financed by his 56.8 percent stake in Campbell Soup that paid him annual dividends of $34 million. (His three sisters were deceased, so the family shares were being held in trust for their children by Jack.) His 49-acre estate in Gladwyne, across the Delaware River from Camden, boasted rows of greenhouses; outdoor sculpture; and a $130 million collection of Impressionists, modern paintings, Chinese art and porcelain, and Russian art and furniture. (His collection decidedly did not include Andy Warhol's Campbell's Soup Can painting, although he later commissioned another soup can painting from Warhol for the company.)

Jack idealized his late father and thought that Campbell Soup was his heritage. He went to the office three times a week even

after retiring from the board in 1984. His three children and
nieces and nephews who were not interested in working at the
company, lacked Jack's intense feelings about Campbell.
However, any thoughts that might have been considered disloyal
by their uncle were unspoken during his lifetime.

Several family members agreed to serve on the Campbell
board at Jack's request. Niece Dorrance "Dodo" Hamilton was
the first of the fourth generation board members and was joined
by her cousin John "Ippy" Dorrance III on his father's retirement.
As the majority shareholder, Jack resisted any consideration of a
company buyout.

As Jack aged, deathwatch speculators kept a lookout on
Campbell's stock. Two days after his death in April 1989, they'd
pushed up the stock price by 20 percent. The hope was that his
heirs—his three children and six nieces and nephews—would sell
the company to the highest bidder. The knowledge infuriated
Ippy, who remarked at his father's funeral, "I hope those Wall
Street arbs lose a lot of money."

Indeed, R. Gordon McGovern, Campbell's CEO since 1980,
had paid courtesy calls on all the Dorrances, fearful that they
might sell the company and that McGovern would lose his control. McGovern heard first-hand that the Dorrance heirs were
unhappy with Campbell's earnings, which had been lower (8.2
percent) than the industry average (12.4) in the decade under
McGovern.

In 1992, the Campbell Soup Company chairman is Robert J.
Vlasic. Vlasic came to the company in 1978, when Campbell
bought Vlasic Foods Inc., the pickle-and-condiment business his
father had founded, and made it a Campbell unit.

The choice of Vlasic over McGovern as chairman was in the
family tradition of choosing a nonexecutive for the chairmanship.
However, it was also seen as a warning to McGovern that the
family was not happy with his leadership.

Shortly before Jack's death, Vlasic approached Ippy and asked
him to consider merging Campbell with another monolith in the
food industry, Quaker Oats. His plan was that McGovern, who
was in his 60s, should retire at the time of the merger. Vlasic
would become chairman of the giant food corporation that would

emerge as the country's second largest, behind Philip Morris Companies.

Eventually, Vlasic would need to gain family approval. Jack, of course, had held a 56.8 percent stake, which was valued at $2.2 billion at the time of his death. These shares were in trust and passed tax free to his three children, who received 31 percent or 10.5 percent each, and to his six nieces and nephews, who together inherited 26.5 percent of Campbell stock. The year before his death, Jack had convinced his four nieces and two nephews to combine this 26.5 stake into a loosely organized voting trust that would enable them to have a stronger voice when communicating with the company. (Jack also left his six grandchildren $30 million each from his estate of $197 million—excluding the value of his Campbell stock.)

The 10.5 percent stake that each of his children inherited was valued at $330 million and gave each of them initial dividends of $13 million. None of Jack's children had ever seemed interested in a career at Campbell Soup, although they had worked there despite their wealth.

Ippy, the oldest, operates a 17,400-head cattle ranch in Wyoming, located at the foot of Devil's Tower National Monument, the site of Steven Spielberg's extraterrestrial contacts in *Close Encounters of the Third Kind*. Ippy had a plan to bring more tourists to the area with a zoo he'd devised for his ranch. It would include such exotic animals as the European boar and the Arctic wolf. Unfortunately for Ippy, the state of Wyoming and his fellow ranchers were fearful of interbreeding between Ippy's escaped exotica and their cattle. They successfully opposed his idea, referred to locally as "Ippy's Dippy Zoo."

Jack's second child, Mary Alice Malone, is an expert horsewoman and breeds "Dutch warmblood" horses at her Iron Spring Farm in Pennsylvania. Her younger brother Bennett Dorrance owns DMB Associates, a Phoenix, Arizona investment and real estate firm. Bennett became a director upon his father's death.

The first two years after Jack's death showed a splintered family. All of Jack's children were interested in keeping Campbell Soup independent. They were also fearful of a merger that would dilute their own shares. (For example, Vlasic's proposed merger of Campbell with Quaker would have reduced the family's total shares from 58 percent to 30 percent.)

But a number of the cousins remained fractious over the company's poor showing under McGovern. The dissidents, as they were termed, were dissatisfied with the low share yield (about 2 percent at the end of 1989) and with McGovern's lackluster performance. They were not opposed to either a merger or a sale if the result would be higher dividends.

The dissidents also became angry when they learned of the secretive courtship of Ippy by Vlasic for the proposed Quaker merger. But although Vlasic had alienated them over Quaker, they indicated they would sell at the right price.

On the opposing side, Jack's children remained insistent that the company remain independent and family controlled. Goldman, Sachs & Company had put together the merger proposal. When Ippy, Bennett, and Mary Alice heard the name of the architect of the plan that would knock down the family company, they were infuriated: Goldman, Sachs was their family's investment banker. Board members Ippy and Bennett wanted to know exactly who Goldman, Sachs was representing.

Now the chance of a merger with Quaker was angrily squashed. In reacting this way, Jack's children may have driven away other suitors. (Other possibilities had been Ralston Purina Company and Philip Morris.) Ironically, every time news of the family squabble reached the press, Campbell stock price was driven upward by investors who hoped for a takeover.

The leader of the dissidents was philanthropist Dodo, the family's oldest board member. Dodo, who had never liked her cousin Ippy and was also worried about estate tax implications of her shares, threatened to sell her 7 percent stake. Joining her was Charles Norris, who was married to Jack's niece Diana. Their stake was 2.8 percent. Hope "Happy" von Bueren, with 6.8 percent of the company, was also a dissident. Together, their shares totaled 17.6 percent.

More speculation ensued when Campbell's CEO McGovern resigned in November 1989, rather than wait a few more years to retirement. Talk of the depth of the family unhappiness over Campbell's course started rumors that McGovern had been fired by the Dorrances. Certainly Campbell faced serious problems:

Operating costs were high, plants were inefficient, and brands and product lines were overexpanded at the cost of their core business. The organizational restructuring that McGovern had been carrying out over the past 18 months was coming to grips with these problems, but in the meantime, the restructuring cut heavily into profits.

In December, Bennett called a board nominating committee and successfully proposed new family members: loyalist sister Mary Alice and neutral cousin Charlotte Weber, whom the press had dubbed "Manhattan's wealthiest woman." These two brought the number of family board members to six of fifteen. (A cousin, George Strawbridge Jr., was also a board member maintaining neutrality and pushing for family conciliation. One of the few family members who was talking to the press, he declared, "My shares are not for sale.")

Not by chance, neither of the new boardwomen was a dissident. Also an odd coincidence was the fact that dissident Dodo had made it clear she couldn't attend a meeting on the date Bennett had called.

Bennett's board action strengthened the mistrust felt by the three cousins who were left out of board membership consideration (Happy, Diana, and Tristam "Tris" Colket Jr.). And it confirmed the negative feelings of the dissidents.

Maybe if the company had been making plenty of money, the seething dissidents would have been mollified. But it wasn't, and the family was still unsure whom the board would choose to replace McGovern. The SEC was kept busy the remainder of December 1989 receiving filings from dissidents Happy and Dodo, who stated that they were reviewing their options, and by separate filings from the Dorrance children, who signaled their determination to keep Campbell independent.

Another SEC filing indicated that the loosely organized voting trust that Jack Dorrance had talked his nieces and nephews into in 1987 had been dissolved. Because the nieces and nephews were divided, there was no point in continuing a trust that was intended to enable them to have a stronger voice—singular. Now each Dorrance descendent was speaking with a separate voice, just as they were each investing their money independently. In trading on the day of the trust's dissolution announcement, Campbell shares soared.

On December 29, 1989 the board chose David Johnson as the company's next CEO. From the beginning, the selection of the Gerber Products Company's CEO looked smart. Johnson had stepped into Gerber, a business with deep organizational problems, and quadrupled earnings and tripled the stock's value. Perhaps as important, he had quelled the unhappy Gerber family members who own roughly 10 percent of Gerber stock. Asked about the Dorrances, Johnson said, "The dispute will certainly complicate my life, but I'm not falling on my sword."

After Johnson's appointment as CEO was announced, Campbell stock jumped again.

New board member Charlotte Weber, thought to have been neutral, said in a letter also signed by her brother Tris that they were thinking of combining their nearly 7 percent stake with the dissident group's 17.4 percent. Charlotte seemed inclined to support Campbell's merger with another company.

During the first half of 1990, the family members kept their traditional positions. Dodo, Happy, and Diana formed a new trust in June with their 17.4 percent stake to seek a sale of the company. Charlotte and Tris declined to join them, despite their statement that they were holding their shares in Campbell, "although we would prefer to maintain that investment as part of a much larger entity. Independence cannot be a goal in itself."

Johnson named himself Campbell's "top spoon" and promptly stirred up some changes. He's credited with a rebound in profits stemming from his reorganization and cost-cutting: the work force was cut by one-fifth; 20 plants were closed worldwide, including the original 1876 Camden plant; and the many unprofitable brands that McGovern had launched were pulled back. By getting back to basics, Campbell's canned-soup market share increased 4 percentage points to 76.5 percent in 1991.

And it seems the gains Johnson was making, along with the sheer force of time, have quelled the family dissidents. In the fall of 1990, Dodo retired. The reasons given for her departure included her 10 years on the board and her husband's illness. She was replaced by a nonfamily member who agreed to support her wish for a company sale or merger, but her absence was generally seen as lessening takeover prospects.

In the spring of 1991, Diana pulled her 3 percent Campbell stake from the dissidents to support management. The remaining hardcore dissidents, Dodo and Happy, together sold a 1.6 percent stake to neutral institutional investors. To some, it looked as if the chance for a takeover had receded. But the company continued to look attractive as David Johnson approached his goals of 20 percent growth in volume, in earnings, in return on equity, and in return on invested cash. As the shares continued to rise, one dissident made a judgment: "We're in a win-win situation."

And the Campbell Soup Company stock price continues to rise.

George Johnson, founder: "My hope is that some sanity will dawn on some of these people and they'll realize what they've done."

Johnson Products Company
Chicago, Illinois

Business:	Ethnic hair care and beauty aids
Best Known Products:	Ultra Sheen, Classy Curl, Soft Touch
Founded:	1954 by George and Joan Johnson, Sr.
Family Executives:	Joan Johnson, Sr., Office of the President Joan Johnson, Jr., Chairman and Treasurer George Johnson, Consultant
Family History:	Second generation
Family Ownership:	61 percent
Family Board Membership:	2 family members of 5 directors
Traded:	American Stock Exchange, JPC
Net Sales:	$38,406,000 1991 33,497,000 1990 29,368,000 1989
Net Earnings:	$3,200,000 1991 2,125,000 1990 2,009,000 1989

JOHNSON PRODUCTS COMPANY

Sibling Rivalry

Johnson Family

Johnson Products, best known for its Ultra Sheen, Soft Touch, Classy Curl, and Gentle-Treatment brand lines, suffered dramatically falling profits in the '80s. Sales dropped 36 percent between 1983 and 1988—the last years of leadership by Eric Johnson's father, George Johnson, who'd founded the Chicago-based company in 1954. (The family controls about 61 percent of the shares.) On the day in 1989 that 38-year-old Eric was named CEO, Johnson stock topped out at its highest since 1987. And the company's 1991 earnings, $2.2 million, stand in testimony to Eric's ability to pull the company from its $2.8 million loss in 1988.

In an interview in 1991, Eric attributed his company's new direction to a transformation that often takes place when second generation management takes charge of a family business. "This company is going through a transition not so much from the George Johnson era to the Eric Johnson era as from the entrepreneurial style to the professional," says Eric.

George Johnson needed that entrepreneurial style in 1954 when he made his move from Fuller Products (then the largest black-owned cosmetic company in the United States) to strike out with his own company, manufacturing and selling hair products for black men to barbershops. To get started, George wanted to go to business's standard source for start-up capital, but no Chicago bank was willing to lend this black man the $500 he needed to produce a chemical hair straightener. A bank did give him half the money after he set aside his pride and changed his request to a personal loan for a vacation. A chemist at Fuller put up the remaining dollars, and George was in business, with his wife, Joan, working by his side. By the early '60s, the company dominated its market, having expanded to sell retail products to both men and women.

Although the company was a little slow in picking up the "black is beautiful" philosophy of the late '60s and missed a timely start-up of natural hair products needed to compensate for the falling sales of the company's hair-straightening products, it soon bounced back with its new product, Afro Sheen. By the early '70s, sales had quadrupled for Johnson Products. George Johnson brought the company public in 1971, making Johnson Products the first black-managed company offered for investment on a major exchange.

There were negatives in the decision to go public, too. Because it was the first ethnic hair care company to trade on the exchange, Johnson's information was widely available for anyone to look at, stimulating interest in this industry. "Yes, it had some financial advantages for George Johnson, but I think it also cost the company dearly in terms of people looking for lucrative markets" and seeing the possibilities in ethnic hair care, Eric says.

But the real problem came five years later, courtesy of the federal government. The Federal Trade Commission required a warning label on those hair-straightening products containing lye, an ingredient in virtually every straightener. While other companies stalled, George immediately complied with the FTC's mandate. Johnson factory workers slapped on the required five-paragraph warning label, scaring off once-loyal customers.

The worst part of this federal requirement, from Johnson Products' point of view, was the FTC's selective enforcement. Johnson Products dominated the field, with 80 percent of the hair relaxer market in 1976. The FTC, looking at the relative market shares of those companies selling straighteners, applied its order immediately to Johnson Products, to Soft Sheen Products Inc. (another black-owner family business in Chicago), and to a small, Southern, white-owned company. The real harm came when the FTC waited 20 months to apply its order to Revlon, using the rationale that the impact of Revlon's product was much smaller than that of Johnson or the other ethnic companies. Eric says that Revlon took advantage of this delay in its advertising. "Revlon for 18 months was able to say, 'Look, our product is safer.'" He mimics their message, "'In fact, we're the safest product on the market, as you can tell. We don't have to have the warning label.'"

The nearly two-year delay gave Revlon the time it needed to break the dominance of black-owned hair companies in the ethnic personal beauty aids market. It was a disastrous period for Johnson Products. George Johnson remembers, "I didn't think we'd ever recover from it." Eric says, "At that point we'd lost 40 points of market share, and the erosion continued." It not only weakened consumer loyalty, but it opened the door for general market companies to come into the industry. "Prior to that, there were none," Eric says.

"I think it also tended to break the spirit of George Johnson. He was never as confident from that day forward, and I think that it had a lot to do with the change in Johnson Products." Eric explains that what Johnson executives once saw as a promising horizon became one clouded with storm warnings. "It can be tampered with by the government as well as by competitors," was the new attitude at Johnson.

This attitude was a shock to the young man who'd seen the golden era of the company when he was a child and teenager. Starting at age seven, Eric had spent his summers at the factory, playing on boxes and occasionally remembering his assigned task of wiping excess cream off the jars for a quarter an hour. Both his mother and father were at the company every day, driving the short commute to the unpretentious factory/headquarters from their house in Chatham, a swank community on Chicago's southside, which boasts the highest average income of any black neighborhood in the country. "I never really thought seriously about doing anything else," Eric says, in contrast to his three younger siblings, none of whom worked at Johnson Products until 1991, when Joan Johnson Jr., 27, received her M.B.A.

After graduating from college, Eric went immediately to Johnson Products but lasted only three months. "Everything I did was okay," he says of life in his father's company. "If I didn't file an expense report, nobody said anything. Everyone looked at me as just the chairman's son."

Eric left for a Johnson sales job in Detroit in an effort to avoid favoritism at headquarters. When the bias continued, he went to the biggest consumer products company with the best sales/mar-

keting program he could find: Procter & Gamble Co. (see JAMES
GAMBLE).

Returning to Johnson Products in the late '70s was not a
pleasant experience for 24-year-old Eric. He saw Johnson executives, still reeling from the one-two punch of the FTC/Revlon
debacle, reacting by following the safest business strategies they
could identify. "Well, in my opinion," Eric says, "there's no such
thing in business as a safe strategy. You're either moving ahead or
you're going to move behind."

The problem was, few others shared Eric's viewpoint. So he
took control of the franchise beauty salons and Johnson's private
label brand lines. Eric says he purposely stayed outside Johnson's
main operations. "Rather than get in there and argue with everybody else, I said, 'Hey, you guys do that. Give me something that I
can build exclusive of the core of the business.'"

"My dad came to me and said, 'Rick, I really need you to run
sales,' and I told him no, I wouldn't do it. He said, 'Well, why not?
Aren't you willing to help in this?'"

Eric said he'd do anything for the company. "But Dad, sales is
not enough. I'm not going to take a sales position and then have to
fight with marketing and production and everybody else. And I
can't play by the rules that I see elsewhere in the organization."

Any strain due to Eric's turndown wasn't eased when George
hired a sales director because sales continued their downward
slide. "Things were going so poorly that I really began to think
about what the place would be like in two years—will there be a
place in two years? When my dad came back again, I said 'Okay, I'll
do it.'"

Things started to change at Johnson Products after Eric took
over sales, but it was by no means a quick turnaround. Eric wanted
to take agressive steps, yet he saw himself surrounded by people
who didn't want to move. He turned this to his advantage. "If
you've got it all laid out, it's a lot easier for them to accept what you
have than to come up with something on their own. And so in
essence, I did at that time get control of marketing. The person
with the title is not necessarily the person who runs the show."

Eric moved into the position of senior vice president, then
executive vice president. Although not officially in charge of marketing while heading sales, in reality he had command. He notes

that sometimes in a family business, persistence and tenacity must be used in business dealings even with parents.

Eric relates this philosophy to the prosperity of Johnson's core product lines. "Every one of the products that are original Johnson products, the concepts and ideas, they do well, they do great. And every one that we copied because we saw someone else doing a good job, they don't do a thing."

"There was an episode on 'Dallas' (you know, you get things from all kinds of places), and I remember Bobby saying to Jock one day, 'But, Daddy, you gave me the power to run Ewing Oil.' Jock looked at him and said, 'Bobby, nobody can give you power.' And that registered."

Eric says "My dad did come to me and he said, 'You're not letting me in on the inner circle. You're not telling me what's going on here. I need to be kept informed. I'm still the CEO of this company.'" Eric leans back and laughs. "I said to him, 'It takes me all day to do it. How much time do you want me to spend with you explaining it?'"

Eric continued to pull Johnson Products through changes in the '80s. (By this time, George and Joan Johnson had moved to suburban Glencoe, and Joan was no longer making the daily commute.) The year 1986 was a bleak one for the company, so Eric pulled in some turnaround specialists who did a cash-in/cash-out analysis that resulted in a considerable downsizing.

Eric saw that this 20 percent reduction of staff was necessary, but it didn't convince him of the value of consultants. "It's a short-term strategy, at best. And what happens after the consultants leave is that people go back to the same things that they've been doing. As a result, the company made a profit that year and then went right back into its losses."

So in 1988, when Eric took over as chief operating officer and president of Johnson Products, he began looking at fresh objectives for the company. "Quality management is the number one key to growth and development. The difficult thing about a small business is that people have to have a broader range of talents. You have to be a doer in a small business, you have to be able to execute things, and you have to be able to know all the pieces."

It's a particularly tough issue in the shrinking manufacturing sector in the United States today. "I can't hire from my competitors," Eric points out, "They're gone." The alternative is extensive training programs.

In 1988, the first year of his presidency, Eric says he didn't want to get to the root of the company's former problems so much as to start afresh.

In that same year, Eric was also watching his parents' 37-year marriage unravel. This was one divorce that made *The Wall Street Journal*. In 1989 George Johnson resigned from the company he'd founded and transferred its control to Joan Johnson as part of the divorce settlement. Prior to the divorce, it was George who'd been the company's principal stockholder, with 49.5 percent of the stock. As a result of the transfer, Joan now controls 61 percent of the company's outstanding common stock, but there was no disagreement about who'd actually manage Johnson Products. The company's board simultaneously announced the change in ownership and named Eric chief executive officer.

George continued at the company as a consultant, and Joan became chairman at the time of the settlement. But Eric was the only one of their four children at the company, a fact he attributes as much to his own competitive level as to their different interests.

In retrospect, Eric's analysis of his siblings is ironic. He points out that one brother promotes rap music and the other is a business consultant. His sister Joanie was married to Dallas cowboy Dennis McKinnon but had filed for divorce by 1992.

When asked if his brothers or Joanie, with her newly-minted M.B.A., might join the company, Eric replies they can "as long as they observe the rules. This is a business first. Maybe first, second, and third it's a business. If family members happen to be in a position to contribute, that's great."

Apparently Joanie believed her contribution to Johnson Products was more valuable than that of Eric, because in early 1992 Eric was pushed out of the company. Their father says that Eric was initially annoyed when Joanie decided to follow her husband to Dallas rather than take a job at the family company. So when she filed for divorce and moved back to Chicago, Eric installed her as director of market research.

Joanie took this as a slight, according to her father. She thought she deserved a more powerful and prestigious position. Joanie began to work on her mother, urging her to bump Eric out of the

CEO spot. And she succeeded at this in early 1992. Now Joanie is one of four executives in a newly devised office of the president.

Eric's denouement was a shock to analysts who credited him with the company's recent success. This was a company that had already seen a shift in control during a family divorce, when George lost the company to Joan. And now the daughter—with the mother—was pushing out the well-liked son. *Newsweek* compared it to a "Dallas" television episode. *Crain's Chicago Business* spoke for many in its editorial that stated "no company run in such an arbitrary and capricious style should be publicly traded."

In another irony, Eric actually had hoped the company could return to private ownership, as *Crain's* suggested. In mid-'91, he had proposed that his mother buy the 39 percent of the company shares outstanding that she didn't own. A potential lawsuit by shareholders nixed that arrangement, though.

At least Eric's fall from grace is cushioned by as much as a $600,000 severance payment, as he pursues other "personal business interests," in the words of his former company.

Eric and Joanie's father, though, is dismayed by the entire episode. "My hope is that some sanity will dawn on some of these people," said George to *Newsweek*, "and they'll realize what they've done."

Willie Farah

Kenneth: "It's really a tragedy. In the end, Willie has no company and no love from his family."

Farah, Inc.
El Paso, Texas

Business:	Multiple apparel lines for men and boys
Best Known Brands:	Farah, Farah Clothing Company, Savene, Process 2000, John Henry (Zodiac)
Founded:	1919 by Mansour Farah as Farah Manufacturing Company, Inc. Incorporated as Farah, Inc. in 1947
Family Executives:	Haleen F. Zweifel, Director
Family History:	Third generation
Family Ownership:	15 percent
Family Board Membership:	1 family member of 10 directors
Traded:	NYSE, FRH
Net Sales:	$151,202,000 1991 139,616,000 1990 239,047,000 1989[a]
Net Earnings:	$(5,508,000) 1991 (6,597,000) 1990 (13,691,000) 1989[a]

[a] *Operations of 1989 includes Generra, sold that year*

FARAH, INC.

No Family and No Company

Farah Family

This is the unhappy story of a family ripped apart by arguments and of a family business, now public, in which family members were cut out in favor of more competent professional managers. More than anything, it is the story of Willie Farah, 73, and his turbulent leadership of the company he had inherited, and from which he was ultimately ousted.

In 1920, Willie's father—Mansour Farah, a Lebanese immigrant—began a workshirt manufacturing business in El Paso. Soon Texas prisons began making shirts more cheaply, and the company turned to manufacturing pants. When Mansour died unexpectedly in 1937, his two sons, James and William (Willie), took over the business rather than finish college. They incorporated the company as Farah Manufacturing Company Inc. shortly after the end of World War II, when the U.S. military services were among their customers. Farah became an early automation leader in an industry with gossamer profit margins.

In the '50s, the company introduced the Farah label in time for an explosive growth in casual slacks. Marketing Farah slacks to retailers was far more profitable than manufacturing anonymously for the military. The '60s were boom years for the company as it became one of the apparel business's fastest-growing manufacturers after its introduction of permanent press pants. The brothers complemented each other, with Willie taking charge of the factory, and James, marketing. But in 1964 James, like his father, died prematurely in the Farah plant of a heart attack at age 47. In 1967 the company went public—a move that foreshadowed the family's problems by increasing its accountability to the business. Initially, the family retained about one-third of its stock.

Willie's son Jimmy worked at Farah for no pay while attending Stanford and the Wharton School. He joined Farah the day after receiving his M.B.A. in 1970. It was made clear immediately that because of his business education, Jimmy would become president rather than either of his two brothers, Kenneth and Robert, who also took jobs at the company. Jimmy told *Family Business* magazine that Farah managers were instructed not to treat him "any differently than anyone else who would eventually be president." Jimmy was given a board seat, as was his sister Haleen.

Jimmy's main problem was his father, who became enraged when Jimmy made suggestions that ran counter to what Willie had already proposed. Kenneth described life with father: "Willie expected blind obedience." Animosity increased. The father and sons would pass each other in headquarters hallways and look the other way. Soon, Kenneth quit the company.

To Willie, the company was his reason for being and he ran it as if it were an extension of his ego. In addition, he was the pit bulldog of decision-making. Managers joked that the company motto should have been, "Where there's a Willie, there's a way."

Another of Willie's strong-willed ways was his rabid chauvinism. In a town teeming with Mexican immigrants, Willie refused to hire foreign labor until the worker had passed his (or more frequently, her) citizenship test. He also refused to do what other apparel companies did to increase margins—build foreign plants. When Willie learned that the nails used to construct his house were a Japanese brand, he had his builder pull each of them out.

In the early '70s, the company endured a two-year labor boycott backed by the winning combination of the Bishop of El Paso and Ted Kennedy. Willie dug his heels in and refused to accede to labor demands even while Farah products were being swept off store shelves by AFL-CIO workers. That year, 1972, Farah Inc. experienced its first loss.

In addition, Willie never had a strong sense for either fashion or marketing. His stubborn viewpoints on those topics left the company stuck with unsalable inventory.

The board of directors stripped Willie of his CEO title in 1976—partly in reaction to the AFL-CIO boycott and partly due to four years of losses—and in protest he resigned as its chairman.

Jimmy was one of those who voted against him. "I didn't want to oppose him," Jimmy said, "but I also couldn't support him."

Farah's creditors took control of the company and installed new outside management. After threatening a proxy fight, Willie was able to return as CEO and chairman. Then in 1978 he successfully sued the creditors for wrongfully assuming control. Besides his reinstatement, he received a $14 million judgment, one of the first that penalized lenders for insinuating themselves into their borrowers' businesses. As soon as Willie returned to the company, he fired a number of employees he believed had been disloyal to him. Armed security guards escorted them out. Jimmy, too, was gone, having left voluntarily.

With Jimmy gone, Willie hired a professional manager as president to help the company rebound. Willie kept the CEO title for himself. Jimmy saw the entrance of a professional manager as a positive sign and was persuaded to return in 1979 as sales manager. His two brothers also reentered. Robert was named head of international operations and Kenneth worked in the accounting section.

Although the new president had stabilized the company, in 1984 he was fired by Willie, who announced that the ultimate goal was for a Farah to resume the presidency. Willie then named Jimmy COO, and Willie himself took over the presidency while retaining his CEO title. Farah's stock fell 25 percent in a single day's trading following the firing.

In 1985, Willie bypassed the two older sons to offer the presidency to the youngest, Robert, who declined in favor of Jimmy. But Jimmy had two problems: He lacked board support, and Willie had said that he would never retire.

There were closed-door meetings to discuss—and argue about—the succession. Willie's children pleaded with him to attend training in family business relations; he refused. They brought in family business experts for group meetings to no avail.

In 1986, Jimmy and Robert talked of selling their Farah stock. Willie accused them of disloyalty. Kenneth discussed a possible takeover with an outsider. When Willie heard of the takeover talk, he summoned his son to his office and called for security guards to eject him from company property. Jimmy and Robert's immediate reaction was to quit once again.

In 1989, the board—unhappy with wavering sales and continued losses—retired William as CEO but left him chairman of the company. Willie continued to battle Farah's new management, so heavily pressuring the board to thwart management that his purpose backfired. In early 1990, the board ousted Willie as chairman. His daughter Haleen was one of the board members who voted against him.

Willie, who then owned a 17 percent stake in the company and still held both a board seat and a consultancy role, retaliated with a lawsuit. The board countersued to remove Willie from the board. Willie came back with a proxy solicitation to unseat seven of nine board members and management, calling them "dummies."

During this stressful period, The *Wall Street Journal* reported that Willie was telling reporters his office phone was bugged and that seemingly innocent passersby were eavesdropping on his conversations. He also went on walkabouts through the plants, informing certain employees that they would be fired after he regained control. "That doesn't do much for morale," one executive commented later.

In August 1990, the proxy solicitation was resolved. The majority share voted to remove Willie, ending his 53-year career at the company his parents had founded. Although Willie's 17 percent stake was valued at about $4 million, he and his wife filed for bankruptcy to protect them from creditors—including their own four children to whom the parents owed a combined $2.3 million.

Since 1990, Farah Inc., with no family members in management (although Haleen retains her board position), is rebounding from its difficulties. It is still considered one of the country's leading men's pants manufacturers. The changes made by new management resulted in improvements in operations and sales in 1991. It looks as if the company has a good shot at climbing back into profitability. Its CEO, Richard Allender, told *Forbes* something that the Farahs seemed to have forgotten: "We're here to run a business."

At 72, Willie has started a new company, WMF Corp. Although he sees Kenneth and Robert, who are now salesmen, he shuns his daughter and his former heir apparent Jimmy, who heads a venture capital firm and has opened a family business consulting practice. Kenneth remarked in 1990, "It's really a tragedy. In the end, Willie has no company and no love from his family."

Bill was the only Koch who reported to a nonfamily member.

Koch Industries, Inc.
Wichita, Kansas

Business: Transports, trades, and refines petroleum products

Best Known Business: Koch Oil, gasoline; Koch Materials Co., asphalt; Koch Oil Co., crude petroleum pipelines

Founded: 1928 by Fred Koch; 1967 as Koch Industries

Family Executives: Charles Koch, Chairman and CEO
David H. Koch, Executive Vice President and Director

Family History: Second generation

Family Ownership: 80 percent

Family Board Membership: 2 family members of 6 directors

Traded: Privately controlled
Sales: $17,190,000,000 (estimated) 1991
16,000,000,000 (estimated) 1990
15,800,000,000 (estimated) 1989

Net Earnings: Will not disclose

KOCH INDUSTRIES, INC.

Blood, Oil, and Money

Koch Family

Feuds, fringe politics, and litigation epitomize the family that owns the largest oil company in the United States and the second largest American private business. The firm's estimated annual revenues ran higher than $17 billion in 1991—and 80 percent of this company is owned by two of the four Koch (pronounced "coke") brothers of Kansas.

The firm is a relatively young one. Fred C. Koch was an engineer who in 1928 originated an efficient refining process that forced a greater amount of gasoline out of crude oil. He was hampered from marketing his refining process in the United States by charges of patent infringement from the major oil companies. In response, he took his process to the USSR and, as part of Stalin's Five-Year Plan, built 15 refineries for that country in the '20s and '30s.

Fred worked with Soviet scientists who were liquidated by Stalin in the murderous purges of the late '30s. Fred was horrified, and his fervid hatred of communism led him to later cofound the John Birch Society.

Fred continued to battle America's larger, established oil firms over his refining process. It took him two decades, but he eventually won more than 40 lawsuits that had been filed against his company. He also bought and sold oil refineries, eventually folding them into Rock Island Oil & Refining, and established vast cattle ranches. When Fred died in 1967, not only did he leave an important oil business but he was reputed to be the largest landowner in America.

Fred had taught his four sons to hunt, shoot, and ride. He also bequeathed to them a company with $250 million in annual revenues. When his sons were teenagers, he told them that their inherited wealth might be "either a blessing or a curse."

Fred's oldest son and namesake, now 59, disappointed his father by having different interests. Young Frederick, for example, was the only male Koch to study English and drama at Harvard and Yale rather than engineering at M.I.T. He was cut out of Fred's will and does not work at Koch Industries. However, a family trust that gave Frederick 14 percent of the company ensures his wealth. Frederick's 14 percent stake also had implications, 15 years later, in the family feud.

The next son is Charles, 57. He was the most aggressive of Fred's boys and liked to challenge his brothers to frequent games of "King of the Hill." This brother who always won the boyhood games now runs Koch Industries.

David and William, 52, are twins. But David's childhood ally was older brother Charles, not his twin. As a result, Bill suffered, and always felt second best.

Each of Fred's three younger sons inherited 21 percent of Rock Island after their father died from a heart attack while duck hunting.

Charles took over the company as CEO at Fred's death and quickly began to build the business that he renamed Koch Industries. He acquired refineries and oil-trading companies and diversified into related businesses. Charles strongly resembled his father, within the industry and in politics; he donated $5 million to the Libertarian Party.

David ran as the Libertarian Party's nominee for vice president in 1980. He had joined the family business in 1970, three years after his father died.

The next year, after earning a doctorate in chemical engineering, Bill also came to work at Koch. By the mid-'70s, rancor began to bubble up between Bill and the other brothers. They say he performed incompetently; he says they're the ones who mismanaged. Another stone in Bill's craw was the contributions to the Libertarian Party. He told *The New York Times*, "Charles was giving as much to the Libertarians as we were paying out in dividends.

"Here I am," continued the man who in 1979 was earning more than $1 million annually in salary and bonuses, "one of the wealthiest men in America, and I had to borrow money to buy a house."

Bill resented his low position in Koch Industries—as vice president for development, he was the only Koch who reported to a nonfamily member. He also wanted to increase shareholder dividends.

Bill turned to a natural ally, fellow outsider Frederick. Together, in 1980 they forced a proxy fight, which would have expanded the board to give Bill majority control. It was speculated that an early action of the refigured board would be to bring Koch Industries public. But the dissident faction lost, and Bill was fired.

In 1982, Bill sued Charles and David, accusing them of committing fraud while fighting against his proxy move. In turn, Charles and David sued Bill in a $167 million libel action and charged him with being mentally unstable. (In the '70s, Bill had been in analysis for three years.)

Then Charles offered to buy Bill and Frederick's shares. Initially, they thought the money offered fell far short of the shares' real worth. Bill eventually settled in 1983 for a rumored $625 million, and Frederick for about $400 million. The company took out long-term loans of more than $1 billion for the stock purchase.

But by 1985, Bill and Frederick felt they'd been taken advantage of and sued Charles and Koch Industries for undervaluing their stock. They didn't, however, get any more money. In 1986, the court dismissed the core of their suit.

Still the feuding continued. In 1988, Bill hired private detectives to gather evidence that Koch Industries was stealing oil from wells on American Indian reservations. A U.S. Senate committee investigated in 1989 and its report concluded that Koch had stolen millions of dollars worth of oil from the Indians, although the U.S. Bureau of Land Management found no evidence of the underpayment.

Charles was horrified. "Why would someone in your own family try to get the U.S. government to brand you a racketeer?" he asked *The Wall Street Journal*.

There have also been lawsuits over such side issues as the ownership of the father's coin collection and the operation of the family's nonprofit foundation. For the foundation suit, Frederick and Bill had their 86-year-old mother Mary served with a subpoenae. Her lawyer told the judge she had just suffered a stroke. Frederick and Bill claimed that was a smokescreen; she had recently been out playing tennis. (She was excused by the judge.)

The litigious activity has ceased, and there is some degree of satisfaction on both sides. After all, Charles and David walked away with the company. Their 80 percent stake in Koch Industries puts their personal joint worth at about $5 billion. Charles also continues political activities through his contributions to the Cato Institute, a Libertarian think tank.

And Frederick and Bill walked away with a great deal of cash. Their joint fortune is estimated at more than $1 billion.

However, after the family break-up, a wistful David missed those family holidays. "Christmas used to be a time when we would all get together," he said to *The Wall Street Journal*, ignoring Christmas Day, 1979, when the sniping of Bill and Charles made their mother leave the Christmas table in tears. "Now it's just Momma, Charles, and myself."

By the '90s, those Christmases were composed of just Charles and David. And before Mary Koch died, she cut Bill out of her will.

But life continues for the dissidents. Frederick picked up a new residence in England to add to those he owns in Monaco, Manhattan, and Philadelphia. To house his art collection, he bought England's historic Sutton Place (see GORDON GETTY).

Bill established the Oxbow Group, a configuration of companies covering energy and real estate. He lives in Palm Beach and outspent Dennis Conner in competing to represent the United States in the 1992 America's Cup races. Bill has expended at least $50 million to build three high-tech yachts and to hire the world's best sailors. Protective of his boats' design, Bill built a dock with metal sides that drop to the bottom of the bay, in order to thwart scuba-diving spies. "It's taken more resources than I bargained for," he said in an understatement.

Of this massive investment, more than $50 million was Bill's own money. When America won the America's Cup, Bill said, "Maybe in a sober moment I'll change my mind. But right now, it's worth it." Of course, Bill also admitted to the *Washington Post* that his donations to the America[3] Foundation would save him "a coupla' million bucks" on federal taxes.

But winning the race wasn't Bill's only motivation. He told a reporter that he felt closer to his sailing team than he ever did to his own family.

In fact, the notoriety of the Koch feud led the Dennis Conner team to approach Charles and David for money to help them race against Bill in the America's Cup, reported *Town and Country*. "Thank God David had the good sense to turn him down," said Louis Cabot, a family friend and business associate (see CABOT INDUSTRIES).

Meanwhile, Koch Industries continues to grow. The company transports oil, petroleum products and chemicals through its more than 20,000 miles of pipeline. It is also an oil trader and refiner, and owns coal mines, gas processing plants, rights for mineral exploration on 800,000 acres, and vast cattle ranches. Under Charles' leadership, its revenues have increased from $250 million to $19 billion.

However, David—even though an ally—still wants to have the last word. "Being big doesn't guarantee survival," he told *Fortune*. "The dinosaurs were big."

Roger (above) and brother Gerrish are worth at least $1.2 billion.

Milliken & Co., Inc.
Spartanburg, North Carolina

Business:	Textile manufacturing
Best Known Products:	Cotton broadwoven fabrics
Founded:	1865 as Deering-Milliken by William Deering and Seth Milliken
Family Executives:	Roger Milliken, Chairman Minot K. Milliken, Vice President and CEO Gerrish Milliken, Director
Family Board Membership:	3 family members of 13 directors
Traded:	Privately held
Net Sales:	$2,500,000,000 1990 (estimated) 2,900,000,000 1989 (estimated) 2,400,000,000 1988 (estimated)
Net Earnings:	Will not disclose

MILLIKEN & CO., INC.

Unraveling the Family Shares

Milliken and Stroud Families

Unlike many family businesses with dissident minority share-holders, Milliken & Co. is an innovative, prosperous company strongly associated with its chairman, Roger Milliken, 77. The business he runs and controls is a textile powerhouse: It's not only the largest in the country but is several times bigger than its next competitor. Milliken ranks among the top 50 largest privately held companies in America, producing more than 48,000 textile and chemical products.

Milliken & Co. is also a tightly held company that is notoriously close-mouthed about its operations. In 1989, *Forbes* assigned a team of journalists to spend several months delving into the company's financial base. They reported the company's revenues as roughly $2.5 billion with a cash flow of at least $400 million. The company is debt-free and has aftertax earnings that average a minimum eight percent of sales—about twice what the rest of the industry can claim.

The company was founded in 1865 by Roger's grandfather Seth, along with William Deering. (It was formerly named Deering-Milliken.) Although Deering left the company to start Deering Harvester (now Navistar), Seth continued as a New England selling agent for textile mills there and in the South. As an agent, he recognized firms that were basically sound but unprofitable. He bought these companies at bargain prices and soon became the owner of a leading mill company.

Seth's son Gerrish continued this practice and added considerably to the company's holdings during the Depression of the '30s. Perhaps the Millikens learned a lesson from the mill owners they bought out. Milliken & Co's. philosophy is lots of cash and no debt.

In its third generation, Gerrish's son Roger became president of Milliken in 1947 and was quickly known for his autocratic ways: After firing his brother-in-law, W.B. Stroud, in 1955, he declared no other Milliken family members would work in the company. The next year, he closed a plant the day after its workers voted to unionize. For 24 years, the company fought the unfair labor practice suit that resulted from the firings. In 1980 it agreed to settle by paying the workers $5 million in compensation.

Although Roger would not win a popularity contest held by supporters of organized labor, the stupendous growth and stability of Milliken is attributed to him. The company manufactures nearly one-third of the stretch fabric used by American sports apparel and swimsuit manufacturers and the cloth for many of the uniforms worn by such service workers as those at McDonald's and Hertz, reported *Forbes*. It also makes about 40 percent of the acetate fabric used in coat linings and 25 percent of the fabric used in automobiles.

In the '80s, Roger attracted attention when he spoke out against textile imports. A conservative Republican who has contributed to the Heritage Foundation (see ADOLPH COORS COMPANY), he has referred to free trade as "a god no other nation worships."

Roger is a man who once equated unionism with communism. His '80s role as spokesman for the industry-union coalition Crafted With Pride Council, which introduced the "Made in the U.S.A." label, came as a surprise to textile insiders, despite his outspoken stand against imports.

With Roger's hand at the helm, the company has always been known for its innovative mill technologies. In fact, Roger's office overlooks Milliken's R&D facilities. Shortly after the Malcolm Baldrige National Quality Award was established in 1987, Roger insisted on competing for it. The company was passed over the first time it entered. Roger systematically set out to improve performance in those areas found to be wanting. As a result, Milliken won the Baldrige Prize in 1989. Milliken's quality control has resulted in greater efficiency: During the '80s, productivity increased by more than 40 percent.

Part of this surge in competitiveness has been attributed to Milliken's first nonfamily president, Thomas Malone. In fact, except for the role of chairman, which may pass to Roger's brother or cousin, it is expected that professional managers will run Milliken after Roger's death.

Although Roger had seen to it years earlier that there would be no family members waiting in Milliken's management wings, he may not have anticipated potential problems of a family fortune so immense and with so many inheritors. The company has 200 shareholders, the majority of whom are family members. Roger, his brother Gerrish, and his cousin Minot account for more than 50 family trusts. Combined with their individual holdings, the three men control 30 percent of Milliken's 420,000 shares of preferred stock and more than half its 4.2 million shares of common stock. In addition, the family owns about 44 percent of the retail chain, Mercantile Stores.

Roger has continued to deny jobs at the family company to his five children and 16 nieces and nephews. Roger's late sister, Joan Milliken Stroud, left her 15 percent company stake to her family. But, cut out from either a chance at management or a place on the board, Joan's children demanded greater dividends. Because their requests reportedly weren't satisfied by Roger and the board, four of the seven children wanted to sell their shares at fair value.

In 1989, the dissident Strouds sold a small part of their stake—500 common shares and 20 preferred shares. The proportion they sold wasn't noteworthy. What did catch Roger's attention was who bought these shares: a group that included Erwin Maddrey and Bettis Rainsford, founders of Delta Woodside Industries—a Milliken competitor.

Roger refused to disclose all the information on revenues and profits that these new shareholders wanted. They said they had the right to take a look at the company's financial information and to disclose it to potential financial backers.

The partial stock sale to Milliken's competitor may have been a strategy engineered by the Strouds to force Roger and the board to buy their shares at an increased value. It's not a question of the company or the three major shareholders not being able to afford this buyout. After all, Roger, his brother, and his cousin are easily members of Forbes 400. Roger's wealth is estimated at about $1.4 billion, Gerrish at around $900 million, and Minot at $450 million.

Rather, if the Milliken share values—which are most likely undervalued as is typical of privately held family businesses—were jacked up, there would be significant estate tax implications. Since Roger, Gerrish, and Minot are no longer young men, this is a situation that is more than problematic. Roger's desire is to keep the entire company intact and family-owned and controlled. Uncle Sam, however, has no such concerns.

The Strouds say they will continue to sell shares, either to outsiders or to the board. Roger has started defensive actions to change Milliken's incorporation so that a change of ownership would require 80 percent shareholder approval, rather than the 75 percent previously required.

Those within the textile industry who are watching Milliken know that Roger has always indicated he would do everything he could to keep his company intact and family-held. That Roger's fiery red hair has turned white is no indication that his resolve has weakened.

Brown-Forman Company History: *"It is the unwritten policy of the Brown family that 'We take care of the sons; the sons-in-law are on their own.'"*

Brown-Forman Corporation
Louisville, Kentucky

Business: Distiller and importer of spirits and wines; fine consumer goods including china and luggage

Best Known Products: Jack Daniel's; Canadian Mist; Early Times; Southern Comfort; Korbel California Champagnes; Lenox china, giftware and crystal; Hartmann luggage

Founded: 1870 by George Garvin Brown and John Forman

Family Executives: W.L. Lyons Brown Jr., CEO and Chairman
George Garvin Brown III, Director
Owsley Brown II, President and Director
Owsley Brown Frazier, Vice Chairman

Family Ownership: 64 percent of Class A voting shares; 29 percent of Class B

Family Board Membership: 4 family members of 8 directors

Traded: NYSE, BF.B

Net Sales: $1,387,780,000 1991
1,303,985,000 1990
1,293,991,000 1989

Net Earnings: $145,233,000 1991
92,505,000 1990
144,497,000 1989

BROWN-FORMAN CORPORATION

Southern Discomfort

Brown Family

Established in 1875 in an area of Kentucky associated with whis-key-making, Brown-Forman produces and markets Jack Daniel's Tennessee whiskey, one of the best-recognized and best selling higher-priced U.S. whiskeys. In 1992, *Business Week* placed Brown-Foreman at number 365 of its 1,000 most valuable U.S. companies. The company's premium spirits and wines—including Southern Comfort—account for three-quarters of its revenue, although it has diversified into other quality goods.

Brown-Forman has gone into fine china, houseware and ta-bleware, and quality luggage. It took over Lenox, which initially fought the takeover for three weeks in 1982. Now the Lenox line of fine china, crystal, and giftware is selling in Japan and is being introduced in Europe. Adding to its Lenox tableware, in 1991 the company signed an agreement to sell Dansk International De-signs Ltd. Hartmann luggage, acquired the same year as Lenox, is also being marketed successfully in Japan.

Overseas business profits for Brown-Forman's beverages as well as its china and luggage have shown strong volume growth. This international emphasis is attributed to the company's leader since 1975, W.L. Lyons (Lee) Brown Jr., 56, who started in the import-export division of Brown-Forman in 1960. Lee is the fifth member of the Brown family to run the business that was founded in 1870 by his great-grandfather, George Garvin Brown.

George's partner was John Forman, who sold his interest to the Forman family in 1902. The men established a business in Louisville producing Old Forester brand bourbon. From the beginning this brand was a higher-priced product than other bourbons. In an era when bourbon quality was uneven, Old Forester benefited from strong sales to consumers who appreciated its consistent quality and guarantee of satisfaction.

The company's first acquisition was the Early Times brand in 1922. Then, during the depression, the company kept afloat by producing alcohol for hospitals. Again, during World War II the company adapted by producing gunpowder while alcohol production was restricted.

After the war, Brown-Forman continued its acquisitions. In 1956, it made a very expensive purchase of Jack Daniel's sour mash whiskey, which had been owned by another family business since its origination in 1866. This appears to have been a wise purchase despite its cost to a relatively small company: Jack Daniel's is probably the most profitable whiskey in America. Jack Daniel's and the company's other whiskey and bourbon brands have also proven very popular with the Japanese.

Brown-Forman accelerated its acquisition rate in the '60s. From that time through the '80s, it has bought Korbel champagne and brandy, Bolla and Cella Wines, Canadian Mist blended whiskey, Southern Comfort liqueur, and California Cooler wine coolers.

The Brown family owns a dominant share of the company—70 percent of the Class A voting stock and 29 percent of the nonvoting Class B stock. The family's shares were valued at close to $865 million at the beginning of 1992.

Family members dominate the leadership of Brown-Forman. They term this control "planned nepotism." The Browns use an affectionate term for family members who work within the company, calling them "nepots." Although the firm is rife with nepots, the man who heads the company—Lee Brown—exerts firm authority over its structure and operations.

There is even an official history of the company that mentions that in-laws cannot marry into nepot status. The history states, "It is the unwritten policy of the Brown family that 'We take care of the sons; the sons-in-law are on their own.'"

And the daughters are excluded entirely—there are no woman Browns at the company or in the wings. Since the daughters are out of the running and their husbands are "on their own," this is a publicly owned club with strict membership clauses indeed.

An example of how family control can be brought to bear by its head was seen in the '80s. Although Jack Daniel's is enviably profitable in the early '90s, sales of its division's three brands had started to slip in the mid-'80s. Lee's younger brother Martin, 54, was then running the brands, serving as Jack Daniel's chairman and the vice chairman of Brown-Forman. Lee thought it was time for the Jack Daniel's brand to be marketed and distributed along with the other Brown-Forman brands.

Martin thought that grouping Jack Daniel's with other company brands would lower Jack Daniel's cachet. In addition, Jack Daniel's Distillery, then located in Nashville, would have to be consolidated into the Spirits unit in Louisville. Besides the move to headquarters, this meant a downsizing of Martin's staff.

The five-member executive committee comprised Lee, Martin, two other family members, and one nonfamily member. The vote was five to one. Martin's nonconcurring vote forced the issue to a board vote. After Martin soundly lost, he resigned from the company and its board.

An anonymous Brown-Forman executive explained Martin's departure to *Advertising Age*: "It's all just a power deal. [Martin] was the kingfish in Nashville, but he'd be just another Brown in Louisville."

A different spin was put on the departure by a Brown cousin, who said to *Fortune* in 1989, "If it is in the best interests of the company that a nepot step aside, then he must. This is something that we all know from an early age."

The last few years have seen a rift in the family, although it's not publicly displayed. Martin and his kin have continued to attend Brown ceremonial occasions. But other than the official functions and, Christmas, you won't catch Martin socializing with Lee.

The nepot next in line is Lee's son W.L. Lyons Brown III, 32, who entered the company in marketing in its international division. Even nepots must earn a graduate degree before entering the company, and Lyons has an M.B.A. from the University of Virginia. Whether or not advanced education will enlighten thinking about family members—including equal opportunity for daughters or their husbands—is yet to be seen.

SECTION VII

THE REBELS

Rebels are creative, productive heirs who want to achieve something radically different from what their parents had planned for them. In fact, many Rebels are perceived as working against family interests. When Gordon Getty dissolved the family trust to go his own way, he forced the sale of Getty Oil to Texaco. Ted Field also wanted to free his money from a trust, which resulted in the sale of the Chicago *Sun-Times* to Rupert Murdoch.

Despite the controversy over their actions, the ultimate results were profitable for these Rebels. Gordon increased his family's wealth by selling Getty shares for a high value. Ted used his proceeds from the trust dissolution—$130 million—to fuel what is now Hollywood's most profitable movie production company, Interscope. It is responsible for such highly commercial films as *Three Men And A Baby* and *FernGully*.

REBELS USUALLY...

1. are ultimately unconcerned when their goals conflict with their family's aspirations for them.
2. are tenacious in their beliefs.
3. are very successful in whatever direction they take.
4. work in fields where they are not tied to 9–5 jobs.
5. are more nonconformist than their siblings.
6. never saw working in the family business as a possible option for themselves.
7. are college graduates who lack graduate degrees— surprising for such introspective heirs.
8. were strongly influenced by the '60s social movements.
9. are conciliatory, after success, with formerly skeptical family members.
10. never doubt they made the right choice in life.

Several Rebels can point to a life's work that varies greatly from what their parents had planned. Adam Hochschild, whose family was instrumental in building the global mineral company AMAX, cofounded the left-of-center magazine *Mother Jones*. George Pillsbury chose a career in alternative philanthropy; George's various foundations fund social action groups that many mainstream philanthropies would consider to be very far left-of-center.

Some Rebels bite the hands that used to feed them. Patrick Reynolds, grandson of tobacco magnate R.J. Reynolds, heads an antismoking foundation. James Gamble, who lives an unpretentious life as an agronomist, used his inherited Procter & Gamble shares to try to stop P&G from buying coffee beans from military-controlled El Salvador. John Robbins, son of the cofounder of Baskin-Robbins, founded EarthSave, which has as its mission the elimination of animal products from our diet. John, in his books and public speeches, links heart attacks, diabetes, strokes, and cancer to the butterfat and sugar found in ice cream and other foods.

Nearly all these Rebels were in college during the '60s and point to the free speech/antiwar/civil rights/women's rights movements as having changed their lives. But it was an older Rebel who expressed these ideas for them.

Michael Butler, an heir to fortunes in both paper and aviation, who's the son of a hidebound conservative, became the spokesman for an entire generation with his production of *Hair*, the most successful musical in history. Michael, the Rebel who says that "freedom and attitude" are the most important things in life, is at 66 one of the oldest heirs in this book.

Which goes to prove that age is only a state of mind.

Gordon: "I picked up my marbles and took them home."

P.A.J.W. Corporation
San Francisco, California

Business: Musical composition; investments made through P.A.J.W. Corporation

Family Companies: Minnehoma Oil Company founded in 1903 by grandfather George F. Getty
George F. Getty Inc. founded in 1920 by grandfather George F. Getty
Getty Oil Company founded in 1916 by grandfather and by father J. Paul Getty; Getty Oil became parent company in 1956

Ownership: Businesses no longer owned by Getty family

Family Executives: Gordon Getty, Chairman

Approximate Worth: $1.3 billion, 1991 *Forbes* 400

P.A.J.W. CORPORATION

Oil Over Troubled Waters

Gordon Getty, Composer (Heir to Getty Oil)

Gordon J. Getty, 57, has turned out to have money-making abilities that would have made his father proud—no mean feat considering that J. Paul Getty was worth more than $2 billion at his death in 1976. But while J. Paul was alive, the father/son relationship was usually rocky. Gordon is contemplative and follows his own agenda, whether it happens to be business or music, while the hard-driving, fortune-building J. Paul was the model for Walt Disney's cartoon figure, Scrooge McDuck.

After J. Paul's death, Gordon, who feared a takeover attempt, forced a sale of Getty Oil, the company his grandfather had founded. The sale of Getty Oil to Texaco Inc. later led to the largest court judgment in American history: $11.1 billion against Texaco for breaking up a proposed merger agreement between Getty Oil and Pennzoil Company. Further fallout included the bankruptcy of Texaco and the dissolution of the family's $4 billion Sarah C. Getty Trust. But the sale of Getty Oil provided Gordon with the opportunity to launch his freelance business career and the freedom to pursue music composition and economics.

Although the Getty Oil buy-out was fraught with corporate and family litigation, and was a debacle for everyone except Gordon, his life is more stable and productive than might have been projected, given the family history. Gordon is the most successful of J. Paul's sons. His incredible income (daily, more than $250,000 in interest alone) allows him the freedom to concentrate on what interests him, whether it's business, music composition, or scholarship in the social sciences. His behavior as a warm family man raising four sons contrasts with his father's and siblings' multiple divorces and acrimonious parent-child relations.

J. Paul was parsimonious in both his finances and his love. He married five times and had five sons by four of his wives. The oldest son, George Franklin II, in 1973 overdosed on drugs and alcohol and stabbed himself in the chest, all in one evening. His triple suicidal efforts were successful.

Jean Ronald, the second son, is a businessman in Los Angeles dabbling in restaurants, real estate, and gas and oil holdings. He was cut off from his father's fortune at age six because J. Paul was angry at Ronald's mother, who bested J. Paul in her divorce settlement.

Eugene Paul, who changed his name to J. Paul Jr., is the third son and Gordon's only full brother. J. Paul Jr. spent a decade addicted to heroin and cocaine, and his second wife, Talitha, died of a drug overdose in 1971. In 1973, his oldest son, Jean Paul III, was kidnapped in Italy and had his ear cut off by kidnappers in a bid to hasten ransom payment. Any sympathy for J. Paul Jr. due to the tragedies that had befallen his wife and son disappeared when news got out that a California court might have to order him to support Jean Paul, now blind and paralyzed from a methadone-induced stroke. (Until J. Paul Jr. agreed to pick up costs, Gordon supported Jean Paul, his wife, and son—now the movie actor Paul Balthazar Getty.) J. Paul Jr.'s daughter, Aileen Getty, 32, formerly married to Elizabeth Taylor's son Christopher Wilding, disclosed in 1992 that her lengthy illnesses were due to AIDS.

Gordon is the fourth son. His mother, Ann Rork Getty, had begun divorce proceedings from J. Paul Sr. before Gordon's birth.

The fifth and last son, Timothy, died at age twelve of a brain tumor. J. Paul, who complained about the boy's medical bills and never bothered to visit him in the hospital, missed his youngest son's funeral because he was in the middle of a business transaction.

Perhaps the best thing Gordon's mother did for him was to divorce J. Paul and not press for a closer bond between father and son. Gordon says that he saw his father about three times a year while he was growing up in Los Angeles and his father was nearby in Santa Monica. After J. Paul moved to Paris, then London, those

visits were reduced to a few hours once a year. Gordon used his
friendship with a schoolchum's large family to supplement his own
nearly nonexistent father/son relationship. Although Gordon's up-
bringing may seem privileged, neither he nor his mother felt the
security of real wealth. There was only basic alimony and child
support payments and, for Gordon, a trust with no income. After
attending a series of prep and military schools, Gordon graduated
from the University of San Francisco with a degree in English
literature in 1956 and joined the Army.

J. Paul had been living as a relatively anonymous oilman when
Fortune, in 1957, revealed that J. Paul was the country's richest man.
This came as a surprise to the American public and to Gordon, age
24, who claims he never knew the extent of J. Paul's wealth until
the *Fortune* revelation. The knowledge didn't diminish Gordon's
desire to join one of the Getty companies after military service.

But Gordon had already begun composing music in his spare
time and was therefore not considered a team player by other Getty
businessmen. In turn, Gordon resented what he termed his
9:00-5:00 "plow horse" duty. He twice quit the Getty companies—to the alleged relief of Getty managers—and twice rejoined. The lack of support given Gordon by Getty Oil
management bore bitter fruit years later when, after J. Paul's death,
Gordon aligned his Getty Oil shares against management.

Although by rejoining Getty Oil Gordon exposed himself to J.
Paul's unrelenting scrutiny, he wanted to remain in his father's
favor. No wonder. A year before Gordon's birth in 1934, J. Paul and
his mother, Sarah Catherine Getty, established the Sarah C. Getty
Trust with $3.4 million in Getty company securities. Its purpose
was to establish family control over the burgeoning Getty Oil
empire and to forbid any trustee to sell holdings unless the sale was
to prevent "substantial loss" of the trust estate. J. Paul's sons were
ultimately to share in the trust (along with the children of disen-
franchised son Ronald) and were also to serve as successor trustees.
(The trust was worth $4 billion at its height in 1984.)

Ironically, the trust had been established to resolve J. Paul's
own arguments with his parents over the family business. George
Getty was an independent oilman who established the troubled
Getty dynasty in 1903. J. Paul, his only child, fought constantly
with both his parents and schemed to oust George from the com-

pany he'd founded. On George's death in 1930, J. Paul discovered that his father had left the bulk and control of the estate not to him but to Sarah, his mother. J. Paul's battles continued with his mother, mostly over his wildcatting in the oil fields by day and tomcatting in clubs by night. The motivation behind the trust was to keep the company's assets away from J. Paul and to preserve them for future Getty generations. The trust's assets could not be sold while J. Paul and his children were living, although 80 percent of the income went to J. Paul.

If a life of rancor was good enough for J. Paul, it was good enough for the men and women who surrounded him. J. Paul liked to set his managers against each other, and as his sons entered his businesses, he enjoyed pitting them against one another, too. J. Paul placed Gordon at Tidewater Oil Company, one of the Getty businesses, in a consultant's "trouble shooting" role, which seemed specifically designed to make Gordon take pot shots at the company's president, half-brother George. Gordon did not have the experience to see that his father had placed him—and George—in a no-win situation.

Watching his sons snipe at each other wasn't enough for J. Paul, who controlled, belittled, and criticized each of them as business-men and as sons. George pathetically described himself as "vice president in charge of failure" and J. Paul as "president in charge of success." As for Gordon, although he hopped around the Getty companies and served erratically in the jobs he filled, he could be aggressive when it came to dealing with J. Paul. Gordon, with 20 percent of the trust's income, had no significant dividend earnings because J. Paul preferred to put Getty Oil's profits back into the business. Getty Oil stock did not pay cash dividends. Gordon coerced his father—through the threat of a lawsuit—to have Getty Oil declare a 10-cents-a-share cash dividend, which would come to Gordon through the trust as a $50,000 yearly income. In retalia-tion, an angry J. Paul removed Gordon as a successor trustee in 1963. George, according to Thomas Petzinger Jr.'s *Oil and Honor: The Texaco-Pennzoil Wars*, gloated to his half-brother, "So it looks like you have gained $50,000 and lost a father."

Gordon badly wanted to be reinstated as trustee, in part because he was truly fond of his father. He continued to seek J. Paul's approval and resisted being branded a troublemaker. A letter this unhappy "plowhorse" wrote to his father in 1965, quoted in *Life*, continued the equestrian metaphors: "You are a cow pony, father, and it seems to me I am too, although vastly less adept. That's a lot different from a bucking bronco."

Gordon soon became dissatisfied with his annual $55,000 in trust income, which he felt was too small a sum for his needs after he married Ann Gilbert in 1964 and they began their family of four boys (Peter, Andrew, John, and William). In 1966, a fearless Gordon sued J. Paul—whose public relations head was then Claus von Bulow—to obtain income from the trust's stock dividends. Gordon wanted the trust's beneficiaries to receive income from the dividends that Getty Oil paid to the trust. This would have increased Gordon's payout nearly a hundred-fold, to $5 million, but would have partially liquidated the trust and led to a tax payment of $25 million.

As the battle heightened, Gordon's wife Ann called J. Paul at his Sutton Place estate in London. "Your lawyer is killing my husband," she entreated. J. Paul called his chief attorney and commanded, "Keep killing my son."

Gordon lost the suit in 1970, and J. Paul's status as head of the country's largest trust was safe. Forbidden to work at the Getty companies, Gordon spent the next decade constructively. He'd studied composition in the '60s at the San Francisco Conservatory of Music and was now prepared to write symphonic music from his Pacific Heights mansion in San Francisco. Gordon also took classes in physics, anthropology, and economics; served on performing arts boards; and, with Ann, raised his four sons. His trust income continued to jump, as his Getty Oil cash dividends increased, bringing Gordon $600,000 annually by 1974.

When J. Paul died in 1976 at 83, he left nearly $770 million as a tax-free gift to Malibu's J. Paul Getty Museum. He also had a portfolio worth $60 million and a collection of paintings and sculpture worth about $200 million. The trust was now valued at $1.3 billion. Without foreseeing its irony, J. Paul had written shortly before his death, "The Getty interests are not about to sell off their shares or dissolve their companies. Those companies have been built into a large and thriving *family* business."

Gordon was the only relative present at J. Paul's deathbed. Truly respectful of his father's fortune-building talents, he'd been successful in being reinstated as a successor trustee before J. Paul's death (partly through Ann's endeavors). Gordon's brothers had been removed as trustees because their father disapproved of their personal lives, their business conduct, or both. Two other successor trustees had been named with Gordon: J. Paul's attorney and Security Pacific Bank (which later withdrew). Gordon also became a director of Getty Oil.

In 1982, the trustee attorney died, and Gordon had control of a trust that held 40 percent of Getty Oil, whose stock Gordon believed was greatly undervalued. In Getty Oil board decisions, Gordon often opposed the chairman and hoped to oust Getty Oil management, men with whom he had little in common. Gordon sought a more active role in the company in order to close the gap between its stock price and what he perceived was its real worth. (Between the income from his dividends and the income from his role as sole successor trustee, Gordon was now reaping $28 million annually from the trust.) Also on Gordon's mind was the fear of a possible takeover from a predator who could join forces with the J. Paul Getty Museum, which owned close to 12 percent of Getty Oil. Gordon himself had attempted to have the museum join with him against Getty Oil management.

However, the board dislocations and Gordon's seeking out oilmen to serve as his mentors served to set Getty Oil in play. It was ripe for assault. Ivan Boesky, the takeover czar, purchased a significant holding. Pennzoil Company made an offer that included Gordon's bringing Getty Oil private and serving as its chairman. Gordon-watchers claimed that Gordon's primary motivation in forcing a sale was to succeed J. Paul as chairman. Indeed, Gordon later admitted he would have enjoyed "the fun" of heading Getty Oil. But Texaco Inc. put more money on the table ($125 a share vs. Pennzoil's $112) as Getty Oil's white knight. Eventually Texaco agreed to pay $128 a share, making the acquisition of Getty Oil, at $10 billion, the largest to date in 1984. Through his actions, Gordon more than doubled the worth of the trust to $4 billion.

Ann and Gordon Getty's financial advisor, Marc Leland, explains Gordon's motives in selling Getty Oil to Texaco: "He was the trustee trying to maximize the value for the Getty trusts. It wasn't a question of somebody trying to save his company. He wasn't attached to the company; he wasn't the CEO. When the price was as high as Texaco was willing to pay, he had no qualms."

After taxes, the Sarah C. Getty Trust value stood at $3 billion. The trust's wealth was so immense that its attempt to put the Texaco proceeds into Treasury bills was delayed because of federal rules that prohibit any one buyer from taking more than 35 percent of each week's bills.

Not everyone was happy at Gordon's sale of the trust's 40 percent ownership to Texaco. Other trust beneficiaries resented the enormous tax bite and Gordon's attempt to appoint trustees who were closely aligned with his own interests (for example, wife Ann) to serve after his death. The daughters of Gordon's late brother, George, sued on the grounds that Gordon violated the trust and abused his power. These women (dubbed "the Georgettes" by the attorneys) resented that they were sharing a mere $35 million annually by 1984 while Gordon, as successor trustee, was then receiving $110 million each year—plus his trustee's fee of $20 million. (The trust's annual income was more than $1 million a day in 1985.)

Gordon's defense of the sale was that it was his fiduciary duty to maximize the trust's wealth and income and to strengthen its position. He could do this only through a sale. And indeed, Gordon struck when oil prices were at their peak. Gordon's actions more than doubled the trust's value.

Fatigued from being embroiled in a family lawsuit—which at one point involved 40 attorneys representing Getty relatives—and being a peacemaker at heart, Gordon agreed in 1985 to split the trust into four parts, each worth $750 million: one for Gordon and his children; one for George's children; one for Paul Jr. and his family; and the last ultimately to benefit Ronald's children. As Gordon described it, "I picked up my marbles and took them home."

Marc Leland points out, "Gordon wanted to split up the trust so each family could have its own block of funds rather than running under one trust when [the children and grandchildren of J.

Paul] had no relationship to each other any longer. Some people might have said, 'No, I want to control all that money. I'd rather keep it under my control.' Gordon just doesn't have that kind of ego-need." Leland also notes that Gordon's personal sense of fairness included Ronald's children in the revamped trust, and that Gordon financed this through his own trustee fee.

During the earlier Getty Oil sale, Texaco had indemnified Gordon from a possible Pennzoil suit. When Gordon was needed to testify when Texaco was sued for $10.3 billion in damages for improperly insinuating itself into the merger agreement between Pennzoil and Getty Oil, he did not have to worry about personal liability. (Texaco sought bankruptcy protection in 1987 but emerged after settling with Pennzoil for $3 billion cash later that year.)

Taking a much-needed breather, Gordon retreated into his music, composing the song cycle "The White Election," based on Emily Dickinson's poems, and "Plum Jack," an operetta based on the Shakespearean character Falstaff. "Composers," Gordon told *Newsweek* in 1985, "are remembered when businessmen are forgotten."

Leland says, "Gordon would consider the music writing and his economics writing as great if not greater than his business accomplishments. Those things are unrelated to what his father was or how much money Gordon may have. You can't buy reviews. You can't buy publication in a scholarly journal."

Ann continued her bicoastal social life but also reinforced her own business interests, buying the publishing companies Grove Press in 1985 and Weidenfeld & Nicolson in 1989. Leland notes that one of the four Getty sons may be interested in joining Grove Weidenfeld or another of the Getty concerns one day. Ann continues to serve as a director of a number of companies, including Revlon Inc. and MGM/UA Communications Company.

———————

By the late 80s, Gordon had revisited the business world. The hackneyed theories that Gordon wants to best his father in money-making continue to crop up with each investment he makes. Leland says that Gordon's business priorities are "making sure he is preserving the fortune by allocating the assets in a diversified way." He directly plays a role in that asset allocation. That's a big part of it. As part of that diversification, he is also involved in direct investment.

"Because oil and gas are something he understands," says Leland, Gordon returned to oil with an investment in DeltaUS Corp., which underwent Chapter 11 in 1989 and reorganized as Delta Drilling Co. Creditors who'd hoped to get at Gordon's assets were disappointed and had to eat $25 million in unpaid debts. Another one of Gordon's oil investments is Chiles Offshore Corp. Gordon's investments were made through his P.A.J.W. Corp. (The initials represent the first names of his sons.)

Gordon also looks at the purchase of businesses that may be undervalued. He joined the Fisher real estate group in 1989 in the hope of taking over the Emhart Corp., losing to Black & Decker Corp. But in the process, Gordon and his team gained a $50 million investment profit. In 1990, he also failed in his raid on British clothing company Aquascutum Group PLC, but he and his associates made $10 million for their efforts.

Gordon joined the Fisher group again to form Chartwell Associates L.P. in an assault on Avon Products, Inc. It acquired 20 percent control of Avon only to give up the siege in early 1991. Unlike the earlier Emhart raid, the attempt to gain control of Avon accrued only a small profit.

Gordon's financial advisor shrugs off the criticism that Gordon hasn't been able to take over every company in which he invests. "It's like the Emhart deal—'Oh, you failed because you didn't take the company over.' But that wasn't really our objective. It was to make money and if we could get it at the right price, take it over." Leland continues, "But *not* to *overpay* for it." In addition, Gordon makes specific direct investments and holds a stock position in the world's largest airline caterer, Caterair Holdings. He also invests in real estate because, as Leland notes, "you have to have that in a large and diversified portfolio."

Leland disagrees with those who say that Gordon is trying to prove himself a better businessman than J. Paul. "His father was building up a fortune, and Gordon is preserving one. Gordon doesn't have to build a fortune.

"Besides, Gordon is a composer," he summarizes. "That's his main business."

Gordon, of course, realizes that however well he preserves his fortune (estimated at $1.2 billion), upon his and Ann's death it will be broken up. Presumably, there will be four parts, each worth $300 million, going to their sons. Obviously, some of his investment rationale must be to build up those parts.

Or it may be the example of hard work that the billionaire parents want to set for their children. After all, in 1989 Ann had a tart response when told by a *Life* reporter that their oldest son Peter, newly graduated from Harvard, quipped that his post-graduation plans were to do "Nothing—until somebody notices."

The quick response from Peter's mother was, "We've noticed, and he's going to get a job."

 is labeled vertically: *Firooz Zahedi*

"*I am not obsessed by carrying the family torch.*"

Interscope Communications, Interscope Records
Los Angeles, California

Business:	Independent film producer and music producer
Best Known Products:	Films: *FernGully, The Hand That Rocks the Cradle; Revenge of the Nerds, Three Men and a Baby, Bill and Ted's Excellent Adventure* Music: *Marky Mark; Primus; Thrill Kill Cult; Nine-Inch Nails*
Founded:	1982 by Ted Field
Family Executives:	Ted Field, Chairman
Family Board Membership:	1 family member
Traded:	Privately held
Net Sales:	Will not disclose
Net Earnings:	Will not disclose
Family Companies:	Marshall Field & Co., founded by great-great-grandfather Marshall Field; Chicago *Sun-Times*, founded 1941 by Grandfather Marshall Field III
Ownership:	Businesses no longer owned by family

INTERSCOPE COMMUNICATIONS INTERSCOPE RECORDS

If the Glass Slipper Fits...

Ted Field, Chairman
(Heir to Field Enterprises)

Frederick (Ted) Woodruff Field, 40, has been described as the Cinderella of the Field family of Chicago. Ted is the second son of Marshall Field IV and the younger half-brother of Marshall V (see MARSHALL FIELD V). The Cinderella imagery seems apt for a man who owns Interscope Communications, a film production company that has produced such light, commercially oriented movies as *Outrageous Fortune, Cocktail,* and *The Hand That Rocks the Cradle.*

But is the metaphor for Ted entirely accurate? It's true that it is Ted's brother Marshall Field V who inherited The Name—although Marshall has said all his name does is guarantee that he's the one stuck with the dinner tab. What may be more important than The Name is The Money, and this Marshall and Ted inherited equally.

Their wealth came from old Chicago money: the Marshall Field & Co. department store empire, filtered through real estate and publishing fortunes. The view of Ted as the below-stairs Field may seem out of focus when you realize he left Chicago in 1984 with more than $130 million in his pocket.

When Ted and Marshall's father died in 1965, he left a personal estate of $25 million to his widow and to the six children—two boys and four girls—he'd had by different wives. His two sons, however, were given a trust, which split equally 80 percent of the stock of Field Enterprises, when they reached 25. It is these shares in Field

Enterprises that eventually realized more than a hundred million dollars for each son.

Immediately after their father's death, Marshall, then 24, came back to Chicago to run Field Enterprises, which included the Chicago *Sun-Times*. Dissolve to Ted, then only 13, living in Anchorage with his mother, the distinguished newspaper editor Katherine (Kay) Woodruff Fanning. (Marshall V had been raised by his own mother in McLean, Virginia and had attended prep school and college in New England.)

Kay had left Marshall IV in 1963, two years before his death. The year Marshall died, she packed 13-year-old Ted and his two sisters in her station wagon for the move to Anchorage. Arriving in Anchorage, Kay regenerated her journalism career at the *Anchorage Daily News* in accordance with the plans she'd made with Larry Fanning, the esteemed former editor of her prior husband's paper, the *Sun-Times*. Kay then married Larry.

Ted had his life's scenario fast-cut from moneyed Chicago to a middle-income Alaskan development called College Village. Instead of day school, Ted now was supposed to adjust to public school at an age where making new friends can be difficult. However, Ted credits the Anchorage years he spent with his stepfather as having opened his mind to democratic ideals.

After high school graduation, Ted segued from Anchorage to Northwestern University, beginning a montage of eight different colleges but not bothering to pick up a degree from any of them. On a cross-country excursion with some college buddies, he ended up in Newport Beach. Ted compared southern California to his experience of Anchorage and Chicago and tasted new pleasures, including race car driving and movie making. Anchorage and Chicago got left on the cutting-room floor.

Initially, Ted was regarded as just another dabbling rich kid. The first sign that he was to be taken seriously was his winning of the 1979 Daytona 24-hour Pepsi Challenge. But race cars and movie scripts were expensive hobbies. By the early '80s, Ted was running through as much as $3 million a year, relying on advances from his Field trust.

In 1983, Field Enterprises had been redesigned, for tax reasons, into a partnership between the half-brothers, now the only shareholders. Ted decided that he wanted out and that he wanted to leave with cash. His racing days were over, and he was moving away from his original 1979 movie partnership with Peter Samuelson to a production-and-development company, founded as Interscope Communications in 1982. Ted needed some serious money to nurture Interscope.

Ted's decision to bow out of Field Enterprises recast Chicago business. His quick response to those who hoped that, as a Field, he'd take center stage was, "I am not obsessed by carrying the family torch."

Chicago had never embraced Ted as it had Marshall, who, after all, was the conservative businessman/philanthropist that the city expected him to be. Additionally, Marshall had toiled in Field Enterprises for years whereas Ted was a relative unknown. When it became known that Ted wanted to break up the partnership—and thus the *Sun-Times*, Chicago's only major Democratic paper—this front-page story cast Ted not as Cinderella but rather as the Wicked Stepmother.

In order to facilitate the fade-out of the partnership, the *Sun Times* was sold to the highest bidder: Rupert Murdoch. Ted's name became anathema to reporters who preferred the liberal Democratic strains of the Field newspaper to the anticipated yellow journalism of Murdoch's rags. Although Marshall himself could have taken steps to pay Ted and retain the paper—or he could have sold it to a lower bidder who was a gentleman and made up the difference himself—it would have meant risking his own fortune. In any case, the media ignored Marshall's role in the sale and zoomed in on Ted.

Ted's defense, "I don't sell properties based on the politics of the buyer," didn't make him any more popular with the liberal media. And again, few hankies were rung over an amateur race car driver/moviemaker who'd pocketed $130 million at 31.

Except for having to endure a short spate of unfriendly articles, Ted remained unaffected. The snickering at Ted's amateur status in the movie community ended with Interscope's first film, the megahit "Revenge of the Nerds." Ted's next step was to buy Panavision, the company that rents the majority of movie cameras to filmmakers. Panavision cost $52 million in 1985; Ted sold it for $142 million two years later.

This man also had the energy to participate in a few of the '80s takeover attempts. Aligning with Sir James Goldsmith, he put $40 million into the 1984 bid for Crown Zellerback, earning him about $45 million in profits for his efforts. The next year, he and Goldsmith went against Goodyear and benefited with more booty. In 1987, he joined with Goldsmith again for a bid on B.A.T. Industries PLC, which ironically owned Marshall Field & Co. at the time. Ted also is a first-rate chessplayer, who started Field's World Professional Chess Promotions, Inc. with plans to televise championship chess tournaments.

Another interest of Ted's has been real estate. He moved his third wife Susie and their three children into Green Acres—the 44-room, $55 million former Harold Lloyd estate—and installed a security system allegedly as tight as at the White House. (Ted and Susie have separated, but he remains in the residence.) Ted also owns four other properties: a 40-acre ranch in Santa Monica, priced at $29 million; a $25 million chalet in Aspen; a Malibu beach house; and a $2.5 million villa in Santa Barbara. Several of these residences hit the market in the early '90s, a reflection of Ted's desire to live more simply. At the same time, Ted also turned over $10 million worth of paintings to Christie's of London for auction.

Ted describes himself as a "fiscally conservative, socially progressive Democrat." To this end, he gives frequent benefits for Democratic candidates, Save the Rainforest, and the U.S. Holocaust Memorial Museum. His guests—and entertainers—at these benefits include such celebrities as Bruce Springsteen, Sting, Goldie Hawn, and Billy Crystal.

In addition to the benefits, he is one of Hollywood's most important philanthropists. A few organizations such as the Pediatric Aids Foundation would not exist if it weren't for Ted's start-up financial contributions and his know-how.

Ted's professional excitement in the '90s focuses on entertainment. With Interscope president and COO Robert W. Cort, Ted negotiated an advantageous distribution contract for Interscope with Walt Disney Corp.'s Touchstone Productions in 1988. In addition, Interscope benefits from a movie-funding pool of at least $200 million, from which fund Disney and Nomura Babcock & Brown Securities Co. plan to produce and market movies together through 1994.

This 1990 shared equity deal gives Ted the clout necessary to green-light any movie project and places him in a select group of Hollywood's largest independent producers. Ted's ability to deal has increased exponentially.

Thanks to the Nomura deal, *The Hand That Rocks the Cradle* was the first film in which Interscope had an equity position. This film cost the company $12 million to make, and within 12 weeks of its release it had made back more than $80 million.

In addition, Ted advanced from movies to music with Interscope Music. He stumbled on a commercially successful rapper—Marky Mark, the little brother of Donnie Wahlberg (one of the New Kids on the Block.) He specializes in hip-hop and opened for New Kids on their summer 1990 tour. Interscope Music is in an explosive breakout, with Marky Mark's album selling more than a million units in its first year.

And as Ted, whose personal wealth has gone well over the half-billion-dollar mark, notes his stunning successes in film and music production, it seems his coach will not turn back into a pumpkin. It looks as if he may live happily ever after, after all.

Jamie and Robert Gamble

Jamie: "I don't identify myself as a Procter & Gamble heir as much as I do with the achievements I've been able to do on my own."

University of Massachusetts
Amherst, Massachusetts

Business: Research technician; Department of Plant
Pathology; State Cooperative Extension
Service; University of Massachusetts

Family Company: Procter & Gamble founded in 1837 by
great-great-grandfather James Gamble and
by William Procter

Ownership: Less than one percent by James Gamble

*Approximate
Worth:* $4 million

UNIVERSITY OF MASSACHUSETTS

Brewing Controversy at P&G

James Gamble, Researcher
(Heir to Procter & Gamble)

Blood spilling from a coffee cup is probably not what James Gamble, cofounder with William Procter of monolith Procter & Gamble Company, had in mind in 1837 when he started the company he would leave to his heirs, including his great-great-grandson and namesake James Gamble, 29. The shocking bloodied coffee mug imprinted "SALE OF SALVADORAN COFFEE" was aired as part of a television commercial on Boston's CBS affiliate WHDH-TV in 1989. The issue-oriented advertisement was an attempt to pressure P&G to stop its Folgers Coffee subsidiary, America's top-selling coffee, from buying coffee beans from El Salvador.

In the commercial, Ed Asner narrated that the beans' purchase brought "destruction" by sustaining wealthy growers who directly or indirectly support right-wing military death squads. He continued, "Boycott Folgers. What it brews is misery and death."

The 30-second spot, which also asked for a stop to U.S. military aid to El Salvador, was sponsored by Neighbor to Neighbor, a San Francisco political advocacy group. The ad identified only the Folgers brand and not any of the other American brands that used beans from El Salvador, like Philip Morris Companies' Kraft General Foods, maker of Maxwell House, and Nestlé S.A.'s Nestlé Foods Corp., which makes Nescafé and Hills Bros. brands. In addition, a print ad, similar to the television commercial, ran in several newspapers.

P&G escalated agitation over the Neighbor to Neighbor commercial when it yanked, for a short time, all P&G advertising at the

Boston station that ran the commercial. The company's move heightened coverage of the boycott and revived perennial questions of media fairness vs. advertising strength. By pulling the ads, P&G extended boycott news to national magazines and trade publications like *Variety*: "Coffee Ad Brew-Ha-Ha Stirring Bean Town."

More important than the television and newspaper ads, however, was the P&G board resolution tendered by James (Jamie) Gamble. Despite his family's lack of managerial involvement in P&G for the past two generations, Jamie led the P&G shareholder effort, backed by Neighbor to Neighbor, to boycott the Salvadoran beans. The hope was that a boycott would pressure landowners to end the political and military turmoil in that country. In its defense, P&G noted that the United States supported the El Salvadoran government (glossing over a controversial situation in itself) and therefore, P&G was unfairly being thrust into a dispute between an activist group and the U.S. State Department. The company also noted that fewer than 2 percent of its Folgers beans were imported from El Salvador.

Of great concern to P&G is its reputation as a corporation that listens to consumers and their needs, whether these consumers want soap that floats (Ivory, 1881) or antidecay toothpaste (Crest, 1955). P&G was the first major company to introduce an 800-number telephone consumer line in 1974. Within a decade, every product line was given its own toll-free phone number and by the early '90s, nearly one million calls were being received annually.

Consumer sensitivity, along with innovative research and development, are the P&G hallmarks that placed their brands first in sales in 22 of 40 product categories in 1991. The company is also the United States' chief advertiser, with $3.2 billion spent on its 1990 ad budget. (The company usually runs neck-to-neck in ad dollars with Philip Morris.)

Most likely, coffee beans were far from the thoughts of James Gamble, a Cincinnati soapmaker who joined his brother-in-law, William Procter, in a partnership in 1837. The agreement stated that the men would manufacture and sell soap and candles. The contract stipulated that the partnership could end after 15 years, if either or both men wished to split up. But it was an equitable relationship, with James taking responsibility for the factory and

William, the office. The partnership was sound for another reason, too: Both candles and soap relied on the same raw manufacturing materials, oil and fat. Each Saturday night, the brothers-in-law would meet at William's house to talk over that week's business while their wives, the Norris sisters, chatted.

James had six sons, three of whom joined P&G: James N., David, and William. James N. travelled to New Orleans on the brink of the Civil War and cornered the rosin market, ensuring that P&G was the only soap manufacturer with an ample supply. When the Union government sought soap and candles for its armies, P&G snapped up the contract.

As the rosin supply diminished, James N. sought a substitute and found it in silicate of soda, which still plays a vital role in soap manufacturing. Similarly, Crisco oil (introduced in 1911) originated from the processes developed as a result of Civil War shortages. P&G was then and is now an innovator in research, spending heavily to develop new products.

By the 1880s, the second generation of Procter and Gamble men was leading P&G, the country's top soap manufacturer in a field of more than 400. The company was earning a yearly net profit of about half a million dollars. Already P&G was shouldering a heavy advertising budget in one of the first ad campaigns addressed directly to the consumer. Wisely, P&G put its money on Ivory soap, which the company introduced in a national magazine in 1879. The soap's initial popularity came from its air bubbles, which caused it to float on the top of the Ohio River where residents did their laundry and bathing. As part of its move toward producing national brands, in 1882 the company registered its "Moon and Stars" trademark (about 100 years before the trademark was erroneously linked with the Reverend Sun Myung Moon and the Unification Church).

The purity of Ivory soap was attested to by prominent chemists hired by P&G. Not only did Ivory soap ensure profitability for the company, the product also marked the beginning of scientific testing for specific product brands. P&G started hiring chemists specifically for quality control, and soon quality control labs were introduced in each of its plants.

Due to the great number of chemists employed by the company, the product list continued to grow. By 1907, a third generation was running P&G. However, when William Cooper Procter, grandson of the first William Procter, retired in 1930, the company ceased to be managed by a member of the founding families. The business was by then one of the 25 largest manufacturers in the United States, with annual revenues of several hundred million dollars. By the time the term of its first nonfamily chairman had expired in 1959, P&G had become the largest seller of packaged consumer goods in America.

P&G had entered the toiletries field, developing Drene and Prell Concentrate shampoos. A breakthrough—nonsoap soap-—was another milestone for the company in 1947. P&G was the first company to develop and market a synthetic detergent. However, the firm was still considered a soap and detergent business until it invaded new markets after World War II.

In the '50s, it entered the food arena, acquiring Duncan Hines in 1956 and Folgers Coffee in 1963. Paper products followed, including P&G's stunning success, Pampers brand disposable diapers. By the '80s, the company had moved into health care and cosmetics through acquisitions of Norwich Eaton pharmaceuticals in 1982, Richardson-Vicks in 1985, and Noxell in 1989. It further cemented its role in cosmetics with the 1991 purchase from Revlon of Max Factor and Betrix.

But the '80s also brought problems to the company. A few of the P&G products, like Duncan Hines cookies, lost market share; disappointing sales from Crush soft drinks led to its sale; and, worst of all, Rely tampons were removed from the market. P&G's ability to make the most absorbent tampon was what tragically linked this product to toxic shock syndrome.

By the end of the decade, P&G was grappling with the coffee bean controversy. Jamie Gamble and several other Gamble family members had started a proxy fight to force P&G to boycott Salvadoran beans. Jamie introduced a resolution at the October 1990 annual meeting for P&G to stop buying these beans "until parties to the Salvadoran conflict fully negotiate a peaceful settlement of the war." Backing Jamie was his brother Robert, his father Walter (a physician), and a nonfamily shareholder.

Although these four were considered substantial shareholders of the company, no one person owns more than 0.5 percent of the shares outstanding. Together, family members own a combined 850,000 of P&G's 338.4 million shares outstanding.

Jamie is a research technician at the University of Massachusetts, having received an associate degree from Stockbridge School of Agriculture. He works in the plant pathology department of the state cooperative extension service, where he helps develop alternatives to pesticides for apple growers.

Although Jamie owns stock valued at more than $4 million, he lives an unpretentious life in Amherst with his wife Sarah and their baby Seth. His house, which he remodeled himself to include a wood-burning stove to reduce the young family's heating oil consumption, has only two bedrooms. The couple drives a Volvo festooned with bumper stickers with slogans such as "Farms, not arms." When news of his shareholder resolution reached Amherst, many of his coworkers at the university were surprised to learn of Jamie's wealth.

"I'm comfortable leading an ordinary life," he was quoted as saying. "I don't identify myself as a Procter & Gamble heir as much as I do with the achievements I've been able to do on my own."

Jamie became interested in social issues through his work in agriculture and the environment. He also attributes his social concerns to having grown up in a family that questions government and bureaucratic authority. As a young adult, Jamie linked up with the Haymarket Peoples Fund (see GEORGE PILLSBURY), a group of young heirs who work for social change through alternative philanthropy. He believed that it would have been hypocritical to support the boycott and not use the power of his shares to try to change P&G policy.

Speaking shortly before the 1990 P&G annual meeting, Jamie told *The Wall Street Journal* that he didn't assume his proxy fight would be successful. P&G's board opposed the Gamble proposal, as did the editorial writers of the *Journal*, who sniffed, "While Mr. Gamble can no doubt afford to savor a pricier brew as he ponders his activist agenda, we doubt he will be toasted by small Salvadoran farmers and workers who would be hurt by the boycott." Also opposing the boycott was the Salvadoran bishops' conference, because of the boycott's potential negative impact on the Salvadoran economy, which is heavily dependent on revenue from coffee beans.

The shareholders rejected the resolution. Gamble's proposal received less than the necessary 3 percent votes to ensure its automatic placement on the following year's ballot. Although the boycott continued, the company claimed it had no effect on Folgers sales.

But some small outlets, including Boston-based Pizzeria Uno, dropped Folgers coffee in response. In late 1991, a P&G sales manager sent a letter to Pizza Hut Inc., stating that the company was developing a coffee blend "that parallels the Folgers flavor profile but contains no Salvadoran beans." P&G said the new blend would be sold under the Maryland Club label, but that Salvadoran beans would continue to be used in some cases under other labels.

Boycotters celebrated their victory prematurely. P&G's chairman and CEO Edwin L. Artzt, who has a reputation for toughness, quickly repudiated the letter. He said the company would continue to use Salvadoran coffee beans, and he rejected the notion that P&G would produce what he termed "boycott coffee" for anybody.

Although the political strife in El Salvador has wound down, and the notorious emblem of its death squads—military leader Roberto d'Aubuisson—died of cancer in early 1992, Jamie has indicated that, because he is still disquieted by the situation in El Salvador, he will carry on his efforts to stop the purchase of Salvadoran coffee beans by U.S. food producers. As he continues his battle as leader of the Folgers coffee boycott, he notes, "I really feel the company wants to do the right thing."

"So much of what came across in our childhood was the social-political activism, and that became kind of a career for all of us to some extent."

The Funding Exchange
New York, New York

Business:	Grant awards to social-change organizations
Grant-making Bodies:	National Community Funds; Paul Robeson Fund; The Saguaro Fund; OUT Fund and 15 community funds serving 26 states
Founded:	1979 by George Pillsbury, Obie Benz, Anne Hess, Sarah Pillsbury, David Crocker, Toby D'Oench and others
Annual Assets:	$12,000,000 1991 12,000,000 1990 6,000,000 1989
Annual Awards:	$6,500,000 1991 3,500,000 1990 3,000,000 1989
Family Company:	Pillsbury Company, founded in 1869 by great-grandfather Charles A. Pillsbury, now part of Grand Metropolitan PLC
Ownership:	Small number of shares owned by family members

THE FUNDING
EXCHANGE

He's Pillsbury—He's Got to Do Good

George Pillsbury, Co-Founder
(Heir to Pillsbury Foods)

George Pillsbury is a rebel with a philanthropic cause. George is the great-grandson of Charles A. Pillsbury, who, in 1869, founded the flour company that had become the world's largest by 1888. Pillsbury Company maintained its competitive position into its second century by expanding into cake mixes and prepared dough, frozen vegetables (Green Giant and Le Sueur) and pizza (Jeno's), premium ice cream (Haagen-Daz), and fast food and casual restaurants (Burger King, Bennigan's, Steak and Ale). George took his inheritance and the values he'd learned from his parents—civic participation and charitable giving—and mixed them together to create a new recipe: alternative philanthropy, which treats the *cause* of social problems, rather than merely their symptoms.

George grew up as the second of four children near Lake Minnetonka, a gentrified area outside Minneapolis. His father George S. Pillsbury worked in the family business for about 20 years and retired as executive vice president in 1968. He was the last Pillsbury to work for the company, remaining on the board until the 1989 sale of Pillsbury to a British firm, Grand Metropolitan PLC, for $5.7 billion.

By the time George was born in 1949, the family had significantly diminished their ownership of the growing Pillsbury company by using their wealth to diversify into other businesses. The Pillsburys owned only two to three percent of the company during George's childhood.

George's father was not only the last Pillsbury in management, but he was also the last family member (for 10 or 15 years) to serve on the board. "With that old a company, and with old wealth, family participation really dissipates," notes George. "My father was pretty active on the board. But of all my 24 first cousins, none of them wanted to go into the family business. It had become just some big corporation."

He thinks his father was disappointed that none of the younger generation was willing to get involved with Pillsbury, but he says, "It had the name, the sentimental value, but we just weren't big players any more in the corporation."

The decision to stay away from Pillsbury was "a little bit of the times too," he adds. "Business wasn't as big a career choice in the early '70s as it was in the '80s. A number of my cousins steered away from business and went into professions. But for my siblings and me, it really was that so much of what came across in our childhood was the social-political activism, and that became kind of a career for all of us to some extent."

The term George uses, "social-political activism," may seem an ironic description of the Pillsbury parents' mix of Republican politics and philanthropy, but it was actually these part-time activities of his mother and father that strongly influenced their four children. "My parents are both very involved in politics and social and civic activities, and so all four of us got involved, too, because of their example," says George.

After leaving Pillsbury management, George's father ran for state office as a moderate/liberal Republican and served in the Minnesota senate for 12 years. His first campaign brought all four Pillsbury children into the political arena. George says, "We were encouraged to be politically involved at a very early age. We were swept into party politics at the ages of eight or nine, involved in a lot of different Republican campaigns throughout the '50s and '60s, putting bumper stickers on cars and passing out leaflets."

George's mother Sally Whitney Pillsbury had always expended most of her energy on volunteer activities, especially on behalf of area hospitals and theater groups. George and his siblings decided that helping others looked more creative and challenging than business. "My social activism comes from their civic and political participation. So it was natural for me, when I got to

college in the late '60s, to get involved in different political campaigns and to do some volunteer work," says this blond, blue-eyed
Yale graduate. "It just turned out that the volunteer work I did was
for the Black Panther party."

George often tells the story of wanting to help the Black
Panthers as an undergraduate but not knowing how to do so. He
showed up at their New Haven headquarters and awkwardly thrust
a check at them for several hundred dollars. "Here, I thought you
could use this," he said to an astonished Panther. But instead of
helping George feel united with a group that was meaningful to
him, the loneliness of his check-writing further isolated him. It was
a pivotal experience because he realized that there must be other
wealthy young people out there who wanted to give to causes their
parents or trust managers would shun, yet were too self-conscious
to make solo contact. George saw he could draw others like himself
to an institution that could act as a grant-giver on behalf of progressive individual donors. Soon George changed his party affilia-
tion from Republican to Democratic.

It was at Yale that George had another key experience: An
article on supporters of the university service workers' strike identified, of the many students present, only one—George Pillsbury.
He realized he could attract attention to the issues he supported
through the use of what he calls his "brand name."

As graduation approached, George cast about for a way to
create a foundation for change to be funded by other like-minded
heirs. George freely discussed his ideas with his parents, whom he
continued to use as role models and reference points even when
some of their ideas were in conflict. The Pillsburys worked hard in
the late 1960s and early 1970s at cementing their mutual respect.
George says, "What we don't agree on is the method to achieve the
change that we both want. I've grown up with a different sense of
how social change can be achieved, so we'll argue about that, but
they're very understanding and supportive of the fact that their
kids are involved in politics and foundations."

Another influence on George was his older brother, Charles, a
Yale upperclassman who was organizing antiwar demonstrations.
Charles is named after the great-grandfather who founded Pillsbury. His college roommate Garry Trudeau, however, ultimately
used Charles as a model for the Doonesbury character in his

newspaper strip. Thus was a second Charles Pillsbury thrust into history.

While George was contemplating his options after leaving Yale, his mother attended a foundation conference in Minneapolis and noticed, as George describes it, "some guy who happened to have a ponytail and Adidas sneakers." Sally Pillsbury was curious, and according to her son, asked "'What's he doing here? What's he about?'"

"She is just the kind of person who would go up and talk to a guy with a ponytail and ask him what he was doing there at a foundation meeting in Minneapolis in 1973," George says. The ponytailed man turned out to be Obie Benz, a Sunbeam Bread heir, who put together the San Francisco Vanguard Public Foundation, one of the original organizations dedicated to alternative philanthropy. Although today Benz spends his energy on writing and filmmaking (he produced the controversial semi-autobiographical movie about sexual mores of the 1960s, *Heavy Petting*), his advice and presence were comforting to George who had thought he was the only family business heir worrying about the best way to use his wealth.

George had found someone with whom he could share ideas on the need for philanthropies to treat the causes of social problems rather than their symptoms. For example, traditional benefactors might give money to a cancer hospital, but these men would direct funds to ending the toxic waste associated with an environmental cause of cancer.

After hearing about Obie's Vanguard Foundation, George took the $400,000 he'd inherited and founded the Haymarket People's Fund in Boston in 1974. Haymarket set up a community-based board so that decisions on funding could be made by local people rather than by professional staff, as is done in traditional philanthropies. Nearly all of Haymarket's funds come from hefty donations made by rich, progressive business heirs. Haymarket is also devoted to "venture philanthropy," giving small amounts of money to groups that have never been grant recipients before in order to get them started.

Haymarket is now one of the largest alternative foundations in the country. More important, the concept advanced by Benz, Pillsbury, and other rich progressives introduced to major gift-giving a new group of donors who otherwise might not have taken part in philanthropy.

After studying tax law at H&R Block in order to solicit funds more knowledgeably, George with a few others (including Obie Benz and Anne Hess, heir to Sears, Roebuck & Co.) founded the Funding Exchange in 1979 as an umbrella group for alternative foundations. The Funding Exchange, which used its national network to give $35 million in its first 11 years, attracts many young family business heirs through workshops covering such practical issues as how to deal with financial advisers when trying to invest responsibly, and how to deal with the "stigma" of being wealthy, especially when one has a famous last name.

These problems may seem slight to most of us, but consider the adolescence of George Pillsbury, who was dubbed "Poppin' Fresh" by his high school classmates. George was 15 when the Pillsbury Doughboy entered the American scene and ever since, George has good-naturedly put up with belly jabs. Even his friends in the antiwar movement couldn't resist dubbing him a "flour child." (Pete Coors also talks about the difficulty of having a "brand name" in ADOLPH COORS COMPANY.)

George knows that he leaves himself open to sarcasm through his much-quoted desire to change "the fundamental inequity of money." He says, "There's definitely been skepticism and some cynicism." *Esquire* and *Forbes* identify him, in a play on his family business and his wealth, as a "doughboy." But George is willing to accept the jibes in exchange for publicity on social activism.

Occasionally, it does seem as if these alternative philanthropic business heirs are consciously biting the hand that has been so generous to them. Look at the films financed by Haymarket: David Crocker, a coal-mining heir, supported the documentary *Harlan County, U.S.A.*, which dramatically exposed the early injustices against coalworkers, and an heir to General Motors stock financed a film about the 1937 Flint strike, *Banners and Babies*. These efforts not only influence moviegoers, but are also artistically successful. *Harlan County* won an Academy Award for best documentary and at least ten other films supported by Haymarket have been nominated for Oscars.

George's younger sister Sarah Pillsbury is the predominant filmmaker of this group. Following her parents' example of service and her brother's example of alternative philanthropy, in 1976 she founded Liberty Hill, a Los Angeles social action foundation. Sarah's main vocation, however, is filmmaking. She began with documentaries like the academy award-winning *Board and Care* and now is a successful producer. She coheads her own production company, Sanford/Pillsbury Productions. Her movies include *Desperately Seeking Susan*, *River's Edge* and *Eight Men Out*. She likes her movies to reflect her values and is, according to George, the most career-oriented of the Pillsbury children.

Today George is development director of National Jobs with Peace Campaign, a grassroots lobby to change federal priorities from excessive military spending to funding human and environmental needs, such as housing and education. "Let's create jobs doing something constructive. You can create more and better jobs doing socially useful things," George believes.

Alternative philanthropy became part of mainstream America when Oprah Winfrey and Phil Donahue wanted to talk about it, and George's parents recognize this. Although George says that they may be most proud of maintaining good family relations through the bumpy years, they would see George's greatest accomplishment as starting the Funding Exchange, the preeminent national network of alternative foundations. It helps that George's work is now nationally recognized. "When their friends tell them, 'Oh, I read about your son George in *The New York Times*,' that makes it real to them. So I think they're proud of that and of what we've done to create this philanthropic network."

George isn't sure that he ever could have influenced Pillsbury Co. if he or his cousins had joined management. The Pillsbury experience shows just how hard it is to maintain control and interest in a family business which is three generations removed from its founder. Charles Pillsbury's company had grown into a conglomerate, in which family members had little input. (In contrast, LEVI STRAUSS & CO. is 16 years older than Pillsbury but still run by a descendent of its founder.) Perhaps the important lesson, however, is that the values that helped keep both the family and the family business on track for so many years can be passed. It was Sally and George S. Pillsbury's belief and practice in giving service to the community that gave the powerful impetus to their children's lives.

"We wanted to do a magazine of progressive politics. And we wanted to do it for a large audience. Somewhat to our astonishment, we did."

Mother Jones Magazine
San Francisco, California

Business:	Muckraking journalism
Type of Organization:	Nonprofit
Financial Supporters:	Subscribers and donors
Key Issues:	Social justice, equal rights, world peace
Frequency:	Six times a year
Length:	80 pages per issue
Founded:	1974 by Adam Hochschild, Paul Jacobs, and Richard Parker
Board of Directors:	18 directors including Adam Hochschild
Circulation:	110,000
Family Company:	AMAX, founded in 1887 with grandfather Berthold Hochschild as part owner and later President and Chairman; father Harold Hochschild, President and Chairman
Ownership:	Small number of shares owned by family members; none held by Adam Hochschild

MOTHER JONES MAGAZINE

An Incompatible Alloy

Adam Hochschild, Co-Founder
(Heir to AMAX)

Adam Hochschild, 50, is a writer and editor best known for having cofounded the progressive political magazine Mother Jones. There seems to be a chasm between Adam's chosen professional life and that of his father Harold K. Hochschild, whose second generation leadership of one of the largest U.S. metals companies gave him a dual status in global business and diplomacy. But unlike the relationship between other fathers and their sons who differ, these two men shared a style that avoided confrontation.

Adam's grandfather, Frankfurt metal marketer Berthold Hochschild, had been sent by his German firm to New York in 1884 to open up metal trading from the western American states. As the bounty of the western copper fields increased, the company formed American Metal Co. (later Amco, now AMAX) in 1887.

Berthold expected his sons Harold and Walter to enter the company in which the Hochschilds had a small ownership stake, and he was not disappointed. The company was already important in its industry, so there was no thought of automatically handing down its leadership to a young man, even if he was the eldest son; Berthold stepped down from the chairmanship and presidency in 1917 and Harold did not succeed to these titles until 1934, when he was in his 40s.

Adam was born in 1942 into a family that was coolly polite, distant, and wary in the way that is characteristic of a portion of America's upper class, especially those with close European ties. Adam grew up as an only child whose daily life was so rigidly structured and overprotected that it could be said that he lacked a childhood.

Adam never developed a casual or comfortable relationship with his father and was instead cosseted by a doting mother (Mary Marquand) and a series of nannies and governesses. In this family, Adam learned to repress his emotions, which, of course, surfaced more obliquely than if he'd been allowed to express them openly. In the presence of his father, Adam wrote later, he felt an overwhelming sense of nausea and would be unable to eat.

Adam's preference for solitary play with his stamp albums or shortwave radio concerned his parents. Friends were brought in to him for play as if these youngsters—some of whom knew their fathers' employment was dependent on Adam's father—were inanimate toys.

Adam was sensitive and intelligent; his ability to see through his parents only added to his discomfort and guilt. He would ask his driver, for example, to let him off before they reached the schoolyard so classmates would think he'd walked to school.

A pivotal moment came when teenage Adam was with his father on a tour of the company's central African mines. Although Amco was an enlightened and benevolent employer compared to many similarly engaged firms, no one would choose an African miner's life.

Adam looked about and made the inevitable comparison between the miners' lives and his own: the home in Princeton (the house was large even by Princeton standards) and Eagle Nest, the family's summer estate in the Adirondacks, with hundreds of acres of pines, a mile-long lake, and a seaplane on which Harold arrived and departed each summer weekend. Although Harold believed that these privileges should be used to do good, his rationale wasn't strong enough for Adam. Simply put, Adam did not believe that he was entitled to reap these benefits.

As a college student, Adam spent a summer working on an antiapartheid newspaper in South Africa. It was a major turning point for him. As Adam wrote in his well-received 1986 memoir, *Half the Way Home*, "South Africa caused me to lose my political virginity."

After studying at Harvard, followed by a brief stint as a civil rights worker in Mississippi, Adam went into the Army Reserve in

1964 to avoid the draft, as the war in Southeast Asia escalated. Several years later, he got soldiers to sign a petition asking for the immediate withdrawal of all troops from Asia, a move opposed by his father only because it might hurt Adam's later career. Harold himself had already had his own letters criticizing the war published by *The New York Times*.

Adam's continuing strained relationship with his father meant he never could have worked with him at the metals company even if he hadn't already rejected the idea for political reasons. Instead, Adam joined the *San Francisco Chronicle* as a reporter, then moved to *Ramparts*, a now-defunct magazine closely associated with the antiwar movement. Adam hadn't yet "come out" as the child of wealthy parents, so even in this environment he was always waiting for the inescapable question that arose as the magazine's writers researched, for example, American corporations in Africa: "Hey, Adam, are you related to the Hochschild who runs AMAX?"

Adam had become more open about his background by the mid-'70s, when he joined with writers Paul Jacobs and Richard Parker to found Mother Jones magazine, named for an early twentieth century labor organizer. The magazine's first issue appeared in early 1976.

"We wanted to do a magazine of progressive politics," Adam says, "a magazine that was concerned with basic issues of social justice. And we wanted to do it for a large audience, not just for a small circle of true believers. We hoped to reach an audience of well over 100,000 readers. Somewhat to our astonishment, we did." The circulation of *Mother Jones* was about 110,000 in 1992.

Mother Jones is published by the Foundation for National Progress. Despite its name, the Foundation is a nonprofit, tax-exempt charity and not a grant-making foundation. Its status enables the magazine to pay a lower postal rate, saving it thousands of dollars each year.

Most people falsely believe that it was Adam who financed the magazine's launch. "I have indeed been a major financial supporter of *Mother Jones*, but oddly enough, this was not particularly true at the very beginning. For the first four or five years of its existence, the number of subscribers grew very rapidly. As a result we had to raise very little money."

Rather than begin the new magazine as a business, Adam says, "We looked around and realized that no political magazine on the left or on the right has turned a profit in the U.S. since the early '20s. We figured that if we were going to lose money, we might as well set up as a nonprofit and not pretend that we were under the illusion of making a profit to begin with."

Adam must have been concerned in 1983 when a local IRS office ruled that the magazine was commercial rather than educational. Although the IRS's National Appeals Office overruled the local decision, the federal action led some to ask why *Mother Jones* with its anti-Reagan articles, rather than, say, *National Geographic*, which has the same tax-exempt status, was challenged.

Mother Jones has evolved through the years, but its left-leaning stance remains. Its pages have been filled with muckraking investigative pieces, such as its early exposés of the now-infamous Ford Pinto, the Dalkon shield, and the drug Benedictin.

Life at *Mother Jones* has not always meant positive publicity for Adam. In 1986, a column in *The Nation* written by Alexander Cockburn took Adam personally to task for having fired editor Michael Moore. Cockburn wrote, "[The rich] think that they can get away with anything. Hochschild is heir to the AMAX mining fortune, and although he has devoted substantial amounts of the family income, originally generated by African wage-slaves, to finance the quasiliberal periodical, he can still behave like a nineteenth century mill owner."

In correcting what he said were Cockburn's misstatements, Adam omitted mention of Cockburn's class-baiting description of him as an heir to the AMAX fortune. Spy magazine in 1992 also described Adam as owning AMAX shares despite Adam's having divested himself of his shares around the time of his father's death in 1981. His mother had died years earlier, and he doubts any of his relatives still own a stake in AMAX. And the family had never owned a significant number of shares to begin with. So much for the AMAX heir description.

By 1987, Adam had ceased doing any editing of *Mother Jones* and no longer sees articles until they appear in print, preferring to concentrate on his own writing. After publishing his childhood memoirs, in 1990 Adam published his second book, *The Mirror at*

Midnight: A South African Journey, about his visit as an adult to the country that had interested him so much as a teenager.

Adam's next book will focus on how the Russians are coming to terms with the legacy of Stalinism. For this book, which will be published in 1993, Adam attended a Russian language school for several months before moving to Moscow with his wife Arlie, a well-known sociology professor at Berkeley who is also a writer (The Second Shift), and their younger son Gabriel, who attended an American school in Moscow. The couple has another son, David, now in college.

Adam is living an emotionally engaged life. It took him some time to be able to do this. While Harold was alive, Adam never seized the opportunity to confront his father. In fact, even today Adam does not want to talk publicly about his childhood.

He does honor his father's memory through serving as a director of the Cedar Fund, Inc., which was established in 1975 to help preserve Harold's beloved Adirondacks and his lodge at Eagle Nest, which is now the Blue Mountain Center for artists and writers. Adam also serves on the board of another family foundation that makes small projects in the field of human rights and the environment.

Adam is now content with his own life and its accomplishments. Although his father would perhaps have preferred Adam to take a law degree and serve in the State Department (the African-American Institute chaired by Harold in the '60s was CIA-backed) Adam is thankful that Harold did not pressure him into joining his company. After all, Harold's loyalty to his business was such that he and his younger brother Walter, who as chairman saw Amco become AMAX in 1957, together served the company for more than 100 years. And with their century of achievement, these men ended the Hochschild family's involvement in the mining, metals, and energy business.

But on Adam's desk, as he describes in his memoir, sits a solid paperweight made of copper, one tangible legacy from his father and the business the family represented for so many years.

"My memories of my father are of seeing a man lying on his back with sandbags pressing on his chest to exercise his lungs, dying of emphysema caused by smoking the Reynolds family's Camel and Winston brands."

Citizens for a Smokefree America
Beverly Hills, California

Goals:	Support of antitobacco education and intervention programs
Founded:	1989 by Patrick Reynolds
Type of Organization:	Nonprofit
Financial Supporters:	Donors
Board of Directors:	7 directors including Patrick Reynolds, Chairman
Family Company:	R. J. Reynolds Company, founded by grandfather R. J. Reynolds in 1875; now part of RJR Nabisco
Ownership:	Small number of shares owned by family members; none held by Patrick Reynolds

CITIZENS FOR A
SMOKEFREE AMERICA

A Breath of Fresh Heir

Patrick Reynolds, Founding President
(Heir to RJR Nabisco, Inc.)

"For every Gordon Getty, for every Patrick Reynolds, for every John Robbins there are 20 or 30 heirs to family businesses who are either alcoholics or in mental hospitals—lost souls. They were never able to overcome their lack of parenting along with the large inheritances that they received," says Patrick Reynolds.

Patrick is both president of the antitobacco organization Citizens For A Smokefree America and grandson of R.J. Reynolds, founder in 1875 of the eponymous tobacco company (now a unit of RJR Nabisco) that is the second largest producer of cigarettes in the United States. (Patrick's uncle founded an aluminum business, now Reynolds Metals Company.)

"My family is a classic example of a founder who is so swept up by his career of being a titan of American industry that he didn't take time to raise his children or teach them the family business," Patrick continues.

When R.J. died in 1919, Patrick's father Richard was only 12 years old. Dick worked at the tobacco company in the '20s as a teenager, but until a few of Patrick's cousins recently joined the company, no family member had worked at the firm since the '40s. Patrick believes of Dick that "too few restraints by his mother were added to the strain of fatherlessness that has lasted through the third generation—my own generation."

Patrick's father also "had the extra burden of receiving a $28 million inheritance in 1934 when he was only 27." Dick led a dissolute, café-society life.

"If someone gives you a lot of money and you're in your 20s," explains Patrick, who himself received $2.5 million when he was 21, "your instinct is to party. You ignore the family business and are not motivated to get a career or start working."

Dick's partying was interrupted only by frequent wedding ceremonies. The second of his four wives was Patrick's mother, the gorgeous movie starlet Marianne O'Brien. They divorced after Marianne's well-publicized affair with Latin playboy Porfirio Rubirosa. Patrick was three. The divorce was surprising because Marianne and Dick had so much in common: partying, smoking, and drinking.

"To have been parented by alcoholics was my lot," Patrick says.

Six years after the divorce, nine-year-old Patrick wrote his father: "Dear Dad, I want to meet you—I'm your son Patrick. Where are you? Love, Me."

Dick responded immediately to the plaintive note.

When people want to know why Patrick, heir to a tobacco fortune, has devoted himself since 1986 to an antismoking campaign, he answers, "My father."

"My memories of my father are of seeing a man lying on his back with sandbags pressing on his chest to exercise his lungs, dying of emphysema caused by smoking the Reynolds family's Camel and Winston brands. I remember him lying there, coughing and gasping for breath, and counting the time he had left to live. That is really all I remember of my father." Dick died of emphysema at 58, when Patrick was 15.

Patrick believes that tobacco has killed many of his relatives: his grandfather R.J., who died of cancer after years of chewing tobacco, and his father, mother, and aunt. He says that his three brothers, all heavy smokers, have emphysema.

Patrick himself was a pack-a-day smoker—he uses the term "addicted smoker"—who realized it was unhealthy even though he couldn't stop. In 1979, he called his broker "with a telephone in one hand and a cigarette in the other" and divested himself of his R.J. Reynolds tobacco stock. He had decided he didn't want to earn his money from a product he associated with sickness and death.

The broker advised him against the move because of the huge capital gains tax Patrick would pay. "Sell it," was Patrick's response.

And, he continues, "I never regretted it, even though my brothers made millions by hanging on to theirs [until shortly before the 1989 LBO of RJR Nabisco by Kohlberg Kravis Roberts]."

Patrick fought hard to rid himself of his addiction to cigarettes, finally winning the 15-year battle in 1986. It took him a little more time before he felt comfortable dedicating himself to an antismoking campaign.

After all, Patrick didn't have to work. He was wealthy through the money his grandmother had left him. His father had left tens of millions of dollars to his fourth wife and not a penny to any of his four children. This was another hurtful legacy for Patrick and his brothers. But with his grandmother's money, Patrick, like his father, went through a rich-kid phase. "I lived in big homes and dated starlets and wanted to be a film director."

Patrick segued from parties to filmmaking and had a short career as an actor. One of his houses, a castle with an artificial waterfall and a paper moon under the famous "Hollywood" sign, was featured in "Nashville," a movie in which Patrick had a small part during his relationship with its star, actress Shelley Duvall.

Trying to find an identity with which he was comfortable, Patrick changed his name and then changed it back to Reynolds again. He realized that dropping the Reynolds name made no meaningful difference; a name change couldn't erase history or memories.

In the early '80s, he married into the European jet set and lost part of his inheritance in an ill-conceived business venture. He returned to acting after his divorce, to star in the 1986 movie "The Eliminators."

The same year, Patrick's friend Larry Miller, a Republican party donor, brought him to Washington D.C. The trip changed Patrick's life. When he was introduced to U.S. Senator Bob Packwood (R, Oregon), he immediately asked the senator why this country had the lowest cigarette taxation rate of any industrial country. But when Packwood invited Patrick to address the Senate committee on the issue of cigarette taxation that same day, he demurred.

Patrick returned home to Beverly Hills and began to educate himself on the tobacco industry. The American Lung Association asked him to testify at the 1986 Senate hearings on tobacco. The hearings were heavily covered when word got out that Surgeon General Everett Koop, who had called Patrick "one of the nation's most influential advocates of a smoke-free America," had been forbidden to testify by President Reagan.

When Patrick started his testimony, flashes illuminated the room and cameras rolled. It was a newswire story: The grandson of the founder of the world's second-largest tobacco business was condemning smoking.

He was besieged with speaking requests, and as a result dropped out of filmmaking. "I didn't want people to think that I was using my antismoking position to publicize an ongoing acting career," he says.

In addition, Patrick thought it was time to associate the Reynolds name with health rather than sickness. With a partner, he started the Reynolds Stop Smoking Program. Its primary product was a behavior modification kit of audio and videocassettes. Although they sold 14,000 kits in the first six months, ultimately Patrick lost more of his inherited wealth on this unsuccessful business.

To pick up the antismoking cause, he founded the Citizens For A Smoke-Free America in 1986 to raise funds for grass-roots, antismoking organizations. As a result, Patrick was recognized by the World Health Organization.

In 1989, attention returned to Patrick with his publication of the juicy Reynolds family history, *The Gilded Leaf*. An unsympathetic *Fortune* article retitled the book *RJR Dearest*.

The tobacco industry has also been antagonistic to Patrick. He, in turn, criticizes the industry for its linkage of smoking to free speech. "When they take out full-page ads to say smoking is a matter of choice, it helps their customers deny how addicted they really are."

Furthermore, Patrick notes that the principal sponsor of the ACLU, an organization committed to free speech rights, is the tobacco industry. "The ACLU retorts that they limit how much one corporation can donate, but it doesn't tell you that five or six tobacco companies together provide it with a lot of money."

But Patrick doesn't want to devote the rest of his life solely to speaking out against the tobacco industry. He'd like to hire professional fund raisers to pick up the staff work of Citizens For a Smokefree America, which he is now doing by himself with a cadre of volunteers.

He's thinking of going back to school to become a psychotherapist. "As long as I had the inherited wealth," he says, "I didn't have to work. I didn't really have to fulfill my potential. Now I want to accomplish whatever I am capable of doing.

"I see the light at the end of the tunnel now, and I'm close to forgiving my father. It took me 10 or 15 years to deal with our relationship, to try to overcome it. Even writing the book wasn't enough.

"Now I want a stable life. A career to recoup my fortune and a family to raise."

When Patrick is asked if he's biting the hand that once fed him, he has a ready answer.

"If the hand that once fed me is the tobacco industry, then that same hand has killed millions of people, and it will kill millions more."

"The thought of selling a product that didn't contribute to people's health was not inviting to me."

The EarthSave Foundation
Santa Cruz, California

Business: Environmental and Health Education

Type of Organization: Nonprofit; 30 local chapters in U.S.

Main Issues: Educating people to eat lower on the food chain; empowering individuals to know their actions can make a difference

Best Known Projects: The YES! Tour (Youth for Environmental Sanity); Lectures, workshops, youth summer camps and river trips; distributes books and tapes on nutrition, environment, and conscious living

Publications: The EarthSave Newsletter with 40,000 readership; Our Food, Our World—The Hidden Realities of an Animal-Based Diet

Founded: 1989 by John Robbins

Family Directors: John Robbins, President
Deo Robbins, Secretary-Treasurer

Family Company: Baskin-Robbins Incorporated, founded by father Irv Robbins and uncle Burt Baskin in 1946; now part of Allied-Lyons PLC

Ownership: No longer owned by family

THE EARTHSAVE
FOUNDATION

Rain Forest Ripple

John Robbins, Founder
(Heir to Baskin-Robbins)

John Robbins, 45, was born with a bright pink plastic spoon in his mouth and a cone-shaped swimming pool in his luxurious backyard in California's San Fernando Valley. He was groomed while a child and young man to take over Baskin-Robbins, the ice cream empire founded by his father and maternal uncle in 1946, one year before his birth. But he's traded the largest chain of ice cream stores in the world for a life that leads to better health through an improved diet—one that does not include high-butterfat, high-sugar ice cream.

"I was being methodically prepared from my childhood to take over the ice cream business," John says. "Anytime I wasn't in school, I was working in the warehouse, in the factory, in a retail store, in advertising. My father wanted me to learn the whole business.

"I enjoyed the work and did it well. Baskin-Robbins was a thriving, growing company, and it was a fun business."

But John's own poor childhood health led him to investigate an improved diet when he was a student at Berkeley in the late '60s. He was married and working vacations at the company founded by Irv Robbins, now 75, and Burt Baskin. And what John learned changed his previous life plans.

"An ice cream cone isn't going to kill anybody. But I realized that the better I did my job, the more Baskin-Robbins ice cream would be sold and consumed. That means the more heart attacks there'd be, the more diabetes, the more strokes, the more cancer.

"The thought of selling a product that didn't contribute to people's health was not inviting to me."

John already had questioned the route that his parents expected him to follow. He had marched in Birmingham and Selma for civil rights, and then on the West Coast to end the Viet Nam War. The assassination of Dr. Martin Luther King knocked out any remaining predisposition John may have had toward business as usual.

"Inventing new flavors seemed pathetic to me," says the man who's credited with helping to originate Jamocha Almond Fudge. "I felt pulled in a different direction.

"I told my dad I wasn't going to run the business for him. He was very hurt, and this made it very hard for me. And I said that I wanted no dependence on his achievement. I did not accept a trust fund, and I didn't want to live relying on his wealth."

John admits, "He was offering me something most young men would have given their right arm for, and he gets the one kid in the country who says no. I must have seemed crazy to him.

"There was a lot of distance between us for many years."

Ironically, John says his older sister Marsha, who has an M.B.A. from Stanford University, would have given "her right and left arm to have the chance that I did." But Irv never thought of his daughters Marsha and Erin (an artist and craftswoman) as possible successors. "He would have been happy to offer their husbands jobs," says John facetiously.

He laughs. "I can't explain it because it makes no sense to me."

Instead, Irv sold the company to United Brands in 1969, one year after John made his declaration. John moved to British Columbia, where he became a therapist after receiving a graduate degree in psychology. He lived simply and his interest in ecology and diet increased.

John continued his research and writing on health issues and started EarthSave Foundation, a nonprofit organization aimed at raising awareness that a meat-centered diet depletes the earth's resources and is deleterious to health. EarthSave is centered in Santa Cruz, California and has a board that includes a mix of scholars, activists, and celebrities: Jeremy Rifkin, Frances More

Lappé, Caesar Chavez, Colman McCarthy, Casey Kasem, River Phoenix, and Olivia Newton-John.

A breakthrough for John—both professionally and personally—came in 1987 with the publication of his first book, *Diet For A New America*. Here was a meticulously researched document that jolted awareness of the health and ecological dangers of America's meat-oriented diet. After its nomination for a Pulitzer prize, John was invited by UNESCO to address the United Nations and received a standing ovation. The book's commercial success brought John, and EarthSave, a tidal wave of publicity.

With the book's royalties and those from his second work, *In Search of Balance*, John and his wife Deo, EarthSave's outreach director, were able to stop drawing their small salaries and become volunteers. In addition, John accepted a role as one of the movement's spokesmen and began talking on the speaker circuit.

John has an updated topic to speak about: his sequel to Diet titled *May All Be Fed: Diet For A New World*, published in the fall of 1992. John received a $360,000 advance for his new book in a heated auction among nine publishers. The advance John accepted was not even the highest bid; however, John was convinced that William Morrow would be the best publisher for *May All Be Fed*.

John's parents did not read his first book until Irv's own cardiologist recommended it to the couple. Irv was nervous about his own poor health—his problems with blood pressure, cholesterol, and diabetes—especially since his brother-in-law and partner Burt had died of a heart attack in 1967 at age 54. So he gave the book a try.

"He began to take some steps by changing his diet, and he got results," says John. "Then he took another step and got more results."

Eventually, Irv was able to decrease his medication dramatically. "On one level, he's a medical miracle. On the other level, these changes are quite predictable," says John. With the improved health came a better understanding of John and his mission.

Irv had retired from Baskin-Robbins in 1980, 11 years after selling the company. He was the last family member in the business. Burt's daughter became a model and Burt's son Richard

Baskin is an artist and musician who made the celebrity columns during the '80s when he was going out with Barbra Streisand.

Baskin-Robbins is now owned by a British conglomerate, Allied-Lyons PLC, with more than 3,413 retail stores globally. Even Muscovites have become accustomed to 31 Flavors. U.S. operations include 2,300 ice cream shops. The company's sale allowed Irv and his wife Irma to retire to Palm Springs where they enjoy a life style that does not tempt John.

"I live in a very small rented house and I drive a '78 Datsun," he says. "That's fine with me.

"I subscribe to Thoreau's philosophy, 'I make myself richer by making my wants few.'"

John had once declared that he planned to reject an inheritance from his parents. Now that he's middle-aged, with a son of his own (named Ocean)—who was instrumental in the founding of Youth for Environmental Sanity (YES!), which gives workshops and presentations for high school students—his thoughts have changed.

"When I was young, I was a child. I didn't have the clarity that I have now. I felt then that I wasn't strong enough to handle the temptation and the power. I look around, and I see that most young people who inherit a lot of money—well, it's just too much for them.

"But now I'm stronger in who I am. I have discovered my identity and my values. Now, if money came my way, I would use it for the causes I believe in.

"Money is a tool to be used," concludes John.

"With attitude, you can do anything."

Theatrical and Motion Picture Production
Chicago, Illinois

Business:	Theatrical producer; real estate; foreign investment adviser
Best Known Activities:	Broadway musical and film Hair
Produced:	1968 by Michael Butler
Current Activities:	Organizer of polo tournament in downtown Chicago; Musical with a Jamaican theme
Family Companies:	Butler Paper founded in 1860 by Julius Butler; Butler Aviation founded in 1945 by Paul Butler
Ownership:	Companies are no longer family-owned

THEATRICAL AND MOTION PICTURE PRODUCTION

From Heir to *Hair*

Michael Butler, Producer
(Heir to Butler Paper, Butler Aviation)

The first Butler to arrive in America was the younger son of the Duke of Ormond, the ranking peer of Ireland. To flee Cromwell, who led parliamentary forces against the monarch during England's Civil War, he set sail in 1654 for America while his father fled to France with young Prince Charles. "We were doubly cursed," says Michael Butler, 66. "We were Irish and we represented the Crown."

Possibly the only Butler tradition Michael has chosen to maintain is a friendship with the English royal family. As recently as 1986, Charles, Prince of Wales, was Michael's guest in Oak Brook, the Illinois village Michael's father founded.

Michael Butler has segued from business to politics to theater and movie production back to business again. Throughout all these shifts, perhaps only Michael's polo playing has remained constant. But Michael is best known for bringing the tribal love-rock musical *Hair* to the Broadway stage in 1968.

Hair ran for five years on Broadway. The show both defined its generation and continues to be the world's most commercially successful musical production.

Michael is descended from a line of patrician businessmen. The Butler Paper Company was founded before the Civil War by Michael's great-grandfather Julius. Michael's grandfather Frank augmented the paper company with a vast cattle ranch and dairy farm. His father Paul added Butler Aviation in 1945 and in 1956 decided to create a town of his own, Oak Brook, with its 17 fields for polo, 20 miles west of downtown Chicago.

Michael grew up in a social scene that was decidedly Anglo in flavor: pink jacket by day for hunting, white tie at night for partying. Michael's parents were divorced when he was young, and his mother remarried five more times. He has a sister Jorie with whom he is close and a brother Frank with whom he is not. The first hint of his nonconformism was his successful petition as a teenager for a name change from Paul Butler Jr. to Michael Butler.

When Michael began work in the early '50s as a paper sales-man in his father's company, there was a hint of the dually profitable and nonconformist life that he would lead. Michael didn't intend to be one of Butler's horde of fine-paper salespeople, so he worked out a gross commission arrangement to sell corrugated shipping containers.

" 'Oh my God,' " Michael quotes as the reaction to his moving out of the fine-paper line. "The only thing that's considered lower class than corrugated paper is waste paper."

Michael's father Paul was eager to move him into management and soon pulled him out of shipping containers to promote him to vice president of sales for the company. The complex relationship between father and son—or between Paul and anyone, for that matter—began to froth. "I discovered I was in the most incredible infighting. It was a corporate war. And my father undercut me in an adversarial way. He would pit people against one another in order to maintain control. He could be a charmer and I love him dearly, but he was pretty difficult."

Michael took off to Europe and soon structured a deal with Axel Wenner-Gren, the ElectroLux heir, which became the overseas operation of Butler Paper. But Michael has never been a one-project man, so he was also dabbling in real estate.

Michael met the young Congressman Jack Kennedy in the south of France, and they became friends. Soon Kennedy was using the well-connected Michael as his observer, especially in the Middle East. "After Jack got elected president, he started to talk with me about whether I wanted to go back to the Middle East as an ambassador," says Michael. "But I told him I wanted to stay here and head the Bureau of Indian Affairs."

" 'Why do you want to get involved in that snake pit?'" was Kennedy's reaction.

"I'd like to disband it and turn the funds over to the Indian chiefs instead of spending it on the agency's bureaucracy," said Michael.

Before this was resolved, Paul called. He and Michael's brother Frank were in a dispute, and Paul needed someone he could rely on at home. "If you come home now, I'll pay your salary for Jack's second term," offered Paul.

Michael accepted and returned to manage Oak Brook Farm, which had been run out of the left hand pocket of the paper and aviation companies. After Kennedy was killed, "the light went out. But Bobby called me one day and asked me to give [Illinois governor] Otto Kerner some help. I was made chairman of the Organization of Economic Development for the state of Illinois and worked on Otto's reelection campaign. I began to get back into politics and ran for state senator for [Oak Brook's] Du Page county in 1966."

Michael lost. "Naturally. They've never elected a Democrat." Michael laughs and adds, "Especially someone like me."

Typically, Michael's political life was not his only interest. Every summer, he'd hire a student to help the regular gardening crew at the farm.

"I discovered that this young chap was growing marijuana in the lower reaches of the garden, so I decided to sample some of his agricultural produce."

As the young man and Michael came to know each other, Michael was exposed to his pacifist philosophy. "I was going through some major changes from being an extremely self-centered, ruthless, military-industrial hawk to swinging in the opposite direction," Michael says.

Michael had to fly to New York City for a meeting on the Civil Rights Commission report with Mayor John Lindsay. He says, "I ran across an ad for an off-off Broadway preview production that said, 'Hair—The American tribal love-rock musical.' "

Looking at the well-known stage photo of five Indian chiefs, and not noticing that two chiefs had the authors' white faces superimposed, Michael says he thought, "My God, the Indians have put a show together!"

"I went down and saw it and thought it was the best antiwar, generational thing I've ever seen."

Michael had induced his father to invest in shows since the '50s. "It was a good deal. He would take the losses, and if there was a profit, we'd split it." He'd talked Paul into investing in *Kismet, Peter Pan, The Music Man,* and *West Side Story.*

"I got Roger Stevens—I'd been involved with Roger in *West Side Story*—to introduce me to Joe Papp." But Papp said he was not interested in a long-term run.

Soon after, Papp changed his mind. *Hair* had opened to such good reviews that bringing it to a wider audience was irresistible. Papp asked Butler to coproduce.

Michael joined Papp, then became sole producer to revamp the show for a larger stage in 1968. Michael also added its infamous nude scene. He rounded up his polo-playing friends to invest in *Hair,* promising them that he'd stay with the show until the movie was made. Michael didn't realize that he'd committed himself to a ten-year deal. After the musical's 1,742 Broadway performances, he says, "I took it through 29 different shows in 17 countries. It has been seen by more people than any other musical."

Paul, who'd invested $100,000 in the musical, was disgusted by the opening-night performance and immediately withdrew his money. The Broadway show ultimately grossed $80 million.

In a sense, the relationship between Paul and Michael was the basis for Michael's interest in *Hair.* He says, "My whole reason for Hair was for communication between the generations." Ironically, the musical—and Michael's resultant wealthy hippie life-style—did not facilitate communication between the Butler generations. "My uncle thought I should be exiled," Michael remembers. "The amazing thing is that I was under attack by the radical right and the radical left."

When Manhattan's St. John the Divine Cathedral invited the cast for its mass, it was the largest crowd the cathedral had seen. Yet the FBI warned Michael to stay away because of rumors that the radical right was planning his assassination during the mass.

"On the other hand, when we opened in Seattle," Michael recounts, "the leftists threatened to blow up the theater if we didn't give them $100,000." Instead, extra security was hired.

Some problems were due to Michael's openness. After the show opened, he was asked to give a charitable performance for the Yippies. "What's the Yippies?" he asked.

"'Oh, just some kids who are working on advanced political thinking,'" Michael said he was told. Then his comptroller warned him that the money was to go to the radical Judson Church. Michael asked for more details.

In walked Jerry Rubin and Abby Hoffman. "One of the reasons we need the money is to teach the kids martial arts," they told Michael. He asked why they needed to learn martial arts.

"'To confront the Man and deal with the pigs,'" was the response.

"Where will the confrontation take place?" asked Michael.

"Chicago," they said. Michael nixed the contribution.

After the movie *Hair* was made, Michael became involved with other productions that had varying degrees of success. He returned to Oak Brook in the early '80s when his father was struck and killed by a drunk driver. Michael took over the real estate developments that his father had left. (Paul had sold the paper company in 1963 to Great Northern Nekoosa for $20 million in stock and, after bringing Butler Aviation public, sold his shares for several million in the late '60s.)

Paul, wishing to maintain control, had never established trusts for his children. That wasn't a problem for Michael, who had always managed to live lavishly and who had increased his spending while he had access to his *Hair* earnings. But marrying and divorcing three times, as Michael did, diminishes a man's bottom line. In addition, a person who is equally at home with King Hussein and Mick Jagger has a considerable style of life to maintain, which ultimately became a problem for Michael.

The estate Paul left his three children was mostly of underdeveloped land worth an estimated tens of millions of dollars. Michael, Frank, and Jorie were hit by a 70 percent estate tax, although they had relatively little cash. In addition, Paul had required in his will that they coadminister the estate—with unanimity required for every vote.

Paul should have known that in his family, peace doesn't guide the planet nor love rule the stars—even when the moon is in the Seventh House and Jupiter aligns with Mars. With both the tremendous tax bite and the need for unanimity among siblings, Paul's legacy to his children fell apart. Litigation ensued regarding the development of the properties. At first, each sibling was against the others, although now Michael and his sister are firmly aligned against Frank.

Overall, the '80s were a painful decade for the Butlers. After more complicated real estate transactions ultimately went bad in a soft market accompanied by wobbly S&Ls, Michael declared bankruptcy in 1990. He was broke to the point of having to use his polo ponies in payment for his attorney fee. This act especially saddened Michael because his only child Adam, 28, has just begun a career as a professional polo player.

Helping to ease the transition into a cash-and-carry world are many friends. A typical bankruptcy does not elicit a personal note of support from, say, the Prince of Wales; Michael's did.

Michael threw himself back into the work world. In 1992, he continued his work on several Chicago business boards, including Business Space Inc., which represents tenants for the restructuring of leases. He's also on the board of a financial clearing house, Stellaris. Michael hasn't abandoned his creative projects, either. He's working on a new musical in Jamaica; considering a few offers to write an autobiography, and establishing polo tournaments for downtown Chicago.

Despite the recent bad luck, Michael remains optimistic. "I've had a wonderful life. It forever changes—I've believed in that all of my life."

But the most important thing to Michael is "Freedom. Freedom and attitude. With attitude, you can do anything."

The one thing that Michael doesn't want to relive again is a political run. And it was the late Chicago Mayor Richard Daley who made him realize it.

Daley and Otto Kerner, in 1968, were trying to talk Michael into running for the U.S. Senate against incumbent Republican Everett Dirkson. Michael says, "They were going to use their influence for me: Otto's down state, and Dick's in Cook County." But then came the fatal comment.

Daley turned to Kerner and remarked, "Mike can win—but he's got to cut his hair."

THE AUTHOR

Jan Pottker has a Ph.D. in sociology and education from Columbia University, where she specialized in organizational dynamics. Her research and writing have led to her inclusion in *Contemporary Authors, Who's Who of Finance and Industry,* and *Men and Women of Science.*

Pottker was raised in Highland Park, Illinois, where both of her parents were involved in family-owned businesses. Her father was a partner with his father- and brother-in-law in a small chain of furniture stores. Her mother was an editor of *The News-Sun* (Waukegan, Illinois), a family-owned county daily.

She is married to Andrew Fishel, Managing Director of the Federal Communications Commission. With their two daughters, they live in Potomac, Maryland.